NOBEL LECTURES PEACE

NOBEL LECTURES

INCLUDING PRESENTATION SPEECHES
AND LAUREATES' BIOGRAPHIES

PHYSICS

CHEMISTRY

PHYSIOLOGY OR MEDICINE

LITERATURE

PEACE

PUBLISHED FOR THE NOBEL FOUNDATION
BY
ELSEVIER PUBLISHING COMPANY
AMSTERDAM – LONDON – NEW YORK

NOBEL LECTURES

INCLUDING PRESENTATION SPEECHES
AND LAUREATES' BIOGRAPHIES

PEACE

1901–1925

VOLUME 1

Edited by

FREDERICK W. HABERMAN

Professor of Communication Arts
The University of Wisconsin–Madison,
Madison, Wis., U.S.A.

PUBLISHED FOR THE NOBEL FOUNDATION
IN 1972 BY
ELSEVIER PUBLISHING COMPANY
AMSTERDAM – LONDON – NEW YORK

ELSEVIER PUBLISHING COMPANY
335 JAN VAN GALENSTRAAT
P.O. BOX 211, AMSTERDAM, THE NETHERLANDS

AMERICAN ELSEVIER PUBLISHING COMPANY, INC.
52 VANDERBILT AVENUE
NEW YORK, N.Y. 10017

LIBRARY OF CONGRESS CARD NUMBER 68–20650
ISBN 0-444-40853-3

PRINTED IN THE NETHERLANDS BY
KONINKLIJKE DRUKKERIJ G.J. THIEME N.V., NIJMEGEN
BOOK DESIGN: HELMUT SALDEN

Foreword

In his foreword to the Nobel Lectures in Physics, Chemistry, and Physiology or Medicine the then President of the Nobel Foundation, Professor Arne Tiselius, wrote:

«The Nobel Foundation has, by agreement, granted the Elsevier Publishing Company of Amsterdam the right to publish in English language the Nobel Lectures for 1901–1962. The lectures in the five Nobel Prize domains: Physics, Chemistry, Physiology or Medicine, Literature, and Peace will appear separately, according to the subject ... Short biographical notes and the presentation speeches will also be included.

The Nobel Foundation has since 1901 each year published *Les Prix Nobel* which contains all Nobel Lectures of that year, always in the language in which they were given, as well as short biographies of the laureates. In addition an account is given of the prize–award ceremonies in Stockholm and in Oslo, including presentation addresses and after-dinner speeches, *etc.*, thus covering the whole field of Nobel Prize events of one particular year.

In the Elsevier series the Nobel Lectures, presentation addresses, and biographies will now be more readily accessible to those who wish to follow the development in only certain of the Nobel subjects, as reflected in the prize awards during the years passed. For practical reasons English has been chosen as common language for this series.

It is the hope of the Nobel Foundation that the volumes to be published by Elsevier Publishing Company will supplement *Les Prix Nobel* and that together they will serve to spread knowledge of those landmarks on the road of human progress that have been honoured by Nobel Prizes.»

The publication of the Nobel Lectures in Peace brings the beginning of this series to completion. It is hoped that these lectures may prove to be a stimulating message from the persons and institutions who, during the years since 1901, have been awarded the Peace Prize for their outstanding achievements in promoting the great idea of fraternity among nations.

Aase Lionaes–Chairman, Nobel Committee of the Norwegian Parliament

Introduction

Only fifty-four weeks before he died on December 10, 1896, Alfred Nobel, the Swedish inventor and business magnate, directed in his will that the bulk of his vast estate should constitute a fund, the interest on which was to be distributed annually «in the form of prizes to those who, during the preceding year, shall have conferred the greatest benefit on mankind.» Four prizes–those in physics, chemistry, physiology or medicine, and literature – were to be administered by Swedish agencies, and one – the Peace Prize–was to be administered by a committee of five persons to be elected by the Norwegian Storting [Parliament] and to be awarded to the «person who shall have done the most or the best work for fraternity among nations, for the abolition or reduction of standing armies and for the holding and promotion of peace congresses.»

To give legal effectiveness to the will, statutes were drawn up which provided for the management of the funds by a Nobel Foundation and for the distribution of the prizes by four prize-awarding bodies, three in Stockholm and the fourth – the Nobel Committee of the Norwegian Parliament–in Oslo.

The Norwegian Parliament approved the basic statutes, and in 1900 the Nobel Committee began its activity. The Committee, exercising its statutory authority to establish a Nobel Institute to assist in the research necessary for making the awards and to promote in other ways the purposes of the Foundation, organized the Norwegian Nobel Institute in 1903. Since 1905 the Institute has occupied its own building in Oslo where it maintains administrative offices and an auditorium, houses an extensive library, and operates a public reading room. In addition to providing library resources, the Institute works for «mutual knowledge and respect, for peaceful intercourse, justice and fraternity among nations» by publishing research studies, particularly in the field of internationalism broadly conceived, and by sponsoring lectures, symposiums, conferences, and courses.

The first task of the Institute, however, is to «follow the development of international relations, especially the work for pacific settlement of them, and thereby counsel the Committee with regard to the distribution of the Prize.» Nominations for the Peace Prize award, due before February 1 of the year in which the award is to be made, may be submitted by people in specified categories: members and former members of the Committee and advisers of the Institute; parliamentarians; members of the International Court of Arbitration at The Hague, members of the Commission of the International Peace Bureau, and members of the Institute of International Law; university professors in the fields of political science, law, history, and philosophy; and recipients of the Peace Prize. The Committee obtains advice on the nominees from an annual report prepared by the director of the Institute and three advisers associated with the Institute, one in political history, one in international law, and one in political economy.

A decision having been made to award the prize, it then remains for the chosen prizewinner to accept and to comply with the Nobel statute which makes it incumbent on him «whenever this is possible, to give a public lecture on a subject connected with the work for which the prize has been awarded... within six months of Commemoration Day... in Oslo.»

The original Statutes of the Nobel Foundation provide that, should the Committee decide no work merits an award in a given year, the amount of the prize money for that year be reserved until the following year; and, if no prize can be awarded even then, that the amount be added to the main fund, or, according to the decision of the Committee, one-third to the main fund and two-thirds to a special fund, the interest from which may be used by the Committee for statutory purposes. However, in accordance with a change made in the statutes on April 10, 1970, this last provision now stipulates that in all such cases the entire amount of the prize money be allocated to the main fund. The statute concerning posthumous awards has also been altered; originally permitting such an award if «death occurred subsequently to a proposal having been submitted, in the manner stipulated, that [the person's] work should be rewarded,» the statute now permits it only if «a prizewinner [should] die before he receives the prize.»

For the original statutes themselves and for the official account of Alfred Nobel and his will, of the Nobel Foundation and its administration, and of the five Nobel Prizes, the reader should see *Nobel: The Man and His Prizes* (Amsterdam: Elsevier Publishing Co., 1962), especially «The Peace Prize» by August Schou, director of the Norwegian Nobel Institute, who categorizes and briefly analyzes the Peace Prizes awarded from 1901 through 1961.

In the seventy years from 1901, when the first Peace Prize was presented, through 1970, the Committee has awarded the prize in whole or in part to fifty-four individuals from fifteen different countries, and to ten organizations or institutions. Among the fifty-four individuals are presidents, premiers, foreign ministers, publicists, scientists, leaders of peace movements, humanitarians, international jurists, religious leaders, civil and human rights spokesmen. They include such diverse proponents of peace as Baroness Bertha von Suttner (1905), who pricked the conscience of the world with her pacifist novel *Lay Down Your Arms*; Woodrow Wilson (1919), who stirred the hopes of the world with his plan for a League of Nations; Archbishop Nathan Söderblom (1930), who led an ecumenical movement looking toward a worldwide religious brotherhood of men; Albert Schweitzer (1952), who put his ideal of «reverence for life» into words and deeds; Albert Lutuli (1960), a tribal chieftain who became the leader of ten million black Africans in their nonviolent protests against the repressive measures of the South African government; Norman Borlaug (1970), who, as a prime mover in the «green revolution», is trying to lessen some of the world's tensions by enabling hungry peoples to feed themselves. Among the organizations are the Institute of International Law (1904), which enlists the brilliant legal minds of the world to research questions of international law and to promote international relations based on law and justice, and, honored three times (1917, 1944, 1963), the International Committee of the Red Cross, that neutral agent of humane intervention dedicated to serving and, indeed, preserving mankind.

The prize itself is awarded at the annual Norwegian Nobel ceremonies which are held on December 10, the anniversary of Alfred Nobel's death, and on December 11. As observed today, they consist of three official functions: the presentation, the banquet, and the lecture. The presentation on Commemoration Day, December 10, usually takes place in the afternoon in the Aula or Auditorium of the University of Oslo, a magnificent hall decorated with murals by the celebrated artist Edvard Munch. In attendance are the king and royal family of Norway, members of the Parliament and dignitaries from foreign embassies, representatives of the Nobel Foundation in Stockholm, representatives of Norwegian scientific institutions as well as of industrial and cultural organizations, and other prominent guests. Music is provided by an orchestra which in recent years has usually placed on its program a symphonic piece by a composer of the laureate's native and. The program itself is impressively simple. The chairman of the Nobel Committee delivers the presentation speech and gives the laureate the diploma and the medal of the Nobel Peace Prize. The laureate then responds in a short speech of acceptance.

The second function is a banquet given by the Committee in honor of the laureate on the evening of December 10. Attended by a distinguished company, the banquet features a toast to the laureate made by one of the members of the Committee, and the laureate's reply.

The third part of the annual ceremony takes place on December 11, usually in the evening, when the laureate delivers his Nobel lecture to an audience gathered in the Festival Hall (auditorium) of the Norwegian Nobel Institute or, in some cases, in the Auditorium of the University of Oslo.

These lectures of the laureates and of the representatives of the recipient organizations constitute an important part of the historical record of twentieth-century man's attempts to live in peace. These responses to the wars, economic depressions, and political catastrophes of this century vary from analysis of the problems to proposed answers, from defense of existing institutions to proposals for new ones, from statements of individualized ethics to pleas for united world action. International law; arbitration of international disputes; pacts and treaties; limitation of armaments or universal disarmament; social justice through assurance of higher living standards for labor and for deprived peoples; social justice through assurance of human and civil rights; the Hague Conventions; preservation of human solidarity through humanitarian aid in times of conflict or disaster; education for peace; brotherly love; the League of Nations; the peace movement as such; interparliamentary action; internationalism *versus* nationalism; the United Nations–all these and more figure in the lectures as ways to peace.

These volumes, sponsored by the Nobel Foundation and the Nobel Committee of the Norwegian Parliament, constitute the first complete collection of existing Nobel Peace Prize speeches of presentation and of the Nobel Peace Prize lectures themselves. The presentation speeches, with few exceptions, are here published in English for the first time. Only a small number of the lectures by the twenty-two laureates or organization representatives who spoke in languages other than English have heretofore been translated into English, and of those some exist only in truncated form.

For each award these volumes contain, in addition to a title page, (1) the speech of presentation or an «equivalent»; (2) the Nobel lecture or, if none exists, an acceptance or the like; (3) a biography or history; (4) a bibliography.

The presentation speech is usually delivered by the chairman of the Norwegian Nobel Committee. In the early years before the prize ceremonies became ritualized, the presentations were brief, sometimes little more than official announcements made by the chairman to the Norwegian Parliament. The laureates were rarely present, choosing to deliver their lectures in Oslo when the weather was better and travel more comfortable; indeed, many of them spoke long after the stipulated six months had elapsed. Since most of the early speeches of presentation are not included in *Les Prix Nobel*, which is the official annual record of the Nobel Prize ceremonies in both Oslo and Stockholm, reporters' versions of them published in the Oslo *Aftenposten* or *Morgenbladet* have been collected here; their versions of toasts, or speeches of introduction, or speeches of welcome have also been used if speeches of presentation as such do not exist. Some of these versions are summaries, some third-person accounts, and some, for long passages at least, virtually verbatim texts. In contrast to these early presentation speeches, those from 1922 on are fully developed discourses, providing biographical information and assessments of the laureate's work, with spatial emphasis upon the particular event, accomplishment, or philosophy which obviously merited the award.

The Nobel lectures make up the bulk of the volumes. They include: forty-two lectures *per se*–that is, forty-two delivered at Oslo and published in *Les Prix Nobel*; two written Nobel «communiqués» sent to the Nobel Committee by Léon Bourgeois (1920) and Ferdinand Buisson (1927) and published in *Les Prix Nobel*; a prepared lecture by Elihu Root (1912) which was never delivered because of the outbreak of World War I but which was later published in a volume of his speeches; and an essay by Ludwig Quidde (1927) who, after delivering his lecture, obtained the reading copy from the Committee and did not thereafter return it but who later published an updated essay version. There are twenty awards for which there are no lectures or the equivalents thereof; it is probable that none were prepared or delivered. *Les Prix Nobel* does not contain lecture texts for these awards, nor are there scripts in the confidential files of the Norwegian Nobel Committee, which were searched for me by the secretary of the Norwegian Nobel Institute. Many of the prizewinners who did not deliver addresses were unable to do so: some were ill–among them, Henri Dunant (1901), Jane Addams (1931), and Cordell Hull (1945); some were committed to duties elsewhere–Nicholas Murray Butler (1931), for example; Carl von Ossietzky (1935) was held in a concentration camp in Germany; Dag Hammarskjöld's award (1961)was given posthumously. To represent these laureates who did not deliver lectures, other pertinent material has been included whenever available: usually their messages of acceptance or the acceptance speeches made on their behalf by others; in one instance an acceptance speech, as well as a banquet speech, made by the laureate himself (Frank B. Kellogg, 1929); and in two instances radio addresses which were major responses by the laureates to their awards (Nicholas Murray Butler, 1931, and Carlos Saavedra Lamas, 1936). In this connection, it should be stated that acceptance speeches (or parts thereof) by or for the lecture-giving prizewinners have been included only for unusual cases: for Theodore Roosevelt (1906) because his was the first on record; for Arthur Henderson (1934) because his answered a point made in the presentation speech; for certain organizations because theirs were given by official representatives other than the lecturers.

For the most part the texts of the presentation speeches and Nobel lectures used in the preparation of these volumes are those appearing in *Les Prix Nobel*. It was not possible to collate these published versions of the lectures with the reading copies since the reading copies have not been retained. But they have been collated with other existing texts whenever possible, and explanations of methods used and results obtained are noted in the appropriate places with each text. These other texts are of various sorts, for example, a photographic copy of a holograph original by Élie Ducommun (1902), a text in the *New York Times* for George Marshall (1953), texts on audio tapes for Ralph Bunche (1950), Georges Pire (1958), Philip Noel-Baker (1959), and Albert Lutuli (1960).

Of the forty-six Nobel lectures, twenty-three were delivered in and have been published in English, and one (Root, 1912) was written and published in English. In these lectures, obvious errors have been corrected, and punctuation, capitalization, and spelling have been normalized in accordance with contemporary American practice. Of the remaining twenty-two lectures, twelve are in French, three in German, three in Swedish, three in Norwegian, and one in Danish. With one or two exceptions, all of the presentation speeches carried by *Les Prix Nobel* are in Norwegian; typically, *Les Prix Nobel* also carries translations, usually in French, but recently in English whenever apropos. All non-English texts have been translated into modern idiomatic English. Naturally, some effort has been made to retain the flavor of the originals, but the twin goals of clarity and ease of understanding have often had to take precedence.

An attempt has been made to make the footnoting of the presentation speeches and the Nobel lectures reasonably complete. Dates have been furnished when they provide a necessary clarity, and historical events referred to are explained briefly; whenever possible, quotations and authors are identified, names of persons and organizations are verified and life dates of the former supplied, and publications mentioned in the speeches are given complete bibliographical citation unless they are listed in the bibliographies, in which case only minimal identification is furnished. Since, for the sake of the selective reader, each speech has been treated as a discreet unit, there is some repetition of footnotes from speech to speech, for the laureates frequently refer to the same people and events.

In the text, titles of organizations or of publications in languages other than English are usually followed by translations in English, which are italicized if they are titles of works published in English translation.

The biographies of the laureates are new and are based on the latest information available. Intended to be brief, factual accounts covering the entire careers of laureates now dead or the activities to date of living laureates (1971), the biographies are designed to complement the information found in the speeches of presentation and in the lectures. Some overlapping has been unavoidable, however, especially in the awards of later years when the presentation speeches became lengthier and more comprehensive in nature. Analogous to the biographies are the brief histories of the organizations or institutions which have won the Peace Prize.

The bibliographies, not intended to be exhaustive, cite revealing biographical and interpretative accounts of the laureates, important publications by the laureates themselves, and, in some cases, pertinent background materials on their work. For the laureate whose native language is one other than English, the bibliography cites most, and in some cases all, of the laureate's writings that have appeared in English translation.

Frederick W. Haberman

Acknowledgments

I record with pleasure my indebtedness to many people who, as individuals or as staff members of institutions, gave me assistance of all kinds in editing these volumes.

The Research Committee of the Graduate School of the University of Wisconsin, together with the Johnson Foundation in Racine, Wisconsin, under the presidency of Leslie Paffrath, provided me with research support in the autumn of 1963. About one half of my time in that semester was spent on this project, the other half in bringing another one to completion. The Johnson Foundation and the College of Letters and Science of the University of Wisconsin collaborated to furnish me with research support in the summer of 1965. The Research Committee gave me full support for the fall semester of 1970–71 and on various occasions between 1963 and 1970 gave me grants to cover certain travel and research expenses.

For six weeks in the autumn of 1963, my wife and I were permitted, through the good offices of the Norwegian Nobel Institute, to live at Pol-høgda, the Oslo home of Fridtjof Nansen (laureate for 1922), now owned by the Fridtjof Nansen Foundation, of which the Institute is a member. We worked daily in the library of the Institute whose staff, headed by Miss Elisabeth Mellbye, was most courteous and resourceful. Mr. Sverre Svanes, secretary of the Institute, was unfailingly prompt and helpful in answering our requests. Mr. August Schou, director of the Institute, placed its splendid facilities at our disposal, and, as the outstanding authority on the Nobel Peace Prize, generously supplied answers then and later to many puzzling questions concerning procedure, history, texts, biography, and the like. Also in Oslo, the staff of the University Library aided me in the search for information in their newspaper holdings, and the Norwegian Broadcasting System presented me with tape recordings of several Nobel lectures.

The staff of Memorial Library of the University of Wisconsin deserves special mention. Gerhard B. Naeseth, associate director, met all emergency requests for research space; Marguerite A. Christensen in the Reference Room, Elizabeth J. Donohue in the Periodical Room, William H. Patch in the Circulation Department and their respective staffs were always helpful; bibliographers Charles Szabo and Erwin K. Welsch put their considerable skills to the solution of some of the difficult reference problems. The Wisconsin State Historical Society Library, with its extensive newspaper holdings and expert staff, also made important contributions to my research.

In the late summer of 1963 and in the autumn of 1970, my wife and I were afforded the inestimable privilege of working in the Reading Room of the British Museum and in its Newspaper Library at Colindale.

At Stanford University in the summer of 1966, I was permitted to work in the Hoover Institution on War, Revolution and Peace whose staff (and in particular Mrs. Wendell G. Cole) was not only helpful but especially delighted to have someone in residence working on peace.

Although I am responsible for the finished translations as they appear in these volumes, I have been forced by the nature of the task to rely heavily on many resources. The Express Translation Service in London, under the direction of W. Brodnicki and T. Dudley, has supplied the basic scripts for most of the translated speeches. All translations from Norwegian, Swedish, and Danish have had the benefit of a reading and consequent correction by August Schou, who also read these volumes in first proof. At one time or another my patient colleagues on the professorial staff of the University of Wisconsin have willingly answered queries on translations: Sieghardt M. Riegel in the Department of German, E. E. Milligan in the Department of French and Italian, Norman P. Sacks in the Department of Spanish and Portuguese, Harald S. Naess in the Department of Scandinavian Studies, and Gerhard B. Naeseth who was always ready to clarify a problem arising in a Norwegian text. Some gifted graduate students whose names are listed elsewhere in this section have also helped, sometimes extensively.

For assistance on various matters I wish to express my gratitude to the following persons and organizations: the International Peace Bureau (Ingeborg Belck) for historical data on the Bureau; the UN Library in Geneva (Sven Welander) for various materials, including a holograph copy of Ducommun's Nobel lecture; the UN Office in Geneva (J. Pommerenck) for biographical materials on Ducommun and Gobat; the Union of International Associations (Robert Fenaux), the Services d'Étude et de Documentation du Sénat de Belgique, and J. Vanderlinden, Faculté de Droit, Université Libre de Bruxelles, for biographical and bibliographical information on La Fontaine; C. F. Coghlan, Fareham, Hants, England, for finding Cremer's baptismal registration; P. de Visscher, secretary-general of the Institute of International Law, for materials on the history of the Institute; the Carnegie Endowment for International Peace for general encouragement and for answers to many questions; the League of Red Cross Societies (Marc Gazay), the Canadian Red Cross Society (Mrs. Terry Watson), and the American National Red Cross (Meyer Mathis) for help on the awards to the Red Cross organizations, and the International Committee of the Red Cross (P. Vibert) for reading the history that serves all these awards; the Jane Addams Peace Association (Ruth Chalmers) and the Swarthmore College Peace Collection (Claire B. Shetter, Ardith Emmons, and Bernice B. Nichols) for information on Addams, Balch, and others; Low Memorial Library of Columbia University for materials and Lindsay Rogers, professor emeritus of public law at Columbia, for advice on Butler; W. Booth of Holbeach, Lincolnshire, England, for confirming Angell's life dates; Knut M. Hansson of Oslo for information on his father, Michael Hansson, who accepted the prize in behalf of the Nansen Office (1938) – and for his generous hospitality as well; Columbus Memorial Library of the Pan American Union for a rare pamphlet on Saavedra Lamas; the Friends Service Council (Elizabeth Spurway) for general data and an original draft of a history which I was permitted to adapt; the American Friends Service Committee (Margaret H. Bacon) for the history of the Committee; the George C. Marshall Research Foundation of the Virginia Military Institute (E. D. Lejeune) for answers to biographical queries on Marshall; the Office of the United Nations High Commissioner for Refugees (J. Colmar) for supplying historical data on the Office; the Heart Open to the World (I. Jolling) in Huy, Belgium, for biographical and bibliographical materials on Father Pire; the Permanent Mission of Sweden to the United Nations (Torsten Örn) for clarifying a point about Hammarskjöld's diplomatic career; Irving Shain of the University of Wisconsin Department of Chemistry for checking technical details in Pauling's biography; William H. Hay of the University of Wisconsin Department of Philosophy and A. H. Johnson of the University of Western Ontario Department of Philosophy for their search for the source of a quotation in King's lecture; the United Nations Children's Fund (Ellen Lukas) for providing extensive historical data and bibliographical suggestions; René Cassin for help in identifying a quotation in his Nobel lecture; the International Labor Office (John Western) for historical and bibliographical information; the Rockefeller Foundation (Marjorie J. Schad) for some pertinent materials on Borlaug, John H. Lonnquist of the University of Wisconsin Department of

Agronomy for explanations of scientific matters connected with Borlaug's career, and Norman Borlaug himself for supplying copies of some of his publications.

I am indebted also to the graduate students at the University of Wisconsin who have worked with me at various times: to Ronald R. Allen, now a faculty colleague, Paul Arntson, Martha Ann Ebert, Thomas B. Farrell, Lars Johnson, Wayne R. Londré, Laurie Schultz, Allen M. Scult, Mark Seiler, Vera Gurk Sheppard, and Sarah Stevenson for their aid on translations or on the research needed for these volumes, or on both; to Daniel S. Hawley for holding copy during some of the proofreading; and in particular, to Anne L. Martin for her assistance in research and in holding copy, and to Joan E. Steck for her help in the reading of both first and second proof. Special recognition is due Felicia Hardison Londré who was my project assistant for some time and who helped in ways too numerous to list.

Mrs. Rosemary Bohannan, of Madison, Wisconsin, both accommodating and skillful, prepared most of the typed manuscript for these volumes.

The editors of Elsevier Publishing Company have been most helpful, and I would like to say that I found it a special personal and professional privilege to work with the late Dr. W. Gaade, vice-president of Elsevier, during much of the preparation of these volumes. Keen, witty, and charming, he was also the embodiment of patience and thoughtful courtesy.

I come finally to my wife. I can only say that she should be listed as co-editor, for she has worked step by step with me from start to finish.

                                                                    F. W. H.

Permissions

I gratefully acknowledge the permissions given by publishers and others to use or reprint several speeches and other material contained in these volumes:

Nicholas Murray Butler, radio address of December 12, 1931, published December 13, 1931. Copyright © 1931 by The New York Times Company. Reprinted by permission.

Dag Hammarskjöld, four lines of poetry from page 31 of *Markings*. Copyright © 1964 translation by Alfred A. Knopf Inc. and Faber & Faber Ltd Quoted by permission.

Johannes Irgens, speech of August 24, 1912. French text in the *Annuaire de l'Institut de Droit International, 1912* (Paris: A. Pedone, 1912, Vol. 25, pp. 539–542) used for translation by permission of the Institut de Droit International.

Fridtjof Nansen, «No More War». Norwegian text in *Eventyrlyst–Ingen krig mere: To taler av Fridtjof Nansen* used for translation by permission of Jacob Dybwads Forlag, Aschehougs Forlag, and the Estate of Fridtjof Nansen.

Elihu Root, Nobel lecture. From *Addresses on International Subjects*, pp. 153–174 (edited by Robert Bacon and James B. Scott, Harvard University Press). Reprinted by permission.

Carlos Saavedra Lamas, radio address of November 29, 1936, published November 30, 1936. Copyright © 1936 by The New York Times Company. Reprinted by permission.

F. W. H.

Volume 1 covers the years 1901–1925; Volume 2, the years 1926–1950; Volume 3, the years 1951–1970.

Contents

ERRATA

p. 11,   2nd line up should read:
         Schilfgaarde (Waszkléwicz), B. van, *etc.*
p. 274, footnote 1, 2nd line should read:
         29, 1916. Archives of the Hoover Institvtion on War, *etc.*

Peace 1901

JEAN HENRI DUNANT

FRÉDÉRIC PASSY

The Occasion of the First Award

The first Nobel Peace Prize was awarded at a meeting of the Norwegian Parliament which took place at ten o'clock on the morning of December 10, 1901. The ceremony was brief, lasting only fifteen minutes. Mr. Carl Christian Berner, president of the Parliament, opened it with this brief address[1]:

«The Norwegian people have always demanded that their independence be respected. They have always been ready to defend it. But, at the same time, they have always had a keen desire and need for peace. Our nation has wished to pursue its material and intellectual development in peace and on good terms with other nations. This basic concept has been put into practice repeatedly and with increasing strength by the Norwegian Parliament. At various times the Parliament has gone on record in favor of the signing of peace and arbitration treaties with foreign powers in order to prevent settlement of possible disputes by armed force and to insure just solutions through peaceful means. We may well believe that this need which motivates the Norwegian people, this ardent desire for peace and good relations between nations, is what influenced Dr. Alfred Nobel to entrust to the Parliament of Norway the important responsibility of awarding the prize, through a committee of five, to the one whose work for peace and for fraternity among nations most deserves it. Today when this Peace Prize is to be awarded for the first time, our thoughts turn back in respectful recognition to the man of noble sentiments who, perceiving things to come, knew how to give priority to the great problems of civilization, putting in first place among them work for peace and fraternity among nations. We hope that what he has done in the interest of this great cause will achieve results which will live up to his noble intentions.»

Upon completing his remarks, Mr. Berner gave the floor to Mr. Jørgen Gunnarsson Løvland, a member of the Nobel Committee and at this time minister of Public Works. Mr. Løvland, in place of Mr. Getz, the Commit-

1. The translation is based on the Norwegian text in *Les Prix Nobel en 1901*, which also contains a French translation.

tee chairman, who had died the previous month, announced that the prize was awarded half to Henri Dunant and half to Frédéric Passy. There was no presentation speech, and after some further official formalities, the Parliament adjourned.

Les Prix Nobel does not record that either of the laureates was present; and neither delivered a Nobel lecture later, each, at his own request, having been released from this obligation by the Nobel Committee.

Biography

Jean Henri Dunant's life (May 8, 1828–October 30, 1910) is a study in contrasts. He was born into a wealthy home but died in a hospice; in middle age he juxtaposed great fame with total obscurity, and success in business with bankruptcy; in old age he was virtually exiled from the Genevan society of which he had once been an ornament and died in a lonely room, leaving a bitter testament. His passionate humanitarianism was the one constant in his life, and the Red Cross his living monument.

The Geneva household into which Henri Dunant was born was religious, humanitarian, and civic-minded. In the first part of his life Dunant engaged quite seriously in religious activities and for a while in full-time work as a representative of the Young Men's Christian Association, traveling in France, Belgium, and Holland.

When he was twenty-six, Dunant entered the business world as a representative of the Compagnie genevoise des Colonies de Sétif in North Africa and Sicily. In 1858 he published his first book, *Notice sur la Régence de Tunis* [An Account of the Regency in Tunis], made up for the most part of travel observations but containing a remarkable chapter, a long one, which he published separately in 1863, entitled *L'Esclavage chez les musulmans et aux États-Unis d'Amérique* [Slavery among the Mohammedans and in the United States of America].

Having served his commercial apprenticeship, Dunant devised a daring financial scheme, making himself president of the Financial and Industrial Company of Mons-Gémila Mills in Algeria (eventually capitalized at 100,000,000 francs) to exploit a large tract of land. Needing water rights, he resolved to take his plea directly to Emperor Napoleon III. Undeterred by the fact that Napoleon was in the field directing the French armies who, with the Italians, were striving to drive the Austrians out of Italy, Dunant made his way to Napoleon's headquarters near the northern Italian town of Solferino. He arrived there in time to witness, and to participate in the aftermath of, one of the bloodiest battles of the nineteenth century. His awareness and conscience honed, he published in 1862 a small book *Un*

Souvenir de Solférino [*A Memory of Solferino*], destined to make him famous.

A Memory has three themes. The first is that of the battle itself. The second depicts the battlefield after the fighting–its «chaotic disorder, despair unspeakable, and misery of every kind»–and tells the main story of the effort to care for the wounded in the small town of Castiglione. The third theme is a plan. The nations of the world should form relief societies to provide care for the wartime wounded; each society should be sponsored by a governing board composed of the nation's leading figures, should appeal to everyone to volunteer, should train these volunteers to aid the wounded on the battlefield and to care for them later until they recovered. On February 7, 1863, the Société genevoise d'utilité publique [Geneva Society for Public Welfare] appointed a committee of five, including Dunant, to examine the possibility of putting this plan into action. With its call for an international conference, this committee, in effect, founded the Red Cross. Dunant, pouring his money and time into the cause, traveled over most of Europe obtaining promises from governments to send representatives. The conference, held from October 26 to 29, with thirty-nine delegates from sixteen nations attending, approved some sweeping resolutions and laid the groundwork for a gathering of plenipotentiaries. On August 22, 1864, twelve nations signed an international treaty, commonly known as the Geneva Convention, agreeing to guarantee neutrality to sanitary personnel, to expedite supplies for their use, and to adopt a special identifying emblem–in virtually all instances a red cross on a field of white[1].

Dunant had transformed a personal idea into an international treaty. But his work was not finished. He approved the efforts to extend the scope of the Red Cross to cover naval personnel in wartime, and in peacetime to alleviate the hardships caused by natural catastrophes. In 1866 he wrote a brochure called the *Universal and International Society for the Revival of the Orient*, setting forth a plan to create a neutral colony in Palestine. In 1867 he produced a plan for a publishing venture called an «International and Universal Library» to be composed of the great masterpieces of all time. In 1872 he convened a conference to establish the «Alliance universelle de l'ordre et de la civilisation» which was to consider the need for an international convention on the handling of prisoners of war and for the settling of international disputes by courts of arbitration rather than by war.

1. The emblem in Muslim countries is the red crescent and in Iran is the red lion and sun. (For a brief history of the Red Cross, see p. 284.)

The eight years from 1867 to 1875 proved to be a sharp contrast to those of 1859–1867. In 1867 Dunant was bankrupt. The water rights had not been granted, the company had been mismanaged in North Africa, and Dunant himself had been concentrating his attention on humanitarian pursuits, not on business ventures. After the disaster, which involved many of his Geneva friends, Dunant was no longer welcome in Genevan society. Within a few years he was literally living at the level of the beggar. There were times, he says[1], when he dined on a crust of bread, blackened his coat with ink, whitened his collar with chalk, slept out of doors.

For the next twenty years, from 1875 to 1895, Dunant disappeared into solitude. After brief stays in various places, he settled down in Heiden, a small Swiss village. Here a village teacher named Wilhelm Sonderegger found him in 1890 and informed the world that Dunant was alive, but the world took little note. Because he was ill, Dunant was moved in 1892 to the hospice at Heiden. And here, in Room 12, he spent the remaining eighteen years of his life. Not, however, as an unknown. After 1895 when he was once more rediscovered, the world heaped prizes and awards upon him.

Despite the prizes and the honors, Dunant did not move from Room 12. Upon his death, there was no funeral ceremony, no mourners, no cortege. In accordance with his wishes he was carried to his grave «like a dog»[2].

Dunant had not spent any of the prize monies he had received. He bequeathed some legacies to those who had cared for him in the village hospital, endowed a «free bed» that was to be available to the sick among the poorest people in the village, and left the remainder to philanthropic enterprises in Norway and Switzerland.

Selected Bibliography

Les Débuts de la Croix-Rouge en France. Paris, Librairie Fischbacher, 1918.

Dunant, J. Henri. His manuscripts are held by the Bibliothèque publique et universitaire de Genève.

Dunant, J. Henry, A Memory of Solferino. London, Cassell, 1947. A translation from the French of the first edition of Un Souvenir de Solférino, published in 1862. The author published the original as «J. Henry Dunant», although he is usually referred to as «Henri Dunant».

1. «Extraits des mémoires» in Les Débuts de la Croix-Rouge en France, p. 72.
2. Taken from a letter written by Dunant and published by René Sonderegger; quoted by Gigon in The Epic of the Red Cross, p. 147.

Gagnebin, Bernard, «Le Rôle d'Henry Dunant pendant la guerre de 1870 et le siège de Paris», bound separately but originally published in *Revue internationale de la Croix-Rouge* (avril, 1953).

Gigon, Fernand, *The Epic of the Red Cross or the Knight Errant of Charity*, translated from the French by Gerald Griffin. London, Jarrolds, 1946.

Gumpert, Martin, *Dunant: The Story of the Red Cross*. New York, Oxford University Press, 1938.

Hart, Ellen, *Man Born to Live: Life and Work of Henry Dunant, Founder of the Red Cross*. London, Gollancz, 1953.

Hendtlass, Willy, «Henry Dunant: Leben und Werk», in *Solferino*, pp. 37–84. Essen Cityban, Schiller, 1959.

Hommage à Henry Dunant. Genève, 1963.

Huber, Max, «Henry Dunant», in *Revue internationale de la Croix-Rouge*, 484 (avril, 1959) 167–173. A translation of a brief sketch originally published in German in 1928.

Biography

Frédéric Passy (May 20, 1822–June 12, 1912) was born in Paris and lived there his entire life of ninety years. The tradition of the French civil service was strong in Passy's family, his uncle, Hippolyte Passy (1793–1880), rising to become a cabinet minister under both Louis Philippe and Louis Napoleon. Educated as a lawyer, Frédéric Passy entered the civil service at the age of twenty-two as an accountant in the State Council, but left after three years to devote himself to systematic study of economics. He emerged as a theoretical economist in 1857 with his *Mélanges économiques*, a collection of essays he had published in the course of his research, and he secured his scholarly reputation with a series of lectures delivered in 1860–1861 at the University of Montpellier and later published in two volumes under the title *Leçons d'économie politique*. An admirer of Richard Cobden, he became an ardent free trader, believing that free trade would draw nations together as partners in a common enterprise, result in disarmament, and lead to the abandonment of war. Passy lectured on economic subjects in virtually every city and university of any consequence in France and continued a stream of publications on economic subjects, some of the more important being *Les Machines et leur influence sur le développement de l'humanité* (1866), *Malthus et sa doctrine* (1868), *L'Histoire du travail* (1873). Passy's passionate belief in education found expression in *De la propriété intellectuelle* (1859) and *La Démocratie et l'instruction* (1864). For these contributions, among others, he was elected in 1877 to membership in the Académie des sciences morales et politiques, a unit of the Institut de France.

Passy was not, however, a cloistered scholar; he was a man of action. In 1867, encouraged by his leadership of public opinion in trying to avert possible war between France and Prussia over the Luxembourg question, he founded the «Ligue internationale et permanente de la paix». When the Ligue became a casualty of the Franco-Prussian War of 1870–1871, he reorganized it under the title «Société française des amis de la paix» which in turn gave way to the more specifically oriented «Société française pour l'arbitrage entre nations», established in 1889.

Passy carried on his efforts within the government as well. He was elected to the Chamber of Deputies in 1881, again in 1885, and defeated in 1889. In the Chamber he supported legislation favorable to labor, especially an act relating to industrial accidents, opposed the colonial policy of the government, drafted a proposal for disarmament, and presented a resolution calling for arbitration of international disputes.

His parliamentary interest in arbitration was whetted by Randal Cremer's success in guiding through the British Parliament a resolution stipulating that England and the United States should refer to arbitration any disputes between them not settled by the normal methods of diplomacy. In 1888 Cremer headed a delegation of nine British members of Parliament who met in Paris with a delegation of twenty-four French deputies, headed by Passy, to discuss arbitration and to lay the groundwork for an organization to advance its acceptance. The next year, fifty-six French parliamentarians, twenty-eight British, and scattered representatives from the parliaments of Italy, Spain, Denmark, Hungary, Belgium, and the United States formed the Interparliamentary Union, with Passy as one of its three presidents. The Union, still in existence, established a headquarters to serve as a clearinghouse of ideas, and encouraged the formation of informal individual national parliamentary groups willing to support legislation leading to peace, especially through arbitration.

Passy's thought and action had unity. International peace was the goal, arbitration of disputes in international politics and free trade in goods the means, the national units making up the Interparliamentary Union the initiating agents, the people the sovereign constituency.

Through his prodigious labors over a period of half a century in the peace movement, Passy became known as the «apostle of peace». He wrote unceasingly and vividly. His *Pour la paix* (1909), which came out when he was eighty-seven years old, is a personalized account–in lieu of an autobiography which he deplored–of his work for international peace, noting especially the founding of the Ligue, the «période décisive» when the Interparliamentary Union was established, the development of peace congresses, and the value of the Hague Conferences.

Passy was a renowned speaker, noted for the intellectual demands he made on his audiences, as well as for his powerful voice, his ample gestures, and his majestic and dignified manner.

Selected Bibliography

«Frédéric Passy», *American Journal of International Law*, 6 (October, 1912) 975–976.

Gide, Charles, «Obituary: Frédéric Passy (1822–1912)», *The Economic Journal*, 22 (September, 1912) 506–507.

Institut international de bibliographie, *Répertoire bibliographique universel: Bibliographie des écrits de Frédéric Passy*. Bruxelles, 1900.

Le Foyer, Lucien, «Un Grand Pacifiste», *Le Monde illustré* (29 juin 1912) 418.

Maza, Herbert, «Frédéric Passy: La Fondation de l'Union Interparlementaire», in *Neuf meneurs internationaux*, pp. 223–239. Paris, 1965.

Obituary, *Le Figaro* (13 juin 1912) 2.

Obituary, the (London) *Times* (June 13, 1912) 11.

Passy, Frédéric. The Passy MSS are in the Library of the Peace Palace at The Hague.

Passy, Frédéric, «The Advance of the Peace Movement throughout the World», *American Monthly Review of Reviews*, 17 (February, 1898) 183–188. An English translation of the original article as it appeared in the *Revue des revues*.

Passy, Frédéric, *La Démocratie et l'instruction: Discours d'ouverture des cours publics de Nice*. Paris, Guillaumin, 1864.

Passy, Frédéric, *Histoire du travail: Leçons faites aux soirées littéraires de la Sorbonne*. Paris, 1873.

Passy, Frédéric, *Leçons d'économie politique*. Faites à Montpellier par M.F.Passy, 1860–1861. Recueillies par MM.E.Bertin et P.Glaize. Montpellier, Gras, 1861.

Passy, Frédéric, *Les Machines et leur influence sur le développement de l'humanité*. Paris, Hachette, 1866.

Passy, Frédéric, *Mélanges économiques*. Paris, Guillaumin, 1857.

Passy, Frédéric, «Peace Movement in Europe», *American Journal of Sociology*, 2 (July, 1896) 1–12.

Passy, Frédéric, *Pour la paix: Notes et documents*. Paris, Charpentier, 1909.

Passy, Frédéric, *De la propriété intellectuelle*. Études par MM.F.Passy, V.Modeste, et P.Paillottet. Paris, Guillaumin, 1859.

Passy, Frédéric, *Sophismes et truismes*. Paris, Giard & Brière, 1910.

Van Schilfgaarde, Waszkléwicz, «Frédéric Passy», in *Mannen en vrouwen van beteekenis in onze dagen*. Haarlem, Willink, 1900.

Peace 1902

ÉLIE DUCOMMUN

CHARLES ALBERT GOBAT

Toast

by Jørgen Gunnarsson Løvland*, Chairman of the Nobel Committee

Dear Mr. Ducommun, when the Committee of the Norwegian Parliament was asked to honor and reward the work of peace, our thoughts immediately turned to the men who have done this work during the long difficult years when it was received with a shaking of heads and a shrugging of shoulders, with apathy, if not with contempt. It was quite natural, then, that three of the first Nobel prizewinners should be Swiss[1]. Your country, Sir, has, in difficult times not so long ago that the older people here cannot remember them, been a place of refuge, an asylum, not only for political refugees, for persecuted fighters for freedom, and for reformers, but also for misunderstood and persecuted ideas of freedom and progress. Thus the idea of peace, humanity, justice, and brotherhood among nations has in your country above all others found sympathy and active support. What we must never forget is this: You Swiss, with your sense of life's realities, have a special gift for taking ideas from the realm of dreams and turning them into realities.

The Swiss were the people who founded the Red Cross[2], and it is two Swiss who now lead two important branches of the peace movement, the parliamentary branch and the popular branch[3]. In you, Sir, we greet the leader of the latter, the untiring and skillful director of the Bern Peace

---

* Mr. Løvland, also at this time minister of public works, offered this speech as a toast to the laureate at the banquet given in his honor on May 16, 1904, the day of the laureate's Nobel address. It is given here in lieu of the usual presentation speech since there is no text or record of such a speech for either the announcement ceremony in 1902 or the occasion of the laureate's address in 1904. This translation is based on the text in German, the language in which Mr. Løvland spoke, printed in the Oslo *Aftenposten* on May 17, 1904.

1. The other two were Jean Henri Dunant (1828–1910), co-recipient for the year 1901, and Charles Albert Gobat (1843–1914), co-recipient for the year 1902.

2. The Red Cross was initiated in Geneva in 1863 largely through the effort of Jean Henri Dunant; see pp. 5–7.

3. Albert Gobat was head of the Interparliamentary Bureau with headquarters in Bern. The Bureau was established by the Interparliamentary Union in 1892.

Bureau and therefore head of the united work of all the peace societies of the world.

The peace societies, whose activities comprise what I have called the popular peace movement, cannot be esteemed too highly. They have participated in the preparation of the ground and in the sowing of the seed which is now showing healthy growth. They have contributed to the creation of the sentiments, feelings, and ideas which shape national opinion and move parliaments, governments, and heads of state to espouse our cause and to achieve our goal.

We offer our homage and our thanks to you and to the peace societies for all that has been thought, written, said, and above all urged in the cause of peace under your leadership. We are still at the beginning, despite all the progress that has been made. There seems to be no end to what still has to be done. We need, and always shall need, sustained and ever increasing work. I shall therefore conclude by expressing the wish that for many years to come we may have the benefit of your great heart, your experience, your knowledge and practical ability, and, not least, your untiring energy at the head of the Peace Bureau in Bern.

To the health of Mr. Ducommun! Long may he live!

ÉLIE DUCOMMUN

The Futility of War Demonstrated by History

Nobel Lecture*, May 16, 1904

War, we are told, shapes character; it resolves the major questions of international politics, consolidates nations, and indeed, constitutes the principal factor in the progress of civilization through its successive stages.

Since all assertions must be carefully examined in order to benefit from what they may contain, let us consult together, if you will, the annals of history to see what war has managed to resolve and consolidate from the earliest times to the present day. This examination will enlighten us concerning the civilizing role which war may have played in the world.

The first theatre of war which history records is the vast expanse of territory comprising Greece and western Asia. In that area, at frequent intervals, there took place repeated migrations of armed tribes or hordes whose only thought was to acquire lands where they might first found tiny monarchies, and then empires. Law and reason were unknown: force was everything, and its abuse checked civilization at every turn by accustoming ignorant peoples to bend their heads before the saber.

To this category of warlike operations whose sole motive was plunder, belong, in chronological order, the expedition of the Argonauts in 1260 B.C., the capture of Troy by the Greeks in 1184 B.C., and later, the migration of the Ionians and the Dorians. Nothing remained of all these expeditions a few years later except the spectacle of devastation and of ruins whose traces had not even disappeared before some new disaster supervened.

These «Dark Ages» saw, among other things, the foundation of the kingdom of Macedonia by the Argive Caranus[1]. Since much revolves around

---

* The laureate, having been granted permission to give his Nobel lecture later than the Statutes ordinarily allowed, delivered this speech on the evening of May 16, 1904, at seven o'clock in the Hals Brothers Concert Hall in Oslo. The translation is based on the French text in *Les Prix Nobel en 1902*, a text that is virtually identical to the holograph original in the Archives of the International Peace Bureau, UN Library, Geneva.
1. Caranus founded the Argive dynasty in Macedonia about the middle of the eighth century B.C.

this unfortunate Macedonian, I ask you to bear with me if I depart from the chronological order of this study in order to follow the harrowing story of the Macedonian martyrology.

In the fourth century B.C., Philip of Macedonia [1], an ambitious princeling, subdued the Greeks, who were no less rapacious than himself, and war ravaged lands whose inhabitants had no reason to slaughter one another. Philip's son, the conqueror Alexander [2] – called «Great», no doubt because of his large-scale massacres – once more subjugated the Greeks, and then vanquished the Persians. With his death, however, the image of war which he had molded from blood and mire disintegrated, and from the ruins of his former empire, now weakened to the point of anemia, were formed the kingdoms of Macedonia and Egypt.

Poor Macedonia who aspired to become queen of the world! Thirty years later she was ravaged by the Gauls, then by the Romans, and the Middle Ages found her under the heel of the Turk. Today in the anguish of a slow agony, her imploring arms reach out in supplication to Europe [3].

Did war, at any stage of her miserable existence, consolidate the political institutions of the Macedonia of Alexander the Great, improve the lot of her peoples, or set her on the road to civilization?

Let us retrace our steps and see what became of other kingdoms which lived by the rule of force – the kingdom of the Medes and the kingdom of the Persians, for example.

About 600 B.C., the kingdom of the Medes conquered Assyria, which had been reduced to a pitiful state by the depredations of armed bands; but fifty years later Media was conquered by the Persians, who also seized Assyria and Egypt. More rivers of blood, more cities in flame, more ruins! Yet all this came to nothing, for after the Persian War, which lasted for fifty-one years, the king of Persia, Xerxes [4], had been defeated by the Greeks, and Philip of Macedonia in his turn destroyed their monarchy, without in any way assuring the future of his dynasty or the supremacy of his nation.

1. Philip II (382–336 B.C.), king of Macedonia (359–336 B.C.).
2. Alexander (III) the Great (356–323 B.C.), king of Macedonia (336–323 B.C.).
3. At the time of the laureate's lecture, insurrection in Turkish-ruled Macedonia–long the prey of raids by rival Serbian, Greek, and Bulgarian revolutionaries–had resulted in intervention by the powers, who were now engaged in argument with the Turkish government over details of a reform program for Macedonia.
4. Xerxes I (519?–465 B.C.), king of Persia (486–465 B.C.).

Again, war had created nothing, consolidated nothing; it had served merely to abase human nature and plunge nations into anarchy.

Ancient Greece is rightly said to have scattered the shadows of these evil times with the light of her arts and literature. True, but far from owing her high degree of civilization to the insistence that might makes right, she became a source of light only when she had repelled the external invasions and renounced the civil wars which threatened to destroy the works of her geniuses. It cannot be said too often that it was to the ultimate establishment of peace that ancient Greece owed her glory and her prosperity.

What can be said of the kingdom of Thrace, set up by the Gauls who had ravaged Macedonia, or of the kingdoms of Pontus, of Bythnia, of Pergamum and of Syria, founded by adventurers after the battle of Ipsus in 301 B.C.? Not the slightest trace is left of these nations which, born in pillage, died in blood.

And what of the Roman Empire? Let us indeed talk of Rome, which for centuries brought ruin to every state then known and which flung at all mankind the challenge of the «civis Romanus»: Surrender or die! How well its legions, who made and unmade emperors, knew how to introduce civilization to the vast lands they overran!

You will say perhaps that the ancient Romans, possessing at home a level of culture unknown to the rest of the human race, carried it with them to whatever part of the world they went. Wrong! People were tired of the ancient anarchy that had dominated their world, and at its end their longing for peace and security was manifest everywhere. But the bloody victories of the Roman emperors continually thwarted this awakening without offering to the vanquished in return even the smallest particle of their much vaunted civilization. The vanquished became no more than wretched slaves.

In support of militaristic ideas, people often cite the example of certain Roman lands whose populations, being far from any of the numerous theatres of war, lapsed into decadence. The fact in itself is true, but the corruption of the foremost families of these lands was precisely a result of the wars of conquest which had led to the loss of their homeland's independence. The conqueror had bent them under his yoke, and its weight crushed any sense of dignity which could have inspired them to rebel. Under the domination of the conqueror, their choice lay between fighting wars for the glory and profit of Rome or becoming shameless lackeys of the master without hope of ever enjoying again the rewards of remunerative labor.

It is certainly true that if ever a colossal and persevering effort was made to build a world empire, it was made by ancient Rome, which drowned whole kingdoms in the blood of the people over many generations. Yet what is left now of this absolute power, this monstrous creation, this crowning achievement of war? After the Punic Wars, the destruction of Carthage, and the conquests of Spain and of Gallia Narbonensis, there followed, as if by way of expiation, the degradation of the Roman Empire by the barbarian invasions. In the fifth century A.D., the Alans, Suevians, and Vandals invaded Italy, Gaul, and Spain. The Visigoths and Burgundians, in their turn, settled in Gaul and the Saxons in Great Britain. Then, toward the middle of the next century, the Heruls put an end to the Western Empire. The Heruls were subsequently overrun by the Ostrogoths, whose own monarchy was soon afterwards destroyed by the Emperor Justinian[1].

And as the din of battle fades away, the work of civilization must start all over again in a world of physical and moral chaos. This, then, is what is known as the ennobling and civilizing influence of war through the ages!

No sooner had the human family begun to recover its balance, to emerge timidly from the ruins, than new wars came to plunge it back into the morass. The inexorable law of the strongest or of the most brazen reasserted itself in the seventh and eighth centuries with the appearance of the Saracen armies who seized Chaldea, Phoenicia, Palestine, Egypt, Cyprus, Rhodes, and a part of Spain. Then, since once again wars of conquest were doomed to achieve nothing permanent, the Saracens were in their turn defeated at Poitiers by Charles Martel[2] in 732. Half a century later, Charlemagne[3] crushed the Lombard empire in Italy and the empire of the Avars in Pannonia (Hungary), overran Spain as far as the Ebro River, and conquered all of Germania.

A powerful empire was founded on the debris of monarchies and peoples. Would it now be possible to recuperate and take up again the thread of civilization which had been broken for so many centuries by bloody struggles of no lasting consequence?

Alas no! The so-called civilized world entered the eleventh century to find that the Furies of war once more awaited it in the form, on the one

---

1. Justinian (I) the Great (483–565), Byzantine emperor (527–565).
2. Charles Martel (688?–741), called the Hammer, Frankish ruler of Austrasia (715–741).
3. Charlemagne (742–814), king of the Franks (768–814), first emperor of the Holy Roman Empire (800–814).

hand, of the first war between England and France under Philip I in 1087[1], and on the other, the First Crusade in 1096.

The hatred fomented by the first hostilities between England and France lasted for more than eight centuries; provinces were lost, retaken, and lost again, but to what useful end? In 1415 Henry V of England was proclaimed King of France[2]. In 1450 the English were expelled from French territory. In 1755 a new Anglo-French war broke out; this was followed by war at sea in 1778 which lasted until 1783[3] when the Peace of Versailles brought a momentary halt to hostilities. These, however, were soon resumed with renewed vigor, continuing throughout the period of the Republic and the Empire. Are we to pretend that such persistent hatred serves the cause of civilization and restores order where disorder prevailed in international relations? The detailed history of these wars gives us proof of the contrary.

And the Crusades? That absurd epic, which originated in 1096, declared its aim to be the deliverance of the lands of the Holy Sepulchre from the Turks. There were seven Crusades, which cut down the flower of Europe's nobility and annihilated innumerable poor serfs for a period of more than 150 years until 1270[4]. At this time the Greeks, having thrown off the Crusaders, revived the Eastern Empire, and eleven years later, the Turkish Empire came into being. The Crusades, it is claimed, brought to the people of the East the civilization of the West. It is more probable that they bestowed upon the West the vices of the East. In any case, it is certain that the peoples of Europe who had taken part in the Crusades were even more ignorant at the end of these distant expeditions than when they had first heard the cry of Peter the Hermit[5]: «God wills it! God wills it!»

Moreover, to gain some idea of the sort of civilization spread abroad among nations by these great and entirely fruitless wars, it is enough to refer

1. William (I) the Conqueror (1027?–1087), king of England (1066–1087), attacked Philip I (1052–1108), king of France (1060–1108) in the Vexin in 1087.
2. Henry V (1387–1422), king of England (1413–1422), defeated the French at Agincourt in 1415 and by the Treaty of Troyes (1420) was designated regent of France and heir to the throne.
3. The Seven Years War (1755–1763) resulted in the loss of most of the French colonial empire; from 1778 to 1783 France joined the Americans against England in the American War of Independence.
4. Some historians identify a total of nine Crusades undertaken between 1096 and 1272, a period of 176 years. The text in Les Prix Nobel reads «durant plus de 250 ans».
5. Peter the Hermit (c. 1050–1115), French monk and preacher; led one section of the First Crusade.

to the state of anarchy prevailing, for example, in France, where the habitual contempt for law led inevitably to armed strife, province against province, town against town, castle against castle; and always, the peasant was the victim sacrificed to the sins of his noble masters.

The dismal night of the Middle Ages is so familiar to us that we need not dwell on its era of violence and human retrogression. This chaotic period, the product of bloody contests whose sole, though unavowed, purpose was spoliation, shows well enough that war can lead only to war and never to progress or civilization.

Let us now go into the history of the formation of the modern state where we will find war once more the evil genie of misery and injustice at every stage of development.

The year 1618 saw the outbreak of the Thirty Years' War, waged by the German States, Austria, Sweden, and France under the pretext of religion. Massacre, pillage, the burning of villages and of whole lands, famine and demoralization—such is the sinister record of over a quarter of a century's folly. After the population of Germany had been decimated, a peace was signed in Westphalia which did no more than reaffirm the original state of affairs except for granting some concessions to princes who did not even know how to preserve them. It was certainly not worth the trouble of tearing one another apart for thirty years just to arrive at the conclusion that nobody knew for what or for whom he had been fighting.

The lesson learned would seem to have been forceful enough to persuade everybody, from then on, to devote himself to establishing the permanent peace so badly needed. However, the waves stirred up by the storm were not so easily calmed, and the end of the seventeenth century was marked by a series of intrigues and truces which continued to the middle of the eighteenth, alternating with periods of so-called general peace which, even then, allowed few people to breathe freely.

We certainly cannot claim that civilization made no progress at all in the course of the centuries following the Dark Ages. Wars, however frequent and destructive they may be, have never been able to kill entirely the intellectual and moral sense which raises man above the beast. The spirit of discovery and the need for solidarity as a prime condition of personal well-being had not been lost in the debris of kingdoms made and unmade by war. Great inventions and important discoveries had broadened the scope of productive activity, first of individuals and then of groups, and mankind was beginning to seek protection against an arbitrary use of violence that served only ignorance and oppression. The relative calm of the second half of the seventeenth and the first half of the eighteenth centuries nurtured this tendency, allowing it to grow–timidly at first among the enlightened–and to spread later among the masses. The concept of justice was emerging, escaping from the shackles of violence.

The Republic which succeeded the Bourbon monarchy in France had to wage wars in order to assert the right of the people to establish for themselves a political regime which would support their chosen internal policy. So it was that the clamor of war finally confused France to the point of making her forget that her role was a defensive one. Militarism reappeared, more ruthless than ever, bringing about the terrible era of the Napoleonic Wars and a reversion to barbarism in full contradiction of the great principles proclaimed by the Revolution of 1789.

There are those who maintain that the war which followed for twenty unbroken years, spreading to every corner of Europe, had the merit of circulating modern ideas even though presented to various peoples on the bayonets of the French grenadiers; who maintain, in short, that the frequent massacres, the sacking of cities and towns, and the crushing of the defeated had this time been the true agents of civilization.

This is a flagrant misconception to be found in extravagantly chauvinistic history books. The principles of the French Revolution would have forced their way into the consciousness of nations more surely and more quickly during peace and prosperity than they could ever have done in an atmosphere of hatred and defiance which encouraged excesses of unwarranted violence.

It is a fact that the end of the wars of the first Empire found populations, that of France above all, drained of manpower and resources of every kind. After dreaming of world domination, leading her armies to the farthest frontiers of Europe, and serving the whims of a despot, France now had to give up a part of her own territory and, under monarchs set on the throne from without, begin the toilsome climb from the depths of the abyss into which militarism had hurled her.

The other countries in Europe, mutilated and devastated by twenty years of war, did not, in the midst of their ruins, seem to appreciate very much the lessons in civilization which were supposedly imparted to them along with the grapeshot. Beyond doubt the people would have accepted these modern ideas of law and justice more willingly and more quickly if they had peaceably discovered their source instead of discovering it while watching their fields laid waste, their homes burned, and their young men killed.

Let no one refer to the sword of Napoleon I as the instrument of progress and civilization!

Some will object perhaps that I have so far spoken only of wars of conquest and will ask me what I think about the wars of independence which broke out in Europe after the Restoration of 1815; no doubt they will demand comment particularly about the intervention on behalf of the Greeks in 1827 and about the aid given by France in 1860 to Italy in her struggle to resist Austrian domination.

Such a question would not embarrass me. The struggles of races and nations to regain their independence are the products of earlier violations of right, which constitute provocation in the eyes of the passive nations. Had the latter not, in the first place, been deprived of their autonomy, been oppressed and cut off from lands to which they had a natural affinity, their people would not have resorted to force in order to rectify an original abuse of force. The Greek war of independence, for example, was no more than the conclusion of an earlier war of conquest; the same is true of every other uprising of a people demanding their right to independence.

These calls to arms are for the purpose of reestablishing the natural order of affairs as it was before its violation by foreign invasions in an era when force superseded law; they are simply the result of these invasions and of the oppressive measures taken to assure their continued effect. These wars would not have occurred, nor would these situations themselves have arisen, if a regime of international justice such as that advocated by the friends of peace had been established rather than repressed for over two thousand years by the apologists of war.

What can we say of other wars of our time which did not have the liberation of oppressed peoples as their primary objective? Fomented by diplomatic intrigues or by private speculation, these intermittent reversions to primitive brutality have produced nothing, apart from the spilling of blood, except the creation of a state of anarchy in international relations and the foundation for future conflicts. In 1855, France, England, and the Piedmont seized Sebastopol in order to weaken Russia and strengthen Turkey[1]. Now, these same powers are allying themselves with Russia in an effort to impose their will on the Sultan with respect to the internal administration of his states[2].

1. In the course of the Crimean War (1853–1856).
2. As in Macedonia, for example. See fn.3, p. 18.

The French expedition to Mexico in 1861 cost the French 800 million francs and exacted untold material wealth and manpower from the Mexicans, only to end in the disaster at Querétaro which erased all traces of the empire on whose throne the French army had placed the Archduke Maximilian[1].

The invasion of Schleswig-Holstein by Austria and Prussia in 1864 had, by 1866, resulted in mutual recrimination between the two who had conspired together in this act of violence, thereby appointing themselves the sole judges of their own cause. Austria, humiliated at Sadowa, later joined hands with Prussia again to form the Triple Alliance[2], which now is scarcely worth the paper it is written on.

Again in Europe, the Russo-Turkish War of 1877 was concluded by the Treaty of San Stefano, which the Treaty of Berlin later nullified and which was even less well disposed to the claims of the Balkan peoples.

As for the Spanish-American War over the possession of Cuba, or the war in the Transvaal, or the combined expedition against China, or the present Russo-Japanese War—all these are too recent[3] for us to be able to draw any conclusions. One thing, however, is certain, and that is that they have contributed appreciably to the discrediting of war. I leave to the militarists the difficult task of trying to explain to us how these wars have served to shape character or to promote the progress of civilization, or to achieve the reign of justice on earth. So far, they have not come forward with the explanation.

In concluding my historical survey, I invite the attention of those who wish to devote some serious study to the relationships between war and the moral and material development of mankind.

One question often asked of pacifists is: Granted that war is an evil, what can you find to put in its place when an amicable solution becomes impossible? The treaties of arbitration concluded in the past few years[4] provide

1. Ferdinand Maximilian Joseph (1832–1867), Austrian archduke and brother of the Austrian emperor.
2. The alliance of Germany and Austria in 1879 became the Triple Alliance when Italy joined in 1882.
3. Spanish American War (April–December, 1898); Boer War (1899–1902); Boxer Rebellion (1899–1900) against foreigners in China was put down by composite forces of all the major powers; Russo-Japanese War (1904–1905).
4. The *Les Prix Nobel* text reads: «Les traités d'arbitrage conclus de ces dernières années...»; the holograph original reads: «Les heureux événements de ces dernières années...».

an answer to this question by showing with what ease, given goodwill on both sides, international disputes can be ironed out and eliminated as cruel preoccupations of our times.

The Convention for the Pacific Settlement of International Disputes[1] signed at The Hague in 1899 by twenty-six nations offers a solution to international conflicts by a method unknown in the ancient world, in the Middle Ages, or even in modern history, a method of settling quarrels between nations without bloodshed. The method is not yet perfect, it is true, but it is an expression of what we were hoping for in bettering the conditions which gave it birth. Let it become a duty to apply its provisions in every case possible, and the friends of peace will be satisfied with this beginning. Later, after some experience has been gained, it will be perfected, and the human conscience, at last awakened, will regard it as the cornerstone of the structure of law and justice which will preside over international relations in the future.

Under the influence of the ideas which have sprung up in opposition to the abuse of force represented by war, several nations, including some of the most important ones, have recently signed treaties agreeing to submit to arbitration at the Court of The Hague any differences which may arise between them. We have welcomed the signing of such treaties between France and Great Britain, between France and Italy, between Great Britain and Italy, between France and Spain, and between The Netherlands and Denmark. Other similar conventions are being drafted by most of the European nations. This is a true sign of the times and, for once, the militaristic mind will be hard put to plunge mankind again into the follies of the past.

That is not all: France and England, taking advantage of the security given them by their treaty of permanent arbitration, have just concluded an agreement with respect to all the colonial questions that might have become a source of friction or dispute between them; namely, those of Egypt, Morocco, Siam, Newfoundland, etc. Let us admit that if all the other signatory nations of the Hague Convention were to draw up arbitration treaties between each other, and then were to settle points that might possibly constitute a source of conflict, there would no longer be any need to declare peace: it would exist *ipso facto*. No longer would the reign of peace be subject to the perpetual contradictions of war, for it would rest on the unassailable bedrock of justice, of law, and of the solidarity of peoples!

1. For detailed discussion of this Convention, see the Nobel lectures of laureates Albert Gobat and Louis Renault, pp. 31–35; 155–158.

Biography

Élie Ducommun (February 19, 1833–December 7, 1906), Swiss journalist, eloquent lecturer, business executive, steadfast advocate of peace, was born in Geneva, the son of a clock maker whose original home was in Neuchâtel. Early in his boyhood he gave evidence of his capacity to make the most of his remarkable talent and intelligence by intense application.

Having completed his early studies in Geneva at the age of seventeen, he obtained a post as tutor for a wealthy family in Saxony, remaining there for three years and becoming expert in the German language. Upon returning to Geneva, he taught in the public schools for two years and then in 1855 at the age of twenty-two, began his journalistic career with the editorship of a political journal, the *Revue de Genève*. In one way or another he was connected with journalistic enterprises for the rest of his life. In 1865 he moved to Bern where he founded the radical journal, *Der Fortschritt* [Progress], which was also published in French under the title *Progrès*; in 1871–1872, he edited *Helvétie*; beginning in 1868, he edited the news sheet, *Les États-Unis d'Europe*, published by the Ligue internationale de la paix et de la liberté [International League for Peace and Freedom]; and after 1891, as head of the Permanent Peace Bureau, he prepared or edited innumerable appeals, pamphlets, reports, news sheets, and the like for the peace societies and the international peace congresses.

He was, indeed, a «literary» man, absorbed for the most part in journalism but finding time, also, to publish poetry and to perform his duties as official translator for the National Council. August Schou, director of the Norwegian Nobel Institute, points out that Ducommun's writing often showed «striking acuity of thought», citing a dialogue he wrote in 1901 in which he refutes the notion current in that day that a war between major powers would be short because of the destructiveness of modern weapons, and predicts, in its stead, a long «war of attrition with alternating advances and retreats, and with operations bound up with a system of trenches and strong-points»[1].

1. *Nobel: The Man and His Prizes* (Amsterdam: Elsevier, 1962), pp. 547–548.

Ducommun was also a political figure of some consequence. In Bern he was a member of the Grand Council for ten years; in Geneva, prior to his leaving in 1865, he was a member of the Grand Council for nine years, becoming vice-chancellor in 1857 and chancellor of state of Geneva in 1862.

He was a business executive as well. For thirty years, beginning in 1875, he was secretary-general of the Jura-Bern-Lucerne railroad, or as it was later called after a merger, the Jura-Simplon line. This position required, according to Frédéric Passy, «the rarest qualities of exactitude, order, activity, and firmness»[1]. When the line was purchased by the state in 1903, Ducommun resigned.

Ducommun, meanwhile, gave virtually every spare moment at his disposal to his work for peace, most notably after 1890 when he consented to organize and to direct the International Bureau of Peace. From the inception of the Bureau until his death, Ducommun devoted himself, at his own insistence without remuneration, to carrying out its purposes of uniting the many different peace societies throughout the world, preserving archives, preparing for the congresses, implementing their decisions, and acting as a clearinghouse for all kinds of information about peace and the activities on its behalf.

Élie Ducommun died at the age of seventy-three of a disease of the heart and lungs.

Selected Bibliography

Dictionnaire historique et biographique de la Suisse. Neuchâtel, 1924–.

Ducommun, Élie. Much of Élie Ducommun's correspondence is deposited in the archives of the International Peace Bureau in Geneva, Switzerland.

Ducommun, Élie, *Derniers sourires: Poésies précédées d'une notice biographique*. Bern, 1908.

Ducommun, Élie, *Discours sur l'œuvre de la paix prononcé à Genève le 23 mai 1893*. Bern, 1893.

Ducommun, Élie, «The Permanent International Bureau of Peace», *The Independent*, 55 (March 19, 1903) 660–661.

Ducommun, Élie, *Précis historique du mouvement en faveur de la paix*. Bern, 1899.

Ducommun, Élie, *Sourires: Poésies*. Bienne, 1887.

Obituary, *Journal de Genève* (8 décembre 1906).

Obituary, *Journal de la paix* (11 décembre 1906).

Passy, Frédéric, «The Recipients of the Nobel Prize of Peace», *The Independent*, 55 (March 5, 1903) 554–557.

1. «The Recipients of the Nobel Prize of Peace», *The Independent*, 55 (March 5, 1903) 556.

Toast

by Jørgen Gunnarsson Løvland*, Chairman of the Nobel Committee

I have the honor to propose the health of our Swiss guest, the Nobel laureate Dr. Albert Gobat. You all know that in his capacity as head of the Interparliamentary Bureau in Bern, he has, ever since the Bureau's founding, directed the activities of the Interparliamentary Union. During this time the Union has grown considerably and is now one of the major factors in international politics. The fact that it has energetically and yet prudently attacked the problems of the present day is due mainly to its eminently practical administration (I was going to say its Swiss administration).

There has always been a governmental diplomatic service, and I am delighted to welcome some of its eminent representatives here. Dr. Gobat himself is in the service of a new type of diplomacy–parliamentary diplomacy. Far from finding himself in opposition, he has already demonstrated that these two kinds of diplomatic service can and do exist in cordial cooperation.

In congratulating Dr. Gobat for the results he has achieved, we also extend our sincere good wishes for the future of his work and we particularly wish him success in the important conference soon to be held in London[1].

* Mr. Løvland, also at this time foreign minister of Norway, introduced Dr. Gobat when the laureate made his speech at the Nobel Institute on July 18, 1906. Since there is no text of his introductory remarks, however, and since there was apparently no presentation speech at the award ceremony itself on December 10, 1902, this brief speech, delivered as a toast by Mr. Løvland at his banquet for Dr. Gobat that evening, is given here instead. The translation is based on the text in French, the language in which Mr. Løvland spoke, published in the Oslo *Aftenposten* on July 19, 1906.

1. The fourteenth Interparliamentary Conference held in London, July 23–25, 1906.

ALBERT GOBAT

The Development of the Hague Conventions of July 29, 1899

Nobel Lecture*, July 18, 1906

It will soon be seven years since the ninth Interparliamentary Conference[1] met here in your capital city. It was a notable assembly whose participants will long remember the magnificent hospitality of Norway. Some time before that meeting the official representatives of the majority of European, American, and Asian powers had gathered at The Hague to discuss the most important questions affecting the law of nations; and on the fourth of August, just as our deliberations here were nearing their close, we received word of the actions taken by the Hague Conference[2]. Our assembly was the first to acclaim this great work, and several of our speakers paid it handsome tribute not far from here in the Chamber of the Norwegian Parliament. No one will deny that this first general congress of world powers was brought about by the efforts of the Interparliamentary Union. It is therefore hardly surprising that the Union should not only submit the resolutions of the Hague Conference to exhaustive discussion, but should also work for the convoca-

---

* Having requested and received an extension of time in which to discharge his obligation as a laureate, Dr. Gobat delivered his Nobel lecture three and a half years after receiving the prize. According to the Oslo *Morgenbladet* for July 19, 1906, he did so in German after being introduced by Mr. Løvland, chairman of the Nobel Committee, at the Nobel Institute in Oslo on July 18, 1906. The *Morgenbladet* remarks that many people attended even though it was the middle of summer. The French text, the only one available, on which this translation is based is taken from *Les Prix Nobel en 1902: Supplément* (Stockholm, 1907).

1. Meeting of the Interparliamentary Union, founded in 1888 through Passy and Cremer (peace laureates for 1901 and 1903) and composed of members of parliaments from various nations. The primary objective of the Union at this time was to promote, via governmental channels, the principle of solving international disputes by arbitration; it also studied other problems related to international law and to peace in general. For a good brief account of the Union and its relations with the universal peace congresses, see F.S.L.Lyons, *Internationalism in Europe 1815–1914* (Leyden: A.W.Sythoff, 1963), pp. 325–330.

2. The Hague Conference of 1899 approved three conventions, three declarations, one resolution, and six *vœux* or recommendations.

tion of a second conference. At our request, President Roosevelt has been kind enough to assume the initiative in this matter [1]. You must agree, then, that it would be difficult for one who has been secretary-general of the Interparliamentary Union for the past fifteen years and who has in this capacity been awarded the Nobel Peace Prize, to select a more appropriate or topical subject than the work of the Hague Conference.

This great assembly of nations drew up three international conventions [2]. Today I shall confine myself to only one of these, that concerning the pacific settlement of international disputes. It can be divided into two parts: preservation of general peace, and international arbitration.

To keep the peace! What a noble and magnificent idea! How many hopes are stirred by the thought that this greatest of all ideals–the maintenance of peace–should be the objective of an international convention bearing the signatures of most of the nations of the world! How sad to relate, then, that it is precisely this part of the Hague Convention of July 29, 1899, which to date has been applied least. For it has averted neither the Boer War nor the Russo-Japanese War [3], not to speak of colonial wars.

For the purpose of preserving general peace, the Convention established procedures for making offers of good offices and for mediation. The first entails an offer made by one or several nations, in the event of imminent war or during the course of actual war, to intercede between the belligerents in an effort to effect conciliation–a very useful procedure and one easily carried out, for all that is required is a diplomatic note. And since, under the terms of the Hague Convention, neither the offer of good offices nor its rejection can be considered an unfriendly act, all powers, especially those favorably disposed to one or the other of the adversaries, should be only too anxious to offer their services. It is highly probable that in most cases war could be avoided or ended. For discussions allow passion to subside; and to persuade alienated neighbors, or at least one of them, to listen to the voice of a conciliator, is a step in the direction of peace.

If we examine the Hague Convention carefully, we see that it considers the offer of good offices a duty of every nation. In other words, such offers

1. See biography, p. 40.
2. The three international conventions were: I. Convention for the pacific settlement of international disputes. II. Convention with respect to the laws and customs of war on land. III. Convention for the adaptation to maritime warfare of the principles of the Geneva Convention of August 22, 1864.
3. Boer War (1899–1902); Russo-Japanese War (1904–1905).

should be made whenever a dispute becomes critical and threatens to explode into war. Article 27 is very clear on this point. Now not only have nations failed in this obligation, but, worse still, when at the beginning of the war between Russia and Japan, the President of the United States[1] was said to be on the point of offering his good offices, the government-inspired Russian press declared that any such act would be regarded as unfriendly. Thus, in this one instance a double violation of the Convention took place: first, by the failure of any nation to offer its good offices, and second, by the Russian government's semiofficial declaration that such an offer would be looked upon as an unfriendly act. But the Convention had already been violated previously, only a few months after the Hague Conference. No government, no head of state made any attempt to avert or arrest the Boer War. Civilization and morality have not yet influenced nations to consider inviolable a promise or agreement, solemnly signed and sealed, when it becomes part of international law. Ordinary citizens are obliged and, if need be, compelled by force to meet their commitments. But let higher obligations of an international order be involved, and governments repudiate them, more often than not with a disdainful shrug of the shoulders.

We can, however, record one very honorable exception: President Roosevelt, in spite of everything, persisted in offering his good offices to the Russians and Japanese. Neither party chose to condemn the offer as an unfriendly act. Exhausted by a terrible war, both accepted, and peace was concluded[2] under the folds of the star-spangled banner. President Roosevelt was the first head of state to apply the rules of the Hague Convention concerning the preservation of general peace. Honor and glory to this eminent statesman!

Since the procedure of offering good offices can effectively contribute to the maintenance of peace, and since the powers seem reluctant to use it voluntarily, there should be a way of organizing it so that it may be applied in all cases. Good offices may be either offered or required. An offer is preferable, but it should not have to depend purely and simply on chance; nor should indifference, false pride, fear, or secret satisfaction at the sight of two nations tearing each other apart prevent this sacred obligation from being exercised in all its dignity. By the organization of good offices I mean the establishment of a convention under the terms of which the powers obliged

1. President Theodore Roosevelt (1858–1919), recipient of the Nobel Peace Prize for 1906.
2. By the Treaty of Portsmouth, New Hampshire, signed September 5, 1905.

to offer them would be designated for each individual case. The signatories of the Hague Convention could be arranged in groups of two or three, the individual groups being nominated in advance to act in given contingencies; in other words, every possible conflict would be covered by a group of states, of whom at least one would be obliged to offer its good offices. Since the number of warlike powers is fortunately limited, it is no difficult matter to determine what possibilities of war exist. The adoption of such a system would mean that hostilities could never break out without the adversaries first having been exhorted to listen to the voice of conciliation.

The second method contained in the Hague Convention for preserving peace is that of mediation. There is a subtle distinction between this method and the one just outlined: whereas good offices are intended primarily to assure preliminary conciliation, the mediating power may go so far as to propose terms of settlement. Everything I have just said about good offices holds true in the case of mediation. Here again, it is a great pity that the Conference, after devoting five articles to it, stopped halfway and did not make mediation compulsory. It should have been stipulated that the conflicting parties must, before opening hostilities, call upon one or more friendly powers to mediate in the dispute. Compulsory mediation was provided for in the Declaration of Paris of 1856; the seven contracting parties [1] undertook to refer to mediation any dispute arising from the implementation of the agreement. Compulsory mediation was also provided for in the draft treaty of arbitration drawn up by the United States and Great Britain in 1897 [2]. These two examples alone give abundant proof that mediation can feasibly be incorporated on a compulsory basis in the Hague Convention. In acceding to this rule of mediation no power would in any way be abrogating its rights to another. For mediation is simply an attempt at conciliation like that which is insisted upon by many civil codes before a case can be taken to court. The mediator's proposals are not a judgment but a simple, friendly presentation. The sovereignty of the states involved remains completely intact, and it would really take a peculiarly obstinate government,

1. The Declaration of Paris, an agreement concerning rules of maritime warfare, was issued by the Congress of Paris which negotiated the Treaty of Paris after the Crimean War; the contracting parties were Austria, France, Great Britain, Prussia, Russia, Sardinia, and Turkey.
2. Signed by Secretary of State Richard Olney and British Ambassador Julian Pauncefote but not ratified by the United States Senate; the treaty was significant because it stated terms on which two nations might henceforth deal with each other.

devoid of all moral sense and concern for intellectual values, to reject mediation in the face of impending war. The state ruled by such a government
would place itself beyond the precincts of civilization.

Compulsory arbitration is a practical instrument of pacification and, as
such, it can and should be enacted by the Hague Conference. By laying
down the procedure and the rules for arbitration, by placing a permanent
court of arbitration at the disposal of conflicting powers, the Conference has
no more than made a start upon its task in the realm of international justice.
All of this is discretionary and left to the goodwill of nations. What is more,
the powers seem to be in no hurry to rally to the idea of general treaties
of arbitration, for only three have concluded such treaties to date: Denmark,
The Netherlands, and Italy[1]. It will be a long while yet, unfortunately, before
the military powers recognize the principle accepted thousands of years ago
in relations between individuals: that nations are obliged to submit their
controversies to the processes of law.

In this sphere of arbitration treaties, the Hague Conference could introduce a ruling that certain categories of international disputes should be submitted to arbitration. In my opinion this is the most that can be hoped for
at present–I repeat, in the sphere of arbitration treaties. It is likely that the
fourteenth Interparliamentary Conference, which is to meet next week in
London, will express this opinion[2]. Under such circumstances, military
powers will still have too many opportunities and too many pretexts to un-
leash the horrors of war. This is what compulsory mediation could prevent.
And even if this very simple and logical method were not accepted, then
another possibility would still remain: compulsory contractual mediation,
whereby nations having incomplete treaties of arbitration would be compelled to insert into these treaties the following clause which the United
States and Great Britain had adopted in their draft treaty of 1897: «In the
event a dispute arises which is not subject to arbitration under the terms of
the present treaty, the contracting parties undertake to request the mediation of one or several friendly powers.» This formula would make an outbreak of war impossible without some attempt at conciliation having been

1. Numerous specific treaties of arbitration had been concluded between various powers since 1899. But only Denmark, The Netherlands, Italy, and later Portugal were,
up to the time of the 1907 Conference, willing to bind themselves to submit practically
all disputes to arbitration.
2. The Conference adopted a model arbitration treaty for powers that did not consider
themselves in a position to submit all international disputes to arbitration.

made first. Now this is crucial. For it is hardly tenable that, once mediation has been accepted, agreement should not finally be reached. Peace negotiations between Japan and Russia were fraught with so many difficulties that success appeared to be out of the question; yet the voice of President Roosevelt prevailed in the end.

Let us restate the principal conclusions we have reached so far. We must:

(1) Organize offers of good offices.

(2) Substitute compulsory for optional mediation in the Convention of July 29, 1899.

(3) In some cases, that is to say when compulsory mediation is not accepted, declare that the mediation clause will always be inserted into every arbitration treaty, subject to the exclusion of certain disputes.

I should now like to consider the Hague Conference as an international political institution.

Before dispersing, the members of that first general congress of civilized states resolved to meet again at some future date. This is in effect the implication of the Final Act of the Conference, which stipulated that three questions[1] be referred for examination to a subsequent conference, and furthermore that the governments concerned should study the question of limiting armed forces and that of the types and calibers of firearms, with a view to reaching agreement. This mention of agreement clearly presupposes a discussion of these problems at another conference. Thus the nations represented at the Conference of 1899, and those who later acceded, affirmed in principle that similar gatherings would be convened in the future. Certainly, one cannot dispute the fact that they are deliberative assemblies, since the first Hague Conference has yielded three important international conventions, a permanent court of arbitration, and an administrative council. We can, therefore, truly say that there is in existence an international political organization whose object is the regulation of common international problems. But this is neither the first nor the only such organization. The international offices for postal (Universal Postal Union) and telegraph services, for railways, and for the protection of intellectual properties are also international political organizations, created to serve particular interests common to the whole of the civilized world. I cite these offices situated in Bern to illustrate how general conferences of states can give rise to the establishment

1. The three dealt with the rights and duties of neutrals, the inviolability of private property in naval warfare, and the bombardment of ports, towns, and villages by naval forces.

of international political institutions equipped with administrative machinery that function for the benefit of humanity in the same way that public authorities in our civilized states function.

Let us for a moment consider the Hague Conference from this point of view. You may perhaps have heard of the proposal submitted last year by the American Group to the Interparliamentary Conference at Brussels, that the latter should organize a kind of world parliament[1]. However alluring the picture of an amphictyonic council embracing all civilized nations may be, I do not believe that our efforts should be directed toward this end, an end whose realization can scarcely be glimpsed even in some dim and distant future. In any case, the Hague Conference can offer to mankind, to civilization, and to justice the same services that an international parliament could offer. And since it already exists, there is no need to create it. What is necessary is to perfect its organization and to ensure its ability to function properly.

In the first place the Conference must be convened. The best method of assuring this is to have it meet at regular intervals. Let it take place every three or every five years. There is no fear of an empty agenda! Nations are linked by so many conventions, agreements, understandings, so many practices and interests that these common concerns alone could fill the program of an entire conference.

Second, the Conference must be arranged in such a way that it can function effectively. For this reason neither the program of the Conference nor its decisions should be subject to unanimous approval. If the majority decides that a question be placed on the agenda, then it should be discussed regardless of any opposition. I grant you that, for the time being, resolutions would be binding only on nations who voted in their favor. But let the future attend to making them universally binding, and let us be satisfied if we reach the point where it will be impossible for one state to thwart the discussion of a question by obstruction or systematic opposition.

Finally, the Conference must be equipped with an administrative organization. This is absolutely vital for any Areopagus which disbands after completing its work but which is to reassemble at a later date. Such an organization presents no problems. As proof of this, I cite the international offices in Bern already mentioned; these are precisely administrative organs that function on behalf of the states forming the international unions charged

1. For this proposal, see *Union interparlementaire: Résolutions des conférences et décisions principales du conseil* by Christian L. Lange (Brussels: Misch & Thron, 1911), pp. 93–94.

with postal and telegraph services, railways, and the protection of literary and artistic works. It is scarcely to be expected that the member nations of the Hague Conference will immediately establish, on a similar scale, an office of international political affairs. But it is certainly possible to guarantee at least the continuity of the Hague Conference as an institution, both in terms of its existence and of its work. Among the duties which could be referred to such an administrative organ I mention the following:

(1) To communicate the decisions of the Conference to the governments of the states which have taken part.

(2) To invite other states to accede to such decisions.

(3) To receive and study claims arising from the implementation of the resolutions and conventions passed by the Hague Conference.

(4) To prepare a memorandum for the next Conference on the subject of these difficulties, if the states themselves have not provided some other method of resolving them.

(5) To prepare the next Conference.

(6) To convene the latter.

The organization in question could be set up in a variety of ways. The Office (president and secretaries) of the Conference, or a committee appointed by it, or a special administrative body such as the International Bureau instituted by the Convention of July 29, 1899 (Art. 22)–any of these could easily handle the assignments involved, especially the last named. For the two cases are highly analogous. Since the International Court of Arbitration is not in fact permanent because it sits only when its decisions are sought, a permanent office[1] has been attached to it. By the same token, a similar office could be set up for the benefit of the Conference itself, which would be meeting only every three or five years.

But I do not wish to impose any longer on your kind attention. What I have said represents the thoughts of a practical politician. It is true that I am not one of those who laugh at utopias. The utopia of today can become the reality of tomorrow. Utopias are conceived by optimistic logic which regards constant social and political progress as the ultimate goal of human endeavor; pessimism would plunge a hopeless mankind into a fresh cataclysm. But though I take my place in the crowded ranks of the optimists, I draw a distinction between the aims which can be realized imme-

1. This Bureau, established by Article 22 of Convention I, served the Court as a record office, as a channel of communication on court meetings, as administrator, and as depository of documents relative to actions by special tribunals.

diately and those for which we are not yet ready. Today one thing is certain: thanks to the marvellous inventions and discoveries of our era, the human spirit has finally awakened a social order long dormant: the solidarity of nations. This solidarity, spurred on by an irrepressible force to assert itself, must be protected in the exercise of its rights and duties. May the Hague Conference be its instrument! May the Conference act as its shield against the modern barbarians who would menace it. Civilization can justly rejoice in possessing in it an institution capable of advancing the aspirations and ideals of mankind. Let us wish this important Conference, so long and so impatiently awaited, every success and prosperity. May the second assembly and those which follow – upholders of the law and custodians of man's happiness – develop, perfect, and consummate the great work so auspiciously begun!

Biography

Charles Albert Gobat (May 21, 1843–March 16, 1914) was born at Trame-
lan, Switzerland, the son of a Protestant pastor and the nephew of Samuel
Gobat, a missionary who became bishop of Jerusalem. A brilliant student,
he studied at the Universities of Basle, Heidelberg, Bern, and Paris, taking
his doctorate in law, *summa cum laude*, from Heidelberg in 1867.

For the next fifteen years, Gobat devoted his time and energy to the law.
He began his practice in Bern and, at the same time, lectured on French civil
law at Bern University. He then opened an office in Delémont in the canton
of Bern, which soon became the leading legal firm of the district.

After 1882, however, he became increasingly absorbed in politics and
education. In that year he was appointed superintendent of public instruction for the canton of Bern, a position he held for thirty years. A progressive
in educational philosophy, he reformed the system of primary training, obtained increased budgetary support to improve the teacher–pupil ratio, supported the study of living languages, provided pupils with an alternative to
the traditionally narrow classical education by establishing curricula in vo-
cational and professional training.

His personal scholarship was concerned with history. He won acclaim for
his erudite *République de Berne et la France pendant les guerres de religion* (1891)
and widespread recognition (as well as large sales) for his more popularly
conceived *Histoire de la Suisse racontée au peuple* [A People's History of
Switzerland] (1900).

Meanwhile, he was pursuing a career in politics. In 1882 he was elected
to the Grand Council of Bern, becoming president of the cantonal government for the 1886–1887 term. From 1884 to 1890 he was a member of the
Council of States of Switzerland and from 1890 until his death a member
of the National Council, the other chamber of the central Swiss legislative
body. In politics as in education, Gobat was a liberal, a moderate reformer.
A major piece of legislation he sponsored in 1902 applied the principle of
arbitration to commercial treaties. By its terms, Switzerland agreed to insert
in all commercial treaties, such as customs agreements, a clause requiring

the parties to submit to the Permanent Court of Arbitration at The Hague any dispute that might arise from the day-to-day operation of the treaty.

The Interparliamentary Union, which held its first major international conference in 1889, provided Gobat with an appealing outlet for his advocacy of arbitration and peace. Founded largely through the efforts of the English parliamentarian Cremer, a Nobel Peace Prizewinner in 1903, and the French Deputy Passy, a co-recipient of the Nobel Peace Prize for 1901, the Interparliamentary Union, then as now, brought together interested members of the parliaments of all countries to discuss international issues and to explore ways to improve collaboration among nations via parliamentary and democratic institutions; at this time, however, its primary objective was to promote international arbitration.

Gobat presided over the fourth conference of the Union convened in 1892 at Bern. This conference officially established a central headquarters at Bern to be called the Interparliamentary Bureau and entrusted its direction to Albert Gobat. As director of the Bureau, a position he filled without remuneration for the next seventeen years, Gobat supervised the details of setting up the annual conferences, prepared the agenda, arranged for the publication of the proceedings (beginning in 1896), edited a monthly publication to which he frequently made personal contributions, encouraged members to sponsor within their own legislatures proposals to improve relations among nations. After the twelfth Interparliamentary Conference of 1904 in St.Louis passed a resolution calling for a second Hague Peace Conference, it was Gobat who acted as the Union's spokesman in asking U.S. President Theodore Roosevelt to appeal to all nations to participate in such a conference [1].

When Élie Ducommun, co-laureate for 1902, died in 1906, Gobat took over the direction of the International Peace Bureau, performing duties for that office during the next eight years analogous to those he had discharged for the Interparliamentary Bureau.

Gobat died with his boots on. On March 16, 1914, while attending a meeting of the peace conference at Bern, he arose as if to speak but collapsed, dying about an hour later.

---

1. Roosevelt responded affirmatively to this request and shortly thereafter had Secretary of State Hay issue a circular to the other nations. For various reasons, however, the credit for convening the Conference of 1907 is legitimately ascribed to Czar Nicholas II of Russia.

Selected Bibliography

Dictionnaire historique et biographique de la Suisse. Neuchâtel, 1924–.

Gobat, Albert, *Le Cauchemar de l'Europe.* Strasbourg, 1911.

Gobat, Albert, *Croquis et impressions d'Amérique.* Bern, Grunau, 1904.

Gobat, Albert, *Développement du Bureau international permanent de la paix.* Bern, 1910.

Gobat, Albert, *L'Histoire de la Suisse racontée au peuple.* Neuchâtel, Zahn, 1900.

Gobat, Albert, «The International Parliament», *The Independent,* 55 (May 14, 1903) 1148–1150.

Gobat, Albert, *La République de Berne et la France pendant les guerres de religion.* Paris, Gedalge, 1891.

Obituary, *Journal de Genève* (17 mars 1914).

Passy, Frédéric, «The Recipients of the Nobel Prize of Peace», *The Independent,* 55 (March 5, 1903) 554–557.

Peace 1903

WILLIAM RANDAL CREMER

Welcome

by Jørgen Gunnarsson Løvland*, Chairman of the Nobel Committee

I have the honor to extend to you a warm welcome. That you have come here, despite your age and despite the long journey in an inclement season of the year, is proof to us of the untiring energy you have for so many years devoted to the great cause which you have served with such enthusiasm and with such success. Our best wish for you is that you may see the ideas of peace and arbitration flourish and gain in strength and influence, and that you–having yourself so nobly given concrete expression to it by the use you have made of your Nobel Prize–may see this work assured for the future.

* Mr. Løvland, also at this time minister of public works of the Norwegian government, introduced the laureate to a large audience in the Hals Brothers Concert Hall in Oslo at 5:00 p.m. on January 15, 1905. He first introduced his guest to the audience in Norwegian in a very short speech summarized in the Oslo *Aftenposten* for January 16, 1905. The newspaper reports that he spoke of Mr. Cremer as being an outstanding member of the British Parliament, a representative of the British people and, in particular, a representative of the British workers. He then welcomed Cremer in English. The text of this speech in English is not extant. The *Aftenposten* for January 16, 1905, however, published a translation in Norwegian which serves as the text for the present translation. It is given here in lieu of the presentation speech since none was made at the award ceremony on December 10, 1903.

WILLIAM RANDAL CREMER

The Progress and Advantages of International Arbitration

Nobel Lecture*, January 15, 1905

For many reasons I regret the delay which has taken place in my appearance here. Ever since the Nobel Committee awarded me the prize, I have been anxious to fulfill the condition which they impose upon the recipient, that he should visit Christiania [Oslo] and deliver an address upon the subject of arbitration and peace.

Several circumstances entirely beyond my control have led to the delay, a delay which I deeply regret and for which I ask you to excuse me.

Travelers anxious to reach their journey's end, occasionally ask themselves how far they have got and how much farther they have to go before they reach the goal of their hopes. The progress they have made can be easily ascertained, but the remaining distance and possible accidents on the way are more difficult to calculate.

In the time at our disposal this evening, we pilgrims of peace might imitate the traveler and note how many milestones we have passed: whether we have made any real progress, whether we have any cause for rejoicing, whether any – and if so, what – real obstacles are still to be overcome.

For a long time the friends of peace were preaching and saying what *ought* to be done. I propose to tell you something about what *has* been done.

First – and I hope that you will agree with me – we have been fortunate in enlisting the sympathies and securing the support of the monarch[1] who sits on the British throne and to whom the world owes a debt of gratitude for using his best influence on behalf of the cause of peace. In the past, monarchs have so rarely used their influence in the cause of amity, that the example set by King Edward is the more notable, and one of the most hopeful signs of the times.

* The lecture text is taken from *Les Prix Nobel en 1903*. The Oslo *Dagbladet* for January 16, 1905, described the laureate as possessing a stocky build, swarthy complexion, bald head, grey mustache, and tinted glasses, and said that he read expertly, his voice strong and distinct.

1. Edward VII (1841–1910), called the Peacemaker, king of England (1901–1910).

Thirty-four years ago, when the organization of which I am secretary[1] formulated a plan for the establishment of a «High Court of Nations», we were laughed to scorn as mere theorists and utopians, the scoffers emphatically declaring that no two countries in the world would ever agree to take part in the establishment of such a court.

Today we proudly point to the fact that the Hague Tribunal *has* been established[2]; and notwithstanding the unfortunate blow it received in the early stages of its existence by the Boer War[3], and the attempt on the part of some nations to boycott it, there is now a general consensus of opinion that it has come to stay – and thanks to the munificence of Mr. Carnegie, this high court of nations will be provided with a permanent home in a Palace of Peace[4].

If evidence had been wanting as to the desirability and usefulness of such a tribunal, the recent «Dogger Bank» incident[5] supplied it. Had there been no tribunal in existence, Russia and Great Britain would probably have taken months to consider whether the so-called outrage was a fit subject to be referred to arbitration, and that delay would have been used by the crimson press to lash the public mind into a state of frenzy and to render a pacific solution impossible. But the very fact that the peaceful machinery was at hand, ready to be set in motion, suggested its employment, and notwithstanding the frantic efforts of some British journals to provoke a con-

1. The International Arbitration League; the proposed constitution of a «High Court of Nations» is carried in pp. 84–85 of *Sir Randal Cremer* by Howard Evans.
2. By the Hague Peace Conference of 1899.
3. 1899–1902.
4. Andrew Carnegie (1835–1919), American industrialist and philanthropist, donated $ 1,500,000 in 1903 for the construction of the Palace of Peace at The Hague as a home for the Permanent Court of Arbitration (Hague Tribunal) and as a library of international law; the building was dedicated on August 28, 1913.
5. The Dogger Bank, or Hull, incident occurred on October 21, 1904, when a Russian fleet on its way through the North Sea fired on English fishing trawlers at Dogger Bank. One vessel was sunk. The remaining trawlers, five of them seriously damaged, put into Hull, England, on October 23, with two killed and six wounded. The Russians claimed to have been attacked by Japanese torpedo boats mingling with the Hull trawlers. Although British public opinion was outraged, Britain referred the matter to an International Commission of Inquiry which, on February 26, 1905, reported its opinion that since «there was no torpedo boat either among the trawlers nor on the spot, the fire opened by Admiral Rozhdestvensky was not justifiable.» On March 9, the Russian ambassador handed to the secretary of state for Foreign Affairs an indemnity of £ 65,000.

flict, the two governments in a few days agreed to resort to the friendly offices of the Hague Tribunal.

During the last century the number of disputes settled by arbitration or friendly mediation amounted to nearly 200. Many of the disputes were of a trifling character. Some, however, were very serious, the most important of all being the great dispute between the United States and Great Britain with regard to the pirate ship *Alabama*[1].

It was not, however, until the year 1887 that the question entered upon what I regard as its practical stage. Up till that time meetings had been held, conferences arranged, and petitions presented to governments; but the difficulty with which the friends of peace were confronted was, who should begin? What nation would take the lead and make a practical proposal? To meet this difficulty and overcome these objections, memorials[2] from members of the British House of Commons were presented to the President and Congress of the United States of America, urging that the governments of the United States and of Great Britain should inaugurate a new era and conclude between them a treaty binding themselves to settle their differences by arbitration.

Of course the scoffers again pooh-poohed the idea that any nations could be found willing to conclude such treaties; but those who ridiculed have been again put to shame, for within the last twelve months, thirteen treaties have been concluded between various nations. The countries that have bound themselves by these obligations are: Great Britain and France; France and Italy; Great Britain and Italy; Denmark and Holland; Great Britain and Spain; France and Spain; France and Holland; Spain and Portugal; Germany and Great Britain; Great Britain, Norway and Sweden; Great Britain and Portugal; Switzerland and Great Britain; Sweden, Norway and Belgium. Seven other treaties have also been drafted, and signed by the government of the United States of America, and the governments of Great Britain, France, Germany, Italy, Spain, Portugal, and Switzerland. With the excep-

---

1. During the American Civil War, a British shipyard constructed the *Alabama* for the Confederacy. Armed with British weapons received at sea and manned by a Southern captain, with a partially British crew, the *Alabama* destroyed Northern shipping in 1863. In 1871 the United States' claims arising from this destruction were submitted to arbitration at Geneva, and in 1872 a decision in favor of the United States was accepted.

2. Memorials (or resolutions) were presented on two occasions, 1887 and 1893, Cremer taking the leading role each time.

tion of the treaties with the United States, which yet await the decision of the Senate, all the others are operative, so that today thirteen treaties have the force of international law.

But, say the skeptics, what use are the treaties now that you have got them? To this I make answer that the treaty between France and Great Britain[1], although only twelve months old, has been followed by a convention between the two governments in which all the differences between the two countries, some of which had lasted for centuries, have been equitably adjusted and the decisions of the convention endorsed by both parliaments. So today France and Great Britain, whose sons had frequently slaughtered each other and wasted the resources of both nations, are now living on terms of the most cordial friendship without a cloud on the horizon.

Another notable instance is afforded of the advantages of treaties of arbitration. The two South American republics, Chile and Argentina, which had been frequently in conflict, having solemnly bound themselves by treaty to settle their disputes by arbitration, finding that they had no use for their iron-clads and vessels of war, have been disposing of them to Russia, Great Britain, and any other power that chooses to purchase them.

The latter affords an excellent illustration of the wisdom of our policy in advocating arbitration first, with the conviction on our part that disarmament would be sure to follow. The one we have always regarded as the *means*; the other as the *end* to be attained.

Amongst the advantages which we have contended that nations would reap from entering into treaties of arbitration are, that when differences arose, the disputants would have time for reflection, because, while the arbitrators were deliberating, the passions of the contending parties would cool, and the chances of war be greatly diminished.

Again, at the first rumors of war, the market price of many necessary commodities is affected, especially articles which are crossing the seas and upon which the premium for insurance is increased, all such increases having ultimately to be paid for by the consumer.

Such treaties would also weaken the baneful influence of panic mongers and serve to protect honest investors from being defrauded by stock ex-

1. The Anglo-French Treaty of Arbitration, first of its kind in history, was signed on October 14, 1903, going into effect before general agreement on pending difficulties was concluded. These difficulties, which included problems in Egypt, Morocco, Newfoundland, New Hebrides, and Siam, were adjusted by April, 1904, and the arguments published.

change gamblers. At the first rumors of war, timid investors in various government stock, being panic-stricken, sell out, to their loss and the gamblers' gain. This evil would be lessened, if not obviated, as investors would not rush to sell out, knowing as they would, that war could not take place until after the dispute had been referred to arbitration.

A notable illustration of the advantages of arbitration is afforded by the late Boer War. If the points in dispute between the two governments had been referred to arbitration, as the Boers desired, the thousands of lives of heroic men and women which were sacrificed, the untimely deaths of 15,378 children in the concentration camps, the devastation wrought, the misery endured, and the 250 millions of money expended, would all have been saved.

So far, I have been referring to some of the good work which has been done, and now I propose to say something about *how* it has been done.

Thirty-four years ago, the British and French workmen inaugurated a series of conferences and meetings and the circulation of mutual addresses to their countrymen in favor of a better understanding between the peoples[1].

These efforts have been continued during the whole of that time and at last have culminated in the Treaty of Arbitration between France and England—the first treaty of that nature concluded between any of the nations of Europe. The example thus set has already led to the series of treaties I have previously referred to.

The victory which has been achieved is therefore a people's victory, and this is the opinion emphatically expressed by the great French orator and popular leader, Mr. Jaurès[2].

I have previously referred to the efforts which were made in 1887 and the following years in favor of an Anglo-American Treaty of Arbitration when two memorials in favor of such a treaty were signed, the first by 234 and the second by 364 members of the British Parliament. These memorials were unique. It was the first instance on record of the members of one

1. In 1871, Cremer formed the Workmen's Peace Association. A similar organization was founded at about the same time in Paris. At a conference in Paris in 1875 fifty British delegates led by Cremer joined with 100 French delegates led by Auguste Desmoulins in establishing the Workmen's Peace Committee to advance the international aspects of the peace crusade.
2. Jean Léon Jaurès (1859–1914), French politician, leader of the Socialists in the Chambre des Députés, founder (with Briand) and editor of *L'Humanité* (1904–1914).

parliament addressing the members of another. These influentially signed memorials were supplemented by a unanimous vote of the British House of Commons.

Ultimately a treaty was drafted [1], signed by both governments, endorsed by a large majority of the Senate, but failed, for want of three votes, to secure the requisite two-thirds majority. At the present moment, however, another treaty has been signed by the two governments and is now being considered by the Senate.

But out of that failure a new force sprang into existence. That force is now known as the Interparliamentary Union.

The Interparliamentary Conferences, which have led to the formation of that Union, began in 1888 with the meeting of thirty-eight British and French parliamentary representatives at Paris. Since then conferences have been held in London, Rome, Bern, The Hague, Brussels, Budapest, Christiania, Paris, Vienna, and last year at St. Louis. From that small meeting in Paris groups have been formed in every parliament of Europe except Spain.

The Union has now nearly 2,000 adherents, and the latest addition is the formation of a group in the Congress of the United States of America.

The influence and power of the Union is now recognized. The conferences are held in senate chambers, and governments make grants toward the expenses.

When the history of the Union comes to be written, it will be found that during the time when there was considerable friction and danger of war between Italy and France, the appeals made by the Union to the members of the Italian Parliament produced an excellent effect and were largely instrumental in preventing strife between those two nations.

It is also a matter of history that the Czar was induced to issue his Rescript, which led to the Hague Convention, by the proceedings of the conference at Budapest [2].

It has also brought into contact with each other and paved the way for a good understanding between the members of the parliaments of Europe and the United States. Its latest achievement was to induce the President of

1. The Anglo-American Arbitration Treaty (1897).
2. There was no official Russian delegate to the seventh Interparliamentary Union Conference in Budapest (September 23–25, 1896), but a Russian consul in Budapest, acting as an observer, sent to the Russian government a copy of the resolutions passed and later, as a member of the Foreign Office, to the Czar when concern about international armaments arose.

that great country to undertake the task of convening another conference of the nations to complete the work which the Hague Convention left unfinished. To the Union, therefore, is due the credit of having brought about the convention at the Hague which systematized arbitration and provided nations with an alternative method of settling their disputes.

To the Union is also due the credit of influencing President Roosevelt[1] to summon another convention, and although the invitations to that convention do not specify that disarmament will be considered, the strong and constantly increasing desire which exists upon the subject – especially in France – will force the convention seriously to consider the cost and danger of armaments and whether they are really peace-preserving, or war-provoking institutions.

The object lesson of the war between Japan and Russia[2], with its unparalleled holocaust, will make it practically impossible for the convention to disregard the question of disarmament.

To the industrial classes, the subject is of supreme importance. The workers have to pay, and the workers have to fight.

The task before us is a mighty one. All the vested interests and people who profit by war will – with the journals they control – resolutely oppose any reduction of armaments.

But science is rapidly becoming a powerful auxiliary of peace; the restiveness of the burden bearers and the growing political power of the people are also factors which will have to be reckoned with in the great struggle between the supporters of barbarism, and the higher civilization.

In this brief summary of efforts made and victories won, I have abstained from any reference to the part which I have been privileged to take in promoting the Anglo-American Treaty of Arbitration, which was the first organized effort ever made for such a purpose and which lifted the question on to a higher plane and brought it within the domain of practical politics.

1. Czar Nicholas II is generally given credit for the actual convening of the second Hague Peace Conference in 1907. Cremer is referring to President Theodore Roosevelt's remarks of September 24, 1904, to delegates from the recently adjourned Interparliamentary Union meetings in St. Louis when he said, «In response to your resolutions, I shall at an early date ask the other nations to join in a second congress at The Hague», and to his fulfillment of this promise in the following month by the issuance of a circular note through Secretary of State Hay to his counterparts in other nations urging the calling of such a conference.
2. February 8, 1904–August 29, 1905.

Incidentally I may state that every senator of the United States has just received a memorial urging that body to ratify the Anglo-American Treaty of Arbitration which is now before it. The memorial is signed by 7,452 officers of industrial organizations in Great Britain, and these organizations have a membership exceeding two and three-quarter millions.

Concerning the long-continued efforts which were necessary to bring the French and British people into line, the initiation and organization of the first Interparliamentary Conferences, the multifarious labors in the cause of peace in which I have been engaged during the past thirty-four years, I express no opinion, leaving my actions and doings to the judgment of my fellowmen.

Some people, however, appear to have lost heart because Japan and Russia are engaged in a sanguinary conflict. But the most ardent advocates of peace never expected that treaties of arbitration would at once put an end to all wars, any more than those who, when mankind was emerging from barbarism, first framed crude laws and set up rude courts of justice, expected that by so doing all men would immediately cease to fight out their personal differences.

Our forefathers, however, were not disheartened. The courts were continued for those who preferred to use them, and now we seldom hear of individual disputes being settled by brute force. What was formerly the universal practice is now regarded as degrading and brutalizing.

That is what we believe will be the ultimate effect upon nations of concluding treaties and setting up tribunals.

It may be that for a long time some nations will continue to fight each other, but the example of those nations who prefer arbitration to war, law courts to the battlefield, must sooner or later influence the belligerent powers and make war as unpopular as pugilism is now.

Gentlemen, if I have not exhausted my subject, I fear that I must have exhausted my audience.

I cannot, however, conclude without heartily thanking the Nobel Committee for having honored me with their suffrages, awarded me the magnificent prize, and afforded me the opportunity of enabling the International Arbitration League to continue its useful work when I am gone.

It has been the great object of my life to build up and endow a great peace organization which should be powerful enough to combat the forces which make for war, and thanks to the Nobel Committee, I have been able to do a great deal in that direction. Nearly the whole of the fund placed at my disposal has been given to and profitably invested for the use of the League.

My only regret is that I am unable to wholly, instead of partially, complete the endowment. I hope, however, that others may be induced to follow my example, and that before I die I may see the dream of my life realized.

There is still a great work before us. The advocates of peace are, however, no longer regarded as idle dreamers, and I trust that I have convinced you that our cause has, especially of late, made wonderful progress and that we are nearing the goal of our hopes.

The world has passed through a long night of tribulation and suffering, millions of our fellow creatures have been sacrificed to the demon of war; their blood has saturated every plain and dyed every ocean.

But courage, friends, courage! The darkness is ending, a new day is dawning, and the future is ours.

Hurrah! Hurrah!

Biography

William Randal Cremer (March 18, 1828[1]–July 22, 1908) was born in the
small town of Fareham, England, not far from Portsmouth, into a working-
class family at a time when intense misery was the workingman's lot. His
father, a coach painter, deserted the family while the boy was still an infant.
His mother, an indomitable woman, raised her son and two daughters despite stringent poverty and even sent her son to school–a church school, for
she was a strong Methodist. At fifteen he was apprenticed to an uncle in
the building trades, eventually becoming a full-fledged carpenter. During
this time he supplemented his meager formal education by attending lectures.
On one occasion he heard a lecture on peace in which the speaker suggested
that international disputes be settled by arbitration, an idea that Cremer
never forgot.

Cremer moved to London in 1852. There his capacity for administration
was recognized in 1858 when, at the age of thirty, he was elected to a council
of those running a campaign for the nine-hour day; later in that year he
was one of seven who directed labor during a lockout of 70,000 men. He
was instrumental in forming a single union for his trade: the Amalgamated
Society of Carpenters and Joiners; he participated in the formation of the
International Working Men's Association but withdrew his support when
the Association was taken over by more revolutionary thinkers.

Inevitably, it occurred to Cremer that labor should be actively represented
in Parliament. He stood for Warwick in 1868 on a liberal platform calling

1. *Les Prix Nobel*, the *Dictionary of National Biography*, the (London) *Times*, *Who's Who*,
the *Guide to Periodical Literature*, and the *Annual Register* give 1838 as the year of Cremer's birth. Sir Randal's biographer, Howard Evans, gives 1828. Investigation confirms
this latter date. The following entry appears in the baptismal register of the Wesleyan
Chapel, Daniel Street, Portsea, Portsmouth (RG4/563): «William Randall, son of
George Morris and Harriett Cremer, was born March 18, 1828, and baptized July 6th,
1828. Residence Fareham by me, W. Toase, Minister.» This information was sent to
the editor by C. F. Coghlan, correspondent and trustee of the Cremer Cottages Charity,
in a letter dated October 21, 1969, Fareham, Hants, England. The name *Randall* is here
written with two «l's», but Cremer always wrote his name with one «l».

for the vote by ballot, compulsory education, Irish disestablishment, direct taxation, land reform, amendment of the laws governing labor unions, creation of courts of conciliation to handle labor-management disputes and of international boards of arbitration to adjudicate disputes among nations. He was defeated then and again in 1874. But after the third Reform Bill of 1885 created the new constituency of Haggerston in suburban London, which consisted almost entirely of workingmen, he was elected to Parliament in 1885, 1886, and 1892. Defeated in 1895, he was reelected in 1900, retaining his seat until his death.

Cremer used his power as a member of Parliament and his prestige as a labor leader to advance his passionate belief that peace was the only acceptable state for mankind and arbitration the method by which it could be achieved. A committee of workingmen which he formed in 1870 to promote England's neutrality during the Franco-Prussian conflict became the Workmen's Peace Association in 1871 and it, in turn, provided the keystone for the International Arbitration League, an association to which he thereafter contributed both his time and his money.

In 1887, two years after entering Parliament, Cremer secured 234 signatures of members of Commons to a resolution addressed to the President and the Congress of the United States urging them to conclude with the government of Great Britain a treaty stipulating that disputes arising between the two governments which defied settlement by diplomacy should be referred to arbitration. In that same year Cremer, heading a delegation of British statesmen, presented the resolution to President Cleveland.

The resolution excited the interest of Frédéric Passy and other French deputies who invited Cremer and his colleagues to an exploratory meeting in Paris in 1888. As a result of this meeting the Interparliamentary Union[1] was formed and its first meeting held in Paris in 1889, with representatives from eight nations in attendance. Cremer was elected vice-president of the Union and secretary of the British section.

Cremer was a lonely man: his first wife died in 1876, his second in 1884; there were no children. He lived simply, enjoyed nature, worked long hours. He was also a generous man. The cash value of the Nobel Peace Prize in 1903 was about £ 8,000. He immediately gave £ 7,000 to the League of which he was secretary and later an additional £ 1,000.

Stricken by pneumonia, he died on July 22, 1908.

1. See biography of Frédéric Passy, co-recipient of the Nobel Peace Prize for 1901.

Selected Bibliography

Cremer, William Randal, «Parliamentary and Interparliamentary Experiences», *The Independent*, 61 (August 30, 1906) 508–513.

Davis, Hayne, «Cremer and the Interparliamentary Union», *The Independent*, 61 (July 19, 1906) 126–131.

Dictionary of National Biography: Twentieth Century Supplement, 1901–1911. London, Oxford University Press, 1912.

Efremov, Ivan N., «La Conciliation internationale», *Recueil des cours*, 18 (1927) 1–148. The Hague, Académie de droit international. The history of arbitration during the Cremer period is covered in pp. 5–62.

Evans, Howard, *Sir Randal Cremer: His Life and Work*. London, T. Fisher Unwin, 1909.

François, M.J.P.A., «La Cour permanente d'arbitrage: son origine, sa jurisprudence, son avenir», *Recueil des cours*, 87 (1955) 457–553. The Hague, Académie de droit international.

Obituary, the (London) *Times* (July 23, 1908) 13.

Ralston, Jackson H., *International Arbitration: From Athens to Locarno*. Stanford, Stanford University Press, 1929.

Peace 1904

THE INSTITUTE OF INTERNATIONAL LAW

Welcome

by Johannes Irgens*, Norwegian Minister of Foreign Affairs

In the name of the Norwegian government and of His Sovereign Majesty, who honors this official opening session with his presence, I have the pleasure of extending to the Institute of International Law a cordial welcome to the capital of Norway.

I assure the Institute and each of its members that it is with the most sincere pleasure that we see them here as our valued and cherished guests.

The noble purpose of the Institute – to encourage the progress of international law – must of itself arouse the most sympathetic response and meet with the keenest interest in every civilized nation. The advancement of the idea of justice among peoples will be a contribution of primary importance in securing peace between states. The Institute's range of activity encompasses the two fields of international law: on one hand, the Institute strives in public law to develop peaceful ties between nations and to make the laws of war more humane; on the other hand, in private law, its aim is to minimize or to eliminate difficulties arising from differences existing in the laws of the different countries.

The realization of the Institute's great work in these two categories of international law will be sought conscientiously and assiduously, we may be sure, by the eminent gentlemen meeting in the session which begins today.

One important and characteristic trait of the Institute is its totally private nature. The Institute is a free association of individuals from nearly every civilized country in the world, united by the lively interest which they

* Since there was no presentation speech at the Nobel award ceremony in 1904, this speech by Mr. Irgens, welcoming the Institute to Oslo in 1912, is given here instead. (For an explanatory note on the occasion, see p.64.) Mr. Irgens presided over the opening session of the Institute which was convened on August 24, 1912, at 3:00 p.m. in the auditorium of the Norwegian Nobel Institute in Oslo. His Majesty Haakon VII, King of Norway, and members of the diplomatic corps, as well as members of the Institute, were present. This translation is based on the French text in *Annuaire de l'Institut de droit international – Session de Christiania – Août 1912* (Paris: A.Pedone, 1912), Vol.25, pp.539–542.

bring to the study of the problems I have just mentioned. We all admire the energy and the dispatch displayed by these distinguished gentlemen who never hesitate at the prospect of taking long, tiring journeys every year or two for the purpose of meeting to carry on these discussions.

And, I should like to emphasize the significant fact that these meetings are organized through private initiative! Free and disinterested discussions among individuals who are bound neither by mandates nor instructions have in their quest for truth a special importance, now and in the future, along with the more official discussions that have also fortuitously ensued during the great peace conferences of our time. The Institute reminds me, in more than one way, of the beginnings of the universities at the end of the Middle Ages, those scholarly communities whose independent studies have contributed so much to the development and the progress of nations.

Let me pause for a moment to point out how useful the work of this unique institute is to the governments of the different nations. Statesmen must continually consult international law. In the various ministries of foreign affairs no long period of time ever goes by without producing some new problem which poses the question: what solution is indicated by international law? Thus the practical actions of statesmen are linked to the principles and requirements formulated by learned specialists. And it is in precisely this area, I think, that the Institute carries out its most important function. All of its members are scholars, but they are not scholars only: most of them are, or have been, practical men of affairs—judges, lawyers, diplomats, government officials, and the like. And that is why the annals of the Institute are veritable mines of information for all those who seek to put into practice the principles of international law. Should a moot question arise in the area of international law today, it would be unusual indeed not to find some clue to its solution in one of the publications of the Institute.

Justitia et pace is the splendid motto of the Institute. But if the ordinary man in our hurried and incessantly active age should stop to think about it, I imagine that what would strike him most about this motto would be its last word: *pace*. And it is by a happy coincidence that the Institute is holding its current sessions in the hall of the Norwegian Nobel Institute. You are undoubtedly aware that the distinguished Swedish philanthropist, in his will, entrusted the Norwegian Parliament with the honorific task of distributing every year one of the five Nobel prizes, the Peace Prize, which is awarded to «the person who shall have done the most or the best work for fraternity among nations, for the abolition or reduction of standing armies and for the holding and promotion of peace congresses»[1]. In 1904 when this prize was awarded to the Institute which we have the honor of seeing assembled here today in this room, the choice was greeted with virtually unanimous approbation, not only here in Norway but all over the world. Through this prize our Norwegian people became still better acquainted with the Institute than we had been previously; and so the news that the Institute had accepted our invitation to hold its session here this year was received enthusiastically.

In conclusion, allow me to express the very sincere hope that the results of these meetings will be fruitful, for the Institute as well as for the progress of international law, and to wish each of the members of the Institute a pleasant stay in Oslo and in Norway.

I have the honor of introducing the next speaker, Minister Hagerup.

1. The translation of this portion of Alfred Nobel's will is taken from *Nobel: The Man and His Prizes*, ed. by the Nobel Foundation (Amsterdam: Elsevier, 1962), p.x.

The Work of the Institute of International Law

An Address*, August 24, 1912

On behalf of the Institute of International Law, whose president I have the honor to be, I would first of all like to express our deep gratitude to His Majesty[1] for honoring this opening of the twenty-seventh session of the Institute with his presence. I also beg to be allowed to convey our sincere thanks to the Minister of Foreign Affairs[2] for assuming the chairmanship of this session, and to the members of the diplomatic corps, to the Norwegian authorities, and to their ladies who have come here at our invitation. We see this large and distinguished gathering as a sign of sympathy not only for the Institute but also, and perhaps above all, for the ideas which it seeks to promote.

Practically no existing movement enjoys such popularity and has such a wide following as the movement for peace in international relations. The undertakings inspired by this aim are numerous and of varied nature. In many civilized countries, societies have been formed to propagate the idea

---

* Delivered by Mr. Hagerup at the Nobel Institute in Oslo, this address was simultaneously the official opening of the twenty-seventh session of the Institute of International Law, of which Mr. Hagerup was the president, and the lecture which the laureate or, as in this case, a representative of the honored organization gives in Oslo after the award of the Nobel Peace Prize. The Institute of International Law had been awarded the prize eight years previously in 1904. Georg Francis Hagerup (1853–1921), Norwegian jurist and statesman who had been minister of justice in the Norwegian government (1893–1895), head of the ministry (1895–1898; 1903–1905), and a member of the Hague Tribunal (1903), was at the time of this address minister plenipotentiary to Copenhagen, Brussels, and The Hague, as well as president of the Institute of International Law and a member of the Nobel Committee. This translation of his speech is based on the French text in *Les Prix Nobel en 1912*, which is identical to the text in *Annuaire de l'Institut de droit international – Session de Christiania – Août 1912* (Paris: A. Pedone, 1912), Vol. 25, pp. 543–555, except for three minor differences. No title has been given to the speech in the printed sources; the title used here embodies the theme of the discourse.

1. Haakon VII (1872–1957), king of Norway (1905–1957).

2. Johannes Irgens (1869–1939), the Norwegian jurist and diplomat – minister of foreign affairs (1910–1913) – who had just delivered the speech of welcome.

of pacifism among the people of the world, and great international meetings are held at frequent intervals. The parliaments of the majority of nations have founded an Interparliamentary Union[1] in order to work together to assure peace, and the same idea has prompted governments to send their representatives to various great conferences.

The part played in this movement by the Institute of International Law has been so considerable that perhaps you will pardon me if I take this opportunity of outlining, as briefly as possible, those aspects of this international work which the Institute can rightfully claim as the fruit of its own endeavors. It is perhaps my duty to do so, for the Nobel Prize awarded to the Institute a few years ago carried with it the stipulation, in accordance with the statutes of the Foundation, that the laureate should go to Oslo and there give a lecture. Now since this statutory rule has, I think, largely influenced the decision of the Institute to hold its present session in the Norwegian capital, it may be maintained that it devolves upon its president to give the lecture in which laureates introduce themselves to the public and justify, from a popular point of view, their claim to the recognition which accompanies the award of a Nobel Prize.

Such an explanation is perhaps not entirely without purpose because the organization and manner of operation of our Institute are necessarily such that it can never aspire to be popular in the broadest sense of that word. The founders of the Institute believed, with good reason, that its deliberations and resolutions would not carry sufficient weight unless its members and associates were more or less restricted to persons of specialized knowledge who represented the science of international law in various countries. The statutes demand that members should have «rendered services to international law in the domain of theory or of practice». The Institute does not open its doors to everybody and consequently does not have the kind of democratic character, so to speak, which in this day and age is generally a prerequisite for popularity. In its day-to-day activities, the Institute can hardly appeal to popular sentiment, nor can it attract to its work the untiring attention of that powerful instrument for expressing and broadcasting such sentiment, the modern press. Our work does not, however, avoid publicity; its results are published in our *Annuaire* [Yearbook], and although in accordance with the statutes its sessions are not public, the Bureau may admit representatives of the press to such meetings. In this connection

1. In 1888. See Cremer's Nobel lecture, pp. 51–52

two additional points are worth noting. In the first place, a large proportion of the work is done, not during the sessions themselves but in the intervals between them, by commissions whose members exchange views on current problems and pave the way for further discussion of them during the plenary sessions. In the second place, it must be admitted that these problems are sometimes so technical that their meaning and significance can be appreciated only with great difficulty by those who are not well versed in international law. In general, one can say that it is through its professional approach to very difficult, often arduous, and consequently rather slow work that the Institute strives to achieve its aim. According to the first article of its statutes, this aim is to «encourage progress in international law», by trying to formulate the general principles of the science so as to meet the standard of the judicial conscience of the civilized world, and by actively supporting every serious effort made toward the gradual and progressive codification of international law.

What is the importance of this work?

To put it briefly, it constitutes the basis necessary for all pacifistic work.

Justitia et pace is the motto of the Institute. It means we cannot hope to achieve peace until law and justice regulate international as well as national relations. It means eliminating, as far as possible, the sources of international friction which result from uncertainties and differences of opinion in the interpretation of the law. It means constructing by unremitting and patient work, block by block, the foundation that will support the rule of law over nations and peoples.

One can scarcely say that the immense importance of such efforts has always been generally understood, or that it is fully grasped even today.

There are two completely different groups that have not given these efforts quite their just due.

On the one hand, there is the group which maintains that in international relations force will always overcome law and that no code of international law can hold its own against the inequalities existing among nations with respect to their means of force. On the other hand, there are those who consider it futile to try to reach the desired goal by following the steep and tortuous path proposed by our Institute and who believe that they can get there by other, more easily accessible roads.

I shall return presently to consider those who are skeptical of international law, but first I would like to say a few words about the utopians of modern pacifism.

It is my opinion that the truly pacifistic movement has no more dangerous enemies than those who believe that they can anticipate natural developments and who try to persuade people to tackle the lofty summit of universal peace by a sort of «flight of Icarus» which would inevitably end, I fear, as sadly as did Icarus himself. Despite the progress of modern aeronautics, the aircraft has yet to be invented which would allow us to dispense with the necessity of following terrestrial paths to achieve practical and lasting civilizing results. Some people are convinced that universal compulsory arbitration in international relations is such an aircraft, just the one to carry us safely into the reign of perpetual peace. I must say frankly that this is a fatal misconception far removed from the true facts of international life. No one will deny that arbitration is an effective instrument for settling many kinds of international disputes, and the ever increasing use of it in our time is one of the most heartening and most promising facets of modern international life. The Institute of International Law would be the last to discount the full significance of this fact. Indeed, it has itself contributed extensively to the development of international jurisdiction. The arbitration procedure adopted by the Hague Conventions[1], for example, is based largely on a system worked out by the Institute. It was also the Institute that supplied valuable preparatory work for the organization of an international prize court whose almost unanimous adoption by the global powers has been called the most notable result of the second Peace Conference[2]. The Institute is including on its agenda discussion of ways in which to extend the application of international arbitration and to resolve certain legal problems which at the last conference at The Hague prevented more general support for the concept of compulsory arbitration. But the Institute's most effective contribution to the development of this idea is the work it has done to establish the foundation without which compulsory arbitration cannot become a reality. We must not lose sight of the fact that international jurisdiction must necessarily take the same role in relations between nations that tribunals play in disputes between individuals. Such jurisdiction is a means of resolving questions of *law*. However, the time is still a long way off when all civilized nations, large as well as small, will be ready to submit to arbitration questions of *interests*, especially of vitally important interests. The situation has been very clearly assessed in a recent

1. For a discussion of these, see Renault's Nobel lecture, pp. 143–166.
2. For a discussion of Convention XII on the creation of this court, see Renault's Nobel lecture, pp. 160–163.

report by an eminent member of this Institute who has devoted much effort to international arbitration: «To settle such questions by arbitration the judges would have to take up positions as gods of battle, of the fortunes of war, and of the fates of armed conflict. They would have to take into account the predominating interests of the nations concerned, the balance of power, and the existence of strength superior enough on one side to determine the outcome of a war. It is fruitless to search for formulas of arbitration which would permit solutions when justice plays so small a part.» One might also add that it would be fruitless to try to find judges who would be universally recognized as being equal to this virtually super-human task.

Those who do not realize that, in the present state of mankind, arbitration is incapable of avoiding or resolving large-scale international conflicts of interests, lay themselves open to cruel disillusionment. Not until the day when international life in its entirety is governed by the principles of law and justice, will it be possible to apply arbitration, universally and without exception, to the relations between nations.

Our Institute can justly claim the distinction of being the first international association to base its work on recognition of the fundamental truth that the advance of international law is the basis necessary to all efforts for peace and justice in international relations. It is only right that I recall at this point the name of the man to whom credit for this distinction is primarily due, the man who first took the initiative in bringing about the realization of the idea, the leading founder of our Institute, the eminent Belgian scholar and statesman Rolin-Jaequemyns[1].

Although I have stated earlier that the importance of «l'idée-force» or guiding principle of our Institute is perhaps not fully appreciated by everyone, I must point out that testimonials from those who do appreciate it are both more numerous and more telling. The Institute has received many such tributes, direct and indirect. Among the former I include words such as those spoken not many minutes ago by the Minister for Foreign Affairs, and certainly I include the Nobel Prize itself. And just recently the directors of that great organization for promoting peace which was created through the generosity of Mr. Carnegie[2] gave the Institute a grant of 100,000 francs

1. Gustave Rolin-Jaequemyns (1835–1902), editor of the *Revue de droit international et de législation comparée.*
2. Carnegie Endowment for International Peace established in 1910 by Andrew Carnegie (1835–1919), American industrialist and philanthropist.

to help it in its work. I wish to take this opportunity to express publicly, on behalf of the Institute, our profound gratitude for this generous recognition of the merit of our work.

The indirect tributes come from those who have focused their efforts on the same goals and who, despite beginning with a point of departure different from that of the Institute, have ended by associating themselves with the actual work of the Institute. Let me call your attention to some remarkable facts concerning this point.

The Interparliamentary Union, one of whose principal aims is to spread propaganda in favor of international arbitration, passed the following resolution at its session in Berlin in 1906[1]: «Whereas, The proper functioning of all international jurisdiction depends on the establishment of generally recognized principles of international law, the Conference is of the opinion that the third conference at The Hague should concern itself with international public law, using as a basis the work already done toward this end and in particular that of the Institute of International Law.»

Even more important is the fact that governments have found problems with which the Institute has been concerned worthy of inclusion in the agenda of major diplomatic conferences.

When, thirteen years ago, the sovereign of a great empire took the generous initiative of convening the first «peace» conference at The Hague[2], the pacifism then envisaged was at first perhaps somewhat different from that which concerns our Institute. But, by necessity, this first conference and the succeeding one in 1907 became in reality what they should also have been called: conferences of *international law*. None will question the great influence which the preparatory work of our Institute has had on the results of these conferences. It is manifest on every page of the Acts of these conferences.

1. The 1906 session of the Interparliamentary Union was held in London. Berlin was the site in 1908 (September 17–19) of the fifteenth Interparliamentary Conference which passed the resolution (Number 7) to which Mr. Hagerup refers. See *Union interparlementaire: Résolutions des conférences et décisions principales du conseil*, 2e édition, par Chr.-L. Lange, secrétaire général de l'Union (Bruxelles: Misch & Thron, 1911). Resolution 7 as reported in *Union interparlementaire*, p. 106, contains three words omitted in both the *Les Prix Nobel* text and the *Annuaire* text of the speech: *de la codification*. These words appear between *s'occupe* and *du droit international public*, so that it reads in English: «...concern itself with *the codification of* international public law...»

2. Czar Nicholas II of Russia whose Rescript to all countries represented at his court resulted in the 1899 Hague Peace Conference.

In the domain of international private law, thanks to the initiative of our eminent colleague Mr. Asser[1], diplomatic conferences have ever since 1893 made use of the material furnished by the Institute's resolutions for international conventions.

One might wonder whether the Institute of International Law has not lost some of its importance through the fact that the subjects for discussion and negotiation between governments have often been the same as its own, particularly after the second Hague Conference recommended that these worldwide meetings become a regular and constant element of international life.

This way of looking at it would not be an objective one, however. As I have just mentioned, the results achieved by the Hague Conferences in the fields of both public and private international law, are to a great extent due to the groundwork done by the Institute. Consequently, far from detracting from the importance of our work, the certainty that its results will be of service to governments for international conventions has increased its significance as well as the responsibility attached to it. Our Institute is fully aware of the special tasks imposed upon it by virtue of its collaboration with diplomatic conferences on international law. At the session in Paris in 1910, it elected a committee to prepare a study for the Institute on matters to recommend for inclusion on the agenda of the next peace conference. This committee's report will be discussed in the course of the Institute's present session.

Moreover, the work of our Institute will never be made redundant by the work of such diplomatic conferences, since the latter use different methods and, at least to a certain extent, different points of view. Through force of circumstances the big conferences can be called only at rather long intervals, often at times dictated by the general international situation rather than by choice. The Institute, on the other hand, works continuously and regularly, so to speak. The program and consequently the resolutions of the big diplomatic conferences are bound to be largely influenced by factors of a non-juridical kind and are very often the result of compromise between conflicting political interests. The Institute, on the other hand, enjoys complete independence and can, without having to look either to right or left, freely maintain points of view which according to the convictions of its members and associates best conform to the demands of law and justice.

1. Tobias Asser (1838–1913), co-recipient of the Nobel Peace Prize for 1911.

Heading our statutes is the following declaration: «The Institute of International Law is an exclusively scientific body, without any official character.»

This independence of any authority or political faction, as well as, generally speaking, of any influence alien to its aims, constitutes the strength of the Institute. The authority and influence of its work are based on this very independence, as well as on the qualifications of competence demanded for admission of its members or associates.

During the forty years since the founding of the Institute, its work has encompassed practically the whole area of international law, both public and private. But we are still far from exhausting all the questions which call for settlement. The development of international commercial and industrial relations, together with current scientific and technological progress, continually gives rise to new problems. There are, for instance, the judicial problems created by modern aeronautics, problems to which the Institute has given serious study and to which it will devote much time during the present session. On the other hand, the progress of scientific research in the field of law itself, along with the general development just mentioned, does not permit the Institute to retain indefinitely the solutions such research may have dictated. After a certain length of time, questions which have already appeared once on our agenda have to be resubmitted for further study whenever theory or practice indicates new points of view concerning them.

Looking back over the development of the concept of law and justice in international affairs during the forty years of the Institute's existence, we have every reason to be satisfied and to view the future with confidence.

Does this mean that we have had no disappointments?

Disappointments, yes, but no failures!

Our disappointments have sometimes been bitter ones indeed. And those to whom any effort to establish a legal basis for international relations is but an object for scorn, have never allowed us to forget them. Who has not heard remarks like this: Rulings of international law have little value since they are broken like spider webs at the first contact with conflicting interests? Even today, many still hold the view expressed by Frederick the Great[1]: «Treaties are like filigree, very pretty to look at but of little practical use.»

1. Frederick II, known as Frederick the Great (1712–1786), king of Prussia (1740–1786).

We have a reply to this. It is true that even today it happens that international treaties are broken or that generally accepted laws are violated. But cast your eyes, you skeptics, upon the vast domains which are today controlled by international conventions or by generally recognized codes of law–domains which include political, economic, philanthropic, artistic, and literary relations which lie at the very heart of the material interests and ideals of nations and which dominate their everyday life. You will see that, compared with the large number of conventional or customary precepts which are scrupulously observed, instances are relatively rare and exceptional in which a treaty is broken by a temporary abuse or a predominating interest. Furthermore, if we want to do justice to these exceptions, we must be truly aware of the relative value of each rule of law– whether it is founded on a convention or on some other source, whether it concerns the internal relations of a country or international life. The purpose of law is to serve, not to thwart progress and development. Even in the internal life of nations such progress cannot always be made without some conflict of interests that cannot be resolved without violation of existing law, either through revolutions or coups d'etat. How many of the numerous constitutions the world has seen introduced in the last century have been able to operate without any infringement of their laws? Should we, on this account, refuse to recognize a constitutional law or deny its judicial character? No sensible person will say Yes. Does this mean then that we must regard violations of international law from a totally different point of view?

As I said earlier, we are certainly not utopians who believe that the reign of justice and peace on earth has long been knocking at our door, and that it is only the obstinate militarists and the plotting diplomats who refuse to open it. If our work has had some success, it is undoubtedly because of our efforts to «calculate the limits of the possible», as one great statesman put it; because of our patience in refusing to advocate premature solutions; and because of our belief in the necessity of developing *gradually* and *progressively* as our statutes bid us.

Without exaggerating our competence, we can perhaps say that the study we have had to devote to the nature of law, to the conditions of its development, and to its place in the progress of human civilization in general, gives us the necessary perspective to judge which factors or events would be most likely to discourage the supporters of international law and justice. We know that what is called the law of nations dates back no further than to the beginning of the seventeenth century, and that this whole system of international conventions which I have just spoken of and which today constitutes an apparently indispensable basis for international relations has its roots only in the last fifty or, at most, the last hundred years. What an infinitesimal fraction of time this is within the entire span of the world's development, past and future! And, if we have managed to achieve so much in so short a time, then what prospects are not open to us for future development?

All attempts to further human progress should have far-reaching aims, and those who wish to take an active part in the effort should not lose patience if the progress sometimes appears to be very slow or even to sustain interruptions and setbacks.

The goal, the undisputed and inviolable reign of law in international relations, is most certainly still a long way off, and we must accept the probability that many generations will perish in the desert before mankind reaches the promised land. But let us take heart in the discerning words spoken by Mirabeau a century ago: «Law will one day become the sovereign of the world.»

History*

Founding. Gustave Rolin-Jaequemyns, a Belgian jurist and editor of the *Revue de droit international et de législation comparée*, provided the initiative for the founding of the Institute of International Law (L'Institut de droit international). In the aftermath of the Franco-Prussian War (1870–1871), he entered into correspondence with some other leading jurists who were also beginning to consider ways of establishing collective scientific action for the promotion of international law–inseparable, in their opinion, from the promotion of peace. In September, 1873, he assembled ten eminent jurists for meetings in the town hall of Ghent: Tobias Asser (The Netherlands)[1], Wladimir Besobrasoff (Russia), J. K. Bluntschli (Germany), Carlos Calvo (Argentina), David Dudley Field (U.S.A.), Émile de Laveleye (Belgium), James Lorimer (Great Britain), P. S. Mancini (Italy), Gustave Moynier (Switzerland), and Augusto Pierantoni (Italy). This group established the Institute, electing Mancini president and Rolin-Jaequemyns secretary-general. The Institute held its first session in Geneva in 1874; its fifty-fifth is scheduled for Zagreb in August–September, 1971.

The Institute of International Law is a purely scientific and private association, without official character, whose objective is to promote the progress of international law by: formulating general principles; cooperating in codification; seeking official acceptance of principles in harmony with the needs of modern society; contributing to the maintenance of peace or to the observance of the laws of war; proffering needed judicial advice in controversial or doubtful cases; and contributing, through publications, education of the public, and any other means, to the success of the principles of justice and humanity which should govern international relations.

Participants. The Institute maintains a reasonably balanced representation from the nations of the world and extends membership only to those who have demonstrated scholarly attainment and who are likely to be free from

* The editor gratefully acknowledges permission to use freely material kindly supplied for this history by the Institute of International Law.
1. Co-recipient of the Nobel Peace Prize for 1911.

political pressures. The statutes and regulations governing the Institute establish three categories of participants: members, associates, and honorary members. The associates – limited to seventy-two – are drawn from candidates «who have rendered service to international law, either in the domain of theory or of practice»[1] and who have been presented either by their national associations or by the Bureau of the Institute. The members – limited to sixty – are chosen from among the associates. The honorary members – not limited in number by the statutes but sparingly chosen in practice – are selected from the ranks of members or associates or from any other persons who distinguish themselves in the field of international law.

All participants share in the scholarly and issue-oriented activities of the Institute. Only the members deal with administrative matters such as finances, decisions concerning the statutes and regulations, election of members and honorary members, or the election of members of the Bureau or of the Council of the Auxiliary Foundation.

To assure representation of the various judicial systems of the world, the Institute permits no state to have more than one-fifth of the members or associates allowed in each category, and the Bureau of the Institute may allocate to candidates from parts of the world which are under-represented, up to one-third of the number of associate memberships open in any given session. As of May, 1971, the Institute had a total of 115 members, associates, and honorary members drawn from forty states, the preponderant number being from Western countries[2].

Organization. The assembly of members and honorary members convened at each session is the sovereign legislative body of the Institute. Executive power is vested in the Bureau of the Institute, an office composed of the president of the Institute, the three vice-presidents, the secretary-general, and the treasurer.

The president, usually chosen from among the members representing the country or institution which is to host the next session of the Institute, and the first vice-president are elected at the end of a given session and remain in office until the close of the following session. The second and third vice-presidents are elected at the opening of each session, remaining in office until the start of the next session. The secretary-general and the treasurer,

1. Statuts de l'Institut de droit international, Article 5.
2. Countries having four or more representatives are: Austria 4, Belgium 8, England 11, France 9, Germany 5, Greece 5, Italy 9, The Netherlands 4, Spain 5, Switzerland 5, United States 6.

elected to serve for three sessions, may succeed themselves. As the principal executive officer of the Institute, the secretary-general directs the daily operation of the Institute, assumes custody of its archives, and supervises publication of its *Yearbook*. His residence is the official seat of the Institute[1].

Finances. For many years the Institute was financed by contributions from its participants. Since the turn of the century, it has gradually built up an endowment from gifts, awards, and bequests, most notably the Nobel Peace Prize funds of 1904 and grants from the Carnegie Endowment for International Peace.

To manage the endowment funds, the Institute in 1947 created, under Swiss law, its Auxiliary Foundation, with headquarters in Lausanne. The funds, derived from the Foundation and administered by the treasurer, are used to reimburse members and associates for travel expenses incurred by attendance at the sessions, to defray organizational costs of the sessions, and to pay for the publication of the *Yearbook*.

Activities. The preoccupation of the Institute is the objective study of existing international law; and its abiding concern is that the evolution of international law proceed in a manner that conforms to the principles of justice and humanity. Since it is a private association, it has no mandate to intervene directly in actual international disputes. The Institute does not, therefore, participate in the settlement of international controversies, nor does it censure governments for the positions they take in particular cases. The only exception to this rule was its adoption of a resolution in 1877 pertaining to the application of international law in the war between Russia and Turkey.

The Institute does not, however, limit its concern to legal abstractions nor its thinking to mere speculation. The Institute has formulated and endorsed specific proposals for the gradual creation of an international community that respects law and justice. Between 1873 and 1969, the pacific settlement of international disputes, for example, has been the subject of

---

1. In the Institute's history of almost a hundred years there have been twelve secretaries-general: G. Rolin-Jaequemyns (1873–1878, Ghent; 1887–1892, Brussels); M. Rivier (1878–1887, Brussels); E. Lehr (1892–1900, Lausanne); Baron Descamps (1900–1906, Louvain); A. Rolin (1906–1913, Ghent; 1913–1919, The Hague; 1919–1923, Brussels); M. Nerincx (1923–1927, Louvain); C. De Visscher (1927–1931, Ghent; 1931–1937, Brussels); F. De Visscher (1937–1950, Brussels); H. Wehberg (1950–1962, Geneva); P. Guggenheim (*par interim* 1962–1963, Geneva); Mme. S. Bastid (1963–1969, Paris); P. De Visscher (1969–, Brussels).

fifteen directly applicable resolutions and of many others indirectly applicable. Among these resolutions are those on treaties of arbitration; on procedures in conciliation; on the establishment, composition, and procedure of an International Court of Justice. On the subject of human rights the Institute has adopted at least eleven directly applicable resolutions, including its declaration of 1929 and the statement of 1947. Between 1873 and World War I, the question of neutrality was the concern of twenty-one resolutions, but it was not revived until half a century later in resolutions of 1963 and 1969. In the domain of international private law, from 1873 to 1969, the Institute has adopted sixty-four resolutions dealing with civil, criminal, and commercial matters.

Although the resolutions of the Institute have no official authority in the chancelleries or the parliaments of the world, they have nonetheless exerted a significant influence on their actions, as well as on international conferences and on public opinion in general. For example, certain international treaties of the 1880's embodied recommendations made by the Institute on the Suez Canal and on the submarine cable; international arbitration procedures incorporated some of its suggestions; the Hague Peace Conferences of 1899 and 1907 utilized its studies on the laws of war, especially those on the codification of land war prepared at its 1880 session in Oxford and thereafter called the «Oxford Manual»; the League of Nations and the United Nations have considered its recommendations on various questions. In the domain of international private law, the Institute's influence can be seen in extradition legislation–to cite only one instance; and the 1969 discussion of pollution of international waters provides direction for research on a pressing, contemporary problem[1].

Selected Bibliography

Abrams, Irwin, «The Emergence of the International Law Societies», *Review of Politics*, 19 (1957) 361–380.

Annuaire de l'Institute de droit international: Session d'Édimbourg, Septembre, 1969. Volume 53, 2 tomes. Bâle, Éditions juridiques et sociologiques S. A., 1970. The first volume of the *Annuaire* was published at Ghent in 1877; the 53 volumes provide a complete record of the Proceedings of the Institute.

1. «Étude des mesures internationales les plus aptes à prévenir la pollution des milieux maritimes» in *Annuaire* (1969), pp. 547–711.

Rolin, Albéric, *Les Origines de l'Institut de droit international (1873–1923): Souvenirs d'un témoin.* Gand, 1923.

Schou, August, *Histoire de l'internationalisme III: Du Congrès de Vienne jusqu'à la première guerre mondiale (1914)*, pp. 311–321. Publications de l'Institut Nobel Norvégien, Tome VIII. Oslo, Aschehoug, 1963.

«Statuts de l'Institut de droit international.» An offprint of pp. xxxiii–lxxv from Tome II of the *Annuaire, q.v.supra.*

«Table des matières: L'Indiquant le titre des Résolutions adoptées par l'Institut au cours de ses cinquante-quatre sessions tenues depuis sa fondation en 1873 jusqu'à 1969.» An offprint of pp. lxxix–xci from Tome II of the *Annuaire, q.v.supra.*

Wehberg, Hans, *Institut de droit international: Tableau général des résolutions, 1873–1956.* Bâle, Éditions juridiques et sociologiques S.A., 1957.

Peace 1905

BERTHA VON SUTTNER

Introduction

by Bjørnstjerne Bjørnson*, Member of the Nobel Committee

On behalf of the Nobel Committee, Bjørnstjerne Bjørnson introduced the speaker, Baroness Bertha von Suttner, to the audience. In a few words he recalled the great influence of the Baroness on the growth of the peace movement. While still young she had had the audacity to oppose the horrors of war [1], and had done so in one of the most militaristic countries in Europe. She had continued this fight all her life and never wearied of crying «*Down with Arms*» [2]. Despite the laughter with which her words had been greeted in the beginning, they did receive a hearing because they were uttered by a person of noble character and because they proclaimed humanity's greatest cause. Many women had since followed in her footsteps and taken up the cause, and the call to lay down arms had become general. Moreover, to all men of goodwill the cause of peace and the women's cause were one and the same movement, striving for the same goal. When the cause of peace prevailed, then too would the women's cause be won.

* Mr. Bjørnson, a leading writer and a friend of the laureate, introduced Baroness von Suttner when she delivered her Nobel address on April 18, 1906. This translation of his introduction is based on the Norwegian précis of it in the Oslo *Aftenposten* of April 19. It is given here because no presentation speech was made on December 10, 1905. This date, the one prescribed for announcing the award, fell on a Sunday when the Norwegian Parliament was not in session. In order to conform to the Statute, the Committee invited Parliament members to attend the inauguration of the new Norwegian Nobel Institute building, which took place on that day, and made its announcement there. Speeches or remarks on this occasion were devoted to Alfred Nobel, the Nobel Foundation, etc. The Committee's decision was also given officially to the Parliament at its session the next day, December 11. Baroness von Suttner was unable to be present at either ceremony because of fatigue incurred during a strenuous schedule of meetings and speaking engagements. A speech in honor of Baroness von Suttner given by Mr. Løvland at the banquet after her address is also included here.

1. The laureate describes herself as being, in her earlier years, either «piously loyal to the military» or completely unconcerned about the horrors of war. See her *Memoirs*, Vol. I, pp. 46; 70–73; 133–136; 173–174; 229–233.

2. *Lay Down Your Arms* is the English title of the laureate's famous novel against war.

Banquet Speech

by Jørgen Gunnarsson Løvland*, Chairman of the Nobel Committee

History constantly demonstrates the great influence of women. Women have encouraged the ideas of war, the attitude to life, and the causes for which men have fought, for which their sons were brought up, and of which they have dreamed. Any change or reformation of these ideas must be brought about chiefly by women. The human ideal of manly courage and manly deeds must become more enlightened; the faithful worker in all spiritual and material spheres of life must displace the bloodstained hero as the true ideal. Women will cooperate to give men higher aims, to give their sons nobler dreams.

Many are the individual women who have set an example in sacrifice and work, who have followed the armies as angels of consolation and healing, tending the sick and suffering. How much more effective it is to do one's utmost to prevent misfortune!

This is where you, Madame Baroness, have taken the lead among women of today. You have attacked war itself and cried to the nations: «Down with arms!» This call will be your eternal honor.

> *Beginning as a murmur in the corn on a summer's day*
> *And growing to a gale through the tops of the forest,*
> *Till the ocean bears it on with thunderous voice,*
> *And nothing is heard but this.* [1]

These stirring words of our great poet apply to your call to action, Madame Baroness. It began as a murmur through the lovely meadow of the Danube

---

* Mr. Løvland, also at this time Norwegian foreign minister, delivered this speech in German at a banquet which he and his wife gave in honor of Baroness von Suttner after her Nobel address on April 18, 1906. The translation is based on the German text appearing in the Oslo *Aftenposten* the next day.

1. From a poem by the Norwegian poet Bjørnstjerne Bjørnson (1832–1910), recipient of the Nobel Prize in Literature for 1903, and the person who had introduced the laureate earlier in the day.

Valley[1], that old highway for the devastating armies of war. We already hear it in the forests in all parts of the world and soon, we hope, its voice, borne by the oceans of people, will permanently drown the sound of war drums and trumpets.

This will take a long time, some will say. We do not know. And it makes no difference to our work. Our task is clear: to combat any act of violence, any war of aggression, and so render even the justifiable defensive war unnecessary. We shall rouse the conscience of man, put justice and morality in the place of war.

We thank you, Madame Baroness, for your firm faith, for your hope and self-sacrifice, for your work. We too, in the lands of the North, women as well as men, need you to light and nourish the flame of faith and work. Good luck to you!

Frédéric Passy, that venerable apostle of peace[2] has called you, Madame Baroness, our general-in-chief. The friends of peace in Scandinavia applaud this salute.

1. The laureate's novel, *Lay Down Your Arms*, was written in the country near Vienna.
2. Frédéric Passy (1822-1912), co-recipient of the Nobel Peace Prize for 1901.

BERTHA VON SUTTNER

The Evolution of the Peace Movement

Nobel Lecture*, April 18, 1906

The stars of eternal truth and right have always shone in the firmament of human understanding. The process of bringing them down to earth, re-molding them into practical forms, imbuing them with vitality, and then making use of them, has been a long one.

One of the eternal truths is that happiness is created and developed in peace, and one of the eternal rights is the individual's right to live. The strongest of all instincts, that of self-preservation, is an assertion of this right, affirmed and sanctified by the ancient commandment: «Thou shalt not kill.»

It is unnecessary for me to point out how little this right and this commandment are respected in the present state of civilization. Up to the present time, the military organization of our society has been founded upon a denial of the possibility of peace, a contempt for the value of human life, and an acceptance of the urge to kill.

And because this has been so, as far back as world history records (and how short is the actual time, for what are a few thousand years?), most people believe that it must always remain so. That the world is ever changing and developing is still not generally recognized, since the knowledge of the laws of evolution, which control all life, whether in the geological time-span or in society, belongs to a recent period of scientific development.

It is erroneous to believe that the future will of necessity continue the trends of the past and the present. The past and present move away from us in the stream of time like the passing landscape of the river banks, as the vessel carrying mankind is borne inexorably by the current toward new shores.

That the future will always be one degree better than what is past and discarded is the conviction of those who understand the laws of evolution and try to assist their action. Only through the understanding and deliberate

---

* The laureate delivered this lecture in the Hals Brothers Concert Hall to a large audience. The Oslo *Aftenposten* of April 19, 1906, reports that the laureate, dressed in black, her voice husky with emotion, held her audience from the first; that she spoke concisely, using no contrived appeals, no gestures, no change of facial expression. The translation is based on the German text published in *Les Prix Nobel en 1905*.

application of natural laws and forces, in the material domain as well as in the moral, will the technical devices and the social institutions be created which will make our lives easier, richer, and more noble. These things are called ideals as long as they exist in the realm of ideas; they stand as achievements of progress as soon as they are transformed into visible, living, and effective forms.

«If you keep me in touch with developments, and if I hear that the Peace Movement is moving along the road of practical activity, then I will help it on with money.»

These words were spoken by that eminent Scandinavian to whom I owe this opportunity of appearing before you today, Ladies and Gentlemen. Alfred Nobel said them when my husband and I visited with him in 1892 in Bern, where a peace congress[1] was in progress.

His will showed that he had gradually become convinced that the movement had emerged from the fog of pious theories into the light of attainable and realistically envisaged goals. He recognized science and idealistic literature as pursuits which foster culture and help civilization. With these goals he ranked the objectives of the peace congresses: the attainment of international justice and the consequent reduction in the size of armies.

Alfred Nobel believed that social changes are brought about slowly, and sometimes by indirect means. He contributed 80,000 francs to Andrée's attempt to cross the North Pole[2]. He wrote to me that this could contribute more to peace than I would believe. «If Andrée attains his goal, or even if he only half attains it, it will be one of those successes that stimulate a spate of talk and excitement which open the way for the generation and acceptance of new ideas and new reforms.»[3]

But Nobel also saw a shorter and more direct way before him. On another occasion he wrote[4] to me: «It could and should soon come to pass

1. The fourth World Peace Congress, August 22–27, 1892. The conversation between Nobel and the laureate on this occasion is reported in *Memoirs of Bertha von Suttner*, Vol. I, pp. 429; 435–439.
2. Salomon August Andrée (1854–1897), Swedish aeronautical engineer and explorer, lost while attempting the first exploration by balloon of the Arctic.
3. This quotation, as well as the story of Nobel's connection with Andrée, is reported by Nicholas Halasz in *Nobel: A Biography of Alfred Nobel* (New York: Orion Press, 1959), pp. 257–258; 262–264.
4. Letter dated January 7, 1893, Paris; quoted in *Memoirs of Bertha von Suttner*, Vol. I, pp. 438–439.

that all states pledge themselves collectively to attack an aggressor. That would make war impossible, and would force even the most brutal and unreasonable Power to appeal to a court of arbitration, or else keep quiet. If the Triple Alliance included every state instead of only three, then peace would be assured for centuries.»

Alfred Nobel did not live to see the great progress and decisive events by which the Peace Idea was brought to life and made to function in a number of organizations.

He was, however, still alive in 1894 when Gladstone[1], the great British statesman, went even further than the principle of arbitration in proposing a permanent international tribunal. Philip Stanhope[2], a friend of the Grand Old Man, delivered this proposition to the Interparliamentary Conference of 1894 in Gladstone's name and succeeded in having a plan for such a tribunal forwarded to the member governments. Alfred Nobel lived to see the forwarding, but it was only after his death that any results were achieved: the calling of the Hague Conference and the founding of the Permanent Court of Arbitration[3]. It was of incalculable damage to the [peace] movement that such men as Alfred Nobel, Moritz von Egidy[4], and Johann von Bloch[5] were taken from it prematurely. It is true that their ideals and their work continue beyond the grave, but had they still been living in our midst, how greatly would their personal influence and the effect of their work have contributed to the acceleration of the movement! With what courage would they have taken up the fight against the militarists who are at the present time trying to keep the shaky old system going!

That system is doomed to failure. Once a new system begins to emerge,

1. William Ewart Gladstone (1809–1898), British prime minister (1868–1874; 1880–1885; 1886; 1892–1894).
2. Philip James Stanhope (1847–1923), member of House of Commons (1886–1892; 1893–1900), member of House of Lords after becoming Lord Weardale in 1905; president of two Interparliamentary Conferences (1890; 1906).
3. Commonly known as the Hague Tribunal, the Court was established by the first Hague Peace Conference (1899).
4. Christoph Moritz von Egidy (1847–1898), German officer and writer; forced to leave the army because of his pamphlet *Ernste Gedanken* which questioned some of the official dogmas of the established church; his broad concept of the Christian ideal involved taking a stand on all problems, including that of peace.
5. Jean de Bloch (1836–1902), Polish-born industrialist, author, and peace advocate; wrote *The Future of War in Its Technical, Economic, and Political Relations* (English trans., 1899) which contends that modern war will become too deadly to be risked.

the old ones must fall. The conviction that it is possible, that is is necessary, and that it would be a blessing to have an assured judicial peace between nations is already deeply embedded in all social strata, even in those that wield the power. The task is already so clearly outlined, and so many are already working on it, that it must sooner or later be accomplished. A few years ago there was not a single minister of state professing the ideals of the peace movement. Today there are already many heads of state who do so. The first statesman in office to pledge his agreement to an interparliamentary conference officially, was, as I recall, Norwegian Prime Minister Steen[1]. It was John Lund[2] who brought this news – which caused a sensation at the time – to the 1891 Interparliamentary Conference in Rome. Moreover, it was the Norwegian government which was the first to pay the traveling expenses of members of the Interparliamentary Union and to make a grant to the Peace Bureau in Bern[3]. Alfred Nobel had good reasons for choosing to entrust the administration of the funds of his peace legacy to the Norwegian Parliament.

Let us look round us in the world of today and see whether we are really justified in claiming for pacifism progressive development and positive results. A terrible war[4], unprecedented in the world's history, recently raged in the Far East. This war was followed by a revolution[5], even more terrible, which shook the giant Russian empire, a revolution whose final outcome we cannot yet foresee. We hear continually of fire, robbery, bombings,

1. Johannes Wilhelm Christian Steen (1827–1906), member of Norwegian Parliament for many years; prime minister (1891–1893; 1898–1902); member of the Norwegian Nobel Committee (1897–1904).
2. John Theodor Lund (1842–1913), member of Norwegian Parliament; member of the Norwegian Nobel Committee (1897–1913). At the banquet honoring the laureate, Mr.Lund proposed the toast to Sweden and the memory of Alfred Nobel.
3. The Interparliamentary Union (1889), composed of members from the various parliaments of the world, had at this time the primary objective of furthering the cause of international arbitration. The Permanent International Peace Bureau (1891), commonly called the Bern Bureau, was an information center for organizations and individuals working for peace and an executive arm for the international peace congresses.
4. The Russo-Japanese War (1904–1905).
5. The Revolution of 1905 in which dissatisfaction with czarist autocracy, spurred by losses in the war with Japan, resulted in a series of strikes, insurrections, and assassinations, along with demands for a constituent assembly; the atmosphere of revolution was still strong at the time of the laureate's speech.

executions, overflowing prisons, beatings, and massacres; in short, an orgy of the Demon Violence. Meanwhile, in Central and Western Europe which narrowly escaped war, we have distrust, threats, saber rattling, press baiting, feverish naval buildup, and rearming everywhere. In England, Germany, and France, novels are appearing in which the plot of a future surprise attack by a neighbor is intended as a spur to even more fervent arming. Fortresses are being erected, submarines built, whole areas mined, airships tested for use in war; and all this with such zeal–as if to attack one's neighbor were the most inevitable and important function of a state. Even the printed program of the second Hague Conference [to be held in 1907] proclaims it as virtually a council of war. Now in the face of all this, can people still maintain that the peace movement is making progress?

Well, we must not be blinded by the obvious; we must also look for the new growth pushing up from the ground below. We must understand that two philosophies, two eras of civilization, are wrestling with one another and that a vigorous new spirit is supplanting the blatant and threatening old. No longer weak and formless, this promising new life is already widely established and determined to survive. Quite apart from the peace movement, which is a symptom rather than a cause of actual change, there is taking place in the world a process of internationalization and unification. Factors contributing to the development of this process are technical inventions, improved communications, economic interdependence, and closer international relations. The instinct of self-preservation in human society, acting almost subconsciously, as do all drives in the human mind, is rebelling against the constantly refined methods of annihilation and against the destruction of humanity.

Complementing this subconscious striving toward an era free of war are people who are working deliberately toward this goal, who visualize the main essentials of a plan of action, who are seeking methods which will accomplish our aim as soon as possible. The present British prime minister, Campbell-Bannerman[1], is reopening the question of disarmament. The French senator d'Estournelles[2] is working for a Franco-German entente.

1. Sir Henry Campbell-Bannerman (1836–1908), British statesman of the Liberal Party; prime minister (1905–1908); advocate of international arbitration and armament limitation.
2. Baron Paul Henri Benjamin Balluet d'Estournelles de Constant de Rebecque (1852–1924), co-recipient of the Peace Prize for 1909.

Jaurès[1] summons the socialists of all countries to a united resistance to war. A Russian scholar, Novikov[2], calls for a sevenfold alliance of confederated great powers of the world. Roosevelt offers arbitration treaties to all countries and speaks the following words in his message to Congress[3]: «It remains our clear duty to strive in every practicable way to bring nearer the time when the sword shall not be the arbiter among nations.»

I wish to dwell for a moment on the subject of America. This land of limitless opportunities is marked by its ability to carry out new and daring plans of enormous imagination and scope, while often using the simplest methods. In other words, it is a nation idealistic in its concepts and practical in its execution of them. We feel that the modern peace movement has every chance in America of attracting strong support and of finding a clear formula for the implementation of its aims. The words of the President just quoted reveal full understanding of the task. The methods are outlined in the following objectives, which comprise the program of a peace campaign currently being waged in America.

(1) Arbitration treaties.

(2) A peace union between nations.

(3) An international body with strength to maintain law between nations, as between the States of North America, and through which the need for recourse to war may be abolished.

When Roosevelt received me in the White House on October 17, 1904, he said to me, «World peace is coming, it certainly is coming, but only step by step.»

And so it is. However clearly envisaged, however apparently near and within reach the goal may be, the road to it must be traversed a step at a time, and countless obstacles surmounted on the way.

Furthermore, we are dealing with a goal as yet not perceived by many millions or, if perceived, regarded as a utopian dream. Also, powerful vested interests are involved, interests trying to maintain the old order and to pre-

1. Jean Léon Jaurès (1859–1914), French politician; leader of the Socialists in the Chamber of Deputies; founder (with Aristide Briand) and editor of *L'Humanité* (1904–1914).

2. Yakov Aleksandrovich Novikov (1849–1912), Russian writer; author of *La Fédération de l'Europe* (1901).

3. President Theodore Roosevelt's fifth annual message to the U.S. Congress, December 5, 1905.

vent the goal's being reached. The adherents of the old order have a powerful ally in the natural law of inertia inherent in humanity which is, as it were,
a natural defense against change. Thus pacifism faces no easy struggle. This
question of whether violence or law shall prevail between states is the most
vital of the problems of our eventful era, and the most serious in its reper-
cussions. The beneficial results of a secure world peace are almost inconceivable, but even more inconceivable are the consequences of the threatening world war which many misguided people are prepared to precipitate.
The advocates of pacifism are well aware how meager are their resources
of personal influence and power. They know that they are still few in
number and weak in authority, but when they realistically consider themselves and the ideal they serve, they see themselves as the servants of the
greatest of all causes. On the solution of this problem depends whether our
Europe will become a showpiece of ruins and failure, or whether we can
avoid this danger and so enter sooner the coming era of secure peace and
law in which a civilization of unimagined glory will develop. The many
aspects of this question are what the second Hague Conference should be
discussing rather than the proposed topics concerning the laws and practices
of war at sea, the bombardment of ports, towns, and villages, the laying
of mines, and so on. The contents of this agenda demonstrate that, although
the supporters of the existing structure of society, which accepts war, come
to a peace conference prepared to modify the nature of war, they are basically trying to keep the present system intact. The advocates of pacifism, inside and outside the Conference, will, however, defend their objectives and
press forward another step toward their goal – the goal which, to repeat
Roosevelt's words, affirms the duty of his government and of all governments «to bring nearer the time when the sword shall not be the arbiter
among nations».

Biography

Baroness Bertha Felicie Sophie von Suttner (June 9, 1843–June 21, 1914), born Countess Kinsky in Prague, was the posthumous daughter of a field marshal and the granddaughter, on her mother's side, of a cavalry captain. Raised by her mother under the aegis of a guardian who was a member of the Austrian court, she was the product of an aristocratic society whose militaristic traditions she accepted without question for the first half of her life and vigorously opposed for the last half.

As a girl and young adult, Bertha studied languages and music (at one time aspiring to an operatic career), read voraciously, and enjoyed an active social life enlivened by travel.

At thirty, feeling she could no longer impose on her mother's dwindling funds, she took a position in Vienna as teacher-companion to the four daughters of the Suttner household. Here she met her future husband, the youngest son of the family. In 1876 she left for Paris to become Alfred Nobel's secretary but returned, after only a brief stay, to marry Baron Arthur Gundaccar von Suttner. Because of the Suttners' strong disapproval of the marriage, the young couple left immediately for the Caucasus where for nine years they earned an often precarious living by giving lessons in languages and music and eventually, and more successfully, by writing.

During this period the Baroness produced *Es Löwos*, a poetic description of their life together; four novels; and her first serious book, *Inventarium einer Seele* [Inventory of a Soul], in which she took stock of her thoughts and ideas on what she and her husband had been reading together, especially in evolutionist authors such as Darwin and Spencer; included is the concept of a society that would achieve progress though achieving peace.

In 1885, welcomed by the Baron's now relenting family, the Suttners returned to Austria where Bertha von Suttner wrote most of her books, including her many novels. Their life was oriented almost solely toward the literary until, through a friend, they learned about the International Arbitration and Peace Association[1] in London and about similar groups on the Con-

1. Founded in 1880 by Hodgson Pratt (1824–1907), English pacifist.

tinent, organizations that had as an actual working objective what they had now both accepted as an ideal: arbitration and peace in place of armed force. Baroness von Suttner immediately added material on this to her second serious book, *Das Maschinenzeitalter* [The Machine Age] which, when published early in 1889, was much discussed and reviewed. This book, criticizing many aspects of the times, was among the first to foretell the results of exaggerated nationalism and armaments.

Wanting to «be of service to the Peace League... [by writing] a book which should propagate its ideas»[1], Bertha von Suttner went to work at once on a novel whose heroine suffers all the horrors of war; the wars involved were those of the author's own day on which she did careful research. The effect of *Die Waffen nieder* [*Lay Down Your Arms*], published late in 1889, was consequently so real and the implied indictment of militarism so telling that the impact made on the reading public was tremendous. And from this time on, its author became an active leader in the peace movement, devoting a great part of her time, her energy, and her writing to the cause of peace – attending peace meetings and international congresses, helping to establish peace groups, recruiting members, lecturing, corresponding with people all over the world to promote peace projects.

In 1891 she helped form a Venetian peace group, initiated the Austrian Peace Society of which she was for a long time the president, attended her first international peace congress, and started the fund needed to establish the Bern Peace Bureau.

In 1892, with A. H. Fried[2], she initiated the peace journal *Die Waffen Nieder*, remaining its editor until the end of 1899 when it was replaced by the *Friedenswarte* (edited by Fried) to which she regularly contributed comments on current events (*Randglossen zur Zeitgeschichte*) until she died. Also in 1892 she promised Alfred Nobel to keep him informed on the progress of the peace movement and, if possible, to convince him of its effectiveness. No doubt she felt that she was beginning to succeed when she received a letter from him in January of 1893, telling her about a peace prize he hoped to found, one which, after his death in 1896, his will showed he had indeed established[3].

1. *Memoirs of Bertha von Suttner*, Vol. I, p. 294.
2. Alfred Hermann Fried (1864–1921), co-recipient of the Nobel Peace Prize for 1911.
3. For a detailed account of the relationship between Alfred Nobel and Bertha von Suttner and a discussion of the Peace Prize itself, including Baroness von Suttner's reactions and opinions concerning it, see Irwin Abrams' article «Bertha von Suttner and the Nobel Peace Prize».

Bertha von Suttner, along with her husband, worked hard to gain support for the Czar's Manifesto and the Hague Peace Conference of 1899, arranging public meetings, forming committees, lecturing. She sent accounts of the Conference itself to the *Neue Freie Presse* and to other papers, in other countries, and in the following year wrote articles and initiated meetings to popularize the idea of the Permanent Court of Arbitration set up by the Conference.

Although grief-stricken after her husband's death in 1902, she determined to carry on the work which they had so often done together and which he had asked her to continue.

She now left her quiet retirement in Vienna only on peace missions, which often included arduous speaking tours. She continued to write, but only for the cause of peace. By 1905 when she received the Nobel Peace Prize – at a fortuitous time financially – she was widely thought of as sharing the leadership of the peace movement with the venerable Passy[1]. In the years that followed she played a prominent part in the Anglo-German Friendship Committee formed at the 1905 Peace Congress to further Anglo-German conciliation; she warned all who would listen about the dangers of militarizing China and of using the rapidly developing aviation as a military instrument; she contributed lectures, articles, and interviews to the International Club set up at the 1907 Hague Peace Conference to promote the movement's objectives among the Conference delegates and the general public; she spoke at the 1908 Peace Congress in London; and she repeated again and again that «Europe is one» and that uniting it was the only way to prevent the world catastrophe which seemed to be coming.

Her last major effort, made in 1912 when she was almost seventy, was a second lecture tour in the United States, the first having followed her attending the International Peace Congress of 1904 in Boston.

In August of 1913, already affected by beginning illness, the Baroness spoke at the International Peace Congress at The Hague where she was greatly honored as the «generalissimo» of the peace movement. In May of 1914 she was still able to take an interest in preparations being made for the twenty-first Peace Congress, planned for Vienna in September. But her illness – suspected cancer – developed rapidly thereafter, and she died on June 21, 1914, two months before the erupting of the world war she had warned and struggled against.

1. Frédéric Passy (1822–1912), co-recipient of the Nobel Peace Prize for 1901.

In accordance with her wishes, she was cremated at Gotha and her ashes left there in the columbarium. The war and its immediate aftermath put an end not only to the plans of the peace movement for the congress in Vienna but to its plans for a monument to Bertha von Suttner.

Selected Bibliography

Abrams, Irwin, «Bertha von Suttner and the Nobel Peace Prize», in *Journal of Central European Affairs*, Vol.22, No.3 (October, 1962), 286–307.

Kempf, Beatrix, *Bertha von Suttner: Das Lebensbild einer grossen Frau*. Wien, Österreichischer Bundesverlag, 1964.

Playne, Caroline E., *Bertha von Suttner and the Struggle to Avert the World War*. London, Allen & Unwin, 1936.

Suttner, Bertha von. Most papers and manuscripts are in the Bertha von Suttner Manuscript Collection in the Peace Archives of the United Nations Library in Geneva, Switzerland. The Nobel Archives of the Nobel Foundation in Stockholm, Sweden, contain communications from Baroness von Suttner to Alfred Nobel.

Suttner, Bertha von, *Bertha von Suttners gesammelte Schriften in 12 Bdn*. Dresden, E. Pierson, 1906.

Suttner, Bertha von, *Briefe an einen Toten*. Dresden, E.Pierson, 1904, 1905.

Suttner, Bertha von, *Inventarium einer Seele*. Leipzig, W.Friedrich, 1883.

Suttner, Bertha von, *Der Kampf um die Vermeidung des Weltkrieges: Randglossen aus zwei Jahrzehnten zu den Zeitereignissen vor der Katastrophe* (1892–1900 und 1907–1914). 2 Bde. Zürich, Orell Füssli, 1917.

Suttner, Bertha von, *Krieg und Frieden: Ein Vortrag*. München, A.Schupp, 1900.

Suttner, Bertha von, *Lay Down Your Arms: The Autobiography of Martha von Tilling*. Authorized translation [of *Die Waffen nieder*]. London, Longmans, 1892.

Suttner, Bertha von, *Marthas Kinder*. Fortsetzung zu *Die Waffen nieder*. Dresden, E. Pierson, 1902.

Suttner, Bertha von, *Das Maschinenzeitalter*. Zukunftsvorlesungen über unsere Zeit von «Jemand». Zürich, Verlags-Magazin, 1891.

Suttner, Bertha von, *Memoirs of Bertha von Suttner: The Records of an Eventful Life*. Authorized translation [of the *Memoiren*]. 2 vols. Boston, Ginn, 1910.

Peace 1906

THEODORE ROOSEVELT

Presentation

by Gunnar Knudsen*, Presiding

As the Nobel Committee meets today, the tenth of December, perhaps for the last time in this hall[1], to announce to the Norwegian Parliament its decision concerning the award of the Peace Prize, it is appropriate to recall that the Norwegian Parliament was one of the first national assemblies to adopt and to support the cause of peace. Twelve or fifteen years ago, Gentlemen, the cause of peace presented a very different aspect from the one it presents today. The cause was then regarded as a utopian idea and its advocates as well-meaning but overly enthusiastic idealists who had no place in practical politics, being out of touch with the realities of life. The situation has altered radically since then, for in recent years leading statesmen, even heads of state, have espoused the cause, which has now acquired a totally different image in public opinion. The United States of America was among the first to infuse the ideal of peace into practical politics. Peace and arbitration treaties have now been concluded between the United States and the governments of several countries. But what has especially directed the attention of the friends of peace and of the whole civilized world to the United States is President Roosevelt's happy role in bringing to an end the bloody war recently waged between two of the world's great powers, Japan and

---

* President Theodore Roosevelt was awarded the Nobel Peace Prize for 1906 on December 10 of that year. He asked Mr. Herbert H. D. Peirce, American envoy extraordinary and minister plenipotentiary to Norway, to accept for him. Having completed his presidency in 1909, Mr. Roosevelt set out on an extensive travel and speaking tour, one of his last engagements being to deliver his postponed Nobel lecture on May 5, 1910, in Oslo. There are two speeches of interest from the ceremony of December 10, 1906, which are given here. The first speech by Mr. Gunnar Knudsen (1848–1928), the Norwegian statesman–and later, prime minister–who was presiding, is one of presentation of the prize to Mr. Peirce. Its translation is based on the text in the Norwegian language in *Les Prix Nobel en 1906*. In the second speech, Mr. Peirce accepts the prize and reads a telegram from President Roosevelt.

1. The hall in which the Norwegian Parliament customarily met. Mr. Knudsen anticipates, no doubt, that future sessions for this purpose would be held in the Norwegian Nobel Institute, which had recently been constructed.

Russia[1]. On behalf of the Norwegian Parliament, I now present to you, Mr. Ambassador, the Peace Prize along with its insignia, and I add the request that you convey to the President the greetings of the Norwegian people and their gratitude for all that he has done in the cause of peace. I would also add the wish that this eminent and highly gifted man may be blessed with the opportunity of continuing his work to strengthen the ideal of peace and to secure the peace of the world.

1. Russo-Japanese War (1904–1905). The laureate offered his good offices to mediate the dispute; the result was the Treaty of Portsmouth signed by Russia and Japan on September 5, 1905, at Portsmouth, N.H., U.S.A.

Acceptance

by Herbert H. D. Peirce, American Envoy

Since President Roosevelt was not present at the award ceremony on December 10, 1906, Mr. Herbert H. D. Peirce [1], American envoy extraordinary and minister plenipotentiary to Norway, accepted the prize on his behalf. Mr. Peirce's speech [2], which included the reading of a telegram from the President, follows:

I deeply regret that my residence in your capital has been as yet too brief to enable me to address you in your own vigorous language. But «had I a thousand several tongues», they would be inadequate to express to you the deep emotion with which I appear before you to receive, on behalf of the President of the United States, this distinguished testimonial of your recognition of those acts which stamp him as preeminent in devotion to the cause of peace and goodwill on earth.

I will not vainly attempt, by any words of mine, to add to the lustre of the name of Theodore Roosevelt. His acts proclaim him, and you, Gentlemen of the Norwegian Storting, by this award of the Nobel Peace Prize, a foundation conceived in God-like love of mankind, have blazoned to the world your recognition of his wise use of his great office in the best interests of humanity.

I quote President Roosevelt's words in a telegram from him, recently received by me, when I say that he regards the award of this prize as one of the greatest honors which any man, in any position, throughout the world, can receive.

Speaking for my countrymen, I may say that this award will deeply ap-

1. Since President Roosevelt was awarded the Peace Prize for his efforts in mediating the Russo-Japanese dispute, it is interesting to note that Mr. Peirce in 1905, as a member of the U.S. Department of State, had charge of arrangements for the deliberations at Portsmouth, N.H.
2. This text is taken from *Les Prix Nobel en 1906* where the speech is printed in English, its original language; some minor errors in the text of the Roosevelt telegram have been corrected by reference to the text in the *New York Times* for December 11, 1906.

peal to the hearts of our people and knit closer those bonds of sympathy which unite us in the brotherhood of nations.

To me, who have enjoyed the inestimable privilege of witnessing in the course of current affairs the earnest desire with which the chief magistrate of my country is imbued to promote the cause of peace, in the interest of all mankind, when peace comports with that honorable self-respect which nations as well as individuals owe to themselves, this award seems most markedly felicitous, and I rejoice greatly in the good fortune which permits me to be the medium of transmission of this token of your appreciation of the profound love for, and lofty sense of duty to his fellowmen which is the guiding principle of his official life.

The President has directed me to read to you, Mr. President, the following message which he has telegraphed to me for that purpose:

«I am profoundly moved and touched by the signal honor shown me through your body in conferring upon me the Nobel Peace Prize. There is no gift I could appreciate more and I wish it were in my power fully to express my gratitude. I thank you for it, and I thank you on behalf of the United States; for what I did, I was able to accomplish only as the representative of the nation of which, for the time being, I am president.

After much thought, I have concluded that the best and most fitting way to apply the amount of the prize is by using it as a foundation to establish at Washington a permanent industrial peace committee. The object will be to strive for better and more equitable relations among my countrymen who are engaged, whether as capitalists or as wage workers, in industrial and agricultural pursuits. This will carry out the purpose of the founder of the prize, for in modern life it is as important to work for the cause of just and righteous peace in the industrial world as in the world of nations.

I again express to you the assurance of my deep and lasting gratitude and appreciation.

Theodore Roosevelt»

Mr. Knudsen then read the telegram in Norwegian, adding the following concluding remarks: «I am convinced, Gentlemen, that the words expressed here by the President of the United States and the aim for which he proposes to work, with the aid of the Peace Prize just awarded him, will gain world-wide approbation. It is incontrovertible, as President Roosevelt says, that peace in all its aspects, peace among mankind, peace between nations, peace between social classes, peace between individuals – all are equally important. The one cannot, so to speak, be divorced from the other. If we are to promote civilization and the well-being of mankind as a whole, we can do it most effectively by securing world peace, for the entire history of the world teaches us that war and devastation are inseparable. The ravages of war arrest the progress of nations culturally, materially, socially, and politically, perhaps for generations. This is why Alfred Nobel has by his testament erected a memorial that will live forever in the minds of men and that establishes him as one of the greatest benefactors of mankind.»

THEODORE ROOSEVELT

International Peace

Nobel Lecture*, May 5, 1910

It is with peculiar pleasure that I stand here today to express the deep appreciation I feel of the high honor conferred upon me by the presentation
of the Nobel Peace Prize. The gold medal which formed part of the prize
I shall always keep, and I shall hand it on to my children as a precious
heirloom. The sum of money provided as part of the prize by the wise
generosity of the illustrious founder of this world-famous prize system, I
did not, under the peculiar circumstances of the case, feel at liberty to keep.
I think it eminently just and proper that in most cases the recipient of the
prize should keep for his own use the prize in its entirety. But in this case,
while I did not act officially as President of the United States, it was nevertheless only because I was President that I was enabled to act at all; and I
felt that the money must be considered as having been given me in trust
for the United States. I therefore used it as a nucleus for a foundation[1] to

* President Roosevelt spoke in the National Theatre in Oslo to an audience of over
2,000. This text is taken from *Les Prix Nobel en 1909*; it is identical to that in *The
Works of Theodore Roosevelt*, Vol. 18, and to that, save for paragraphing, in the *New
York Times*, May 6, 1910. After his salutation, Mr. Roosevelt prefaced his formal remarks
with a tribute to Bjørnstjerne Bjørnson, Norwegian author and member of the Nobel
Committee which awarded Roosevelt the prize, who had died only nine days before.
The reporter for the *New York Times* says that Roosevelt read the speech, departing
from the script to repeat in the same words or in somewhat different words the ideas
he had just expressed. On the evening of May 5, despite hoarseness which became
evident during the course of his speech in the afternoon, Roosevelt spoke at a banquet
in his honor, reviewing his presidential actions concerning problems in Cuba, Santo
Domingo, Panama, and the Philippines. This speech, recorded stenographically and
printed under the title «The Colonial Policy of the United States» in *African and
European Addresses by Theodore Roosevelt*, taken in conjunction with the Nobel address,
constitutes what may be called his theory of «peace with action».
1. The $36,734.79 prize was held in trust for Roosevelt's intention by a committee
which included the Chief Justice of the Supreme Court and the Secretaries of Agriculture, Commerce, and Labor. They made no use of the money, and it gathered
interest until 1917 when Roosevelt asked Congress to return it to him for distribution
among various charities in the United States and Europe which were providing relief

forward the cause of industrial peace, as being well within the general purpose of your Committee; for in our complex industrial civilization of today
the peace of righteousness and justice, the only kind of peace worth having,
is at least as necessary in the industrial world as it is among nations. There
is at least as much need to curb the cruel greed and arrogance of part of
the world of capital, to curb the cruel greed and violence of part of the world
of labor, as to check a cruel and unhealthy militarism in international relationships.

We must ever bear in mind that the great end in view is righteousness,
justice as between man and man, nation and nation, the chance to lead our
lives on a somewhat higher level, with a broader spirit of brotherly goodwill
one for another. Peace is generally good in itself, but it is never the highest
good unless it comes as the handmaid of righteousness; and it becomes a
very evil thing if it serves merely as a mask for cowardice and sloth, or as
an instrument to further the ends of despotism or anarchy. We despise and
abhor the bully, the brawler, the oppressor, whether in private or public
life, but we despise no less the coward and the voluptuary. No man is worth
calling a man who will not fight rather than submit to infamy or see those
that are dear to him suffer wrong. No nation deserves to exist if it permits
itself to lose the stern and virile virtues; and this without regard to whether
the loss is due to the growth of a heartless and all-absorbing commercialism,
to prolonged indulgence in luxury and soft, effortless ease, or to the deifica-
tion of a warped and twisted sentimentality.

Moreover, and above all, let us remember that words count only when
they give expression to deeds, or are to be translated into them. The leaders
of the Red Terror [1] prattled of peace while they steeped their hands in the
blood of the innocent; and many a tyrant has called it peace when he has
scourged honest protest into silence. Our words must be judged by our
deeds; and in striving for a lofty ideal we must use practical methods; and
if we cannot attain all at one leap, we must advance towards it step by step,
reasonably content so long as we do actually make some progress in the
right direction.

to victims of the World War. In August of that year, the total sum – $ 45,482.83 – was
so distributed.
1. The «Terror» is a term characterizing the conduct of power in revolutionary France
by the second Committee of Public Safety (September, 1793 – July, 1794), sometimes
identified as the «Red Terror» to distinguish it from the short-lived «White Terror»,
which was an effort by the Royalists in 1795 to destroy the Revolution.

Now, having freely admitted the limitations of our work and the qualifications to be borne in mind, I feel that I have the right to have my words
taken seriously when I point out where, in my judgment, great advance can
be made in the cause of international peace. I speak as a practical man, and
whatever I now advocate I actually tried to do when I was for the time being
the head of a great nation and keenly jealous of its honor and interest. I ask
other nations to do only what I should be glad to see my own nation do.

The advance can be made along several lines. First of all there can be
treaties of arbitration. There are, of course, states so backward that a civilized
community ought not to enter into an arbitration treaty with them, at least
until we have gone much further than at present in securing some kind of
international police action. But all really civilized communities should have
effective arbitration treaties among themselves. I believe that these treaties
can cover almost all questions liable to arise between such nations, if they
are drawn with the explicit agreement that each contracting party will
respect the other's territory and its absolute sovereignty within that territory,
and the equally explicit agreement that (aside from the very rare cases where
the nation's honor is vitally concerned) all other possible subjects of controversy will be submitted to arbitration. Such a treaty would insure peace
unless one party deliberately violated it. Of course, as yet there is no adequate safeguard against such deliberate violation, but the establishment of
a sufficient number of these treaties would go a long way towards creating
a world opinion which would finally find expression in the provision of
methods to forbid or punish any such violation.

Secondly, there is the further development of the Hague Tribunal, of the
work of the conferences and courts at The Hague. It has been well said that
the first Hague Conference framed a Magna Charta for the nations; it set
before us an ideal which has already to some extent been realized, and towards the full realization of which we can all steadily strive. The second
Conference made further progress; the third should do yet more[1]. Meanwhile the American government has more than once tentatively suggested
methods for completing the Court of Arbitral Justice constituted at the
second Hague Conference and for rendering it effective. It is earnestly to
be hoped that the various governments of Europe, working with those of

1. First Hague Conference (May 18–July 29, 1899) which established the Permanent
Court of Arbitration, known as the Hague Tribunal; second Hague Conference (June
15–October 18, 1907); a third conference was planned for 1915, but planning ended
with the outbreak of World War I in August, 1914.

America and of Asia, shall set themselves seriously to the task of devising some method which shall accomplish this result. If I may venture the suggestion, it would be well for the statesmen of the world, in planning for the erection of this world court, to study what has been done in the United States by the Supreme Court. I cannot help thinking that the Constitution of the United States, notably in the establishment of the Supreme Court and in the methods adopted for securing peace and good relations among and between the different states, offers certain valuable analogies to what should be striven for in order to secure, through the Hague courts and conferences, a species of world federation for international peace and justice. There are, of course, fundamental differences between what the United States Constitution does and what we should even attempt at this time to secure at The Hague; but the methods adopted in the American Constitution to prevent hostilities between the states, and to secure the supremacy of the Federal Court in certain classes of cases[1], are well worth the study of those who seek at The Hague to obtain the same results on a world scale.

In the third place, something should be done as soon as possible to check the growth of armaments, especially naval armaments, by international agreement. No one power could or should act by itself; for it is eminently undesirable, from the standpoint of the peace of righteousness, that a power which really does believe in peace should place itself at the mercy of some rival which may at bottom have no such belief and no intention of acting on it. But, granted sincerity of purpose, the great powers of the world should find no insurmountable difficulty in reaching an agreement which would put an end to the present costly and growing extravagance of expenditure on naval armaments. An agreement merely to limit the size of ships would have been very useful a few years ago, and would still be of use; but the agreement should go much further.

Finally, it would be a masterstroke if those great powers honestly bent on peace would form a League of Peace, not only to keep the peace among themselves, but to prevent, by force if necessary, its being broken by others. The supreme difficulty in connection with developing the peace work of The Hague arises from the lack of any executive power, of any police power to enforce the decrees of the court. In any community of any size the authority of the courts rests upon actual or potential force: on the existence of a police, or on the knowledge that the able-bodied men of the country

1. Articles III and IV of the Constitution of the U.S.

are both ready and willing to see that the decrees of judicial and legislative bodies are put into effect. In new and wild communities where there is violence, an honest man must protect himself; and until other means of securing his safety are devised, it is both foolish and wicked to persuade him to surrender his arms while the men who are dangerous to the community retain theirs. He should not renounce the right to protect himself by his own efforts until the community is so organized that it can effectively relieve the individual of the duty of putting down violence. So it is with nations. Each nation must keep well prepared to defend itself until the establishment of some form of international police power, competent and willing to prevent violence as between nations. As things are now, such power to command peace throughout the world could best be assured by some combination between those great nations which sincerely desire peace and have no thought themselves of committing aggressions. The combination might at first be only to secure peace within certain definite limits and on certain definite conditions; but the ruler or statesman who should bring about such a combination would have earned his place in history for all time and his title to the gratitude of all mankind.

Biography

Theodore Roosevelt (October 27, 1858–January 6, 1919) was born in New York into one of the old Dutch families which had settled in America in the seventeenth century. At eighteen he entered Harvard College and spent four years there, dividing his time between books and sport and excelling at both. After leaving Harvard he studied in Germany for almost a year and then immediately entered politics. He was elected to the Assembly of New York State, holding office for three years and distinguishing himself as an ardent reformer.

In 1884, because of ill health and the death of his wife, Roosevelt abandoned his political work for some time. He invested part of the fortune he had inherited from his father in a cattle ranch in Wyoming, expecting to remain in the West for many years. He became a passionate hunter, especially of big game, and an ardent believer in the wild outdoor life which brought him health and strength. In 1886 Roosevelt returned to New York, married again, and once more plunged into politics.

President Harrison, after his election in 1889, appointed Roosevelt as a member of the Civil Service Commission of which he later became president. This office he retained until 1895 when he undertook the direction of the Police Department of New York City. In 1897 he joined President McKinley's administration as assistant secretary of the Navy. While in this office he actively prepared for the Cuban War, which he saw was coming, and when it broke out in 1898, went to Cuba as lieutenant colonel of a regiment of volunteer cavalry, which he himself had raised among the hunters and cowboys of the West. He won great fame as leader of these «Rough-Riders», whose story he told in one of his most popular books.

Elected governor of the state of New York in 1898, he invested his two-year administration with the vigorous and businesslike characteristics which were his hallmark. He would have sought reelection in 1900, since much of his work was only half done, had the Republicans not chosen him as their candidate for the second office of the Union. He held the vice-presidency for less than a year, succeeding to the presidency after the assassination of

President McKinley on November 14, 1901. In 1904 Roosevelt was elected to a full term as president.

In 1902 President Roosevelt took the initiative in opening the International Court of Arbitration at The Hague, which, though founded in 1899, had not been called upon by any power in its first three years of existence. The United States and Mexico agreed to lay an old difference of theirs, concerning the Pious Foundations of California, before the Hague Tribunal. When this example was followed by other powers, the arbitration machinery created in 1899 was finally called into operation. Roosevelt also played a prominent part in extending the use of arbitration to international problems in the Western Hemisphere, concluding several arbitration treaties with European powers too, although the Senate refused to ratify them.

In 1904 the Interparliamentary Union, meeting in St. Louis, Missouri, requested Roosevelt to call another international conference to continue the work begun at The Hague in 1899. Roosevelt responded immediately, and in the autumn of 1904 Secretary of State John Hay invited the powers to meet at The Hague. Russia, however, refused to participate in a conference while engaged in hostilities with Japan. After the peace of 1905, the matter was placed in the hands of the Russian government, which had taken the initiative in convening the first Hague Conference.

In June, 1905, President Roosevelt offered his good offices as mediator between Russia and Japan, asking the belligerents to nominate plenipotentiaries to negotiate on the conditions of peace. In August they met at Portsmouth, New Hamsphire, and after some weeks of difficult negotiations concluded a peace treaty in September, 1905.

Roosevelt's candidate for president, William Howard Taft, took office in 1909. Dissatisfied with Taft's performance, Roosevelt bolted the regular Republican Party in 1912 and accepted the presidential nomination by the Progressive Party. He outpolled Taft, but Woodrow Wilson outpolled each of them. In 1917 Wilson refused his offer to raise and command a division to fight in World War I.

Roosevelt was an historian, a biographer, a statesman, a hunter, a naturalist, an orator. His prodigious literary output includes twenty-six books, over a thousand magazine articles, thousands of speeches and letters.

In 1919, at the age of sixty, he died in his sleep.

Selected Bibliography

The Theodore Roosevelt Collection in the Library of Congress contains some 150,000 Roosevelt letters besides drafts of state papers and speeches. The Roosevelt Memorial Association Collection at Harvard University contains his diaries, some original MSS, microfilms, and most of his publications.

Beale, Howard, K., *Theodore Roosevelt and the Rise of America to World Power*. Baltimore, Johns Hopkins Press, 1956.

Beers, Henry A., «Roosevelt as Man of Letters» in *Four Americans*. New Haven, Yale University Press, 1920.

Bradford, Gamaliel, «The Fury of Living: Theodore Roosevelt» in *The Quick and the Dead*. New York, Houghton Mifflin, 1931.

Dennett, Tyler, *Roosevelt and the Russo-Japanese War*. New York, Doubleday, 1925.

Hagedorn, Hermann, ed., *The Works of Theodore Roosevelt*. 24 vols. Memorial ed. New York, Scribner, 1923-1926.

Harbaugh, William H., *The Life and Times of Theodore Roosevelt*. New York, Straus and Cudahy, 1961.

Lorant, Stefan, *The Life and Times of Theodore Roosevelt*. New York, Doubleday, 1959.

Morison, Elting E., ed., *The Letters of Theodore Roosevelt*. 8 vols. Cambridge, Harvard University Press, 1951-1954.

Pringle, Henry F., *Theodore Roosevelt: A Biography*. New York, Harcourt Brace, 1931.

Richardson, James D., ed., *Messages and Papers of the Presidents*. Washington, D.C., 1908. Volumes X and XI, along with a Supplement (1910), contain texts of all Roosevelt's state papers.

Roosevelt, Theodore, *African and European Addresses*. New York, Putnam, 1910.

Roosevelt, Theodore, *African Game Trails*. New York, Scribner, 1910.

Roosevelt, Theodore, *An Autobiography*. New York, Scribner, 1913.

Roosevelt, Theodore, *Oliver Cromwell*. New York, Scribner, 1900.

Roosevelt, Theodore, *The Rough Riders*. New York, Scribner, 1898.

Roosevelt, Theodore, *The Winning of the West*. 4 vols. New York, Putnam, 1889-1896.

Wagenknecht, Edward C., *The Seven Worlds of Theodore Roosevelt*. New York, Longmans, Green, 1958.

Peace 1907

ERNESTO TEODORO MONETA

LOUIS RENAULT

Presentation

by Jørgen Gunnarsson Løvland*, Chairman of the Nobel Committee

Ernesto Teodoro Moneta was born in Milan in 1833. At the age of fifteen he took part in the war of liberation against the Austrians, and in 1859 he fought at Garibaldi's side in both North and South Italy[1]. In 1866 Moneta was an officer in the war with Austria, but after that campaign he retired from the army and has since devoted himself to journalism. In his thirties he became editor-in-chief of the Milan newspaper *Il Secolo*, one of the most important newspapers in Italy, and since 1898 he has published the periodical *La Vita internazionale*.

Since 1870 Moneta has belonged to the international peace movement and is its most important Italian representative. He has been a member of the Commission of the International Peace Bureau since 1895. With his prominent position in the Italian press, he has enjoyed excellent opportunities to promote his views. Special emphasis must be placed on his work in the press and in peace meetings, both public and private, for an understanding between France and Italy – work which dates back as far as the beginning of the modern-day enmity between these two countries.

In 1887 Moneta founded the Lombard Peace Union, of which he is now president. He has organized several peace meetings in Italy and in 1906 presided over the fifteenth International Peace Congress in Milan.

* On December 10, 1907, at the Norwegian Nobel Institute, Mr. Løvland, also at this time Norway's foreign minister, welcomed the audience and paid tribute to the memory of King Oscar II of Sweden (the last king to reign over the union of Sweden and Norway before its dissolution in 1905) who had died two days before. After a speech on «The Second Peace Conference» by Committee member Francis Hagerup, Mr. Løvland announced the joint winners of the Peace Prize for 1907, Mr. Moneta and Mr. Renault. He followed his announcement with a biographical sketch of each. That of Mr. Moneta is given here as the presentation speech. The translation is based on the Norwegian report in the Oslo *Aftenposten* of December 10, 1907.

1. See biography and the laureate's lecture.

ERNESTO TEODORO MONETA

Peace and Law in the Italian Tradition

Nobel Lecture*, August 25, 1909

When on the afternoon of December 10, 1907, I received the happy news, soon to be made public in the newspapers, that you had conferred upon me the Nobel Peace Prize, the satisfaction of all Italians was reflected in the many marks of affection and esteem I received from people in every walk of life, and in particular from His Majesty King Victor Emmanuel[1], who, in his telegram congratulating me on this great honor, reaffirmed «his ardent desire that the great cause of peace should triumph». For all the honors I have received and for a public acclaim as great as any man could wish for, you have placed me in your debt; indeed, the years of life still left to me are too short in which to demonstrate to you, by renewed activity in my propagandist work, my undying gratitude.

Your choice was all the more pleasing to my fellow countrymen in coming from a country we have loved for a very long time for its devotion to truth and beauty, for its civic institutions, and for its poets and dramatists, such as Ibsen and Bjørnson[2] who are among the most admired and most widely read in Italy. It was they who focused the world's attention on the admirable way of life, so full of vigor and sincerity, of your wonderful country. It was they who evoked anew your courageous ancestors, the Vikings, who with their small boats and indomitable courage were sailors and warriors truly worthy of being immortalized in legend; conquerors,

---

* Although awarded the prize in 1907, the laureate asked, for reasons of health, to give his lecture later, preferably in the summer of 1909 when he could also attend a peace congress in Stockholm. He therefore delivered this lecture on August 25, 1909, at the Norwegian Nobel Institute where he was introduced to a large audience by Mr. Løvland, chairman of the Nobel Committee. This translation is based on the text in French (the language in which Mr.Moneta spoke) published in *Les Prix Nobel en 1907*.

1. Victor Emmanuel III (1869–1947), king of Italy (1900–1946).

2. Henrik Ibsen (1828–1906), Norwegian poet and dramatist. Bjørnstjerne Bjørnson (1832–1910), Norwegian poet, novelist, dramatist; recipient of the Nobel Prize in Literature in 1903 and one of the original members of the Norwegian Nobel Committee.

not mercenaries, they astonished the world by the boldness of their fighting exploits in the days when war was honorable.

I say, without adulation but with the profound conviction that I am truly expressing what the world thinks of you and of your country (especially what the inhabitants of my own country think, and it is well known that foreigners, in their judgment of the affairs of others, are often as impartial and truthful as posterity)—I say to you, in all sincerity, that your civic life today is as worthy of admiration in our time as was that of the bold Vikings in the days of war and armed conquest.

This is because, caught up in the daily struggle, your nation faces ever changing reality with a clear eye and rejects old practices accordingly. It does not cling to customs which no longer have a reason for being; it is constantly readjusting itself to new needs and necessities. That is why your country is today in the vanguard of the world peace movement. Your Storting was the first parliament to uphold officially the idea of universal arbitration, to set aside funds for the Interparliamentary Union and for the Bureau in Bern[1], and, ever since 1890, to encourage the King to lend support to arbitration treaties between Norway and the small nations. Furthermore, the memory of the recent attainment of your independence, for which you strove so long in the midst of the gravest difficulties, is still fresh in all our minds[2]. Your independence, achieved as it was without violence or bloodshed, is a living example of good sense and wisdom, prudence and great tenacity, and brings everlasting credit both to you who obtained it and to those who did not refuse it to you.

Pacifism—as we have always advocated it, and as you are practicing it—does not seek to obliterate countries by throwing them into the melting pot of cosmopolitanism, but to organize them, if this is not already the case, according to the dictates of justice.

In varietate unitas! The more each nation contributes to world society

1. The Interparliamentary Union (1889) was organized in 1888 through the efforts of Frédéric Passy (co-laureate for 1901) and William Randal Cremer (laureate for 1903); composed of delegates from the different parliaments of the world, its primary aim originally was to further the cause of international arbitration. The Permanent International Peace Bureau began its work late in 1891 at Bern as a clearinghouse and information center for the many organizations and individuals working for peace, and as an executive arm for the international peace congresses.
2. In 1905 Norway achieved complete independence from Sweden; from 1815 to 1905, the king of Sweden was the sovereign of Norway as well, although Norway had her own constitution and parliament.

from the wealth of its own aptitudes, its own race, and its own traditions, the greater the future development and happiness of mankind will be.

And now, allow me to say a few words in respectful tribute to the memory of Alfred Nobel whose last act is responsible for my being here with you. Although Alfred Nobel was Swedish, he wished the choice and award of the Peace Prize to be in the hands of the Norwegian Parliament, which, as I have already said, was the first parliament in Europe to support the idea of international arbitration.

The service done our cause by Nobel was immense; for here was a man of science, a man of industry, always in search of practical goals, who rejected the old cliché that peace is an unattainable utopia, capable only of seducing the minds and souls of sentimental idealists.

The inception of the Nobel Peace Prize put an almost immediate end to the scoffing of skeptics and pseudo-intellectuals; and ever since then, our ranks have been reinforced by newcomers from all sides: politicians, industrialists, merchants, bankers–all hitherto aloof, now sympathetic to our cause.

The gravest difficulties faced by our Society[1], however, occurred at the very beginning of its existence when our members, who had founded it to combat a militant nationalism which imperialist politicians wanted to foster in Italy, were denounced by our adversaries as the «stateless ones».

This accusation was totally inconsistent. Before devoting ourselves to the propaganda of peace, my friends and I had first taken part in Italy's battles of independence, and by defending peace and brotherhood among peoples we were faithfully interpreting the great men who had planned and instigated our revolution. Like them, we proclaimed our primary obligation to be that of liberating our country, believing with Immanuel Kant[2] that to hasten the great and beneficial advent of united mankind, it is first essential to restore nations to their natural frontiers.

Our revolution did not explode in a sudden uprising of people intolerant of a tyrannical regime; it was the result of a long period of intellectual and moral evolution, brought about by men of great talent and of rare spiritual qualities, poets and philosophers, true educators of the people. In speaking of liberty and patriotism, all of them taught that liberty may be won by risking death, but it is preserved only by adherence to the principles of justice and through acts of civic virtue.

1. See biography, p.139.
2. Immanuel Kant (1724–1804), German philosopher.

I was a young man when, in March, 1848, Milan along with the other cities of Lombardy rose in revolt against the ruling government's rejection of its offer of «peace and fraternity» in return for national representation for Lombardy and Venice. While the tocsin sounded, we were putting up the barricades; we fought, mingling cries of joy with the shots and the crash of tiles and bricks thrown from windows. If this magnificent and epic struggle, which passed into history under the name of the «Five Days»[1], demonstrated the courage of our people in the face of danger, it also demonstrated their generosity in the face of victory, which was free of reprisals even against the most notorious police agents. They fought heroically but without hatred for the poor foreign soldiers who were obliged by discipline to fight in spite of themselves. For our fighters it was practically a cause for celebration whenever, by catching the enemy unawares, they were able to capture them without bloodshed. The enemy prisoners and wounded were all well treated.

One day when my father and brothers were absent, I watched, from the windows of my home, three Austrian soldiers fall amid a hail of bullets. Apparently dead, they were carried away to a neighboring square. I saw them again two hours later: one of them was still in the throes of dying. This sight froze the blood in my veins and I was overcome by a great compassion. In these three soldiers I no longer saw enemies but men like myself, and with remorse as keenly suffered as if I had killed them with my own hands, I thought of their families who were perhaps at that very moment preparing for their return.

In that instant I felt all the cruelty and inhumanity of war which sets peoples against one another to their mutual detriment, peoples who should have every interest in understanding and being friends with each other. I was to feel this way many times as I looked at the dead and the wounded in all the wars for our independence in which I took part.

I was not alone in thinking and feeling this way. On the day following the victory of the people, the government set up after the insurrection issued a manifesto to the peoples of Europe, in which it said[2]:

1. Austrian rule of Lombardy and Venice came under attack during the «Five Days of Milan» (March 18–22, 1848) when the Milanese forced the occupying Austrian troops to retreat.
2. Manifesto published by the Milanese revolutionaries on March 23, 1848. The translation of the quotation is taken from «The Peace Prize» by August Schou in *Nobel: The Man and His Prizes*, ed. by the Nobel Foundation (Amsterdam: Elsevier, 1962), p. 539.

«The day is probably not far distant when all nations will forget old quarrels and rally to the banner of international brotherhood, putting an end to all conflict and enjoying peace and friendship, strengthened by the bonds of commerce and industry. We look forward to that day. Italians! Free and independent we shall seal the peace of brotherhood with our own hands, not least with the nations which today constitute the Austrian Empire, if only they are willing.»

We can almost identify these vows as the heritage of, or better still, as the development of a civic way of thinking which, manifest from time to time in Italian life from its very beginning, considers law and justice the basis of true social harmony and of all human relations.

The same idea played a leading part in the common rites of the Etruscans, Volscians, Sabines, and Latins when magistrates representing forty-seven towns gathered together at the temple of Jupiter on the Mons Albanus[1]. These early Italian peoples formed confederations whose only purpose was to present a united front against aggression by their neighbors and against the demands of collective municipalities, never to promote aggression of their own.

The concept that flourished during the most glorious periods of republican Rome and that appeared in the Twelve Tables of the Law[2] as one of the first, though as yet imperfect, affirmations of the rights of man, inspired the struggle between patricians and plebeians. The plebeians were eager to gain equal rights with the patricians, and the patricians were anxious not to let the government of the Republic slip from their grasp since they could foresee from the first victories Rome's great destiny.

This was a conflict that rarely degenerated into civil war. It instituted the tribunal, the right of appeal to the people, and the arraignment of magistrates who abused their powers. It was a conflict dominated by patriotic feeling so intense that it stirred those involved in it to fantastic feats of heroism and sacrifice which the world may perhaps equal but never surpass.

Governed as it was by a senate always eager to spread the influence of the city, Rome soon became a militant conqueror. It should, however, be given credit for the *jus fetialium*[3], which originated among the first Italian

1. Mons Albanus is the highest point in the Alban Hills, which lie a few miles southeast of Rome.
2. The Twelve Tables (450 B.C.) embody the earliest codification of Roman law.
3. *Jus fetialium* was a branch of early Roman law concerned with embassies, declarations of war, and treaties of peace; it was administered by a college of *fetiales*, that order of priests who discharged the duties of ambassadors.

races, particularly among the Etruscans and Sabines, and which Cicero called «*sanctissimum jus*».

This law was a true *ius gentium*[1] for its day, an important affirmation of the supremacy of justice, equity, and peace. Although it dealt primarily with legal form and ceremony, it marked great progress nevertheless, for it removed legal procedure, which constitutes so great a part of law, from the domain of the arbitrary. Functioning as guardian of this law was a college of priests responsible for declaring war, making alliances, arraigning those who violated the law of the people, keeping the peace by ensuring respect for treaties.

When Rome became omnipotent after the Punic Wars[2], it no longer looked to the «Collegium Fetialium» for approval, regarding it as a superfluous and antiquated institution.

But though sheer force of arms opened the way to a world empire, though the exploits of Roman consuls and of the Senate were not without frequent incidents of cruelty to towns like Numantia, which put up heroic resistance[3], the first and already vigorous protests came from the Roman people themselves.

Histories of ancient Rome, such as those by Livy[4] and Dionysius of Halicarnassus[5], are full of accounts of popular protests and of episodes concerning the way in which the common people of Rome resisted the warmongering and conquering policies of the Senate; it was, indeed, the Latin poets and philosophers who called war «horrida bella» or «bella matribus detestata»[6].

Even though Rome came to dominate the world through a series of often

1. *Jus gentium*, in early Roman practice, became that part of the law of nations, «regulating the transactions of men who reside in different countries and carry on the intercourse of nations independently of the local customs and municipal law of particular states». Palmer D. Edmunds, *Law and Civilization* (Washington, D.C., 1959), p. 152.

2. The three Punic Wars, fought between Rome and Carthage in the second and third centuries B.C., resulted in the destruction of Carthage and the domination of the Mediterranean by Rome.

3. An ancient fortress town in northern Spain which withstood an eight-month siege but finally fell to the Roman armies in 133 B.C.

4. Titus Livius (59 B.C.–A.D. 17), Roman historian whose life work was his *History of Rome*.

5. Dionysius of Halicarnassus (fl. 1st cent. B.C.), Greek rhetorician and historian, among whose important works is *Antiquities of Rome*.

6. Literally: «horrible war»; «war detested by mothers».

unjust wars, it was its civic and assimilative virtues, which it never lost, that enabled Rome to maintain its position and to be of service to humanity. Behind the legions came the merchants and farmers who, as conquest spread, implanted the civic standards, the name, the language, and the institutions of the mother country in the new territories. While assimilating some of the character and customs of the vanquished peoples, Rome imparted to them some of its own, thus fusing all peoples, lands, and cultures into a homogeneous entity and finally, as its crowning gift, granting citizenship, first to the Italian people themselves and later to all nations within the Roman Empire.

This explains the rapidity with which the conquered provinces became absorbed and Romanized, and how imperial Rome with its handful of legions was able to keep under control the immense populations of its enormous empire. And if it is with some justification that later aspirations of certain warrior kings to conquer the world have been attributed to the splendor of the Roman conquests, it should also be remembered that when the Republic declined and the Empire began, it was Rome who gave the world the doctrine of the rights of man and of nations.

One of the advocates of this doctrine was the philosopher and teacher Cicero who, even prior to Alberico Gentili and Grotius[1], sowed the first seeds of international law. Cicero was against all wars unless they were absolutely unavoidable.

«Disputes», he said, «can be settled in two ways: by reason or by force; one way belongs to man and the other to the beasts; one should employ force only when reason proves impossible.»[2] He possessed a much greater breadth of vision than Aristotle, who justified slavery and believed that it would last until doomsday. «Beneath the cloak of the slave», said Cicero, «breathes a man who is not just a thing, but a person who hires out his services and who has a right to decent treatment and a fair wage.» He wanted all people to be equal in the eyes of justice: «True law is reason, just and consistent with nature; it imposes obligations and forbids fraud; it cannot be different in Athens from what it is in Rome.»[3]

---

1. Marcus Tullius Cicero (106 B.C.–43 B.C.), Roman orator and statesman. Alberico Gentili (c.1550–c.1608), Italian jurist whose book *De jure belli* paved the way for the work of Hugo Grotius (1583–1645), Dutch statesman and jurist, who wrote *De jure belli ac pacis* (1625), the first systematic text on international law.
2. *De officiis* i.11.
3. *De republica* iii.33.

Although in the realm of ethics Cicero was far ahead of his time, he was not alone in propounding such ideas. The Epicurean poet Lucretius, in his poem about the Roman world[1], marked the contrast of its internal strife and the horrors of its wars with the placid tranquillity of the sage who, from the heights of the austere temple of knowledge, contemplates the senseless conflicts of men. And when Augustus brought these conflicts to an end, there was a host of high-minded individuals, such as Vergil, Horace, Pliny, Seneca, and all the Stoics, who extolled the peace[2].

No one painted a more accurate picture of military depredation than Vergil. Inspired though he was by the Latin spirit and by his pride in Rome, he nevertheless glorified Rome's true mission as one of providing the world with the rules of peace and justice.

These ideas of peace and justice were a prelude to Christianity which, while preaching brotherhood among all men, established its principal center in Rome. When the Empire fell under the sword of the barbarian, the ideal of humanitarianism and peace survived in Italy by finding refuge and support in the Roman church. The church set out to educate even the barbarians; it opposed the cruelty of the times with the Christian law of love; and it almost always used its moral authority, intensified by the very violence and rampant anarchy of the day, to foster the free and civil association of peoples. This international arbitration, which, for want of any communal law, we still regard as the best protection of peace today, was practiced by the best and greatest of the pontiffs of the early Middle Ages who censured injustice and the corruption of the aristocracy and who defended the liberty of the common man.

The *Truces of God* which at certain times of the year punctuated any continuous wars between neighboring countries, or between communities, or even between factions within the same community, were also a beneficent inspiration of the Roman church. They sprang into existence and multiplied in a feudal society whose aristocracy, beyond our mountain ranges, gloried in celebrating any event, joyous or sad, with battles and massacres.

---

1. Titus Lucretius Carus (c.99 B.C.–c.55 B.C.), Roman didactic poet whose *De rerum natura*, referred to here, presents the Epicurean philosophy in verse.
2. Augustus (63 B.C.–A.D.14), first Roman emperor. Vergil (70 B.C.–19 B.C.), Roman poet. Horace (65 B.C.–8 B.C.), Latin lyric poet. Probably Pliny the Elder (A.D. 23–79), Roman scholar. Seneca (c.3 B.C.–A.D. 65), Roman philosopher, statesman, dramatist.

When, however, following the Donation of Constantine[1], the popes became temporal sovereigns and began to concern themselves more with their own material interests than with the moral interests of the people, they gradually lost the authority which, to the benefit of society at large, they had previously wielded in civic matters.

The last days of the Empire saw the growth of our free towns, composed for the most part of a Roman element (which was never suppressed), of a Christian element, and of a new Germanic element.

During the Middle Ages it was these free towns that kept the torch of freedom alight in Italy. They aroused and sustained in their citizens the sentiment of human dignity and they insured the protection of their cottages by forcing the nobility to abandon their castles and to live among the free citizens in the towns and villages. It was they who, even before the birth of the Hanseatic League, formed the Lombard League to defend their rights against the Empire[2]. And it was they who, after defeating Barbarossa's army at Legnano, then for the sake of peace and of compliance with customary law, acknowledged in Barbarossa imperial authority in all «except», said they in the presence of Pope Alexander III, «what concerns the honor of Italy»[3]. «Moreover», they added, «we will never allow ourselves to be deprived of our liberty. This we have inherited from our fathers and our ancestors and this we will yield only with life itself; we would rather die than live in slavery.»

This devotion to the free towns, strengthened by a religious feeling which prompted each town to seek for itself a patron saint, produced in Italy a galaxy of republics, all flourishing in commerce, industry, and the arts at a time when the rest of Europe was still in the grip of feudalism. However,

1. A supposed grant of extensive temporal authority made to Pope Silvester I and his successors by the Roman emperor Constantine I (274?–337), which was later used as a basis for larger papal claims. Accepted as genuine during the Middle Ages, its authenticity was questioned during the Renaissance, and by 1800 it was commonly admitted to be a forgery.

2. The Hanseatic League, organized in the 14th century and dissolved in the 17th, was a loose confederation of German towns in a mercantile league formed for protection against pirates and foreign competition. The Lombard League united rival towns of Lombardy in 1167 to defy the extension of imperial authority by Frederick I; successful at first, the League was defeated in 1237 by Frederick II.

3. Frederick I or Frederick Barbarossa (c.1123–1190), German king and Holy Roman emperor (1152–1190), was defeated in 1176 at Legnano, a Lombard city near Milan. Alexander III (?–1181), pope (1159–1181), supported the Lombard League.

formation of one strong and unified Italian state was impossible, for no Italian prince could obtain the slightest support for it from the people, who were more concerned with the liberty and sovereignty of their own town than with any notion of national greatness.

Dante saw the danger and the pity of this division into jealous and antagonistic city states. In his poem, attacking parties, he says in an immortal line that Italy, «no longer the mistress of provinces,» has become the slave of cruel and pitiless sects[1].

This masterpiece in which Dante sets forth the fundamentals of his doctrine can be said, if one discards the now obsolete part which was adapted to his own day and to the metaphysics of Aristotle, to present the rules of government and of humanitarian life under *one* law; to this end, he wanted the Empire transferred to Rome, for he perceived in the Romans those qualities most suited to governing the world.

The purpose of civilization, he said, is to put man's intellectual potential to practical use, in short, to develop his faculties to their fullest extent. So too, do universal peace and the free functioning of public bodies and of nations coordinate in aiming for the ultimate establishment of a universal society.

Translate these highly philosophical words into common parlance and you see outlined the way to attain universal peace and, at the same time, to attain the greatest possible universal perfection.

I will not now speak of Pietro Belli[2] nor of Alberico Gentili who, in imposing limitations and applying rules to war, were the predecessors of H. Grotius and who, in holding peace to be the ultimate goal desired by all civilization, went far beyond him.

To conclude this already considerable digression, let me repeat the words of one of our eminent historians and publicists of today: «It has always been the concern of all the great Italian political leaders to preach: *peace, love, unity,* and *concord.*»

---

1. Dante Alighieri (1265–1321). The laureate probably refers to lines in Canto VI of the *Purgatory*. As translated by Thomas Okey, p.225, in the Carlyle-Wicksteed translation of *The Divine Comedy of Dante Alighieri* (New York: Modern Library, 1932), these lines read: «Ah Italy, thou slave, hostel of woe, vessel without pilot in a mighty storm, no mistress of provinces, but a brothel!»

2. Pietro Belli (1502–1575), Italian jurist, counselor on international law to Charles V and other rulers; wrote *De re militari et bello tractatus* (1563).

With the decline of the freedom and sovereignty of the city states came a reawakened interest in Greek and Roman letters and through it the Renaissance which, scorning politics and disdaining military glory, held the supremacy of the mind and of the cult of truth and beauty to constitute the ideal life. It paved the way for the association of nations by creating a fellow-feeling among scholars and men of science.

But this purely intellectual pacific existence, coupled with the disuse of arms, was fatal for Italy.

While in neighboring territories great monarchies possessing new permanent armies were consolidating, the premature pacifism in our country left her once more wide-open to invasion; as a result, the richest and most beautiful parts of our peninsula came under the domination now of Austria, now of Spain.

Since we are deeply concerned with the present, with all its dangers and contradictions, you may think it strange that I have talked to you about ancient Italy and about the Italy of the Middle Ages rather than about the place and purpose of today's Italy within the complicated framework of modern Europe.

I do not regard a look at the past as fruitless, however, for it was from the past that the forerunners and the first apostles of our revolution drew their inspiration. The idea of a legal system for the whole world, pursued by the pacifists in Europe and America during both the last century and this one, is to be found back in the history of Rome and in the minds of our greatest thinkers.

Both pagan and Christian Rome regarded national law as the foundation and keystone of the law of nations. That is why nationalism, in whose name Italy rose in rebellion, is not jealous, is neither shut up within itself nor greedy for the acquisition of foreign territories. It is, on the contrary, sympathetic toward all nations who live and flourish in liberty, or who aspire thereto.

After Giuseppe Mazzini[1] had founded the «Giovine Italia» [Young Italy], whose objective was unification and liberation of Italy, he went on in 1834 to found the «Giovine Europa» at Bern in collaboration with German and Polish exiles. In accordance with his instructions to its initiators, this group strove «to organize human society in such a way as to enable it through

1. Giuseppe Mazzini (1805–1872), Italian patriot and revolutionist.

continuous progress in the shortest possible time to discover and apply the law of God by which it should be governed»[1].

Later, Mazzini founded another such committee with Ledru-Rollin and other French, German, and Hungarian exiles[2].

Perhaps you would now be interested to hear what Pasquale Stanislao Mancini[3], leader of the modern Italian juridical school, was teaching in regard to *the new law of nations* as early as 1852 when he held a professorship at the University of Turin. «Humanity is our concern,» he said, «and it is essential that mankind attain a unique organization of sufficient versatility to enable it to fulfill its destiny on earth. But in the human world an element of diversity exists: nations in which individual talents and abilities are educated become developed nations, civilization is advanced, and the rule of law becomes a reality.»

After the revival and reconstitution of Italy, Mancini, along with other jurists such as Corsi, Buzzati, and Pasquale Fiore[4], never tired of advocating the reform and codification of *the law of nations*, or, in a word, the establishment of international justice in the interests of peace and the progress of civilization.

So far, this plea from our jurists and lawyers has not been answered; so international justice is still the high objective of our world congresses and of our propaganda.

A great deal of credit for the development of the study of international law in nearly every civilized country belongs to the Italian school; from this study was born the Institute of International Law to which you so rightly awarded the Nobel Prize in one of the first years after you began to function[5].

But Italy has done more than this.

Anticipating the beginning of a codification of international law—and

1. From Principle 3 of the *Pact of Young Europe*. See E.E.Y.Hales, *Mazzini and the Secret Societies* (London, 1956), pp.136–140.
2. In 1850 in London, Mazzini, along with Alexandre Ledru-Rollin, a French lawyer and politician, Arnold Ruge, a German political writer, and Albert Darasz, a Polish political reformer, founded the European Democratic Central Committee.
3. Pasquale Stanislao Mancini (1817–1888), Italian jurist and statesman; professor of international law at Turin (1849 ff.); minister of justice (1876–1878) and minister of foreign affairs (1881–1885).
4. Nineteenth-century Italian scholars of international law.
5. Founded in 1873 by a group of international lawyers, the Institute was awarded the prize for 1904.

indeed we have even now at The Hague a tribunal for its application[1] –
Italy, since her unification, has introduced into positive legislation almost
all of the principles concerning private international law set up by her
juridical school. The legislation has established not only that «a foreigner
may enjoy the same civil rights as those held by Italian citizens» (Article
III of the Italian Civil Code), but also that in civic matters, he is, while
in our country, governed by the laws of his own nation. In this important
respect we have preceded other nations in eradicating the differences, as far
as civil law is concerned, between nationals and foreigners and have thereby
founded the principles of our doctrine concerning the rights of the human
individual in the provisions of jurisprudence. Thus theory is put into practice, as is further demonstrated by the fact that Italy is the first, and so far
the only one, among the bigger nations to have abolished the death penalty
from its penal code.

It is evident then that Italy offers the best conditions for the continuous
development and perfection of private international law, which provides
the surest route to public law.

It is not patriotic vanity that has prompted me to bring up these facts.
It is because on the day when an international parliament proclaims the
judicial unity of nations, followed by a related disarmament, the day awaited
by all pacifists, I believe that all nations, Norway no less than Russia,
England as well as France, will be able to prove that they have contributed
in one way or another to this great event.

But I must also provide facts to show that our first educators did not
teach us in vain that Italy would have to undergo a rebirth not only to
gain her own rights, but also to fulfill her obligations toward other nations.

Unfortunately, like all other nations, Italy has had to yield to the hard
necessity of armaments which from time to time must be increased because
they are considered essential for the conservation of peace in the present
state of world turmoil.

The situation is so strangely anomalous that we see even allies fortifying
and arming themselves one against the other; we cannot, however, blame
Italy for this.

Of the many examples I could cite to show how strongly the Italian soul
is opposed to the idea of war, I will be content to give you two of the
most eloquent ones.

1. The Hague Tribunal was set up as a court of arbitration by the 1899 Hague Peace
Conference.

As the leader of the government in 1865, General La Marmora[1], who was a true product of the old Piedmontese militarism, initiated confidential negotiations with the court of Vienna in an effort to procure the surrender of Venice in exchange for a sum of millions to be established; that these talks never went beyond the preliminary stage was not La Marmora's fault.

The second example is even more typical.

Garibaldi, who was the most sublime personification of Latin genius and military valor of our day, won the battle of the Volturno at the end of September, 1860[2], and on the following day, in his capacity as dictator of southern Italy, sent a message to the powers of Europe, exhorting them to put an end to wars and armaments by uniting in a European confederation.

With the same hand that had but a little earlier wielded the sword of liberation, he wrote: «In waging war, we differ little from primitive men who killed one another to snatch each other's prey. We spend our lives (today as then) continually threatening one another while in Europe the large majority, not only of great minds but of all sensible men, understand perfectly that we could easily go through life without this perpetual menace and mutual hostility and without the necessity–which seems to have been fatally imposed on nations by some secret and invisible enemy of mankind– of slaughtering each other with such science and refinement.»

He closed by expressing the hope that France and England, setting aside old rivalries and uniting, would form the nucleus of a European confederation which all other nations of Europe would soon join.

Garibaldi's hopes for a French and English unity that might serve as a nucleus of a European confederation have been realized. The future will tell whether or not the other nations will gradually rally round them.

Incarnating the highest ideals which he always put into action, fighting in a hundred battles for the freedom of all peoples, Garibaldi in 1870, in the same spirit, despite his distress over the transfer of his native town of Nice to France, hastened with his companions to the aid of a France abandoned by all Europe–and this only a few years after he had attended the

1. Alfonso Ferrero, Marchese di La Marmora (1804–1878), Italian general and statesman; prime minister (1864–1866).
2. Giuseppe Garibaldi (1807–1882), Italian soldier and patriot, hero of the 19th-century movement for political unity in Italy; his army of 1,000 selected volunteers, known as the «Mille», defeated the Neapolitans in the Battle of the Volturno on October 1–2, 1860 (the date usually given).

first Congress for Peace and Liberty in Geneva[1], which he opened with these words: «All nations are sisters and war between them is therefore inconceivable. Italians as citizens of other countries, men of other countries as citizens of Italy–that is the goal we should reach...»

These sentiments are the same ones expressed by the Italian people in the culminating moments of the revolution, but I would be dishonest were I to claim that they are those of the majority of my fellow citizens in ordinary times. Had that been the case, our pacifist propaganda would never have been necessary and would not at present be necessary.

On the contrary, because Garibaldi, having become universally known and admired, said himself on several occasions that he had always drawn inspiration «from the great qualities and magnanimous deeds of the Roman people», there arose in Italy a generation of patriots who, dreaming of an impossible return of Roman splendor, would have liked to make modern Italy a military power of the first rank rather than a nation outstanding for its great freedom and advancement.

To begin with, they would have liked to annex the canton of Ticino[2]; then they set their sights on the Ethiopian Empire whose coinage they had already got as far as minting[3].

Irritated at seeing France enter Tunis in spite of the French government's last assurances to our government that she would not[4], these patriots believed that with the aid of Germany they could make war against France and wrest Nice and Corsica from her.

It was at this stage that we, the former followers of Garibaldi together with patriots from other parties, all of us friends of France, formed the Lombard Union of Peace to counteract this mad Gallophobia.

By exposing the nefarious schemes of the sowers of discord, by reviving memories of Italy's debt of gratitude to France, by holding conferences and forming pacifist propaganda committees in the cities where they were most needed, we succeeded in obliging the government of that time to modify

1. The congress which founded La Ligue internationale de la paix et de la liberté was convened on the initiative of Charles Lemonnier in September of 1867.

2. An Italian-speaking canton annexed by Switzerland in the 16th century.

3. Italian efforts in the 1880's and 1890's to establish a protectorate over Ethiopia led to war and eventually to the Italian defeat at Adua and the Treaty of Addis Ababa (1896) recognizing Ethiopian independence.

4. The Treaty of Bardo (1881), establishing a French protectorate over Tunis, initiated a long period of Franco-Italian tension, with relations becoming particularly strained in the late 1880's.

its policy and to silence those newspapers which seemed bent on creating a rift of hatred between Italy and France.

You know the result of our work. For several years there has been no trace of Gallophobia in Italy; and a warm friendship for our western neighbor has taken its place. We had clear proof of this last June on the fiftieth anniversary of the liberation of Milan and Lombardy. The streets, the squares, and the theaters were filled with crowds vibrant with memories of the political events and the feats of bravery that had freed our country. The warmest and most unanimous demonstrations were those saluting France and her army–several of whose gallant representatives were among us–for the generous assistance lent us during that memorable campaign in 1859, assistance which played so large a part in securing our emancipation.

Clearly, a people who, after a half-century of extraordinary and occasionally unfortunate events, can preserve intact their deep appreciation of the benefits received from another nation, can be neither a boorish people nor one oblivious to the obligations that bind them to the society of other nations.

Although today this society of other nations has no actual political existence, it has a virtual one. We Italians were made very aware of this when, struck by the terrible disaster which buried Messina, Reggio, and many villages in Calabria and Sicily[1], we were consoled by receiving touching proofs of affection and prompt aid from every part of the world.

Such is the voice of the universal human soul which, in times of great calamity, ignores the artificial barriers created for reasons of state and testifies to the goodness and nobility of human nature.

And during the celebration of our national jubilee we did not forget the great demonstration of compassion and active sympathy that came to our country from your magnanimous Norway, as indeed from all the civilized nations.

The orator of the «Mille» himself, the poet Abba[2], in the presence of the King at Rome, commemorated that great event by expressing the thought which was then and still is uppermost in the minds both of the people and of the government; he closed his speech by saying that Italy had risen again to accomplish the mission of peace with which history and her position in Europe had charged her. It is now known, even outside Italy, that there is no longer in our country any party agitating for war.

1. The earthquake of December 28, 1908.
2. Giuseppe Cesare Abba (1838–1910), Italian poet, one of Garibaldi's «Mille».

Even so, there is no lack among us, particularly among the military, of people who, though not expressly wishing for war, would not be displeased were war to come; they hope that the laurels of victory, denied to Italy at the time of her wars of independence, which were fought by bands of Italians [rather than by an organized Italian army], might now come to crown Italy as a nation. This idea, held by a small number of our fellow citizens, has been rejected by all those of us who have any human feelings and is contradicted by the history of nearly every modern nation which has managed to become great, prosperous, and respected in spite of the fact that its military chronicles record a larger number of defeats than of victories.

When, by the virtue of its people and the valor of its fighting men, a nation manages in a few years to throw off all governments that have enslaved and divided it and to accomplish a rebirth that would have taken other nations over a century; when, not since the Greek insurrection against Turkish domination[1], has there been a single war of national independence in Europe or America in which Italians have not shown their brotherhood by fighting on the side of liberty; when the bravery of our soldiers was always remarkable even in the battles which we lost, like the Prussians at Jena[2] and the French in the [Franco-Prussian] War of 1870–1871, through lack of organization and the fault of commanders-in-chief–when all these things are true, then new wars are not needed to demonstrate to the world that if our independence and our national honor are again endangered, our people and our army will know how to perform their duty to the bitter end.

However, it is not glory in war that Italy or any other nation should seek today.

It is sad to think that the peace which has now prevailed in Europe for many years can be maintained only at the price of ever increasing armaments whose enormous economic weight prevents nations from developing themselves fully and freely; and sad to think that this peace exists only on condition that very serious questions be ignored–a situation that, after a few vain protests, allows the abuse of force which would not occur if *law* were in control.

No man of sense and feeling can fail to see the grave dangers of this situation or to shudder at the thought of the terrible conflagration it could lead to if we delay much longer in finding the remedy.

1. From 1821 to 1827.
2. The Prussian army was defeated at Jena by Napoleon in 1806.

It is urgently necessary that some ray of truth and love fall upon the three or four men who are today the arbiters of peace and war, so that a peace rich in justice and well-being for Europe may replace the present armed truce.

Ever since Muraviev, chancellor of the Russian Empire, acting for the ingeniously inspired Czar Nicholas, addressed his famous circular to the powers inviting them to a conference aimed at disarmament and peace[1], we have believed that the great day of proclaiming universal peace was close at hand.

The frequent exchange of visits in recent years between the sovereigns of England, Germany, Russia, and the president of the French Republic, the often attempted conciliation between France and Germany, the demonstrations of friendship made both in England and in Germany to dispel the clouds of suspicion and enmity which unhealthy prejudices raise from time to time between the two–all these indicated the good intentions of the heads of state as well as of the people and encouraged us to go on hoping. But almost immediately the dark, proud, and provocative arrogance of nationalism reared its ugly head, and the ground we believed ourselves to have gained in the direction of a general peace seemed lost again.

Will it always be like this? Will the day foretold by the prophet never come, that day when no nation will ever again take up arms against another and when lances and swords will be beaten into plowshares?

Was it in vain that Jesus of Nazareth came into this world to herald peace and goodwill among men and died on the Cross so that one day all men would recognize each other as brothers?

Consider the French Revolution which should have introduced the ideals of peace, equality, and fraternity into international relations and instead, two years after the Declaration of the Rights of Man, let loose a tempest of war such as the world had not seen since Attila[2]. Consider the fact that

1. The Czar's Rescript, dated August 12, 1898 (New Style, August 24), was handed by the Russian minister of foreign affairs, Count Muraviev, to all foreign diplomatic representatives accredited to the Court at St. Petersburg; along with the Russian follow-up circular of December 30, 1898 (New Style, January 11, 1899), it resulted in the calling of the first Peace Conference at The Hague in 1899.
2. The French Revolution, which began in 1789, and its Declaration of the Rights of Man, which was adopted as part of the French constitution of 1791, were followed by the French Revolutionary Wars and they in turn by the Napoleonic Wars. Attila (406?–453), leader of the Huns, ravaged much of central Europe (451–452).

two years after the founding of the Society of the Friends of Peace in France[1], which was greeted warmly by men of letters, by statesmen, and by workers' associations throughout France and Germany, came the outbreak of the Franco-German War, disastrous not only for France, but also for the cause of peace throughout Europe. And then remember that our distinguished master Frédéric Passy was not returned to office by his electors[2], perhaps on account of his grievous sin in having become the most fervent apostle of international peace. Notice too that not one of our most eminent pacifists has ever been summoned to lead a government or to direct foreign policy. Note that the Pope, the vicar of Christ on earth as he is called, shuts himself up like a voluntary prisoner in the Vatican in protest against loss of temporal power[3]; yet when his voice should have rung out above every other in true Christian love and anguish in an effort to avert war at its inception, it was either never raised at all, or else too late, or too feebly, just as were the voices of his most recent predecessors. Consider the way that poets, with few exceptions, pay court to fame and popularity by singing the praises of war and massacre. Consider again how the most sublime virtues are always associated with the national flag while cruelty is ascribed to the enemy alone–this in order to sustain mistrust, hatred, and enmity between nations. Remembering and pondering all this, oh, I confess to you that I too have had moments of discouragement, wondering whether the idea to which I devote and have for years devoted all my time and energy might be no more than an illusion of my poor mind, a dream like Thomas More's *Utopia* or our own Campanella's *City of the Sun*[4].

But these were fleeting moments! And I was soon telling myself that if work for a future of peace and justice, a future of continual progress and of fruitful and useful labor for all men and all nations was indeed an

1. Société française des amis de la paix (later known as Société française pour l'arbitrage entre nations) was founded by Frédéric Passy in 1867 under the name La Ligue internationale et permanente de la paix.

2. Frédéric Passy (1822–1912), co-recipient of the Nobel Peace Prize for 1901, was elected a French deputy in 1881 and again in 1885 but was defeated in 1889.

3. After the French troops left Rome in 1870 to fight in the Franco-Prussian War, the city was annexed to Italy; stripped of the papal states, the Pope refused to accept the terms offered by the government and withdrew to the Vatican where he and his successors remained voluntary «prisoners» until 1929.

4. Sir Thomas More (1478–1535), British author and statesman, published *Utopia* in 1516. Tommaso Campanella (1568–1639) published *Civitas solis* [*City of the sun*] in 1623.

illusion, it was still an illusion so divine as to make life worth living and to inspire one to die for it.

But it is not an illusion. I felt this deep within me, and the history of human evolution as well as everyday experience confirmed it for me. Reasonable ideas which find their sanction in the conscience of the righteous do not die; they are consequently realities and active forces, but they are so only to the extent that those who profess them know how to turn them to account. It depends on us, then, and on our judgment and steadfastness whether or not the idea of peace will root itself ever more firmly in public awareness until it grows into the living and active conscience of a whole people.

Today, unfortunately, what many facts indicate only too well is that universal peace, as we conceive of it, still lies far in the distant future, and in view of the growing greed for the lands of others, the weaker countries can no longer trust the stronger ones.

«Keep your powder dry and always be ready to defend yourself»; this is for Italy, as well as for others, a hard necessity at the present time.

I do not believe that there is at the moment a single government in Europe which is actually planning war, but the time could come when those who are thinking of it least might find themselves embroiled in war by force of circumstances. We had a classic example of this in France in 1870 when, one month before the war, no one dreamed of or could have imagined such a thing; but once it had started no one knew how to stop it.

Meanwhile, one thing seems certain: alliances today are made not for war, but for peace. We see proof of this in the fact that one nation belonging to a given group of allies can establish and maintain friendly relations with nations making up another group, without protests or complaints from the allies.

There are still of course many people dominated by old prejudices who conceal under the mask of civilized man, the barbarian who sees any foreigner as an enemy and war as a good speculation.

It is up to us pacifists to expose these backward mentalities by making people aware of what war really involves–just how many tears, how much blood, and how much torture unfortunate populations have to pay as the price of victory.

Meanwhile, the situation in Europe is so involved, the old bitterness between certain nations still so alive, that no one can guarantee the future.

It is very strange, however, that while progressive men of science have succeeded in overcoming the resistance of the winds and in cleaving a way through the air on artificial wings, not one of their counterparts among progressive statesmen–and there are still many in the various countries–has so far found out how to overcome the resistance of evil passions and antisocial interests that together block the inevitable advance of nations toward the common goal of peace, justice, and well-being.

I do not know what the governments of the principal powers will do today, tomorrow, or later to find a way out of a situation whose weaknesses, instability, and dangers they themselves recognize.

Nor am I any more able to predict what government and what policy could bring about a different form of parliamentary action in our own country. I can assure you of one thing, however, for I know the spirit of our people. It is that Italy will never take up arms or bring influence to bear in the service of causes condemned by the conscience of free men who have a feeling for justice and for the conditions of universal progress.

One recent event is a good omen for the future: When in 1870 the very popular king, Victor Emmanuel II, out of a sense of chivalry wanted to send 100,000 men to reinforce the army of Napoleon – then waging war on Prussia in an effort to prevent the unification of Germany–our people opposed it unanimously, and the 100,000 soldiers remained in Italy.

Later, when the Crispi government seemed bent on war against the French Republic, Cavallotti[1] spoke out in the name of Italian democracy and all the friends of peace, saying that the Italian soldiers would have to march over our dead bodies before they could cross the French frontier. As a result, Crispi was forced into changing his policy to one that made such a war impossible.

Again, a few years later, the same minister planned to send an entire army to Africa to regain the prestige which, according to the militarists, had been lost by our forces in the unfortunate battle of Adua. But threatened with revolution by the people if this senseless and unjust war were continued, he was compelled to hand over power.

I do not, however, wish to conceal from you the fact that, although our people have many good qualities, they are also impressionable and impulsive, and since some of their agitators are equally so, it has occasionally happened that some of them, particularly the students, have indulged in rash demonstrations which could have compromised Italy's good relations

1. Felice Carlo Emmanuel Cavallotti (1842–1898), Italian writer and politician, an opponent of Crispi (premier 1887–1891; 1893–1896).

with neighboring states. But these were commotions that the majority of the people never had anything to do with. They were not provoked by thoughts of revenge nor were they stirred up in answer to taunts; almost without exception they were the result of insults and injuries suffered by Italians outside the frontiers of our kingdom: «Blood is thicker than water.»

Gentlemen, I'm sure you know how I am going to end my lecture.

Italy, the youngest and the smallest among the great powers, has contributed to international life her fair share of political ideas, juridical concepts, and moral ideals which have been both sound and productive and which have served as her compass in dark and stormy days; they will be her strength, her glory, and her driving spirit in times to come.

The Italian Revolution was fought first of all to obtain the liberty and unity of the nation, and then, with that achieved, to join the freest and most advanced nations in inaugurating a new era of peace, justice, and joint cooperation in the work of civilization.

So far, only the first goal has been attained; Victor Emmanuel II, who was king of tiny Piedmont, made his contribution by assuming the crown of Italy in Rome.

It remains now to realize the second ideal.

If King Victor Emmanuel III (who deserves recognition from civilization for founding the International Institute of Agriculture[1], which will certainly yield benefits useful to all in the future world economy) will lend his support to the fulfillment of the Italian Revolution with respect to Italy's place in the world, he will gain added renown for himself and his subjects and at the same time strengthen the bond of affection between himself and his people.

«Courage ever high and ever for liberty, for justice, and for peace among peoples.» This is the motto with which both people and sovereigns can face all obstacles and strive to reach the highest goals.

I speak here without mandate, but I speak as a man who has followed closely (sometimes as one of the lesser participants) every phase of the political renaissance of his country and who has in the supreme moments of our national epic felt the stirrings of the Italian soul.

Gentlemen, at this most solemn moment of my life, before you citizens and representatives of this illustrious Norway whose example has taught

1. Acting on an idea advocated by David Lubin, an American agriculturist, Victor Emmanuel III convened the 1905 international conference in Rome which initiated the Institute, the opening of which took place several years later.

all nations, large and small, how to achieve without violence the greatest civil victories – in view of the patriotic and humanitarian ideals in the name of which Italy has come into its third existence, and in memory of the long list of heroes and martyrs who died on the battlefields, in prisons, or on the scaffold for those ideals – I give the solemn assurance, as a seal to my speech, that Italy will never fail in the commitment she made before the world: to be, once free to control her own destiny, an element of order and of progress, of pacification and of civilization in Europe. Yes, I am fully convinced that she will never fail, for one can say of Italy what your great Ibsen said of your country:

> *After a heavy sleep,*
> *She awoke renewed in strength, ready for the word of command,*
> *And now she is the race which has the will and the faith,*
> *Will and faith in the peaceful progress of mankind.* [1]

1. These lines paraphrase the last part of Ibsen's poem «Ved tusendårs-festen».

Biography

Ernesto Teodoro Moneta (September 20, 1833–February 10, 1918) had a personality as paradoxical as the term «militant pacifist» which was so often applied to him. He was a nationalistic internationalist, a deeply religious anticlerical propagandist, a crusader for physical fitness who daily took a tram to avoid walking across a square to lunch in a restaurant opposite his office.

Born of aristocratic Milanese parents, he spent his childhood in two country houses where his impoverished family could still live on a patriarchal scale, although without luxury. He was profoundly affected by his experiences in the uprising against Austria when, at the age of fifteen, he fought next to his father to defend his family home and saw three Austrian soldiers die nearby. It was probably then that Moneta's dual advocacy of peace and yet of fighting for his own kind of nationalism was born. From 1848 to 1866 he spent a great deal of his time in efforts for Italian independence and unification, fighting with Garibaldi in 1859 and 1860 and later under General Sirtori whose aide-de-camp he became. Disillusioned by the campaign of 1866, however, he cut short what seemed to be a promising army career and returned to civilian life, although he remained personally loyal to General Sirtori all his life.

Moneta was a handsome, warm, cheerful man who enjoyed riding horses, acting in amateur theatricals, and contributing play reviews to *Il Secolo*, a daily newspaper founded in 1866 by Edoardo Sonzogno. When two of his friends took over *Il Secolo* in 1867, he accepted the position of editor, which he held from 1867 until 1895. Journalism proved to be the ideal outlet for Moneta's dynamism and idealism, his career as a pacifist being an organic outgrowth of his daily intellectual stimulation and passionate commitment as editor of *Il Secolo*.

A man of strong personal convictions, Moneta was respected for his integrity as much as for his courage and willingness to accept innovations. He forged *Il Secolo* into a powerful instrument for shaping public opinion without compromising its editorial balance. Although he respected religion and was a practicing Catholic, he permitted *Il Secolo* to adopt an anticlerical stance because he believed for many years that specific abuses among the clergy were impeding Italian unification and social progress. He became virtually estranged from his wife – and from his two sons during her lifetime – largely because she was unable to accept this apparent inconsistency in her husband's attitude toward the religion which meant so much to her.

Since Moneta understood and sympathized with the problems of the Italian army, he campaigned vigorously in the columns of *Il Secolo* for reforms which public opinion could bring about. He contended that the lengthy basic training of recruits and conscripts was wasteful and inefficient, that organized athletics, target practice, and civilian drills in the villages could drastically cut down the time needed to train recruits, that militarism could be de-emphasized, yet the effective strength of the army actually increased.

During the last thirty years of the nineteenth century, Moneta gathered material and insights for his opus *Le guerre, le insurrezioni e la pace nel secolo XIX* [Wars, Insurrections and Peace in the Nineteenth Century], which he published in four volumes in 1903, 1904, 1906, and 1910. The part of this work which remains of greatest interest is the first volume, in which he describes the development of the international peace movement during the course of the century. Moneta concentrates his interest on military rather than on social or economic issues throughout the work and utilizes the point of view and approach of the journalist, narrating in a first-person, anecdotal style. His recurrent theme is the lack of substantive results achieved by wars and militarism. Yet, during his career as editor of *Il Secolo*, Moneta was one of the most vocal nationalists in Italy. He managed to make his intense patriotism and his devotion to the cause of national defense and of Italian unification consistent with his dedication to the fostering of international peace and arbitration, becoming a full-time pacifist immediately upon his retirement from *Il Secolo*. Although his highly personal brand of nationalism almost approached chauvinism, he fought for years against the contempt for Austria displayed by many *Il Secolo* readers and against the «Gallophobia» which swept Italy during the 1880's.

The range of activities in which Moneta engaged for the propagation of world peace is impressive. In 1890 he began to issue an annual almanac called *L'Amico della pace*. After his retirement as editor of *Il Secolo*, he continued to contribute to its columns from time to time and to republish many of his articles in pamphlets and periodicals. Ever aware of the value of propaganda for peace, he even printed one-page tracts and distributed them to rural schoolmasters. In 1898 he founded a fortnightly review, *La Vita internazionale*, which gained sufficient prestige to ensure publication on a regular basis for many years during a period when most such periodicals languished in Italy for lack of interest and financial support.

His work for peace was not solely of a literary nature. He became the Italian representative on the Commission of the International Peace Bureau in 1895. He attended peace congresses for many years, and his courtly, deceptively diffident presence became increasingly familiar and respected. He had encouraged l'Unione lombarda per la pace e l'arbitrato internazionale [the Lombard Union for International Peace and Arbitration] since its foundation in 1887[1], and had himself founded, besides several organizations of an ephemeral nature, the Società per la pace e la giustizia internazionale [Society for International Peace and Justice][2], which lasted from 1887 until 1937[3], long after his death. He lectured at the newly founded Italian Popular University. In 1906 he planned and had constructed a Pavilion for Peace at the Milan International Exposition, during which he presided over the fifteenth annual International Peace Congress.

From 1900 until his death in 1918, Moneta suffered from glaucoma, and he spent long periods in the country recuperating from eye operations which barely prevented total blindness. Physical suffering refined Moneta's high sense of purpose but did not diminish his essential exuberance, even in advanced age, or his ability to state vigorously his convictions. During World War I, for example, supporting Italy's role in the war, he said[4]: «I, as an Italian, cannot put myself *au dessus de la mêlée*. I must participate in the life of my country, rejoice in her joys, and weep in her sorrows.»

1. He contributed to it the financial bonus his publisher awarded him after 20 years with *Il Secolo*. As editor of a politically significant newspaper, he could not become a board member, but he met with the founding president Francesco Viganò and founding secretary Angelo Mazzoleni when Hodgson Pratt came to Milan to found an Italian branch of his International Arbitration and Peace Society; and after he left *Il Secolo*, he became active in the Union itself–often referred to as the Lombard Peace Union. For a discussion of Moneta's complicated relationship to this organization and to the one he founded in 1887, see Maria Combi, *Ernesto Teodoro Moneta* (especially the Foreword, pp. 7–13, and Chapter V, pp. 77–107).
2. Whose functions were less politically sensitive, although those who met with Moneta in founding it were virtually the same as those founding the Lombard Union.
3. It was revived in 1945 by Doro Rosetti, nephew and collaborator of Moneta.
4. The (London) *Times* (February 11, 1918) 7.

Moneta succumbed to pneumonia in 1918 at the age of eighty-five. The monument which his friends erected to him in 1925 was carted off to a warehouse during the Fascist regime, thus escaping destruction when a bomb fell on the site during World War II. The inscription on its base preserves the essential paradox of his life, for it honors him both as a partisan of Garibaldi's and as an apostle of peace.

Selected Bibliography

Combi, Maria, *Ernesto Teodoro Moneta: Premio Nobel per la pace 1907*. Milano, Mursia, 1968.

Moneta, Ernesto Teodoro, *Dal presente all' avvenire*. Milano, 1913.

Moneta, Ernesto Teodoro, *Le guerre, le insurrezioni e la pace nel secolo decimonono*. Compendio storico. 4 vols. Milano, 1903–1910.

Moneta, Ernesto Teodoro, *L'ideale della pace e la patria*. Milano, 1913.

Moneta, Ernesto Teodoro, *Irredentismo e gallophobia*. Milano, 1903.

Moneta, Ernesto Teodoro, *La nostra pace*. Milano, Bellini, 1909.

Moneta, Ernesto Teodoro, *Patria e umanità*. Milano, Sonzogno, 1899.

Pinardi, Giuseppe, *La Carrière d'un pacifiste: E.T.Moneta*. Le Havre, Publication de «L'Universel», 1904.

Schou, August, *Histoire de l'internationalisme III: Du Congrès de Vienne jusqu'à la première guerre mondiale (1914)*, pp. 355–359. Publications de l'Institut Nobel Norvégien, Tome VIII. Oslo, Aschehoug, 1963.

Presentation

by Jørgen Gunnarsson Løvland*, Chairman of the Nobel Committee

Louis Renault was born in 1843 at Autun (Saône-et-Loire) and since the age of twenty-five has been professor of international law, first at Dijon and then in 1873 in Paris, where he has lectured both at the Faculty of Law at the University and at the Free School of Exact Sciences, which trains aspiring diplomats and members of the consular service. Since 1890 Renault has also been legal counselor to the French Ministry of Foreign Affairs.

Although Renault has not been a prolific writer, he is the author of a number of articles on international law, some published as monographs, some in periodicals; and in collaboration with a colleague he has produced a treatise on commercial law which is very highly regarded. His principal activities have been those of university lecturer–he may be said to have been the guiding genius in the teaching of international law in France–of counselor to the French Ministry of Foreign Affairs, and finally of France's representative at a large number of international meetings, among them: the conferences in Bern and Paris on the protection of literary and artistic property[1]; the important series of conferences at The Hague in 1893, 1894, 1900, and 1904 on agreements about international civil legal conditions; the conference in Geneva in 1906 for the revision of the 1864 Geneva Convention[2]; and last, but not least, the two international Peace Conferences at The Hague in 1899 and 1907.

At all these conferences Louis Renault has played an outstanding part. As a rule he has been the *rapporteur* of the meeting and as such has drafted

* Mr. Løvland delivered this speech on December 10, 1907, at the Norwegian Nobel Institute, following his announcement of the award of the Peace Prize for 1907 to Mr. Moneta and Mr. Renault. This translation is based on the Norwegian report in the Oslo *Aftenposten* of December 10, 1907. (For a note on other details of the occasion, see p.113.)

1. Bern: 1886; Paris: 1896.

2. The first Geneva Convention for the Amelioration of the Condition of Soldiers wounded in Armed Forces in the Field (signed on August 22, 1864) was revised at this 1906 conference which was called by the Swiss in response to a request made at the time of the 1899 Hague Peace Conference.

reports and recommendations; consequently, he has had a decisive influence upon the agreements and the form they took. At the Hague Peace Conference in 1899, Renault was reporter for the commission working on the problem of applying the provisions of the Geneva Convention to naval warfare, and for the drafting committee which drew up the Final Act of the Conference.

Renault's participation in the Peace Conference at The Hague[1] was even more important. He was spokesman on the following problems:

(1) Opening of hostilities
(2) Application of the Geneva Convention to naval warfare
(3) Obligations and rights of neutral countries in the case of naval warfare
(4) The International Prize Court of Appeal

The last two, in particular, are of far-reaching importance, as well as of extremely delicate nature. Renault was also chairman and spokesman of the drafting committee of the Conference and, as such, had enormous influence upon the final wording of the Conventions; by the outstanding part he played in the debates, probably greater than that of any other member, he also made his mark on the work of the Conference as a whole.

The president of the Conference, Mr. Nelidov[2], described Renault as its «principal worker» and on one occasion said that his dictionary had run out of words of praise with which to describe Renault's share in the work of the Conference.

Louis Renault is a member of the Institute of International Law and of the Institut de France.

1. In 1907.
2. Aleksandr Nelidov (1838–1910), Russian diplomat, president of the 1907 Hague Peace Conference.

Louis Renault

The Work at The Hague in 1899 and in 1907

Nobel Lecture*, May 18, 1908

As you can imagine, I have been looking forward to this opportunity of expressing publicly to the Nobel Committee my deep gratitude for the signal honor they have conferred in awarding me the Peace Prize; I look upon it as the greatest honor of my life. I should like also to keep a promise made to my distinguished colleague Mr. Frédéric Passy[1] when I saw him on the eve of my departure, by conveying to you his regrets that age has prohibited him from discharging the same duty.

My debt of gratitude to you all has been further increased by the warmth and friendliness of your welcome, a welcome which has gladdened my heart even more than it has flattered my vanity. I cannot help adding that I ought also to thank Norway for the moving experience afforded me by the spectacle of her national festival. It was not by chance that I was present; guided by friendly advice, I had indeed *chosen* the date for my visit here. However, in spite of all I had been told, what I had the good fortune to see yesterday far surpassed all my expectations.

In the morning under a dazzling sun all the gay young people in their varied and picturesque costumes, stepping so briskly and waving their flags so joyously, made me think of the springtime of life on its march into the future. In the afternoon the scene took on a more serious aspect, and the sky was less radiant; it all seemed more like autumn. I was deeply moved to hear the national anthem sung by everybody with almost religious fervor, and to see the banners of so many societies and associations dipped in universal salute to the highest representative of the country.

So it was that I saw the two faces of Norway's noble image–the one gay, the other serious, but both equally engaging. My eyes and my heart were fully satisfied.

You have shown me every kindness and no doubt you will now think

---

* Mr. Renault delivered this lecture at the Nobel Institute on May 18, 1908, at 6:00 p.m. The French text in *Les Prix Nobel en 1907* has been used for this translation.
1. Frédéric Passy (1822–1912), co-recipient of the Nobel Peace Prize for 1901.

me only too quick to take advantage of your patience. Forgive me and understand that I am repaying a debt of gratitude.

It is not only on my own behalf that I thank you; I thank you also on behalf of all the jurists who have devoted their efforts to the study of international law, and to whose services in the interest of better international relations you have seen fit to testify so appreciatively. These services had already been collectively honored by the award given to the Institute of International Law[1], an award which excited universal interest. From this pacifist army of internationalists you have now singled out one soldier who, for many years, has fought for the concept of law, both in teaching and in practice.

For too long the diplomats and the theorists of international law ignored each other and disdained each other; as a result of this mutual scorn, now fortunately ended, both theoretical studies and diplomatic agreements have suffered. International relations have become so complex that, if they are to be regulated effectively in view of the many interests at stake, the cooperation of various jurisdictions is indispensable. This is especially true now that the scope of conventional law has been extended to include almost all aspects of political, economic, juridical, and administrative affairs. As we have found in recent conferences, we must now call upon experts in all categories. By doing so we create a climate for the successful collaboration that is so necessary.

Since you have chosen to honor a jurist, it is as a jurist that I address myself to you now, and I beg forgiveness in advance for the aridity of an account which seeks only to be clear and accurate. Unluckily for you, the qualifications of the professor do not necessarily correspond to those of the orator who, as we saw at the Peace Conference, has the knack of making even the most involved problems sound alluring.

I shall not delve into the historical background of the Peace Conferences, the political aspects and organizational details of which have an importance all their own. In this very place, the first Norwegian delegate to the Conference of 1907, my distinguished colleague Mr. Hagerup[2], made this the

1. Recipient of the Nobel Peace Prize for 1904.
2. Georg Francis Hagerup (1853–1921), Norwegian jurist and statesman (twice premier of Norway) and member of the Nobel Committee (1907–1921), who spoke on the second Hague Peace Conference at the Peace Prize award ceremony in 1907.

subject of a talk on an occasion that I shall never forget. I have no desire to repeat what he has already told you, and told you with an authority that I cannot even pretend to possess. I should like, however, to make some observations of a general nature, in fact to present the philosophy of the Peace Conferences. I shall not enter into any controversy. I merely speak as a man who has always been a keen observer of these events, now and again taking a modest part in them, and as one who has profited from the time that has elapsed to evaluate, at a distance from the heat of discussion, the results achieved through strenuous effort.

What, in my opinion, characterizes what I call *the work at The Hague* is the progressive development of the concept of law in the relations between peoples, in short the *juridical organization of international life*.

Here I call to mind what has been done at The Hague in the last fifteen years in the fields of private international law and public international law: the Conferences of 1893, 1894, 1900, and 1904 dealt with the former, those of 1899 and 1907 with the latter.

There are, unquestionably, great differences among the matters treated, yet they share a common characteristic. Such conferences seek to substitute law for the arbitrary; they are concerned with relations between individuals as well as with those between states. The difficulties involved are not the same in both cases, but they are equally great. To resolve them, each country must give up stubborn adherence to its own ideas and concede whatever it can without actually injuring its own essential interests. Let me pay tribute here to a Norwegian magistrate, Mr. Beichmann [1], with whom I have on many occasions had both the pleasure and the profit of working in the field of private law.

Curious, at first glance, is the fact that codification of public international law was begun before that of private international law. The interests of the individual undoubtedly suffered in the absence of rulings in cases of conflicting civil law, but complaints were not lively enough to attract the attention of the various governments. It was the initiative of The Netherlands government, prompted by an eminent jurist, the Minister of State Mr. Asser [2], that finally led the nations of Europe to discuss the conflicts

1. Frederik Valdemar Nicolai Beichmann (1859–1937), Norwegian jurist; chief justice of the Appellate Court in Trondheim (1904–1927).
2. Tobias Michael Carel Asser (1838–1913), co-recipient of the Nobel Peace Prize for 1911.

of civil law; the action this inspired was blessed with favorable results, and we can say that in Europe the codification of private international law is well on its way.

The codification of public international law can be traced back to the Congress held in Paris in 1856 following the Crimean War. The diplomatic act of April 16, 1856, known as the *Declaration of Paris*, contains four rules relating to maritime warfare which are universally accepted today. They brought about great progress, particularly in reconciling on two important points two widely varying systems, that of France and that of Great Britain. This rapprochement, at first forced by the necessity of waging a common war and later maintained after the peace, was established under conditions that complied with both justice and the general interest. Each country gave up practices in its system which seemed, if not unjust, then particularly harsh; the result was entirely favorable to the neutrals, who comprised the largest group concerned: the flag covered the cargo without confiscating it. It is in such a way that all conciliations should be worked out.

However, it is not the Declaration of Paris itself which I want to examine here; rather, it is the procedure that was followed to achieve its extraordinary result, that is to say, the adoption by the whole world of the rules it laid down.

The powers represented at the Congress of Paris–namely, the five big European powers, Austria, France, Great Britain, Prussia, and Russia, together with Sardinia and Turkey who took part in their capacity as belligerents– agreed, after deliberation, on terms which were *ipso facto* binding on themselves and which they later asked the other powers to accept. To be sure, an agreement reached among governments of such widely divergent political, economic, and geographical backgrounds provides certain assurances, for it presents every opportunity for the variety of interests involved to find some sort of satisfaction; so the subsequent adherence by other governments to the terms agreed upon can be easily understood. Nevertheless, the nonparticipating powers could have contributed some pertinent observations both in their own and in the general interest. The adherence procedure, however, put them in the position of having to choose between outright acceptance or outright rejection of rules adopted in their absence.

The same procedure was followed in 1864 for the *Geneva Convention* concerning military wounded on the battlefield and in 1868 for the *Declaration of St. Petersburg* which involved banning the use of explosive bullets, except that in these cases, the procedure was not confined to the great powers alone.

A real step forward was taken by the Brussels Conference which was convened[1], on Russia's initiative, to attempt the regulation of the laws and practices of war on land. No longer were the great and secondary powers the only ones represented at the discussions; the smaller nations were also invited to take part. Obviously these small nations have special interests to protect in that they do not have the same military organization as the large nations and are more likely to be invaded than to invade. However, it should be noted that, in spite of this extension of participation in discussion, the movement remained exclusively European. The United States of America was not represented, despite the initiative it had taken in 1863 through the promulgation of its famous instructions to armies in the field[2].

Once again it was Russia who took the lead in making yet another change by persuading twenty-six nations to send delegates to the first Peace Conference in 1899; thus the movement spread beyond Europe to include nations in America and Asia: the United States, Mexico, China, Japan, Persia, and Siam. The halfway point had been reached. The decision as to which nations were to be invited was arrived at somewhat arbitrarily by the Russian government, which compiled its list on the basis of whether or not the respective powers had ambassadors at the Court of St. Petersburg. The last stage was completed in 1907 when forty-six nations were invited and forty-four actually took part. This time almost the entire civilized world was represented at the conference which some daring journalist, not surprisingly, dubbed the *Parliament of Mankind*–certainly an incorrect title in many respects, but a striking one just the same.

Apart from congresses such as the postal or telegraphic conferences which are primarily concerned with administrative matters, I think one can say that no diplomatic gathering purporting to have matters of political interest as the main items on its agenda had ever before been so well attended. Such a congress is clearly qualified to pass laws intended for universal application; all parties have an equal opportunity to voice their opinions and to defend their own interests, and it is with a full knowledge of the facts that they adopt any resolution. This general participation in discussion is unquestionably more in keeping with the independence and equality of states than was the previous procedure. But along with these theoretical and practical

1. In 1874.
2. General Order 100, 1863, dealt with martial law, protection of persons and property, deserters, prisoners, spies, flags of truce, etc. (*Regulations of the Army of the United States and General Orders in Force*, Washington, D.C.)

advantages come many difficulties which have to be surmounted, first during the *discussions* themselves and then in connection with the passing of the *resolutions*, as all who attended the Conference discovered. By pointing out these difficulties I do not mean to condemn the system, but merely to draw attention to their inescapable consequences and to the care which must be taken to mitigate them. The equality of nations, except in matters of material strength, is juridically incontrovertible, but this equality pushed to the last limits of literalness becomes absurd. To give an example which should offend no one, Great Britain and Luxembourg are two states equal before the law, yet would it not be ridiculous if the voice of Luxembourg carried as much weight on a maritime issue as that of Great Britain? The small nations have a most useful and honorable part to play in these conferences; they are most frequently the true representatives of justice, precisely because they do not have the strength to impose injustice. However, if they wish to see maintained the tradition of these conferences to which they are invited, they would do well to exercise a certain restraint and to avoid the fallacious belief that obstinacy, not to say obstructionism, is the best way of asserting their independence. Please forgive the great liberty I have taken in thus expressing myself; it is a liberty taken by a jurist influenced by a sincere love for justice and not by any political considerations. I am less concerned with criticizing the attitude of this or that delegation than with paying homage to that of a delegation which has correctly understood the role it should play. I shall return to this matter later.

Unanimity is basic to any diplomatic conference, for the goal of such a conference must be the alignment of equal but distinct wills; in a parliamentary assembly, on the other hand, it is the expression of a single will, that of the nation represented, which must be obtained. This necessity for unanimity is a constraining factor since it can lead to the exercise of the *liberum veto*, in short to a stalemate, but it is also an indispensable safeguard against hasty decisions and against coalitions of interests. It allows compromise in the sense that a resolution can represent the will of the conference as a whole, in spite of some disagreements. It is a matter of tact and prudence; such delicate problems are not resolved mathematically. The main point is that no nation should be forced into anything against its will.

One has only to think about it to appreciate the difficulties bound to arise in any attempt to draft a formula which will be acceptable to the representatives of so many nations differing in interests, customs, and institutions.

Even when there is a solid basis for agreement, there are always innumerable nuances suggesting diversity in attitudes of mind, ways of thinking and of reasoning. People may even speak the same language, but they do not speak it identically nor give to words the same shades of meaning. It is necessary indeed to accept compromises and to agree to conciliatory schemes which the logical, critical mind and which the learned scholar at his desk would not tolerate. I hasten to plead extenuating circumstances on behalf of one who has often used the pen and who knows, better than anyone else, that the end result is not perfect. Had he been as uncompromising in the drafting of resolutions as he would be in the formulating of a purely scientific work, he would have achieved nothing.

In short, sometimes, instead of laying down a hard-and-fast rule, we must limit ourselves to a recommendation, indeed to a kind of prayer. The resolution is binding «insofar as is possible», «insofar as circumstances permit», etc. Then, you will say, it is no longer a legal obligation, but merely a moral duty. True, but it is no small matter that a moral duty be recognized by the majority of nations. By force of circumstance, it eventually becomes a part of custom and compels as much acknowledgment as if it had constituted a strict obligation in the first place. Assistance to enemy wounded was a charitable duty generally recognized even before the Geneva Convention of 1864 made it a legal responsibility. We must not move too fast or believe that, in our age of rapid communication, minds can be reshaped as quickly and easily as matter. There are some forms of resistance and even of hesitation that only time, allied with education, can overcome. Jurists and journalists can do a great deal to pave the way for the reform of nefarious practices. They can succeed – and there are examples of this – in influencing a nation to give up barbaric measures which its government has been unwilling to renounce.

Finally, in considering the work of a conference, we are wrong to take into account only what has produced definite, clear-cut results, ignoring what has been done to prepare the way for future achievements. There can be no harvest without the seed. We may well heed the instructions given to the United States delegates before the second Peace Conference in the name of one whom I take pleasure in remembering here – President Roosevelt[1]: «You should always keep in mind the promotion of this continuous process through which the progressive development of interna-

1. Theodore Roosevelt (1858–1919), president of the United States (1901–1909); recipient of the Nobel Peace Prize for 1906.

tional justice and peace may be carried on; and you should regard the work of the Second Conference, not merely with reference to the definite results to be reached in that Conference, but also with reference to the foundations which may be laid for further results in future conferences. It may well be that among the most valuable services rendered to civilization by this Second Conference will be found the progress made in matters upon which the delegates reach no definite agreement.»[1] Here is practical wisdom that has been lacking in all too many of those who disparage the Peace Conferences.

I have no intention of commenting on or analyzing the various resolutions formulated at the Conference of 1907. The delegates drew up thirteen *conventions* proper and one *declaration*, not to mention the important *voeux* or recommendations and the general acknowledgments contained in the Final Act. I should like merely to single out certain essential facts that show the extent to which the concept of law was strengthened and developed.

Let us first of all consider the resolutions pertaining to war. To begin with, does it not seem paradoxical to be so occupied with war at a conference for peace? Indignation and mockery are easily evoked and given full rein; they are not the more justified for this reason. The name «Peace Conference» was chosen somewhat irrationally by a section of public opinion which, on the strength of the first Russian message[2], expected the Conference to bring about partial, if not total, disarmament and, consequently, everlasting peace. Eventually the name passed into official usage. I must confess I regretted this fact wholeheartedly since I doubted very much that the public, having failed to obtain from the Conference what it had unreasonably expected, would then attach any importance or value to the actual useful results.

Is this to say that the term «Peace Conference» is entirely unjustified?

1. Quoted from Elihu Root [U.S. secretary of state and recipient of the Nobel Peace Prize for 1912], «Instructions to the American Delegates to the Hague Conference, 1907», Department of State, Washington, D.C., May 31, 1907.

2. Dated August 12 (New Style, August 24), 1898, the first message stated the belief «that the present moment would be very favorable for seeking, by means of international discussion, the most effectual means of insuring to all peoples the benefits of a real and durable peace, and, above all, of putting an end to the progressive development of the present armaments.» (James Brown Scott, *The Hague Peace Conferences of 1899 and 1907*, Vol.II [Baltimore: Johns Hopkins Press, 1909], p.1.)

I do not believe so. Anything that contributes to extending the domain of law in international relations contributes to peace. Since the possibility of future war cannot be ignored, it is a *farsighted* policy that takes into account the difficulties created by war in the relations between belligerents and neutrals; and it is a *humanitarian* policy that strives to reduce the evils of war in the relations between the belligerents themselves and to safeguard as far as possible the interests of noncombatants and of the sick and the wounded. Whatever may be said by those who scoff at the work undertaken in this field by the Peace Conferences, wars will not become rarer by becoming more barbarous.

For a long time discussion has centered on the question of whether a government on the verge of war has an obligation to warn its adversary before opening hostilities. This question has led to frequent recriminations between belligerents. The Conference agreed unanimously that «hostilities must not commence without previous and explicit warning, in the form either of a reasoned declaration of war or of an ultimatum with conditional declaration of war.»[1] The future will show whether it is possible to go a step further, as certain delegations have asked, by requiring a specified time-lapse between the receipt of the warning and the start of hostilities.

The Convention dealing with the laws and customs of war on land is the Convention of 1899 carefully revised[2].

Let me select a few points which indicate significant progress.

Article 23.h of the Statute forbids belligerents to «declare abolished, suspended, or inadmissible in a court of law, the rights and actions of the nationals of the hostile party». This would seem to satisfy a theoretical rather than a practical necessity because, with our modern concept of war and its effect on civilians, it would be difficult to imagine a civilized country's declaring void or suspended the rights of enemy subjects.

In accordance with a new provision added at the end of the same Article 23, «a belligerent is likewise forbidden to compel the nationals of the hostile party to take part in any operations of war directed against their own country, even if they were in the belligerent's service before the commencement of the war.» This provision results from the same concern that in-

1. Peace Conference of 1907: Convention III (relative to the opening of hostilities), Article I.

2. Convention II in the Peace Conference of 1899; Convention IV in that of 1907.

spired the new Article 44: «A belligerent is forbidden to force the inhabitants of territory occupied by it to furnish information about the army of the other belligerent or about its means of defense.» This touches on the question of forced guides, one of the most painful raised by the practice of war. Is it, after all, logical to forbid a belligerent to conscript an inhabitant of enemy territory into its army, and at the same time permit it to force the same inhabitant to serve it as a guide, thereby compelling him to do his country even greater harm? Is this not an outrage against the most honorable aspect of patriotism? Should we not, then, commend the majority of the Conference for refusing to be sidetracked by technical arguments and for persisting in comdemning the present practice? Undoubtedly, certain delegations had their reservations with regard to the provision. It is open to question whether their governments would dare, should the occasion arise, to resort to a practice censured by the vast majority of the civilized world. What happened in the case of the «dum-dum» bullets offers an argument worth considering [1].

Article 52 now ends with the provision that requisitions in kind must be paid as soon as possible; this is a real advance toward achieving respect for private property.

Lastly, and most important of all, is the inclusion in the Convention of an article under whose terms any belligerent party violating the provisions of the Statute will be subject to penalties. In addition, the belligerent will be held responsible for all acts committed by members of its armed forces. The inclusion of this new clause resulted from the doubts held in certain quarters about the compulsory character of the Statute, since comparison of its provisions with those of the Brussels Conference seemed to indicate that neither possessed more than moral weight. All doubt has been removed now that the terms of the Statute are supported by the obligation to make amends for any injurious consequences which might result from their violation. Moreover, the belligerent's responsibility for acts committed by members of its armed forces is clearly defined. Is this not a great step for-

---

1. The «dum-dum» bullets, named for the city of Dumdum in India where they were first made, were outlawed by Declaration 3 of the 1899 Peace Conference. The laureate may be referring to the fact that the U.S. and Great Britain were recorded as opposed to its adoption, the U.S., at least, through a technicality: its delegates, objecting to the wording of the proposed declaration, presented an amendment which they considered more inclusive, but the original motion, being put to the vote first, passed, with the U.S. and Great Britain recorded as opposed.

ward, and is it not calculated to make the belligerent more vigilant in observing the Statute?

The Convention concerning the rights and duties of neutral powers and persons in war on land[1] implemented a recommendation of the Conference of 1899. It clarifies certain principles and, in doing so, gives guarantees to neutrals perpetually exposed to the demands of one or both of the belligerent parties. Again, this facilitates the maintenance of peace.

Naval warfare presents many difficulties on many points, since it involves the relations between the belligerents themselves and those between belligerents and neutrals. There is always some vagueness which the belligerents take advantage of to further their own interests. These interests are, or seem to be, very divergent, and the divergence unfortunately results primarily from geographical situation, which no one can do anything about. It would have been useless, therefore, to hope for general agreement on many of these matters. That negotiations became possible at all constituted an achievement in itself, since the great seafaring nations had for a long time automatically refused to be drawn into discussion on this subject.

A great effort was made on all sides. Understanding was reached on several points; the field of controversy was limited, to the advantage of all concerned; and a basis for future discussion and agreement was established. It now remains for each country to undertake a serious examination of its own real interests and to determine how far it can go in bringing about the accord that is so desirable.

In order to show just what has been attempted or achieved, I should have to delve into minute details and technicalities, but I shall confine myself to the broad outlines.

The question of laying automatic submarine contact mines[2] had stirred public opinion ever since the last war because of the threat these mines posed to peaceable shipping even long after the end of hostilities. If no completely satisfactory answer has been given, it is because the technical questions involved have not as yet been satisfactorily answered; there is bound to be some groping in the dark. Rules offering certain guarantees concerning bombardment by naval forces have also been formulated[3]–not

1. Convention V, 1907.
2. Convention VIII, 1907.
3. Convention IX, 1907.

without difficulty. Both of these delicate matters were handled by a sub-committee presided over by Mr. Hagerup.

The right to seize private property in the course of war at sea has long been a point for argument. Pursuing its traditional policy, the United States of America proposed the abolition of this right and succeeded in rallying the majority of nations to its point of view. However, since the remaining minority included the great seafaring nations, the proposition could have no immediate practical results. On the other hand, if the principle of abolition itself did not triumph, at least certain important restrictions were brought to bear on the exercise of the right of seizure[1]. For example, postal correspondence found on either enemy or neutral ships was declared inviolable–to the distinct advantage of both belligerent and neutral commercial relations. Coastal fishing boats and local shipping of light tonnage were exempted from seizure. The treatment of the crews of captured enemy merchant vessels was regulated advantageously. These results can well be appreciated by any country which, like Norway, is greatly concerned with fishing and shipping.

Norway, like all maritime nations intending to remain neutral, was particularly anxious to have a comprehensive and precise ruling covering the rights and duties of neutral powers during naval warfare, especially with regard to the governing of belligerent warships visiting neutral ports. A convention was drawn up, thanks partly to the efforts of the late Count Tornielli, Italy's first delegate[2]. This Convention appears, on the whole, to provide a fair settlement of the matter. It is to be hoped that agreement can eventually be reached on the points which certain powers still have reservations about. This would mean real progress in the interests of peace, for it would reduce the danger of any extension of hostilities resulting from conflicts between belligerents and neutrals.

In connection with this train of thought, I would just like to mention the Convention for the adaptation of the principles of the Geneva Convention [1864] to naval warfare[3]. Agreement was easily reached. The Convention of 1899 was carefully reviewed in the light of the amendments to the Geneva Convention which went into effect in 1906. The same spirit

1. Convention XI, 1907.
2. Convention XIII, 1907. Count Joseph Tornielli Crusati di Vergano (1836–1908), Italian ambassador to Paris (1895–1908) and head of the Italian delegation to the second Conference.
3. Convention III in 1899; Convention X in 1907.

of goodwill dominates both Conventions, the one concerning the sick and wounded in land warfare and that dealing with them in naval warfare. Differences of application occur in some cases, but only because of the difference in milieu.

I come now to those points which have a direct bearing on the maintenance of good relations between nations and which naturally claim the special attention of all friends of peace.

How much did the second Peace Conference attempt, and to what extent did it succeed in contributing to this cause?

First of all, it had to consider the Convention for the pacific settlement of international disputes which had been drawn up in 1899 and signed by nearly all the nations of the civilized world[1]. I shall deal only with those aspects of the Convention that concern arbitration. For certain problems, arbitration had been recognized as the fairest and most efficient instrument for settling disputes not resolved through diplomatic channels. Its use remained optional, but it still constituted a piece of legal machinery easily set in motion – something not to be disdained. When two powers agree to settle a dispute legally by arbitration, it is preferable that they should not first have to discuss details of the organization of the tribunal or of procedure. Such discussion can easily become a source of friction which, although completely dissociated from the dispute itself, makes settlement of the dispute that much more difficult. How much better it is to be able to use an instrument set up in advance when there was no particular dispute in view, and no objective except that of finding the best means to serve the general cause of justice!

To appreciate fully the benefits derived from the Convention of 1899, we should consider not only its material and tangible results, but also the imponderable influence which it has exerted on the chancelleries, an influence which has made itself felt in two important ways. In the first place, when a dispute does arise, the idea of settling it by arbitration is now readily accepted, whereas previously those who proposed such a solution were regarded by men of action as pure theorists, I can confirm this from personal experience. In the second place, there have already been numerous applications of Article 19 of the Convention, by the terms of which the signatory powers reserved the right to conclude new standing agreements of their

1. Convention I in both 1899 and 1907.

own which would apply compulsory arbitration to all cases in which they deemed it appropriate. I am happy to say that it was the Franco-British Convention of October 14, 1903, which was the first to be signed under these terms and that approximately sixty such agreements have been signed up to April 6 of this year. One of the latest is, I believe, the Convention of April 4 between Norway and the United States.

So far only four arbitration cases[1] have been adjudicated at The Hague itself in conformity with the procedure adopted in 1899. There have been others which were dealt with more simply. The important thing is that arbitration be used to avoid conflict; whether it is used here or there, whether through this or that procedure is of little consequence. Let me add, however, that we should not want too many such arbitrations. Undoubtedly, it is better to plead than to fight; but it is better still to come to a direct understanding without having to plead. It is the fear of arbitration and possible public censure by a tribunal, however, that prompts a government to be prudent enough to relinquish an unfounded claim.

This 1899 Convention was revised in 1907 and many improvements in its details were made. I mention only the introduction of a summary procedure for minor matters and of the carefully drawn up procedures adopted by the International Commissions of Inquiry whose effectiveness was demonstrated in a striking manner on the occasion of the Hull incident[2]; this in itself would have been enough to exonerate the 1899 Convention from the reproach of having done nothing useful.

I come now to what the 1907 Conference did about compulsory arbitration, a subject which it discussed thoroughly if not always happily.

1. The Pious Fund case (Mexico *vs.* United States): agreement to submit to the Hague Tribunal on May 22, 1902; award made on October 14, 1902. The Venezuelan Preferential case (Germany, Great Britain, Italy *vs.* Venezuela – eventually involving Belgium, Spain, United States, France, Mexico, The Netherlands, Sweden, Norway): agreement to submit on May 7, 1903; award on February 22, 1904. (See fn.1, p.159) The Japanese House Tax case (France, Germany, Great Britain *vs.* Japan): agreement to submit on August 28, 1902; award on May 22, 1905. The Muscat Dhows case (France *vs.* Great Britain): agreement to submit on October 13, 1904; award on August 8, 1905.
2. In 1904, during the Russo-Japanese War, the Russian fleet fired on English fishing trawlers in the North Sea, claiming Japanese torpedo boats were among the trawlers; the ensuing English-Russian dispute was referred to and satisfactorily settled by an International Commission of Inquiry.

It had been proposed at the 1899 Conference to introduce this measure with limited applications, but the proposal had to be withdrawn in the face of overwhelming opposition. In 1907 the proposal was advanced again, and again was dropped, with the result that the Convention itself was not amended on this point. Does this mean that we are still exactly where we were in 1899 and that no progress at all has been made in a matter which so deeply concerns all peace-loving people?

To say this would be to exaggerate unfairly. I shall try to clarify this point and to explain the positions adopted at the Peace Conference.

No attempt was made to present arbitration as a means of resolving all disputes, no matter what their nature, at least not in a general Convention. There is nothing to prevent two determined nations that may be able to foresee the possible nature of their future disputes, from going far beyond the scope of a Convention like the one I have just mentioned; indeed, many instances of this kind can be cited. However, some delegates believed that by taking precautions it was possible to introduce compulsory arbitration for certain types of disputes under terms extending to all nations; they were vigorously opposed. I am certain that the problem had never before been examined in such detail. By gathering together all the possible objections to it and thereby forcing everyone to face the problem in all its aspects, the adversaries of compulsory arbitration have, probably unwittingly, rendered an invaluable service to the very cause they so relentlessly attacked; for to face the problem is to take the first sure step toward its solution. I firmly believe that none of the objections is truly fundamental and that the principle must therefore triumph in the end. Jurists and diplomats will do well to devote some careful study to these lively, sometimes impassioned, but always courteous discussions of 1907. They will gain a clearer insight into the difficulties that must be overcome and so be better able to work out the proper solutions.

What has actually been the result of the discussions I have just described?

Thirty-two nations agreed to the drafting of a Convention instituting compulsory arbitration: first, for a range of general cases which would be subject to the traditional reservations covering vital interests and national honor; and second, for a number of specific cases which would not be subject to such. Some of those present indulged in lighthearted banter about a few of these cases, asking if anyone really supposed they could lead to war. In the first place, however, wars very frequently spring from petty incidents, and arbitration can be of value in dealing with these as well as with the more serious cases. We must become accustomed to making it function in relatively minor affairs before we come to more serious ones. In any event, some of the eventualities covered were not as trivial as they might seem, a case in point being the assessment of the sum of an indemnity once the onus of responsibility has been admitted. Experience has shown that arbitration in such a matter would prevent exaggerated claims. Be that as it may, the minority, invoking the rule of unanimity, opposed inclusion in the Final Act, of the agreement formulated along the lines just mentioned, and supported, as I have said, by thirty-two nations. There could clearly be no possibility of incorporating it in the same Convention that all the nations were prepared to sign. No one could be satisfied with this purely negative result; so the following declaration was inserted in the Final Act: «The Conference, actuated by the spirit of mutual agreement and concession characterizing its deliberations, has agreed upon the following declaration, which, while reserving to each of the powers represented full liberty of action as regards voting, enables them to affirm the principles which they regard as unanimously admitted: It [the Conference] is unanimous, first, in admitting the principle of compulsory arbitration and, secondly, in declaring that certain disputes, in particular those relating to the interpretation and application of the provisions of international agreements, may be submitted to compulsory arbitration without any restriction.»

Thus, no power now directly attacks compulsory arbitration; it only remains for certain nations to restudy their positions in order to decide in which cases they are prepared to allow it. The other thirty-two nations are prepared, as of now, to be bound by specific categories, and no further obstacle stands in the way of their signing an agreement to that effect. Can we say then that the situation is the same as it was in 1899? To do so would be to ignore the evidence. We can safely say that the future of compulsory arbitration is assured.

The Conference of 1907 succeeded moreover in introducing a certain form of compulsory arbitration in a case which is not without significance; I refer to the Convention concerning the limitation of the use of force for the recovery of contractual debts[1]. In principle, contractual debts claimed from the government of one country by the government of another as owed to its nationals may not be recovered by force. However, this stipula-

1. Convention II, 1907.

tion would not apply if the debtor nation refused or ignored an offer of arbitration or if, in the event of acceptance of such an offer, it obstructed the implementing of a compromise or, after arbitration, failed to comply with the decision given. Here, surely, is a case of compulsory arbitration in that the creditor nation must propose arbitration at the very outset and that it depends only on the debtor nation to accept. Those nations possessing powerful means of coercion renounce their use to start with, in the arrangement described. This is no mean advantage for the weaker nations. Objection has been made that the procedure suffers from a lack of complete reciprocity because a strong nation against whom a weaker one makes a claim could either ignore it or refuse arbitration, knowing that the only possible recourse for the weaker state would be the use of force, an absurd expedient in view of the disproportion of strength. This cannot be denied, nor can the fact that only in a limited way did the Convention allow such compulsory arbitration. However, it would be wrong to suppose that it is always the weaker nations who call for such arbitration and the strong ones who refuse it. The reverse was the case in 1902 at the time of the claims by European powers against Venezuela[1].

The United States proposed the setting up of a judicial arbitration court which would be truly permanent as opposed to the one instituted by the Convention of 1899 which is permanent in name only; the framework alone [of the latter] is permanent since the tribunal is essentially mobile, having to be convened for each individual case and then dissolved immediately after pronouncing its verdict. A great deal of work was done to define the jurisdiction of the court and the procedure to be followed in sessions. The proposal encountered an insurmountable obstacle when it came to the composition of the court. The sponsors of the plan believed that, to be a truly effective instrument, the new tribunal should not include too many judges, and a total of fifteen to seventeen appeared to be the absolute maximum. If we compare this total with the number of nations represented at the Conference, we can understand the difficulty. How could one provide for

1. In 1902, Germany, Great Britain, and Italy blockaded Venezuelan ports to enforce payment of claims which they and other nations (which had abstained from hostile action) held against Venezuela. Venezuela then agreed to a certain method of paying the claims but refused to give preferential treatment to the blockading powers. In May, 1903, the question was submitted to the Permanent Court of Arbitration which decided unanimously in favor of the blockading powers.

each nation's sharing in the appointment of fifteen or seventeen judges? It is easy to foresee the various factions, whether they be of the great or of the lesser powers, colliding in opposition. All hope of reaching agreement in the Conference had to be abandoned and action restricted to the inclusion of the following recommendation[1] in the Final Act: «The Conference calls the attention of the signatory powers to the advisability of adopting the annexed draft Convention for the creation of a judicial arbitration court, and of bringing it into force as soon as an agreement has been reached respecting the selection of the judges and the constitution of the court.» It is to be hoped that we will succeed in arriving at an understanding obviously requiring compromise and the setting aside of unreasonable demands. The proposed permanent court would be of valuable service, particularly in its setting up of a delegation of three members to settle quickly a large number of minor disputes. The fact that three great powers, none of them particularly noted for idealism – namely, Germany, England, and the United States–jointly put forward the proposal is significant.

I end my review of the work of The Hague with the Convention relating to the creation of an international prize court[2]. This is concerned largely with the rules of war; but the draft of the Convention was also referred to the First Commission entrusted with examining questions relative to international justice, since the matter involves the means of settling serious international disputes through litigation. I have kept this Convention for the last because it seems to me that it best demonstrates the general spirit of the second Peace Conference, the development of the concept of law, and the influence of the times.

For centuries it has been accepted that a captured enemy merchantman or a seized neutral ship becomes a prize in fact only after confirmation by a judicial authority: all prizes must be adjudicated. The competent jurisdiction has been that of the captor who arranges the prize tribunals as he sees fit. It is hardly surprising that the decisions of these tribunals have often given rise to objections and sometimes even to actual conflict. Indeed, these tribunals exercise the laws set down by their own governments, laws which may well be arbitrary. Furthermore, since their own national interests are deeply involved, they are not inclined to find illegal the acts perpetrated

1. This is the first of four «voeux» or recommendations contained in the Final Act of the 1907 Conference.
2. Convention XII, 1907.

in serious or even dangerous circumstances by officers of their own national navy. Surely there is no better way of working for peace than by attempting to obtain a greater measure of justice for those wronged in the course of maritime warfare, and thus to eliminate some serious causes of conflict. The smaller nations, whose voices can sometimes hardly be heard among those of the powerful belligerents, would derive real benefit from a change in such practice.

For a long time, publicists have been clamoring for reform. The Institute of International Law had drawn up a comprehensive proposal, but it was looked upon as belonging to the realm of pure theory, without a chance of realization. One would scarcely have thought that a group of great seafaring nations, who have an interest in preserving their freedom of action if they are belligerents and who are in a position to make themselves heard if they are neutrals, would take the initiative in this matter. Nevertheless this is precisely what happened. From the very start of the Conference, Germany and Great Britain each advanced plans aimed at establishing an international court for dealing with prizes. They were, however, motivated by such divergent ideas that a conciliation was at first thought to be impossible. A compromise was nevertheless attained, and a comprehensive, carefully drafted proposal was submitted to the Conference in the name of four great powers, Germany, the United States, France, and Great Britain. With only a few amendments relating to points of detail, it was accepted by the main body of the Conference. The only opposition came from one non-European nation[1].

I cannot even think of embarking on an analysis of a Convention which touches on so vast a number of technicalities and which in fact constitutes a code for the new institution. I shall confine myself to two points of primary importance.

I. Composition of the Court

The court consists of fifteen members supplied by forty-four nations. Comparison of the two figures gives an immediate indication of the difficulty of the problem. Here is a brief outline of the system adopted. Eight powers—Germany, Austria-Hungary, the United States, France, Great Britain, Italy,

1. Of the 44 nations polled, 37 voted for the convention, 6 abstained, and 1 (Brazil) opposed.

Japan, and Russia—all appeared to have a predominating interest by virtue of the size of their navies, the tonnage of their merchant shipping, and the importance of their maritime commerce; so they will select the regularly presiding judges. For the other powers, rotation determines a table appended to the Convention which lists, year by year, their respective judges and deputy judges. The system is inevitably arbitrary, both in itself and in its applications, and it is immediately open to criticism concerning its departure from the concept of the equality of all nations in law. But is it logical to wish to give equal control over the composition of the court to Germany, Montenegro, and Siam? Is it not the major powers who make the greatest sacrifice in agreeing to a revision of the decisions of their own prize tribunals? Lastly, granted that the nature of its composition is defective, does not the new jurisdiction at all events herald great progress, and does it not assure all nations, particularly the secondary powers, certain guarantees absent in the present state of affairs? Therein lies a decisive point not immediately grasped by the majority of the interested parties. I am happy to recall that the delegation of one nation, which is of secondary political importance but which possesses one of the largest merchant marines, declared that its government, in spite of reservations which it could have made on the subject of its participation in the selection of judges, accepted the proposal for the sake of the significant progress which it promised.

II. Applicable Law

What rules of law will the new jurisdiction put into effect? This a crucial question posed by the fact that the laws of maritime warfare are far from being codified and that, in spite of the efforts of the 1907 Conference, uncertainty persists with regard to a great many points, some of them very important. When there are conventional rules that bind the nations concerned, or when rules have become so well established by custom that they can be regarded as the expression of the tacit will of these nations, international jurisdiction need only apply or interpret such rules. But a situation may well arise in which the law of nations, actual or customary, is silent; what then is the duty of international jurisdiction? Such a situation gives pause for thought. Here is the set of rules proposed by Great Britain which, after doctrinal scruples were expressed by certain delegates, was adopted by the Conference without serious objection:

«If a question of law to be decided is covered by a treaty in force between the belligerent captor and a power which is itself or whose subject or citizen is a party to the proceedings, the court is governed by the provisions of the said treaty.

In the absence of such provisions, the court shall apply the rules of international law. If no generally recognized rules exist, the court shall give judgment in accordance with the general principles of justice and equity.» (Art. 7, par. 1 and 2.)

This is unquestionably a bold solution, but also one likely to exert the most beneficial influence on the development of international maritime law. The judges are thus set a delicate task, but we must trust the powers to choose them carefully enough that we can rely on the wisdom and moderation of their views. They will know how to amend a practice without overthrowing it. Such a provision reflects great credit on both the power which proposed it and on the Conference which voted for it. I emphasize this because it seems to me to signify outstanding progress for the concept of law in international relations.

Thus the Conference of 1907 has created the first international judicial organism of a permanent nature in the sense that, as soon as redress from decisions of the prize tribunals is sought, the new institution will function on its own without there being any need for a new agreement between the nations concerned. I consider it auspicious for the development of compulsory arbitration that this agreement could be reached in view of the fact that it means submitting to a court of justice disputes deeply involving vital interests and national prestige, matters usually subject to the traditional reservations. Even though the whole problem was perforce related to the idea of war, it was, I feel, well within the domain of a Peace Conference.

The first Peace Conference had made it incumbent upon the one that would succeed it to pursue the study of certain questions. The second Conference was honorbound to execute this legacy insofar as practicable. It followed the example of its predecessor and referred various problems to the consideration of a third Conference. The calling of the latter has been expressly provided for by several Conventions, and the Final Act ends with these words:

«Finally the Conference recommends to the powers the assembly of a Third Peace Conference, which might be held within a period corresponding to that which has elapsed since the preceding conference, at a date to be fixed by common agreement between the powers, and it calls their attention to the necessity of preparing the program of this Third Conference a sufficient time in advance, to ensure its deliberations being conducted with the necessary authority and expedition.

In order to attain this object, the Conference considers that it would be very desirable that, some two years before the probable date of the meeting, a preparatory committee should be charged by the governments with the task of collecting the various proposals to be submitted to the conference, of ascertaining what subjects are ripe for embodiment in an international regulation, and of preparing a program which the governments should decide upon in sufficient time to enable it to be carefully examined by the countries interested. This committee should further be entrusted with the task of proposing a system of organization and procedure for the conference itself. »

I regard this recommendation as important for two reasons: it establishes the fact that the holding of regular international conferences is now a universally accepted idea and that suggestions based on experience should be made to ensure that these conferences take place under the most favorable conditions. Certain delegates had been in favor of providing an actual link between the second and third conferences by setting up a committee which would have been the executor, as it were, of the outgoing conference and the prime mover of the conference to come. This idea had to be promptly abandoned in favor of the formula I have just read, the drawing up of which was not an easy matter. In spite of the purely diplomatic prudence which inspired it, it contains several interesting points.

The date of the next conference was not and could not be fixed since nobody can ever control the course of events, and since the year nominated might well prove totally unfavorable for a meeting of this kind. The interval provided for is fairly elastic. A certain amount of time must be allowed for the decisions of the 1907 Conference to take effect: the period allowed for signing does not expire until June 30; the agreements signed will have to be ratified and, in a number of countries, the ratification of these agreements, or at least of some of them, will require the approval of parliament; and finally, in some cases special executive laws will have to be passed. All this naturally requires considerable time. Only after that can we start thinking about the next conference, and it is in this connection that practical experience has pointed the way. A diplomatic conference must be prepared carefully and the problems awaiting solution subjected to careful study in the various countries so that the delegations can come equipped with precise instructions about the main issues, thus avoiding the necessity of referring them to their respective governments at every stage. The agendas of 1899 and 1907 were too extensive and too vague. A committee of competent persons, formed well in advance, could render a signal service in collecting the various proposals, classifying them, and suggesting a program which would of course be decided upon by the governments themselves. Furthermore, regulations covering organization and procedure should be drawn up. In the wise recommendations made, which will, one hopes, find a receptive audience, there is an intentional omission: nothing has been said about the composition of the preparatory committee which will raise problems similar to those I have mentioned in connection with the court of arbitration. Let us hope that excessive touchiness does not thwart its appointment.

Finally, you will note that the calling of a third conference is provided for in only a general way; nothing is said about initiating it or about the place where it is to be held. The institution exists independently, and each power can on its own responsibility take the necessary steps to activate it. From the legal point of view this is a sign of progress because no longer do meetings considered useful appear to depend on the goodwill of any particular power. As a jurist, however, I cannot make such a statement without also stating that Russia deserves the recognition of all nations for the initiative which she took in 1899 and which she has valiantly tried to preserve in the aftermath of a terrible war, thus continuing a glorious tradition. She has shown the way once and will not hesitate to do so again, but she does not intend to monopolize the role of herald for the civilized world. As for the meeting place, if The Hague is not chosen it will not be because we have forgotten its gracious hospitality but because of consideration for The Netherlands government which cannot be tied up for years at a stretch. All legitimate sensitivities have been taken care of by a formula accepted by everyone.

It is more than time for me to conclude. I have attempted to give an objective account of what has been achieved and of what has been done to prepare for future achievement. Let us be patient and let us have confidence in the beneficial effect of time in consolidating what is already decided and in developing what is only anticipated. Time can indeed be a «galant' uomo», to use the Italian phrase, but we must not leave it to work on its own; we must help it along. So let all of us who can exert any influence on international relations, be it in the sphere of theory or of practice, set to work. Let us devote ourselves neither to blind enthusiasm nor to blind disparagement of what has been done, but to constructive criticism that can lead the way to improvement; let us give properly measured considera-tion to every attempt and to every suggestion made to achieve success. Let all of us in each country search carefully for the real interests involved in any given question and for the changes in practice that might be effected by compromise–for habit is often a poor counselor, encouraging unjustified opposition to measures which would be to the general good.

I need hardly say that I confine myself to my own field, that of juris-prudence, and that I do not mean to encroach upon that of the statesman.

In closing, if I may be permitted to include the personal as I did in be-ginning this lecture, I promise you that I will devote to the task I have described the years of work still left to me. I would like to try in this way to justify the distinguished honor you have conferred upon me and to show my living gratitude to a country which welcomes me so warmly.

Biography

Although his active participation in efforts to solve the problems of international law brought him honor and respect from around the world, Louis Renault (May 21, 1843–February 8, 1918) was, in his own words[1], «a professor at heart». Born at Autun in the Saône-et-Loire district of France, he received his love of learning as a heritage from his Burgundian father, a bookseller by vocation and bibliophile by avocation. Intellectually gifted, Renault was first in his class at the Collège d'Autun, taking prizes in philosophy, mathematics, and literature before going on to the University of Dijon for his bachelor's degree in literature. For seven years, from 1861 to 1868, he studied law in Paris, receiving three degrees, the highest of them the doctoral and all of them with extraordinary honors.

In 1868 he began the career in the academic world which he never deserted. Twenty-five years old in 1868, he returned to Dijon as lecturer in Roman and then in commercial law. He joined the Faculty of Law of the University of Paris as an acting professor of criminal law in 1873, but he found his true field the next year when the opportunity arose to fill a temporary vacancy in international law. Although at first loath to change his primary field of interest, he continued in the new milieu and so distinguished himself in the next seven years by his teaching and by his publication of some fifty notes and articles and a book, *Introduction à l'étude du droit international*, that he was offered the chair of international law in 1881.

Renault's scholarly output during his lifetime was extensive, making him the outstanding French authority on international law. He delivered countless lectures, wrote dozens of reports, published upwards of 200 notes and articles, most of them in law reviews and political science journals, and produced several books, of which the most important, in collaboration with his colleague, Charles Lyon-Caen, is the nine-volume *Traité de droit commercial* (1889–1899). Devoted to teaching as well as to research, he lectured for some years, concurrently with his appointment at the University of

1. From a statement to his class in 1906; quoted by Paul Fauchille, *Louis Renault*, p. 2.

Paris, at the School of Political Sciences and at two of the military schools; he directed 252 doctoral theses[1]; he taught many students who later held important diplomatic posts in France and abroad.

Prior to 1890, Renault had participated in the solving of practical problems of international law, notably those of proprietary rights in literature and art and of the regulations governing submarine cables, but in the following years, having been appointed a legal consultant to the Foreign Office by Minister Alexandre Ribot, he became the «one authority in international law upon whom the Republic relied»[2]. For the next twenty years he was a French representative at innumerable international conferences held in Europe, figuring prominently in conferences on international private law, international transport, military aviation, naval affairs, circulation of obscene literature, abolition of white slavery, commercial paper used in international transactions, revision of the Red Cross Convention of 1864. In recognition of this and other services, Renault was accorded the titular rank of Minister Plenipotentiary and Envoy Extraordinary in 1903.

When the Hague Tribunal was opened to conduct cases of international arbitration, Renault was named one of its panel of twenty-eight arbiters. Voluntarily selected more times than any other member of the panel in the first fourteen years of the tribunal's existence, Renault was involved in six of the court's thirteen cases: the Japanese House Tax case between Japan on the one hand and Germany, France, and Great Britain on the other (1905); the Casablanca case between Germany and France (1909); the Savarkar case between France and Great Britain (1911); the Canevaro case between Italy and Peru (1912); the Carthage case between France and Italy (1913); and the Manouba case between France and Italy (1913).

At the first Hague Peace Conference of 1899, Renault was the reporter for the Second Commission, which was concerned with various questions governing naval warfare, and the principal drafter of the Final Act–the «summary»–of the Conference. A dominant figure at the second Hague Peace Conference in 1907, he was the reporter for the Conventions relating to the opening of hostilities, to the application of the Geneva Convention to naval warfare, to the creation of an international prize court, and to the defining of the rights and duties of neutral nations in naval war, as well as being on the drafting committee for the Final Act, which he presented.

1. According to the list compiled by Fauchille, *op.cit.*, pp. 235–243.
2. Scott, «In Memoriam: Louis Renault», *American Journal of International Law*, 12 (1918) 607.

The recipient of many honors for his accomplishments as teacher, scholar, judge, and diplomat, Renault was named to the Legion of Honor and to the Academy of Moral and Political Sciences in France, awarded decorations by nineteen foreign nations and honorary doctorates by several universities, and chosen to be president of the Academy of International Law created at The Hague in 1914.

Renault never retired. After teaching his last class on February 6, 1918, he went to his villa in Barbizon for a brief holiday, was taken ill, and died on the morning of February 8.

Selected Bibliography

Fauchille, Paul, *Louis Renault (1843–1918): Sa Vie, son oeuvre.* Paris, Pedone, 1918. Contains a bibliography of Renault's publications.

Renault, Louis, *La Conférence navale de Londres: Déclaration relative au droit de la guerre maritime.* Paris, Rousseau, 1909.

Renault, Louis, *Les Conventions de La Haye (1896 et 1902) sur le droit international privé.* Paris, Librairie de la Société du Recueil général, 1903.

Renault, Louis, *Les Deux Conférences de la paix de 1899 et 1907: Recueil dex textes arrêtés par ces Conférences et de différents documents complémentaires.* Paris, Rousseau, 1908.

Renault, Louis, *First Violations of International Law by Germany: Luxembourg and Belgium,* translated from the French by Frank Carr. London, Longmans, Green, 1917. (*Les Premières Violations du droit des gens par l'Allemagne: Luxembourg et Belgique.* Paris, Librairie du *Recueil Sirey,* 1907.)

Renault, Louis, *Introduction à l'étude du droit international.* Paris, Larose, 1879.

Renault, Louis, *L'Oeuvre internationale de Louis Renault, 1843–1918: In Memoriam.* 3 Tomes. Paris, Les Éditions internationales, 1932–1933.

Renault, Louis, «War and the Law of Nations in the 20th Century», translated from the French by George D. Gregory, in *American Journal of International Law,* 9 (1915) 1–16. [«La Guerre et le droit les gens au XXe siècle», *Revue générale de droit international public,* 21 (1914) 468.]

Renault, Louis, et É. Descamps, *Recueil international des traités du XIXe siècle.* Paris, Rousseau, 1913.

Renault, Louis, et Charles Lyon-Caen, *Manuel de droit commercial spécialement destiné aux étudiants des Facultés de droit.* Paris, Cotillon, Pichon, Durand-Auzias et Pichon, 1887.

Renault, Louis, et Charles Lyon-Caen, *Précis de droit commercial.* 2 Tomes. Paris, Cotillon, 1884–1885.

Renault, Louis, et Charles Lyon-Caen, *Traité de droit commercial.* 9 Tomes. Paris, Cotillon, Pichon, Durand-Auzias et Pichon, 1889–1899.

Renault, Louis, et Charles Lyon-Caen, *Traité du droit maritime*. Paris, 1894–1896.

Renault, Louis, et Charles Lyon-Caen, *Traité des sociétés commerciales*. Paris, 1892.

Schou, August, *Histoire de l'internationalisme III: Du Congrès de Vienne jusqu'à la première guerre mondiale (1914)*, pp. 451–453. Publications de l'Institut Nobel Norvégien, Tome VIII. Oslo, Aschehoug, 1963.

Scott, James Brown, «In Memoriam: Louis Renault», in *American Journal of International Law*, 12 (July, 1918) 606–610.

Peace 1908

KLAS PONTUS ARNOLDSON

FREDRIK BAJER

Presentation

by Jørgen Gunnarsson Løvland*, Chairman of the Nobel Committee

On behalf of the Nobel Committee of the Norwegian Parliament, I have the honor to extend a welcome to all who have assembled here on this occasion commemorating the great Swedish patron and benefactor, Alfred Nobel, who gave the whole of his large fortune to the solution of problems concerning the future fate of mankind. Since we last met here, one of the winners of the Peace Prize, Randal Cremer, has left us forever[1]; but he has left behind the memory of a great personality and of a warm friend of peace and of mankind. I invite you all to honor his memory by standing.

This year the Nobel Committee has unanimously decided to divide the Peace Prize between former member of the Swedish Parliament, K. P. Arnoldson, and former member of the Danish Parliament, Fredrik Bajer.

It is a great pleasure for the Committee to award the prize to these gentlemen, since it is convinced that its choice accords with the general desire in the Scandinavian countries. They have both been untiring advocates of the ideals of peace.

K. P. Arnoldson was born in Gothenburg in 1844 and in his youth was in the service of the Swedish Railways. At the same time, however, he also worked for the press as a journalist and author, one of his favorite subjects even then being the cause of peace. From 1882 to 1887 Arnoldson was a member of the Lower House of the Swedish Parliament. In 1883 he put forward a proposal for an address to the king, petitioning for a declaration of permanent neutrality by Sweden. The proposal was not adopted, but the House recommended that the government should continue to work

* Mr. Løvland gave this speech on December 10, 1908, at the Norwegian Nobel Institute before presenting the Nobel medal and diploma to Mr. Arnoldson, who gave his Nobel lecture a few minutes later. The translation is based on the report of the speech published in the Oslo *Morgenposten* of December 11, 1908. Although probably not verbatim (the account says that Mr. Løvland delivered «approximately the following speech»), the text is obviously that of the actual speech insofar as the reporter was able to take it down.

1. Sir William Randal Cremer (1828–1908), recipient of the Nobel Peace Prize for 1903, died on July 22, 1908.

along the lines of the proposal. In the same year Arnoldson helped to found the Swedish Peace and Arbitration Association [Svenska freds-och skilje-domsföreningen], which recently celebrated its twenty-fifth anniversary. Arnoldson was secretary of the association for the first few years and edited its paper.

Arnoldson's work also extended to Norway. The success of his speeches in several of our cities in 1889 and 1890 indirectly encouraged Parliament in 1890 to adopt his arbitration address to the king.

Arnoldson has published a number of important works on peace, several of which have been translated into other languages. His most important is *The Hope of the Centuries: A Book on World Peace*, an account of the growth of the idea of peace among nations and in international relations.

Mr. Arnoldson, along with Mr. Fredrik Bajer, was nominated for the Nobel Peace Prize this year with the unanimous support of the Swedish Interparliamentary Group and a number of Norwegian members of Parliament.

KLAS PONTUS ARNOLDSON

World Referendum

Nobel Lecture*, December 10, 1908

Like many such legends in many nations, an old Nordic saga tells of a time when the streets were paved with gold without tempting anyone to sin, a time when human beings were good and their customs and laws mild, inspired by the spirit of wisdom. The whole world lived a life of happiness. This paradise was buried in a mire of conflict and degraded values. However, the hope of finding it again is not yet lost. The nature of man provides a guarantee of this. Man's nature is fundamentally good, or perhaps it is neither good nor evil. In any case, man is something to work on. We must hold fast to this fact–man is something to work on.

The age of our race can perhaps be reckoned in millions of years. So it is probably true that the human brain has now reached a state of high development and that after an immeasurable process of evolution it is now biologically and physiologically similar in all peoples and races.

Accepting this as a scientific fact, one necessarily comes to the conclusion that every normal human being must be as susceptible to the light of knowledge as he is to the light of the sun. It is in his nature to want peace rather than war. Education is the only certain road to the final goal of peace. And there is no higher goal.

«In truth,» someone replies, «the rule of law is higher; and so are personal freedom and national independence.» But for these, as for all the other good things of life, peace is perforce a prerequisite.

This idea confuses those who lack understanding. «Surely», they say, «one has to defend oneself.» And they add: «National defense can be likened to fire insurance» or «Nobody wants his house to stand open to thieves and murderers» or «Nobody wants to walk unarmed in the woods, surrounded by robbers and brigands.» And so on. Seductive phrases! For civilized peoples are not gangs of brigands, and their rulers not robber barons.

* This lecture was delivered by Mr. Arnoldson in the auditorium of the Nobel Institute just after he had received his prize. This translation is based on the Swedish text in *Les Prix Nobel en 1908*.

Of course, it is not a question of giving up one's national independence. We hold on to that which is dear to our hearts, but we must see things in their true perspective. Without peace there is no freedom, individual or national. War and hostilities are a form of slavery. Under such conditions, the laws are silent. Without peace there is nothing truly human. Peace is harmony. And harmony is the highest ideal of life.

For a long time this fact has been clear to seekers of the lost paradise, those thorn-crowned servants of humanity. Unnoticed by the world, their work has persevered through the ages, just as, slowly and quietly in a dark crevice of the earth, the forming of a brilliant diamond goes on for thousands and thousands of years. No sound rises from the silent depths while atom fuses with atom and the crystal slowly grows, finally to gleam and glitter in a royal crown.

Thus the concept of peace, mankind's most brilliant treasure, has at last been disclosed to the eyes of us all. No one now denies its beauty; all extol its worth. But these tributes have all too often taken the form of words alone, seldom that of actions as well.

At last, however, it has dawned on many people in all countries that militarism lies like a heavy curse over the land. Perhaps, though, the reason for this does not lie entirely in the unutterable woe of war—woe which defies description. Unfortunately we have not yet reached the stage where militarism is condemned on these grounds.

We do not yet consider it beneath ourselves to invent and develop tools of destruction. We have not yet been seized with a holy wrath against evil, against militarism's coarsening influence on our inner selves, an influence which darkens our view of life and nurtures that frightened and insidious distrust which beguiles us into inflicting on each other so much suffering, so much wrong and sorrow.

Rather, it is with the economic weight of the militaristic systems that many people are concerned. It is estimated that for each minute of the nineteenth century, 1,350 Swedish kroner were spent on armaments in Europe. The burden of armaments on the great powers between the first and second conferences at The Hague—that is to say, in the eight years 1899–1907–increased by sixty-nine million pounds sterling. And the increase is still continuing. As far as the smaller states were concerned, in Sweden for example, the annual military expenditure increased from 27.7 million Swedish kroner to 84.3 million over the years 1888–1908; in other words, it more than trebled in two decades. Ample evidence of this increase may be obtained; for instance, from the International Peace Bureau in Bern or the Nobel Institute in Oslo.

The relation between the pressures of militarism and the deterioration of social conditions becomes more and more apparent. Vast resources are absorbed by militarism, without benefit to anyone. If these were set free, we could double the harvests of the nourishing earth, harness the power of roaring rivers for mills and factories, and open up undreamt of opportunities to challenge the finest talents possessed by man.

That something must be done to eliminate this evil now seems clear even to those in power in the world.

The Czar of Russia issued a Peace Manifesto[1] which led to the creation of the Permanent Court of Arbitration at The Hague, and the President of the United States is encouraging the nations to use it[2]. The aged ruler of Austria-Hungary[3] is often called the «Emperor of Peace» on account of his character. The young Italian monarch[4] has created an International Agricultural Institute which he maintains with his own private means, and has also offered to pay for the marble for the Palace of Peace at The Hague. The British head of state[5] is at the forefront of an entente policy which seeks to anticipate complications leading to hostility. King Edward greeted the World Peace Congress in London[6] with words to the effect that the heads of state could not aim at any goal higher than that of fostering a common spirit of understanding and warm friendship between nations, such being the surest means of realizing the highest ideal of humanity; and he further promised that «to achieve this goal would be [his] perpetual endeavor». Kaiser Wilhelm[7], in a telegram to the Interparliamentary Con-

1. The Czar's Rescript of 1898, proposing to all governments represented at his Court an international conference on the means of insuring peace, resulted in the Hague Peace Conference of 1899 which created the Permanent Court of Arbitration.
2. Theodore Roosevelt (1858–1919), U.S. president (1901–1909) and a proponent of mediation and of arbitration in all its forms, took the initiative in having an American-Mexican dispute submitted to the Court in 1902; this was the tribunal's first case.
3. Francis Joseph I (1830–1916), emperor of Austria (1848–1916), king of Hungary (1867–1916).
4. Victor Emmanuel III (1869–1947), king of Italy (1900–1946).
5. Edward VII, called the Peacemaker (1841–1910), king of Great Britain and Ireland (1901–1910), helped prepare the way for arbitration treaties with various nations and for ententes with France and with Russia.
6. Held in the summer of 1908.
7. Wilhelm II (1859–1941), emperor of Germany and king of Prussia (1888–1918).

ference in Berlin[1], said that he took the blessings of peace very much to heart, and the Crown Prince echoed these words, stating on behalf of his father, that the latter's greatest concern was the maintenance of peace, «which is, and shall ever be the foundation of all true cultural progress». The president of the French Republic[2] finds it natural to continue to advocate world peace, and the Japanese sovereign[3] neglects no opportunity to convince the world of his love of peace.

At every suitable opportunity, the heads of smaller states express themselves in the same spirit to the world press, as also do the responsible ministers in parliament when accompanying their heads of state to the more and more frequent peace conferences.

An ever increasing volume of intercourse is occurring between the various nations through their representatives in science and art, health care and education, communications, trade and industry, and all other cultural fields. The human feeling of spiritual affinity is the fundamental motivation of all these international congresses and conferences. This idealistic impulse shared by all peoples is leading to real agreements and to laws which are incompatible with war and militarism.

Now, at last, active pacifists from all classes of society are receiving considerable assistance from the modern labor movement, which participates in the effort to forestall war by advocating arbitration and disarmament. At the Stuttgart Congress in the spring of 1908, 900 representatives of ten million organized workers from all the states of the world unanimously accepted a resolution to try to abolish all militaristic systems and to prevent all international acts of force. Furthermore, at the meeting of the International Socialist Bureau in Brussels last autumn, it was unanimously declared that one of the main tasks of the labor organizations would be to try to avert the danger of war.

It is thus obvious that in such matters the interests of the governments and of the governed are identical. This fact receives constant confirmation at the international meetings of sovereigns and peoples. The persistence of a state of suspense and anxiety in the world must therefore be imputed to other interests, which achieve this result through rumors of war which

1. Held in September, 1908.
2. Clément Armand Fallières (1841–1931), president of the French Republic (1906–1913).
3. Mutsuhito (1852–1912), emperor of Japan (1867–1912).

appear now and then. It would be much wiser to try to expose the meaning of such rumors than to let ourselves be taken in by them.

Nowadays it is probable that no subject of international disagreement would lead to war if it were first submitted to examination by experts. This procedure is as a rule adopted by the responsible governments of states in the case of vital international questions. Of course, Europe in particular is still divided into certain power groups, but when anything vital is at stake, there is immediate cooperation, as seen in Morocco, the Balkans, Crete, etc.[1] Then too the new Scandinavian treaties are peaceably and tranquilly succeeding in providing greater security[2]. Such an approach is also likely to be applicable to colonial policy, despite what the «know-it-alls» say about trade wars and the like.

America poses no threat. She is gathering her strength. Washington recently saw the laying of the cornerstone of a palace for the Pan-American Bureau, which will be a shrine to the idea of a peace uniting the whole of the western hemisphere[3]. Nor is there any threat from Japan, which is now reducing her annual military expenditure by 360 million Swedish kroner. Warlike adventures do not suit the peaceful nature of the Chinese. The «Yellow Peril» is probably not all that perilous! The Sultanate of Turkey is developing into a great civilized state, a powerful center of peace for

---

1. The Morocco incident occurred when Germany, testing the Anglo-French Entente of 1904, demanded an international conference to consider Moroccan independence; the Conference met at Algeciras in 1906 and reaffirmed Moroccan independence. In the Balkan crisis of 1908–1909, threatened war was averted when Serbia and Russia accepted Austria's annexation of Bosnia and Herzegovina after intervention by the powers, and especially by Germany. Crete at the same time added to the crisis by breaking with the Ottoman Empire and uniting with Greece.

2. The Norwegian Integrity Treaty, November 2, 1907, was effected between Norway and certain strategic powers, including Great Britain, Germany, France, Russia, and Sweden, to protect Norway's new independence. The Baltic Treaty was signed on April 23, 1908, in St.Petersburg by Russia, Germany, Denmark, and Sweden, respecting rights in the Baltic Sea. The North Sea Treaty was signed on April 23, 1908, in Berlin by Germany, Denmark, France, Great Britain, The Netherlands, and Sweden, respecting rights in the North Sea.

3. Its cornerstone laid on May 11, 1908, the Pan American Union building was a gift from the American industrialist Andrew Carnegie, with contributions from the United States and other nations, to the International Union of American Republics (name changed in 1910 to Pan American Union), which was organized 1889–1890 to promote pan-American cooperation.

all of the Moslem world. In addition, South Africa constitutes a new peaceful confederation within the British Empire[1].

Many of these far-flung nations are graphically united by an «arbitration» map drawn by the French Foreign Ministry, on which a red line joins the capitals of those thirty-five, or rather thirty-two, states[2] which voted for a complete plan of compulsory arbitration of international disputes at the second conference of governments at The Hague in 1907. No less does the following resolution[3], which was passed at the same conference, correspond to this ideal: «The Second Peace Conference confirms the resolution adopted by the Conference of 1899 in regard to the limitation of military expenditure; and inasmuch as military expenditure has considerably increased in almost every country since that time, the conference declares that it is eminently desirable that the governments should resume the serious examination of this question.»

If the whole of humanity is now weary of the burdens of war, something more effective than a mere «serious examination» is required if we are to lighten these burdens and perhaps finally eradicate them. If this is regarded as impossible, it is not so much because of certain technical difficulties as it is because we lack strong moral fiber.

We demand too much of others and too little of ourselves. No one wishes to be the first to take the straight and narrow path. In addition, there is a tendency to overrate our own goodwill and underestimate that of others. «Of course *we* want to live in peace», we say. «But our neighbor and the others!» If only we would worry a little less about others and a little more about ourselves, ask a little less of others and more of ourselves!

This applies to all nations. It also applies first and last to individuals, especially in the context of their citizenship. They should each of them carry

1. After the Boer War (1899–1902), the Transvaal and the Orange Free State were incorporated in the British Empire, becoming part of the Union of South Africa in 1910.
2. The thirty-two nations voting in favor of a proposal for compulsory arbitration were: United States of America, Argentine Republic, Bolivia, Brazil, Chile, China, Colombia, Cuba, Denmark, Dominican Republic, Ecuador, Spain, France, Great Britain, Guatemala, Haiti, Mexico, Nicaragua, Norway, Panama, Paraguay, The Netherlands, Peru, Persia, Portugal, Russia, Salvador, Servia, Siam, Sweden, Uruguay, and Venezuela. Opposed were: Germany, Austria-Hungary, Belgium, Bulgaria, Greece, Montenegro, Rumania, Switzerland, and Turkey. Abstaining were: Italy, Japan, and Luxembourg.
3. From the Final Act of the Hague Peace Conference of 1907.

the responsibility for the welfare of their country and for the whole of mankind. This, then, is the original idea which I have very much at heart, and now is the time and opportunity to proclaim it to the world.

If a present-day prophet were to exhort the peoples to peace and common sense, he would speak as one human being to others. With the power of the law and the gentleness of the Gospel, he would speak thus: «Patriotism is a noble feeling, insofar as it approaches that which is purely human, but the very reverse the further it is removed therefrom. No interests, however great, are higher than those common to the whole of mankind. Among them, the foremost is the old commandment, as old as the oldest documents of any nation: Thou shalt not kill! You are all of one blood. Love one another. People can. Nations can. All this is eminently possible because love is as natural as national hatred is the most unnatural of all human feelings.»

Inspired by such a spirit, I wish to suggest that the peoples of the earth should be exhorted to unite in a common aim.

In all countries an appeal should be issued for every adult man and woman to sign the following declaration: «If all other nations will abolish their armed forces and be content with a joint police force for the whole world, then I, the undersigned, wish my own nation to do the same.»[1]

This appeal would probably be answered by the well-informed elite in all countries, perhaps to a larger extent than anyone can now imagine. If this were to happen, a new great power would emerge–the united will of the peoples. Then, at their next peace conference, the governments would receive moral support powerful enough to enable them to agree to an effective commencement of general disarmament.

Much work would be necessary. At first, a genuine effort would have to be made to interest as many men and women as possible in helping to publicize the plan throughout the nations and in many languages, even at a considerable cost in time and money.

It might be unnecessary to wait for a resolution to be passed by one of

---

1. Immediately following this paragraph, the text of the lecture carries a parenthetical paragraph which reads as follows: «Arnoldson later suggested the following as an alternative: I, the undersigned, desire peace on earth. I want all armed forces to be abolished. I want a joint police force to be created, to which each nation should contribute according to the size of its population. I want that force to be subject to an International Supreme Court. I want all states to be in duty bound to refer any kind of international controversy to this court, and subject themselves to the judgments of the court. »

the international peace organizations–by an institute, a directorate, a congress, or a conference. This might make a simple matter too complicated and irksome. It would insure a minimum of delay in beginning the task if a well-known man of peace, able to unite belief in the cause with financial resources, having no authority other than his own as a member of the human race, were to send out a referendum accompanied by petition forms for signatures, together with administrative directions for their distribution.

The more simply this could be done, the better. The petition forms for signatures should consist of only one sheet, bearing a declaration on the front, together with columns for names, titles, and addresses, and on the reverse side a short and extremely simple explanation of its purpose. [1]

The lists should be distributed in many ways, not the least being as newspaper supplements, and should be returned as soon as possible, with the greatest possible number of signatures, to the peace association committees of the individual countries, through whom the returns could systematically be communicated to the International Peace Bureau in Bern, as well as to the respective governments at their next peace conference.

Once the principle of this measure is clearly grasped and strongly adhered to, incidentals would look after themselves. Everyone would answer for himself and hold to his word; that is the principle of this worldwide referendum.

People may object: «We already know that all men want to live in peace. There is no need to ascertain this fact.» If that were true, they should not be dangerous to each other. However, since militarism still flourishes, this objection must be proved. The answer has to be obtained, not from groups, but from individuals; we must not hide behind the backs of others, but bravely step forward to confirm our will with our own signature.

People may object: «This is all too easy.» But it is very easy, also, to understand the necessity of cleanliness, sunshine, and fresh air for our health. Nevertheless, it took a very, very long time before this understanding became generally accepted practice.

Thus also, the real meaning of Christianity, insofar as it departs in some

1. At this point another parenthetical paragraph is inserted in the text: «Arnoldson suggests that the reverse side might carry, instead, an alternatively worded declaration, together with columns for names, titles, and addresses as on the front page. The referendum would thus be designed to cover, on the one hand, those whose desire, that something be done, is in some way conditional, and on the other, those for whom this desire is unqualified and who demand the drawing up of a definite program.»

measure from strict reality, creates an eternal source of contention, although in the near future it will be clear that its essential message, untrammeled by the disputes of theology, is a true religion of peace; that this natural and easily comprehensible religion is absolutely incompatible with all war and military organization; and that it is exemplified, better than by all the sermons in the world, by the statue of Christ which two South American peoples have erected on top of the mountain separating their countries, to proclaim that war between them is now a thing of the past.

We are not here concerned with a question of faith, which so often gives rise to differences and schisms, but with one of love, which equalizes and unites. Thus, individual religious and social interests must not on any condition become involved in this cooperation of all peoples.

A foreseeable objection is this: «If less than half the adult population of a country votes against military organization, this will be considered proof of its acceptance by the majority.» Such a view, however, attributes to a mass of people who lack willpower an importance which they do not possess. In a case like this it is not the inert majority that counts. Even ten percent of the population would represent a sizeable expression of opinion. Furthermore, the average man can grasp a simple idea easily enough, but if he should be dependent on authority even in such a simple matter as this, then he must be awakened by the vigilant and by those who have seen the light.

«In any case,» some may protest, «this will take a long time even in the free countries, not to mention the backward ones.» It is not, however, proposed that a campaign which concerns all civilized peoples should be concluded hurriedly. Nor is it the intention to be precipitate, though it is important to make the best use of the time available until 1914 or 1915, when the third peace conference of the governments is likely to take place[1].

A further objection may arise: «In the hard struggle for the necessities of life, men in general are not conscious of things which go beyond or above their daily cares, nor do they have the time to attend to such matters. There are far too many who, in their dark and straitened circumstances, are never able to look toward bright and wide horizons.» True enough, and for a long time to come, the old, persistent lamentation about the burdens and adversities of life will not be silenced.

But if, in fact, the world is so gloomy, it is to be hoped that many of

1. Preparations to hold this conference had been started but were cancelled with the outbreak of World War I in August, 1914.

those who complain will, at least once in their lives, make a sacrifice for the establishment of a better state of affairs in this world, the sacrifice of a minute to be occupied in reading and signing a declaration which favors taking an axe to the root of the evil. Otherwise, all their laments are in vain.

The last objection may be: «My vote, being but a drop in the ocean, means nothing.» It does, however, mean everything to every responsible human being, for all those who are powerless individually gain power beyond measure when they are united. Many small rivulets make a great stream, the stream becomes a river and the river a great sea, a pacific ocean around this world of ours.

A new power is emerging from the depths and slowly spreading over land and water. It is the concept of peace of the ancient sagas, enriched by new and immense cultural progress. Those who seek after the lost paradise can see it shimmering in the sunrise of a new era, presaging the fulfillment of the Christian prayer and the heathen saga, presaging the kingdom of peace which we pray for in saying «Our Father–Thy kingdom come» and which the old inhabitants of the North sensed in the happy era of the ancient sagas–when the streets were paved with gold which remained untouched and when human beings were good, their customs and laws mild and wise.

Nowadays, to pave the streets with gold would be quite unsafe. It is certain, however, that the gold which has now been placed in my path shall not rest untouched. It gives me the opportunity of devoting more work and more time to the idea of the world referendum which I have proposed here. It also enables me to serve the cause of peace in yet other ways and with even stronger perseverance. So will I try to carry my burden of gratitude, and to discharge the mission to which I have been called.

Biography

Klas Pontus Arnoldson (October 27, 1844–February 20, 1916), the Swedish journalist, pacifist, and proponent of Scandinavian unity, was a man of humble origin. Born at Göteborg, the son of a caretaker, he was obliged to discontinue his formal education in the public schools of Göteborg at the age of sixteen because of family financial difficulties after the death of his father in 1860. For the next twenty-one years he worked for a railroad, first as a clerk and then for ten years as a station inspector in Jonsered, Älgarås, and Tumba.

During these years, Arnoldson continued his studies, reading widely in history, religion, and philosophy; observed the political events of his day, especially the Danish–Austrian–Prussian War of 1864 and the Franco-Prussian War of 1870–1871; and evolved the ideas on religion, politics, and peace that he developed in detail in his voluminous writings.

Arnoldson was a liberal in theology. Familiar with the humanistic tenets of religious movements originating in the nineteenth century in Great Britain and in the New England section of the United States, he decried fanatic dogmatism and espoused essentially Unitarian views on truth, tolerance, freedom of the individual conscience, freedom of thought, and human perfectability. These views he published in the *Nordiska Dagbladet* [Northern Daily] which he edited for a short time in the early 1870's, and in *Sanningssökaren* [The Truth Seeker], a monthly journal devoted to the exposition of «practical Christianity», as well as in books and pamphlets.

Arnoldson was also a liberal in political philosophy, committed to the practical application of the principle of democracy and individualism. From 1882 to 1887, as an elected member of the Parliament, he introduced legislation to extend the franchise and when it failed to pass, supported legislation which later succeeded; favored the extension of religious freedom; pursued an antimilitaristic policy; drafted a controversial resolution asking the government to investigate the possibility of guaranteed neutrality for Sweden [1].

1. For an analysis of his position, see August Schou, *Histoire de l'internationalisme III* (Oslo: Aschehoug, 1963), pp. 517–518.

Outside Parliament Arnoldson carried on work for peace even more vigorously. Originally attracted to pacifism because of his repugnance for the wars of 1864 and 1870–1871 and because of his religious beliefs, Arnoldson was one of those instrumental in founding the Swedish Peace and Arbitration Association in 1883, occupying the position of secretary of the society and becoming the editor of *Tiden* [The Times], a medium for peace information and free debate. Not at his best in a managerial capacity, Arnoldson resigned from *Tiden* in 1885 when it ran into financial difficulties, and from his office with the peace society in 1887 when he felt himself being overwhelmed by financial problems, the pressure of work, and emotional depression. Arnoldson edited *Fredsvännen* [The Friend of Peace] from 1885 to 1888 and the *Nordsvenska Dagbladet* [North Sweden Daily] from 1892 to 1894. For the most part, however, he kept himself free of administrative and political duties, devoting his energies to speaking and writing on behalf of arbitration. In 1888 he mounted a campaign for a popular petition addressed to the king favoring arbitration agreements with foreign nations. Extending his agitation to Norway in 1890, he spoke to receptive audiences throughout the country and provided some of the impetus for the Norwegian Parliament's passage of a resolution on arbitration addressed to the king.

In the political controversy of 1895 between Norway and Sweden and in the final constitutional crisis which resulted in dissolution of their Union, Arnoldson sympathized with Norway. This was not popular in Sweden. When Arnoldson was named a Nobel peace laureate in 1908, some Swedish newpapers were incensed, saying that the award was an «outrage» against Sweden, a disgrace to «every Swedish man who takes pride in his national honor», and, to add injury to insult, was paid for with «Swedish money» given by a Swedish countryman. In reply, Løvland, chairman of the Norwegian Nobel Committee, pointed out that Arnoldson's candidacy had been proposed by the unanimous vote of the Swedish Group of the Interparliamentary Union[1].

Throughout his life, Arnoldson complemented his day-to-day political activity by writing. In his early years he wrote mainly journalistic pieces; in the last three decades of his life, he produced some major works. An historical essay on international law, *Är världsfred möjlig?* [Is World Peace Possible? translated into English under the title of *Pax mundi*], appeared

[1]. Oscar J. Falnes, *Norway and the Nobel Peace Prize* (New York: Columbia University Press, 1938), pp. 252–254.

in 1890; *Religionen i forskningens ljus* [Religion in the Light of Research] in 1891; a history of the pacifist idea, *Seklernas hopp* [The Hope of the Centuries], in 1901. He also wrote polemical fiction, putting his pacifist message into novelistic and dramatistic form.

Although Arnoldson suffered from periods of illness throughout his life, he lived to be seventy-two, dying of a heart attack in Stockholm in 1916.

Selected Bibliography

Arnoldson, Klas Pontus, *Maria Magdalena: Fredsberättelse*. Stockholm, Bohlin, 1903.

Arnoldson, Klas Pontus, *Neutralitetsfrågan*. Stockholm, 1883.

Arnoldson, Klas Pontus, *Pax mundi: A Concise Account of the Progress of the Movement for Peace by Means of Arbitration, Neutralization, International Law and Disarmament*. Authorized translation from the Swedish. London, Swan Sonnenschein, 1892. (*Är världsfred möjlig?: En historisk framställning af sträfvandena för lag och rätt mellan folken*. Stockholm, Fröléen, 1890.)

Arnoldson, Klas Pontus, *Religionen i forskningens ljus*. Sundsvall, Forlagsforeningen Fria Ordet, 1891.

Arnoldson, Klas Pontus, *Seklernas hopp: En bok om världsfreden*. Stockholm, Wilhelmsson, 1901.

Arnoldson, Klas Pontus, *Unitarismens apostel: Fyra föreläsningar*. Stockholm, Bjorck, 1882.

Svenskt biografiskt lexikon.

Svenson, Axel, *En lifsgerning för freden: Några erinrande ord på K. P. Arnoldson sixtio-årsdag den 27 oktober 1904*. [Stockholm], 1904.

Presentation

by Jørgen Gunnarsson Løvland*, Chairman of the Nobel Committee

Fredrik Bajer was born in 1837. Like Tolstoy and many other fighters for peace, he began his career as an officer and from 1856 to 1865 was a lieutenant of Dragoons. He then began his study of foreign languages, becoming an elementary school teacher and later a translator. Already in the 1860's he was maintaining contact with the peace movement and was in touch with Frédéric Passy, who in 1867 founded the first French peace society[1]. From 1872 to 1895, Bajer was a member of Parliament for Horsens and during that time did much work for the cause of peace and for women's rights.

Mr. Bajer has been an extraordinarily prolific writer, and in his many articles and pamphlets about and in favor of the cause of peace, he has dealt with practically all the problems involved in the peace movement. Norwegian newspapers have also enjoyed the benefit of his able pen.

Special mention should be made of his great study of the question of neutrality. In 1882 he was also responsible for the foundation of a peace society in Denmark, at first called the Society for the Promotion of Danish Neutrality and later the Danish Peace Society[2].

At a very early date Mr. Bajer took an active part in the European peace

* Mr. Løvland gave this biographical sketch of Mr. Bajer as the last part of his speech at the award ceremony in the Norwegian Nobel Institute on December 10, 1908. The first part of his speech (which included introductory remarks, the award announcement itself, and a similar sketch of Mr. K. P. Arnoldson, who shared the prize for 1908 with Mr. Bajer) will be found in the Presentation for Mr. Arnoldson, pp. 173–174. Since illness prevented Mr. Bajer from being present, his Nobel medal and diploma were accepted in his behalf by Mr. Grevenkop Castenskiold, the Danish minister. The translation of Mr. Løvland's speech is based on the Norwegian report of the speech published in the Oslo *Morgenposten* of December 11, 1908; see asterisk footnote concerning this report, p. 173.

1. Frédéric Passy (1822–1912), co-recipient of the Nobel Peace Prize for 1901, founded the Ligue internationale et permanente de la paix, later known as the Société des amis de la paix, and then as Société française pour l'arbitrage entre nations.

2. The Danish title of the organization was Foreningen til Danmarks Neutralisering, later changed to Dansk Fredsforening.

movement. In 1884 he participated in the International Congress in Bern and in 1889 he took part both in the International Congress and in the Interparliamentary Conference, held during the Great Exhibition in Paris; since then there have been few of these meetings in which he has not participated. It was at his instigation and suggestion that in 1891 a permanent International Peace Bureau was established in Bern. Bajer was president of its Board of Administration until last year when he declined reelection and was instead named honorary president.

Since 1891 Bajer has also had a seat on the council which controls the Interparliamentary Union.

He has always shown a great interest in cooperation between the Nordic countries in the cause of peace. He has invariably taken part in the Nordic peace meetings, and it is mainly due to his efforts that a Nordic Interparliamentary Union has been founded[1].

Fredrik Bajer was nominated this year as a candidate for the Nobel Peace Prize by the Danish Interparliamentary Group, among others, and, together with K.P.Arnoldson, by the Swedish Interparliamentary Group and a number of members of the Norwegian Parliament.

1. In 1908.

F R E D R I K   B A J E R

The Organization of the Peace Movement

Nobel Lecture*, May 18, 1909

Yesterday was the seventeenth of May, Norway's great day of national celebration [1]. Today's date, the eighteenth of May, should sometime become an occasion of great international celebration, for on this day ten years ago the first Peace Conference opened at The Hague. I regard it as a good omen that the Nobel Committee has allowed me to present my address on this particular day.

There is no contradiction between a nation's strong self-esteem and its will to internationalize itself (to use a current expression) with other peoples in order to promote better understanding – the supreme aim of peace. This concept of international understanding is what Alfred Nobel called «fraternity among nations». It is not enough to cry out, «Lay down your arms» [2]; and this, incidentally, is not the same as «Away with armaments.» We must also shout, «Lift up your hearts!»

The address which I am about to give I have entitled «The Organization of the Peace Movement». My role has not, in the main, been that of a propagandist, but rather that of an organizer whose work has been discharged behind the scenes.

I could, perhaps, have called my lecture «The Organization of Peace». To describe briefly my understanding of the organization of peace, a structure which has been built on a foundation laid by the peace movement, I would compare it to a house of three stories.

The first story belongs to the peace associations. They hold an annual conference, known as «le congrès universel» or *the international congress* [3].

---

* The laureate, having missed the presentation ceremony of December 10, 1908, because of illness, delivered this lecture on May 18, 1909, in the auditorium of the Norwegian Nobel Institute. This translation is based on the Danish text in *Les Prix Nobel en 1908.*

1. Norway's Independence or Constitution Day.

2. The novel of this title (*Die Waffen nieder*, 1889) by Bertha von Suttner, recipient of the Peace Prize for 1905, had had great influence on the peace movement and by 1909 had become a slogan for many pacifists.

3. The peace societies or associations scattered throughout the world had held inter-

The next story is the *Interparliamentary Union*[1], which generally also holds one meeting a year, *the interparliamentary conference*. Finally, the third story, which we hope will not be the last, is *the intergovernmental peace conference*[2]. An easy but less precise labeling of the situation is: there are *peoples*, *parliaments*, and *governments*. These three stories I shall now consider rather more closely.

In speaking of the peace movement, I could also use another metaphor. The distinguished Chairman referred in his introductory words to my being an old soldier, and I shall therefore use a military one. There are three columns marching forth: the *international*, the *interparliamentary*, and the *intergovernmental*. These three columns must maintain contact with one another. In battle, it is useless to attack alone, however courageous one may be; one has to maintain contact to the left and to the right; otherwise nothing of great moment can be achieved. This contact, this organization, is of the utmost importance if results are to be achieved in the peace movement.

I shall not deal in great detail with the subject of the mutual contacts required. Various proposals have been made. On many occasions, pacifists have expressed the wish that a bond of association be formed linking all those who work for the cause of peace, both individuals and institutions. To this end they have suggested the appointment of a common supreme authority. I do not believe, however, that this solution would be successful. I do not believe that such a joint supreme authority is desirable. And it would scarcely prove practical.

When the London International Peace Congress was under preparation in 1890, I studied its program[3]. Coincidentally, this was in the same place where I sat as a cadet in 1854. As a result of my study, I came to the con-

national peace congresses intermittently since 1843. In 1889 their representatives met in a «Universal Peace Congress» in Paris at almost the same time the first Interparliamentary Conference, composed of parliamentarians from different nations, met in the same city. Both were presided over by Frédéric Passy. An unofficial connection was thus established between the two groups, and it became customary thereafter for the international peace congresses and the interparliamentary conferences to meet periodically (almost annually in fact) at practically the same time in the same city. The peace congresses were variously called «international», «universal», or «world»–terms often used interchangeably.

1. Founded in 1888 and composed of members of the parliaments of various nations.
2. Two international Peace Conferences, to which many governments sent delegates, had been held at The Hague, one in 1889 and one in 1907.
3. The second regular Universal Peace Congress met in London, July 14–19, 1890.

clusion that a common supreme authority was undesirable. I would rather propose a bureau somewhat similar to that which we have in the Universal Postal Union[1]. Strangely enough the same idea had been introduced previously, unbeknown to me. During the Paris World Peace Congress in 1878, the elderly Charles Lemonnier[2] defended this concept against all the rest of those assembled. The others wanted to have a joint authority, but he maintained that there should be only a bureau as a common bond of association. I attempted to promote this idea in London. Although unsuccessful, I did not give up hope. I worked on, and I shall report briefly how the matter developed.

At the Congress in Rome on November 13, 1891, an International Peace Bureau was set up[3]. This bureau was, in my mind, originally intended as a sort of focus for the whole peace movement, forming a bond of association between all institutions and individuals who desired to cooperate for peace, and serving as a source of information. But it soon developed that the Interparliamentary Conference, which was held immediately afterward, would not agree to anything of this kind. In the following year, however, in 1892 in Bern, the conference explored the setting up of an interparliamentary bureau[4]. Since that time small rifts have appeared; a kind of dualism has asserted itself between the international and the interparliamentary work for peace. I believe that this dualism is in the process of being smoothed out, and the trend should rapidly gather momentum. The proposals which are adopted at [peace] congresses should be referred to the [interparliamentary] conferences, and in turn the congresses should strive to influence the people and to implement the decisions which are taken at the interparliamentary conferences. It would, moreover, be desirable for some persons to be members both of the Interparliamentary Council and of the Board of the World Peace Bureau (just as I am myself).

I wish, figuratively speaking, to pause for a moment at the lowest story of the structure of peace, that of the peace associations, and raise the ques-

1. The Universal Postal Union (first called the General Postal Union) was initiated by 22 nations meeting in an International Postal Congress in Bern in 1874.
2. Charles Lemonnier (1806–1891), French pacifist; founded the International League of Peace and Liberty (Ligue internationale de la paix et de la liberté) in 1867 at Geneva.
3. Held in Rome, November 11–16, 1891, the Congress set up the Bureau international permanent de la paix in Bern as a permanent office to conduct the business of the peace congresses and to serve as a general clearinghouse for the peace movement.
4. The fourth Interparliamentary Conference, held in Bern, August 29–31, 1892, created its own central office, the Bureau interparlementaire.

tion: Should they be political? Yes or no? This is a moot point. They should be political insofar as the cause of peace, like all else which concerns the activity of the state, also concerns politics. But they should not be party-political. A sign that a peace association is going adrift is its exclusion of other political parties, with whom it could collaborate effectively on most of the problems besetting the cause of peace. Leave well enough alone and let each have his own opinions about domestic policies! In this respect, the interparliamentary groups, in which all shades of political opinion meet, are good models. In the Danish Parliament, all members of the Lower House, without exception, are members of the interparliamentary group, and so are all but eleven members of the Upper House.

Now first of all, we have–and I again revert to the military metaphor–recruitment, so as to encourage membership in the peace associations. I am reminded of an incident that took place a good many years ago. A young man came up to me and said, «I have heard talk of this Nobel Peace Prize and I would very much like to have it. Can you tell me how I should set about it?» «With the greatest of pleasure,» I replied. «Please sit down, and I will help you.» I then asked, «Are you a member of the peace association?» «No.» «Well, that is the first step!»

Once members have been brought into the association, they should then be informed and educated, for there is much to learn. On joining such a movement, one should not think that he is wiser than all those who have been working for it for a long time. One must be informed. Ordinary and annual meetings are arranged by the groups. At the national meetings which are held in most countries, representatives are chosen for the annual peace congresses. These representatives, in turn, receive further information. They return and report what they have heard. In this way a process of mutual education comes into operation.

One of the first documents that the Bureau in Bern sought to prepare was a set of statistics on the existing peace associations. Since it is difficult to obtain accurate data on the effective membership of these associations, it would not be amiss if at some time we could afford to appoint an inspector-general who would travel around to determine how many of the members included in the statistics are in fact active.

Propaganda is a topic of particular concern to peace associations. This is a matter of educating the population in general, and not least the voters. The voters elect the people's representatives who will enter the interparliamentary groups forming the Interparliamentary Union. For this reason, the peace associations have often approved their members' asking prospective candidates if they, upon election, would join the interparliamentary groups. I believe that at present no further commitment is required, for election automatically brings membership, at any rate in Denmark.

With regard to the task of education, I shall touch on the question of literature. There are those who believe we have need of more literature, of a large international publishing house, of a great peace newspaper, or the like. I am rather skeptical about this idea. We already have an immense literature. I could name a whole series of excellent periodicals in England, America, France, and Germany; and in addition we all have in common *La Correspondance bimensuelle*[1], with its factual announcements, issued by the Peace Bureau in Bern. No, it is not this that we need so much. Indeed, peace literature is almost exclusively read, though to good effect, by pacifists, while what is needed is the canvassing of those who have not so far been won to the cause. Up to now, we have had too much of what the French call «prêcher aux convertis»–preaching to the converted. We should direct special efforts toward those who still remain unconverted. In this connection, I got an idea not long ago from a bird called the cuckoo: It lays its eggs in other birds' nests. I have, therefore, applied to the Danish Ministry of Justice for permission to deposit a sum of 1,000 kroner in the Public Trustee Office–this being the safest place to invest money in Denmark–the income from which will go to the person who, in the course of the preceding calendar year, has written for a national newspaper or journal the best article, in the opinion of a certain committee, in the cause of peace on an appropriate theme, such as «folkens förbrödrande» [fraternity among nations]. The articles in competition must have appeared in the daily press. As you can see, to obtain this prize the person concerned must first persuade an editor to accept his essay. The task of the committee which is to judge the articles is lightened by the fact that the press will have already rejected those efforts which are totally unacceptable. This experiment is to be made in Denmark and, if it succeeds, I hope that the example will be followed elsewhere.

There is another form of propaganda which I shall call the «letter movement». I give it this name since it is directed at some higher authority which is to be influenced. As an old parliamentarian, however, I know that this

1. A bimonthly newsletter concerning current developments in the peace movement and any new literature on peace.

method seldom has much effect. There are many members of parliament present here who know as well as I do that, if a man has not already been converted, it will require a great deal more than a letter of appeal to achieve conversion. Nevertheless, this type of propaganda has a special value, for it serves to convince those who sign the appeal, of the necessity for carrying on propaganda; so a corps of propagandists, if I may use the term, is thus trained. It is important, however, to find the right objective for such an appeal. It must not be anything remote; it must be something which can be envisaged by those to whom it is addressed, something which can be accomplished in the not too distant future. Let me give you an example. At the last Hague Conference, a step in the direction of compulsory ar-bitration of international disputes was proposed. In the end, thirty-two nations were persuaded to vote for arbitration[1], and a proposal was then advanced–I believe its sponsor is among us today–that these nations be prevailed upon to unite. In most cases, of course, unanimity is required at diplomatic conferences, but in this instance a number of states could clearly unite with advantage, and others could later be added to their number.

This is the task, I think, of a letter movement. But it should be set up only in states where a significant response can be achieved, for a letter movement necessarily presupposes a strong organization. We have had such a letter movement on two occasions in Denmark when more than a quarter of the adult Danish population participated. Such an achievement, however, demands a really great effort and also a great deal of money. If an excellent organization had not already been in existence, these projects could scarcely have succeeded.

I shall touch quite briefly on another method, that of mutual international visits. Such visits have been made in the past, of course, and have proved to be of great value, particularly those between England and France and between England and Germany–the Scandinavians, of course, have been visiting in Paris for five years. This is a very costly method, and I am sure I may say that, while work and play may go together, there should not, however, be too much play. I believe that if this method is to be worthwhile, it should be pursued somewhat more assiduously than has hitherto been the case. The same applies also to conferences generally and to the interparliamentary conferences in particular, for they tend, as I have indicated, to resemble meetings of tourists rather than conclaves of jurists.

1. Of the 44 nations represented, 32 voted for, 9 voted against, and 3 abstained.

Always we must bear in mind that law has to be substituted for power, that care must be taken to serve the interests of law. Naturally, business and pleasure can be readily combined, but a certain balance should exist, and the latter should not predominate over the former.

There is one criticism which cannot be leveled at interparliamentary conferences but which is applicable to a great extent to peace congresses: the meetings waste time. Peace congresses often start by dealing with some of the less important questions in excessive detail, so at the end there is no time to discuss the most important problems. One even occasionally sees, as I have seen at a congress in Milan, a chairman left with a number of proposals in his hand, like a handful of playing cards, saying, «You may just as well adopt all the resolutions without discussion–they are quite straightforward.»

The aspect of congresses and such meetings generally to which I attach the greatest importance is the discussion. That is why people assemble: to hear different opinions, rather than to pass resolutions. To read the report of a discussion in which arguments for and against are presented, in which a subject has been covered from different points of view, with new ideas advanced–this is far more instructive than to read a brief account of the resolution passed on the matter. Here we can learn something from the Swedes who, if they fail to reach agreement after discussing a matter, often conclude their meetings with a vote that «diskussionen är svar på frågan» [the discussion is a reply to the question].

One serious obstacle to the smooth working of congresses is the language barrier. At the first peace congress in Paris in 1889[1], only French was used. When the initial session had ended, the Englishmen got together and asked that everything be translated into their language. President Frédéric Passy[2], however, said that he could not accede to this request because the Germans would then demand a German translation, and so on. It has since been agreed that speeches given in English will be translated into French and vice versa, and even into German and Italian when necessary. No doubt translations into Esperanto will also soon be in demand. If everyone understood Esperanto, this language could be used everywhere, but that is surely a long way off. I would have thought it possible to choose delegates for these larger conferences who, even if they could not speak the principal languages, could at least understand them or could have friends seated

1. The first of the *regularly* held congresses. See fn. 3, p. 190.
2. Frédéric Passy (1822–1912), co-recipient of the Peace Prize for 1901.

beside them who could keep them informed on essential points. It is quite unbelievable how much time is wasted otherwise. I ask your indulgence for making all these criticisms, but I wish to take this opportunity to express them while speaking to this gathering in the hope that my words will reach not only those present but also those farther afield.

I have omitted to add that, although many decisions have been made at these congresses, the participants nevertheless accomplish too little. The congresses have now taken over the Peace Bureau at Bern for special services. This bureau has not become what I originally hoped it would: a central office for all, congresses, conferences, and so forth. It has been reserved mainly and almost exclusively for the world peace congresses. In this respect it is no doubt of great value, but it cannot accomplish everything asked of it. It is not a patient pack mule upon which everything possible may be loaded. When a matter cannot be brought to a conclusion at a congress, it is referred to the Bern Bureau, and the bureau then tries to find a solution. It circularizes proposals to appropriate institutions and individuals – for example, to the ministers of foreign affairs. Unfortunately, not many reply and those who do, confine themselves to an acknowledgment of receipt. Last time, only one foreign minister sent a really thoughtful reply such as might be expected from a friend of peace, and this was the Norwegian foreign minister.

The interparliamentary conference should, in my opinion, direct its particular attention to the preparation of the next Hague Conference, the diplomatic conference, the conference of governments. For this reason I proposed at Berlin last year [1] that each of the different parliamentary groups should set up a commission which would list, on the one hand, those older questions which had received favorable consideration but which had not been fully discussed at the 1907 Hague Conference, and, on the other, any new questions which they thought should be debated at the next conference. I had a suspicion at the back of my mind, however, that this measure would not succeed, since parliamentarians have much, almost too much, to do attending to their own affairs, with little time to spare for other matters such as this. Nevertheless, I wanted to make the proposal in order to emphasize the need for a different approach. Since it now appears that nothing has been done, the governments will have to make this analysis themselves. There are, as was pointed out at the Hague Conference, a great many

1. The Interparliamentary Conference was held in Berlin, September 17-19, 1908.

problems which have to be studied nationally before they can usefully be studied internationally.

I now propose to discuss the third story, the peace conference at The Hague. The assembly is composed of a great many people, many of whom have never seen each other before. I prepared statistics for the first of the Hague Conferences, showing that there were 138 representatives in all. Of this number no less than seventy-seven were diplomats. With all due respect to diplomats, who can be good or even excellent, I feel that one can have too much of a good thing and that a smaller proportion of diplomats would be beneficial at future conferences. There were also thirty-six military officers, twenty-two from the army and fourteen from the navy. Of real politicians there were only thirteen, of whom twelve were experts on international law, six of them members of the Institut de droit international[1]. If you were to read the Proceedings, you would find that the remaining twenty-five were those who really carried the load. These were the men who presided over or chaired the different commissions. I have no similar figures for the last Hague Conference, the Proceedings of which have not as yet been published in their entirety. I believe, however, that an analysis would reveal like results. I mention this because I firmly believe that governments should see to it that future representation to Hague Conferences be such as to make them more fruitful.

An advantage that the Hague Conferences lack, in contrast to the peace associations and the Interparliamentary Union, is a bureau. The International Court of Arbitration at The Hague has its central office, but the conference itself has none. This was pointed out by an earlier winner of the Nobel Peace Prize, namely Dr. Gobat, who delivered his lecture here, to the best of my memory, on the eighteenth of July, 1906[2]. The last Hague Conference has in the meantime expressed its opinion that a body should be established which could prepare for the work involved more effectively than has hitherto proved possible. I interpret the resolution taken at The Hague as confirming the desirability of setting up such a body within the next two years, one capable of carrying out preparatory work prior to the assembling of the next conference. Immediately, a number of difficulties arise. It becomes apparent, I believe, when this stage has been reached, that there will be a question as to who is to set the machinery in motion. No

1. Institute of International Law, recipient of the Nobel Peace Prize for 1904.
2. The date is correct; Albert Gobat shared the prize for 1902 but delivered his lecture in 1906.

one government has been given this responsibility. Moreover, how is the commission itself to be constituted? It is of course impossible to call upon representatives from all states.

I would suggest a method which I think could work and which I shall designate by the Swiss term, the «Vorort» system[1]; it consists in yielding the presidency to each of the participant states in turn. Naturally, it would be an honor for the state which is appointed first. After all, up to the present, only Russia has had the presidency. It could, however, pass to another state whose government would appoint a commission and take the responsibility for the preparatory work.

A similar arrangement has already been introduced in the Nordic Inter-parliamentary Union, which was set up last year. Its council and its executive are elected by the three Scandinavian groups. The council consists of nine persons. The first two from each country are the president and the vice-president of each of the three groups, and a third member is then chosen from each of them – an elected member. I have had the honor of being elected for two years by the Danish group.

When we met in Copenhagen on the fourteenth of September last year to constitute the council, we agreed to establish the presidency in such a way that one man could not be reelected president time after time, and to do it by using the so-called «Vorort» system. This year it is Sweden which presides and which is therefore responsible for convening the meeting of delegates, which number forty-five in all, including the three triads already mentioned. They are to meet in Stockholm this year on the twenty-seventh of August, or perhaps a little later. Next year Norway has the presidency, and it is up to the Norwegian group to decide whether an assembly of delegates or a conference will be convened and how it is to be organized. The following year, 1911, Denmark will assume the leader-ship, the presidency, the «Vorort». A similar method is used in Switzerland when the peace associations of the various cantons hold their joint annual meeting. The presidency passes from state to state, in turn: Bern, Neuchâtel, Lucerne, and so on. At each annual meeting, the «Vorort» for the following year is named.

Before I proceed with my observations on the Hague Conferences, I want

1. The «Vorort» (a term derived from *vorderster Ort*–in this case, «first canton») system was that used by the early Swiss Confederation; in this system any canton could be designated as the Vorort, which held the presidency of the Diet and accepted the responsibility of administering federal affairs between sessions of the Diet.

to comment on a term which I have not originated but have adopted from someone else. This is the word «pacigérance» or «waging peace» in contrast to «belligérance» or «waging war». I have taken it from a famous and distinguished Belgian writer, Baron Descamps[1], who is at present Belgium's minister of science and art. In 1898 he wrote an excellent book in which he developed the legal principles which should apply to neutral and non-neutral states in time of war and which he calls «pacigérat» or «pacigérance». According to French etymology, however, «pacigérat» must signify a condition, a legal status; whereas «pacigérance» denotes an action, an activity, something to be done, performed. Later Descamps used the word «pacigérat» only in the former sense.

I requested and received his permission to borrow the word «pacigérance» and to use it in another sense. Waging war we understand, but not waging peace, or at any rate less consciously so. It should, however, be better understood, and we should direct the attention of states to the matter of «waging peace» with other states; this should be one of the ways by which we seek to further the cause of peace and in particular to put the results of the Hague Conferences to practical use. I am convinced that this work will gain increasing momentum.

We have long possessed the art of war and the science of war, which have been evolved in the minutest detail. Warfare has been marvelously developed. It will soon be impossible to raise it to further heights. Indeed, whenever a new idea is developed, as for example ballooning, warfare immediately takes possession. On the other hand, the waging of peace as a science, as an art, is in its infancy. But we can trace its growth, its steady progress, and the time will come when there will be particular individuals designated to assume responsibility for and leadership of this movement. There are in most states one or two ministers of war, one of whom is the minister of naval affairs. I would not wish on any account to abolish them; as long as the status of international law is no better than it is at present, we cannot very well do without them. But I feel convinced, and I venture even to prophesy in this regard, that the time will come when there will also be a minister of peace in the cabinet, seated beside the ministers of war.

Among the problems confronting the waging of peace, «pacigérance», I would return to one already mentioned, that of obtaining agreement

1. Édouard Eugène François Descamps (1847–1933), Belgian statesman and jurist, who wrote Le Pacigérat (Brussels, 1898).

between the states whose delegates at The Hague voted for compulsory arbitration of international disputes on the seventh of October, 1907.

I would also mention another matter which in my opinion could be further refined. All who have followed later developments know that last year–I believe it was on the twenty-third of April–a so-called «entente» was concluded among the North Sea Powers and among the Baltic Sea Powers, whereby they guaranteed each other's coastal areas[1]. There is, however, an extraordinary definition in this agreement, namely, that the North Sea ends where the Baltic begins. But the agreement does not state where the North Sea does in fact end. Since the whole question remains obscure, I believe that it is desirable to try to bring these two «entente groups», that for the North Sea and that for the Baltic, into a closer association. A first step has to be taken; there is a need to «treatify», if I may coin this expression, the waterways–the French call them «canaux inter-océaniques»–which connect the two seas. These are the Sound, the Great Belt, and the Little Belt. Clearly, when such waterways are concerned, it is necessary to define precisely what rights and duties are invested in those who use them. To use a logical approach to the problem, I would say: Let us begin with one waterway; for example, the Kaiser Wilhelm Canal, the North Sea-Baltic Canal. There is no doubt that Germany exercises control of it. If we then turn to the Little Belt, I believe it would be natural to say: This is both a Danish and a German coastal area; so Denmark and Germany have to agree on what is to happen to it. And, by analogy, a similar situation must exist in the case of the Sound. The Sound has, however, already been the subject of a treaty, the treaty of 1857 (concerning the toll levy)[2]. This treaty, I believe, should be interpreted so that it relates only to politico-commercial circumstances and not to strategic ones. I believe that great master of international law, Bluntschli[3], is right when he says that, when two states border on the open sea and also have overlapping coastal areas, they are then obliged to support each other in the event of war. It would be of tremendous importance and would also affect Danish domestic affairs, if the Sound could be «treatified» in such a way that in

1. See Arnoldson's lecture, fn. 2, p. 179.
2. Sixteen powers were represented at the Conference of Copenhagen in 1857; in return for a lump-sum compensation Denmark agreed to discontinue the collection of Sound dues which she had collected since the 15th century from foreign ships using the Sound.
3. Johann Kaspar Bluntschli (1808–1881), Swiss legal scholar and statesman.

the event of war between powers inside or outside the Baltic, the Sound would remain open as a commercial waterway but be closed to the warships of belligerent powers. The warships would then have to be diverted to the Great Belt, which in any case is the only available route for large warships whose draft is too deep to allow them to pass through the Sound. In time of war, ships sail in squadrons. It is thus no sacrifice to use the Great Belt, which is a passageway through which, both in time of peace and of war, all types of shipping ought to be able to sail. The Baltic must not become a «closed sea». Indeed, this is a matter which merits very detailed study in view of the many important and intricate problems involved. I do not in any way pretend to have found the answer; but I should mention that I have spoken to many experts about it, and they have agreed with the idea that the Sound be prohibited to the warships of belligerent powers in wartime so that it can then remain an assured commercial seaway. I might mention that as early as 1887 I wrote a treatise on this subject published in the Danish naval officers' journal, the *Journal of Naval Affairs*. I also offered a resolution about it which was accepted at the Lucerne Peace Congress in 1905. It is one of my pet subjects, and therefore, I should not like to let pass this opportunity of reiterating my views. I believe that it is of particular significance at present. Norway may be geographically somewhat remote, but as a seafaring nation with a large merchant fleet she is nevertheless interested in seeing the Sound closed [to warships] in case of war between powers within or without the Baltic.

I wish, finally, to touch on a question which was recently raised in the Danish Parliament but which has received relatively little attention. Fourteen members of Parliament, with Mr. Sveistrup [1] as their spokesman, submitted a proposal that the cause of peace be supported by a very substantial monetary grant. There are now very few people who believe that the cause of peace should be entirely unsupported by government funds. It seems to me that the cause of peace serves international political ends, ends which also strongly affect the domestic affairs of a state, to such an extent that the state should supply funds for its support. In this connection, Norway led the way as early as 1890 by granting traveling expenses for its delegates to the interparliamentary conferences. Denmark has also been generous of late. But on this last occasion, an appropriation of no less than a quarter-million kroner was proposed. This caused considerable astonishment, but

1. Poul Sveistrup (1848–1911), Danish social statistician, politician, and peace worker.

the present Danish president of the Council, Neergaard[1], was on the whole favorably disposed and said that when the purpose for which the funds were to be used had been specified in greater detail, he would not oppose the motion. He referred particularly to the interparliamentary delegate meetings of which our Nordic delegates are a part. I hope this matter will be discussed there also.

What I have called «pacigérance» is clearly part of the larger struggle for civilization which is progressing on an increasingly broad front: it is civilization's battle between rule by law and rule by power. In this context, pacifists should stress more and more that it is the rule of law for which they are fighting. It is quite usual to maintain that treaties become just so much wastepaper when war breaks out. This is a military concept that pacifists should not tolerate. We should do everything within our power to insure that the idea of law conquers. What contributes largely to the confusion of ideas is the accepted division of the world into major powers and small states. We understand a «power» to be a state which has a large population and well-developed armed forces, army and navy, and so on. This is comparable to believing that a great man is a very tall and big man. By a great man, however, we mean a man who, because of his spiritual gifts, his character, and other qualities, deserves to be called great and who as a result earns the power to influence others. By the same token it must follow that the state we now call a small state is in reality a power if it plays such a role in the development of civilization that it marches in the front ranks and wins victories in the fight for law which surpass those of the so-called great powers.

I do not think that I dare tire my distinguished audience any longer. I have touched on various matters, many of which would have merited discussion as separate topics. I ask you to forgive me for a lecture which has been rather fragmentary. It is true that I have kept a thread running through it with my metaphor of the three stories and the three columns, but apart from that I have expressed random thoughts which I must characterize as details and which may seem, for the most part, of quite secondary importance. If this is so, I would recall, turning again to the military, the words of that great general, Frederick II of Prussia[2]. Very fond of expressing

1. Niels Neergaard (1854–1936), Danish historian and statesman; prime minister (1908–1909; 1920–1924).
2. Frederick II of Prussia, known as Frederick the Great (1712–1786), king of Prussia (1740–1786).

himself in French, he once said, in another context naturally, that one should not turn up one's nose at details, that details should be noted and attended to, for they constitute the first step to victory.

Aimez donc ces détails! Ils ne sont pas sans gloire.
Ce sont les premiers pas menant à la victoire.

I must now thank you for the attention you have shown, and I wish to offer special appreciation to the Head of this State[1] who has honored the lecture with his presence. And last but certainly not least, my thanks to those to whom I owe the privilege of standing here today: the Nobel Committee of the Norwegian Parliament.

1. King Haakon VII.

Biography

The Danish pacifist, Fredrik Bajer (April 21, 1837–January 22, 1922), was born in Vester Egede, near Naestved, Denmark. The son of a clergyman named Alfred Beyer, he adopted the altered spelling of his surname in 1865.

Bajer entered the Sorø Academy in 1848 and six years later a military school. In 1856 he joined the army as a lieutenant in the Dragoons, stationed first in Naestved and then in Holstein, interrupting his service for two years in 1860 to take advanced courses in another military school. During the 1864 war against Prussia and Austria, he commanded troops in northern Jutland, winning attention by his ability and conduct and earning promotion to the rank of first lieutenant. Despite his record, he was discharged from the army in June of 1865 during a general reduction of troops at the end of the war. Even before his dismissal, however, he had begun to think, as his autobiography shows, that he was more cut out for a philosophical than for a military way of life.

Between the ages of twenty-eight and thirty-five, Bajer laid the foundations of his later career. He studied languages, mastering French, Norwegian, and Swedish; established himself as a teacher and translator in Copenhagen; supplemented his income by free-lance writing; spoke and wrote on the subjects which were thereafter to claim the major share of his attention; and entered politics in 1872. In that year he was elected to the Folketing, the Danish House of Representatives, retaining his seat there for the next twenty-three years.

In politics Bajer displayed liberal tendencies, but, disliking party discipline, remained independent of political affiliation. The main causes he supported in his political life were those with which he had already become prominently identified: international peace and Danish neutrality, Scandinavian unity, women's rights, and education.

In the field of education, Bajer was professionally interested in linguistics, particularly in orthography and phonation, but he was concerned with school organization as well; he was a member of the governing board of the Pedagogical Society and played an important role in the first Scandinavian conference of schoolmen held in Göteborg in 1870.

Bajer was one of Denmark's leading spokesmen for women's rights, helping to found the Dansk Kvindesamfund [Danish Women's Society] in 1871 and supporting legislation in the Folketing on behalf of equality for women, especially in economic matters.

In 1870 Bajer started the Nordisk Fristats Samfund [Society of Nordic Free States], dedicated to the promotion of Nordic unity and cooperation, and for two years edited its weekly journal Folkevennen [Friend of the People]. Eventually, his ideas on Scandinavian unity became inextricably associated with his evolving ideas on neutrality and peace.

Bajer was introduced to the organized peace movement of his day through his study of languages and became especially interested in the efforts of the French peace leader, Frédéric Passy, and the work of the Ligue internationale et permanente de la paix founded in 1867, offering his help in distributing its literature. Perceiving one aspect of peace in terms of neutrality, he founded the first Danish peace society in 1882 under the name Foreningen til Danmarks Neutralisering [Society for Promotion of Danish Neutrality], serving as its president until 1892. (Later this association became the Danish Peace Society, and still later the Danish Peace and League of Nations Society.) Using his military training to advantage, he cited the danger the Nordic countries faced in the event of a European war because of the strategic importance of the water routes adjacent to their borders and proposed that Scandinavian neutrality, modeled on that of Switzerland and Belgium, be internationally recognized. Between 1883 and 1889 his proposal was adopted in principle by several international organizations, but later Bajer came to believe that neutrality should be a way of life for Denmark to pursue independently without relying on other states to guarantee it.

Bajer rapidly became a major figure in the flourishing international peace movement. He participated in the European Peace Congress at Bern in 1884, shared the initiative with those who called the first Scandinavian Peace Meeting in 1885, attended the first regular World Peace Congress at Paris in 1889 and regularly represented the Danish Peace Society at the congresses until 1914, and also in 1889 attended the first meeting of the Interparliamentary Union held in Paris. At the second World Peace Congress in London in 1890, Bajer proposed the creation of a permanent bureau, with headquarters in Bern, to act as a focus for the peace movement and a clearinghouse for pacifist information. The proposal was approved in 1891 at the congress in Rome, and Bajer was named the first president of its governing board. Bajer founded the Danish Interparliamentary Group in 1891, acting as its secretary for twenty-five years, and prepared the way for the creation of the Scandinavian Interparliamentary Union in 1908.

Believing that arbitration was a mechanism which could satisfactorily supplant that of war in settling differences among nations, Bajer guided through the Danish Parliament in 1888, a carefully, if somewhat cautiously, worded proposal to establish arbitration agreements with Sweden and Norway.

To his active participation in all these causes Bajer constantly added the support of his writing, publishing many articles, pamphlets, and books in the course of his activity.

After 1907, Bajer's health deteriorated. In that year he resigned from active office on the board of the Peace Bureau to become its honorary president, and in 1916 from his various duties in connection with the Interparliamentary work. An invalid in his last years, he still kept informed on world events and, even while observing World War I, resolutely maintained his faith in the pacifist cause. He died in Copenhagen in 1922.

Selected Bibliography

Bajer, Fredrik. Collections of Bajer's papers are held by the Royal Library of Copenhagen and the Royal Library of Stockholm.

Bajer, Fredrik, *Dansk Fredsforenings Historie*. København, Gjellerup, 1894.

Bajer, Fredrik, *Idéen til Nordens, saerlig Danmarks, vedvarende Neutralitet*. København, 1900.

Bajer, Fredrik, *Klara-Rafael Fejden*. København, Topp, 1879.

Bajer, Fredrik, *Livserindringer*, udgivne af hans Søn. København, Gjellerup, 1909.

Bajer, Fredrik, *Nordens politiske Digtning, 1789–1804*. København, Topp, 1878.

Bajer, Fredrik, *Nordens, saerlig Danmarks, Neutralitet under Krimkrigen*. København, Schultz, 1914.

Bajer, Fredrik, *Nordiske Neutralitetsforbund*. København, Studentersamfund Forlag, 1885.

Bajer, Fredrik, *Om Årsager til Krig og Voldgift i Europa siden År 1800*. København, Gjellerup, 1897.

Bajer, Fredrik, *Samlinger til jaevnførende nordisk Lyd-og Retskrivningslaere*. København, Gad, 1871.

Bajer, Fredrik, *A Serious Drama of Modern History: How Danish Slesvig Was Lost*, trans. from the Danish by P.H.Peckover. London, Peace Society, 1897. (*Da det danske Slesvig gik tabt*. Under pseudonym Bjarke Frode. København, 1896.)

Bajer, Fredrik, *Tactics for the Friends of Peace*, trans. from the Danish by P.H.Peckover. Wisbech: Poyser, 1891. (*Fredsvennernes Krigsplan*. København: Möller, 1891.)

Dansk biografisk Leksikon.

Privatarkiver Politikeren Fredrik Bajer og Hustrus Arkiv. Foreløbige Arkivregistraturer Serie 8. København, 1963. Contains brief bibliography.

Schou, August, *Histoire de l'internationalisme III: Du Congrès de Vienne jusqu'à la première guerre mondiale (1914)*, pp. 510–515. Publications de l'Institut Nobel Norvégien, Tome VIII. Oslo, Aschehoug, 1963.

Peace 1909

AUGUSTE MARIE FRANÇOIS
BEERNAERT

PAUL HENRI BENJAMIN BALLUET,
BARON D'ESTOURNELLES
DE CONSTANT DE REBECQUE

Presentation

by Jørgen Gunnarsson Løvland*, Chairman of the Nobel Committee

Auguste Beernaert was born in 1828[1]. After completing his legal studies he began practice as a barrister in Brussels in 1853. In 1859 he was appointed counsel at the Belgian Supreme Court of Appeal. He entered politics at an early date and in 1873[2] was elected deputy for Thielt. His unusual talents and political ability promised a great political future. In 1875[3] he was named minister of public works, an office he held until 1878 when the Liberal Party won the election. When his Clerical Party returned to power in 1884, he was made head of the Department of Agriculture, Industry, and Public Works, and a few months later became finance minister and head of the cabinet. In 1895 he was elected president of the Chamber of Representatives.

Beernaert has played a leading role in Belgian politics. It was through his efforts that the Belgian Chamber agreed that King Leopold[4] should become sovereign of the Congo State, and it was thanks to him that fortifications were constructed on the Meuse to protect Belgium's neutrality. This experienced politician also played an important part in the revision of the Belgian constitution. His work for the cause of peace is widely known in

* Mr. Løvland opened the award ceremony of December 10, 1909, in the auditorium of the Norwegian Nobel Institute, with a welcome to the audience and an introduction of Mr. Christian L. Lange, secretary to the Committee, who had just been named secretary-general of the Interparliamentary Bureau. Mr. Lange delivered a speech on the Interparliamentary Union, reviewing its twenty-year history. After thanking Mr. Lange for his speech and for his years of service to the Committee, Mr. Løvland announced the joint winners of the Peace Prize for 1909, Mr. Beernaert and Baron d'Estournelles de Constant, and gave a brief biographical sketch of each. The translation of that of Mr. Beernaert, given here, is based on a reporter's version of it which appeared in the Oslo *Aftenposten* of December 10, 1909; certain apparent errors of date in the text are noted as they occur. There is no indication in *Les Prix Nobel en 1909* or in the *Aftenposten* that the laureates were present at the ceremony. Neither laureate delivered a Nobel lecture.

1. According to all sources checked, Beernaert was born in 1829.
2. According to all sources checked: 1874.
3. According to all sources checked: 1873.
4. Leopold II (1835–1909), king of Belgium (1865–1909). See biography of Beernaert.

Europe, and his name renowned in the international Peace Conferences. At the first Hague Conference he was chairman of the commission set up to formulate proposals for the restriction of armaments.

Beernaert is also a member of the Permanent Arbitration Commission, a member of the Institut de France and of the Belgian Academy. He is honorary president of the Société de droit international, active president of the Association for the Promotion of International Maritime Law, and honorary president of the International Law Association.

Each of these men [Mr. Beernaert and Baron d'Estournelles de Constant] holds a prominent position in the international movement for peace and arbitration, and it is therefore fully in keeping with the spirit of Nobel's intentions that the prize should be awarded to them.

Biography

Auguste Marie François Beernaert (July 26, 1829–October 6, 1912) was born in Ostend, Belgium, in a middle-class Catholic family of Flemish origin. His father was a government functionary whose changing appointments took the family from Ostend to Dinant and then to Namur, where Auguste and his sister spent their childhood. Their early education was undertaken by their mother, a woman of outstanding intelligence and moral character. Admitted to the University of Louvain in 1846, Beernaert took his doctorate in law in 1851 with the highest distinction. Awarded a traveling fellowship, he spent two years at the Universities of Paris, Heidelberg, and Berlin, studying the status of legal education in France and Germany and upon his return to Belgium submitting a report of his findings–later published–to the minister of the Interior.

Admitted to the bar in 1853, he clerked for a time for Hubert Dolez, a prominent lawyer and former president of the Chamber of Representatives, then set up an independent practice, specializing in fiscal law. In the next twenty years his essays in legal journals earned him a reputation as a scholar, and his practice a comfortable fortune. Consequently, there was some surprise expressed in Belgian legal circles when he gave up his practice in 1873 to become the minister of public works in Jules Malou's conservative Catholic cabinet. In the next five years Beernaert proved to be an able and energetic administrator. He improved the country's rail, canal, and road systems, established new port facilities at Ostend and Anvers, and beautified the capital, but he failed in his attempt to end child labor in the mines. In June of 1874 he lost a contest for a seat in the Senate but three months later won an election in the west Flanders town of Thielt, a constituency which re-elected him until his death.

When the Catholic Party, defeated in 1878, was returned to power in 1884, Beernaert was named minister of the Department of Agriculture, Industry, and Public Works in the new cabinet. Four months later, after some resignations from the cabinet, King Leopold II entrusted Beernaert with the direction of the government.

Beernaert was prime minister of Belgium and finance minister for the next ten years. Under his administration the budget was balanced; the Flemish language was protected; the independent State of the Congo was created in 1885 and the title of sovereign of that land given to Leopold who had personally been largely responsible for its development; social and judicial reforms designed to protect the welfare of the workingman were instituted in 1887 in the wake of riots in that year; military fortifications on the Meuse were constructed in order to defend Belgian neutrality; the constitution of 1831 was revised, the right of suffrage being granted to ten times the number of citizens who had formerly enjoyed it.

On another constitutional question, that of proportional representation, the cabinet fell in 1894. Although he returned to his law practice, Beernaert continued to serve in the government. He accepted the advisory post of minister of state and from 1895 to 1900 served as the president of the Chamber of Representatives, being elected by his colleagues. A lifelong patron of the arts, he was selected to head the Commission of Museums and Arts. During this period he engaged actively in international attempts to abolish slavery and solidified into active opposition his dismay at the exploitation of the Congo that had troubled his relationship with Leopold in the last part of his tenure as prime minister.

One of Belgium's leading pacifists, Beernaert became an active member of the Interparliamentary Union after he resigned from the prime ministry, presided over several of its conferences, and served as president of its Council after 1899 and of its Executive Committee after its creation in 1908. At the Peace Conference at The Hague in 1899 he presided over the First Commission on arms limitation; at the Conference of 1907, over the Second Commission on codification of land war. He was a member of the Permanent Court of Arbitration; he represented Mexico in 1902 in the dispute with the United States, the first case to be brought before the Court; and on many occasions he acted as arbiter of international quarrels. Beernaert was the primary force behind proposals to unify international maritime law; those resulting from the international conferences of 1885 and 1888, convened on his initiative, failed of adoption by the several nations, but the conventions dealing with collision and assistance at sea drawn up in 1910 at the conference in Brussels under his chairmanship were soon signed by many nations. He exemplified his own aphorism: «The first virtue of politics and the first element of success is perseverance.»[1]

1. Henri Carton de Wiart, *Beernaert et son temps*, p.139.

On his way home from the 1912 Geneva conference of the Interparliamentary Union on the prohibition of air warfare, Beernaert was hospitalized in Lucerne where he died of pneumonia. He was buried at Boitsfort with the simplest of ceremonies, as he had requested.

Selected Bibliography

Beernaert, Auguste Marie François, *De l'état de l'enseignement du droit en France et en Allemagne: Rapport adressé à M. le Ministre de l'Intérieur*. Bruxelles, Lesigne, 1854.

Beernaert, Auguste Marie François, *Discours prononcé à l'occasion de l'inauguration des quais d'Anvers, le 26 juillet 1885*. Paris, Chaix, 1885.

Carton de Wiart, Edmond, *Auguste Beernaert: Sa Vie et son œuvre*. Gand, 1910.

Carton de Wiart, Edmond, *Léopold II: Souvenirs des dernières années, 1901–1909*. Bruxelles, Goemaere, 1944.

Carton de Wiart, Henri, *Beernaert et son temps*. Bruxelles, La Renaissance du Livre, 1945.

Carton de Wiart, Henri, «Notice sur Auguste Beernaert», *Annuaire de l'Académie Royale de Belgique*, 105 (1939) 293–364. Contains a bibliography.

Collin, Paul-Victor, «Un Homme d'état: Auguste Beernaert, 1829–1912», *Res Publica*, 3 (1961) 251–254.

De Ridder, A., «Léopold II, M. Beernaert, et la défense nationale», *La Revue Générale*, 104 (juillet 1920) 30–48.

Jaspar, Henri, «Auguste Beernaert: Discours prononcé à Ostende à l'inauguration de monument», *La Revue Belge*, 4e année, Tome IV (15 octobre 1927) 181–192.

Lettenhove, H. Kervyn de, «M. Beernaert: Ami et protecteur des arts», *La Revue Belge*, 4e année, Tome IV (15 octobre 1927) 111–122.

Lyon-Caen, Charles, «Notice sur la vie et les travaux d'Auguste Beernaert (1829–1912», *Séances et travaux de l'Académie des sciences morales et politiques: Compte-rendu 89e année*, Paris, Alcan, 1929, pp. 33–57.

Mélot, Auguste, «Beernaert et le Congo, 1884–1894», *La Revue Générale*, 127 (février 1932) 147–167.

Mélot, Auguste, «Beernaert I: Le Régime bourgeois et la législation sociale», *La Revue Générale*, 118 (août 1927) 129–144.

Mélot, Auguste, «Beernaert II: L'Introduction du régime démocratique», *La Revue Générale*, 118 (septembre 1927) 299–314.

Passelecq, Ferdinand, *Auguste Beernaert—sa carrière et son œuvre politique: Notes pour servir à l'histoire de l'évolution des idées dans le parti catholique belge après 1878*. Bruxelles, Dewit, 1912.

Van der Smissen, Édouard, *Léopold et Beernaert d'après leur correspondance inédité de 1884 à 1894*. 2 Tomes. Bruxelles, 1920.

Woeste, Charles, *Mémoires pour servir à l'histoire contemporaine*. 3 Tomes. Bruxelles, Dewit, 1927–1937.

Presentation

by Jørgen Gunnarsson Løvland*, Chairman of the Nobel Committee

Paul Henri Benjamin d'Estournelles de Constant is still in the prime of life. Born on September 22, 1852[1], at La Flèche (Sarthe), he belongs to the old French aristocracy. As Baron de Constant de Rebecque, he can trace his ancestry back to the Crusaders.

He was educated at the Lycée Louis le Grand in Paris and later studied law; he is a Licentiate of Law and also holds a diploma from the School of Oriental Languages.

At the age of twenty-three he became attaché in the French Foreign Office and two years later was sent to the Balkans. When he was twenty-nine he became secretary-general of the French Residency in Tunis; on the basis of his experience there he wrote *La Politique française en Tunisie*[2]. While in Tunis, d'Estournelles de Constant performed most valuable organizing work.

He returned to Paris and became assistant director for the Levant in the Department of Foreign Affairs. At thirty-eight he went to London as counselor to the Embassy, with the title of minister plenipotentiary. As chargé d'affaires he was involved in averting threatened war between France and England during the conflict between King Chulalongkorn of Siam and the French fleet[3].

---

* Mr. Løvland gave this biographical sketch of Baron d'Estournelles de Constant, along with one on the co-laureate Mr. Beernaert, on December 10, 1909, at the Norwegian Nobel Institute. The translation is based on a reporter's version of the speech which appeared in the Oslo *Aftenposten* of the same date. (For a note on other details of the occasion, see p. 211.)

1. According to all sources checked, d'Estournelles was born on November 22, 1852.

2. Published in 1891, the book won a prize from the French Academy.

3. In 1893 during French-Siamese border disputes, the Siamese, under Chulalongkorn (Rama V, 1868–1910), fired at gunboats sent to enforce French demands. A French ultimatum, rejected by the Siamese, was followed by a blockade which, in turn, brought opposition from the British who refused to remove a gunboat stationed at Bangkok to protect British subjects. The crisis, brief but acute, ended when the Siamese were obliged to accept the ultimatum and the blockade was raised.

Since then he has become thoroughly dedicated to the movement for peace and arbitration, and he has written a number of books and articles on the subject.

He entered politics in his own country, and in 1895 the republican Baron stood for his native Sarthe. He was elected senator in 1904.

In 1899 d'Estournelles de Constant was named a French representative at the first Hague Conference, and in 1903 he founded the Groupe parlementaire de l'arbitrage international. It was this work which determined his later political attitude. A practical result of his efforts was the arbitration treaties between France and other countries, and he saw his policy adopted beyond the frontiers of France. He believed that foreign policy should be controlled by parliaments and that consequently parliamentary arbitration groups should be developed and strengthened.

His work for peace has not been performed blindly. As a diplomat he has learned to understand international policy and has planned his efforts accordingly.

In this country d'Estournelles de Constant is a well-known and very welcome visitor ever since the last visit of the French parliamentarians[1].

[For the concluding paragraph of the speech, which concerns both laureates, see p. 212.]

---

1. The laureate was an advocate and organizer of reciprocal visits between parliamentary groups of the various nations; his own group had just visited Norway in the preceding summer.

Biography

Paul Henri Benjamin Balluet, Baron d'Estournelles de Constant de Rebecque (November 22, 1852 – May 15, 1924), the son of an aristocratic family tracing its ancestry back to the Crusaders, was born at La Flèche in the Sarthe district of the Loire valley. A diplomat and politician, d'Estournelles, immensely energetic, found time to engage in fencing, yachting, and painting, and to pursue a keen interest in the automobile and the airplane after those machines had made their debut.

He attended the Lycée Louis le Grand in Paris, completed his legal studies, received a diploma from the School of Oriental Languages. Entering the diplomatic corps in 1876 as an attaché in the consular department of the Ministry of Foreign Affairs, d'Estournelles represented France in the next six years in Montenegro, Turkey, The Netherlands, England, and Tunis. Recalled to Paris in 1882, he assumed the assistant directorship of the Near Eastern Bureau of the Ministry of Foreign Affairs.

D'Estournelles was named chargé d'affaires in London in 1890 and both there and back in Paris helped to avert a possible war between England and France over a conflict of interests in Siam. Reflecting later on those days, in a speech in Edinburgh in 1906, d'Estournelles said he became convinced of the general impotence of those in the diplomatic service and resolved to abandon the «gilded existence of the diplomatist in order to undertake the real struggle... against ignorance» by obtaining an elective seat in the legislature and attempting to remedy the situation in which «the silent majority allow themselves to be persuaded that they know nothing of ‹Foreign Affairs› »[1]. And so, on May 19, 1895, he began his political career as deputy from Sarthe, elected by the same constituency that had years earlier elected his famous great-uncle, the author Benjamin Constant de Rebecque. Elected senator from the same region in 1904, he held that seat as an active Radical-Socialist until his death.

From the time that he was chosen to serve on the French delegation to

1. Baron d'Estournelles de Constant and others, *International Peace* (Edinburgh: Edinburgh Peace and Arbitration Society, 1906), pp. 5 and 6.

the first Hague Peace Conference in 1899, d'Estournelles devoted himself almost exclusively to working for peace and arbitration. At the Peace Conference he led the successful struggle to strengthen the language dealing with arbitration and the court in Article 27 of Convention I, and in 1902 scored a notable success for arbitration when, during a visit to the United States, he was influential in persuading President Theodore Roosevelt to submit a U.S. dispute with Mexico to the Hague Tribunal.

In 1903, d'Estournelles founded a parliamentary group composed of members of the French Chamber and Senate irrespective of party, dedicated to the advancement of international arbitration, and employing as its chief method, the exchange of visits with foreign parliamentarians. A goodwill mission to London under his chairmanship in 1903 – and a return visit to Paris by British parliamentarians – helped pave the way for the Franco-British Entente Cordiale of 1904; a visit to Munich gave birth to the Franco-German Association in 1903. In 1905 at Paris he founded the Association for International Conciliation, with branches abroad.

D'Estournelles' long-range solution for European problems was a political one – the formation of a European union. But meanwhile he continued to pursue those of a diplomatic and juridical nature – as an active contributor to the work of the Interparliamentary Union, as a member of the French delegation to the second Hague Peace Conference of 1907, as a member of the Permanent Court of Arbitration, as president of the European Center of the Carnegie Endowment for International Peace.

During the First World War, d'Estournelles supported the French effort, interesting himself particularly in measures against German submarines and turning his home – the Chateau de Clermont-Créans on the Loire – into a hospital for the wounded. In 1918 he denounced the armistice as meaningless as long as German soldiers remained on French soil. At the same time, however, he continued his campaign for international understanding: he joined Léon Bourgeois (Nobel Peace Prizewinner for 1920) in presenting a plan for the League of Nations to Clemenceau in 1918, and in later years he never ceased trying to bring together parliamentarians of various nations, especially those of France and Germany.

Throughout his career d'Estournelles proved a gifted writer and speaker. He published translations from the classical Greek, as well as a book on Grecian times; wrote a play based on the Pygmalion myth; won the French Academy's Prix Thérouanne in 1891 with a book on French politics in Tunisia; produced speeches, pamphlets, and articles covering topics that ranged from French politics to feminism, from arbitration to aviation. Possessed of an admirable command of English–helped, no doubt, by his marriage to an American, Daisy Sedgwick-Berend–he made a number of lecture tours in the United States and published in 1913 a comprehensive review entitled *Les États-Unis d'Amérique* [*America and Her Problems*]. He became, indeed, a leading French authority on the United States.

D'Estournelles died in Paris in 1924 at the age of seventy-two and was interred in the Père-Lachaise cemetery. Two days after his death, his final speech, commemorating the twenty-fifth anniversary of the first Peace Conference, was read by his son Paul at The Hague.

Selected Bibliography

À la Mémoire de son président-directeur, d'Estournelles de Constant, 1852–1924. Paris, Centre Européen de la Dotation Carnegie, 1924.

d'Estournelles de Constant, P.H.B., *America and Her Problems,* translated from the French by George A.Raper. New York, Macmillan, 1915. (*Les États-Unis d'Amérique,* Paris, Colin, 1913.)

d'Estournelles de Constant, P.H.B., *La Conciliation internationale: Discours prononcé au Palais de Westminster, à Londres, le 22 juillet 1903.* La Flèche, 1904.

d'Estournelles de Constant, P.H.B., *Le Devoir et l'intérêt des États-Unis: Publications de M.d'Estournelles de Constant aux États-Unis.* Paris, Delagrave, 1915.

d'Estournelles de Constant,P.H.B., *La Politique extérieur de La France: Le Respect des autres races.* Paris, Delagrave, 1910.

d'Estournelles de Constant, P.H.B., *La Politique française en Tunisie: Le Protectorat et ses origines, 1854–1891.* Paris, Plon, 1891.

d'Estournelles de Constant, P.H.B., *Pour la Société des Nations.* La Flèche, Dépot des Publications de la Conciliation, 1921.

d'Estournelles de Constant, P.H.B.,*Pygmalion.* Paris, 1907.

d'Estournelles de Constant, P.H.B.,*Vie de D.Coray,* traduite du grec. Paris, 1887.

d'Estournelles de Constant, P.H.B., *La Vie de province en Grèce.* Paris, 1878.

d'Estournelles de Constant, P.H.B.,*Woman and the Cause of Peace,* translated from the French. New York, American Association for International Conciliation, 1911. (*Les Femmes et la paix.* Paris, Delagrave, 1910.)

d'Estournelles de Constant,P.H.B., and David Jayne Hill, *The Result of the Second Hague Conference.* New York, American Branch of the Association for International Conciliation,1907.

Schou, August, *Histoire de l'internationalisme III: Du Congrès de Vienne jusqu'à la première guerre mondiale (1914),* pp. 458–461. Publications de l'Institut Nobel Norvégien, Tome VIII. Oslo, Aschehoug, 1963.

Peace 1910

THE PERMANENT INTERNATIONAL
PEACE BUREAU

Presentation

by Jørgen Gunnarsson Løvland, Chairman of the Nobel Committee*

Chairman of the Committee Løvland then announced that the Peace Prize for this year had been awarded to the permanent Peace Bureau in Bern.

He then briefly reviewed the peace movement in Europe which, as we all know, has made steady headway since the great Napoleonic Wars. The idea had earlier been championed by men like Kant[1] and Rousseau[2]. First attempts were made to form organizations in America and in England. The cause was supported by Garibaldi[3] and his comrades-in-arms and by the writer Victor Hugo[4].

The Permanent International Peace Bureau (Bureau international permanent de la paix) was founded in 1891, with its headquarters in Bern. It was clear from the annual peace congresses that a central office was needed to act as a link between the peace societies of the various countries, and in particular to help the local congress committees to organize the world rallies. To make the Bureau a legally constituted body empowered to receive dona-

---

* Mr. Løvland announced the award of the Peace Prize for 1910 on the afternoon of December 10, 1910, in the auditorium of the Norwegian Nobel Institute. There is no original text of his speech extant, but the Oslo *Aftenposten* for December 10, 1910, carries a reporter's version of the speech which is here printed in full in English translation. It would appear that the reporter in the first two paragraphs is summarizing Mr. Løvland's remarks, and that thereafter he is striving to record the speech as delivered.

1. Immanuel Kant (1724–1804), German philosopher; wrote *On Perpetual Peace* (1795).

2. Jean Jacques Rousseau (1712–1778), French philosopher; wrote *The Social Contract* (1762), outlining the political principles of a governmental utopia.

3. Giuseppe Garibaldi (1807–1882), Italian patriot and soldier; supported, mostly by personal correspondence and letters to the press, an International Court of Justice, a United States of Europe, free education, and other plans to promote international understanding.

4. Victor Hugo (1802–1885), French author; was associated with peace movements in the mid-19th century–for example, he chaired the Peace Congress held in Paris in 1849 and in his welcoming speech made his famous allusion to the «United States of Europe».

tions and legacies, it was made the agency of a society (Société du Bureau international permanent de la paix) in accordance with Swiss law. Admission to membership is open to any institution, association, or individual upon a simple declaration of agreement with the objectives of the society.

The Bureau is now under the control of a Commission of thirty-five members from the various countries under a president, at the present time Belgian Senator Henri La Fontaine[1]. Three members must live in Bern where the offices of the Bureau are situated and supervised by an honorary secretary-general. Nobel Prizewinner Élie Ducommun[2] held this office from the time of the Bureau's founding until his death in 1906, a period during which he rendered most valuable services to the organization.

The present secretary-general is Nobel Prizewinner Dr. Gobat[3], member of the [Swiss] Federal Council. Both men have worked without compensation.

The economic position of the Peace Bureau has been difficult. In addition to the interest on a capital of about 40,000 francs, it has for some years received smaller fixed annual grants from Switzerland, Denmark, Sweden, and Norway. With some private contributions, it has about 8,000 francs per annum. Most of this is spent on the publication of the journal *Correspondance bimensuelle*, which gives news of the peace movement and lists new literature on the subject of peace. The Bureau issues a yearbook, *Annuaire du mouvement pacifiste*, with valuable information and papers on international affairs, institutions, and personalities. Since 1894 the Bureau has had an affiliated American office in Washington.

It is the function of the Bern Bureau to facilitate communications between the societies and individuals, and to collect information on the peace movement; it has a record office and a library; it also prepares the questions to be put before the annual world peace congresses and implements the decisions of the congresses.

It has long been the common wish of all those in the peace movement throughout the world that the Bureau be awarded the Peace Prize. The World Peace Congress in Munich in 1908 directed a general request to all those entitled to make nominations, to name the Bureau.

The Nobel Committee has also received recommendations from, among others, the Swedish and Danish Peace Unions.

1. Henri La Fontaine (1854–1943), recipient of the Nobel Peace Prize for 1913.
2. Élie Ducommun (1833–1906), co-recipient of the Nobel Peace Prize for 1902.
3. Albert Gobat (1843–1914), co-recipient of the Nobel Peace Prize for 1902.

We are convinced that this award is entirely in the spirit of Alfred Nobel's plan; he wanted his money to be used to support, accelerate, and promote the peace movement.

We firmly hope and expect that this year's prize will further this aim and that the fruits of the award will be harvested in the years to come.

.

The Nobel lecture usually delivered by the prizewinner was not given in this case.

History*

The International Peace Bureau (IPB) was founded as a result of the third Universal Peace Congress in Rome, 1891, with Fredrik Bajer[1] one of its principal founders and its first president. Established at Bern as the central office and executive organ of the International Union of Peace Societies «to coordinate the activities of the various peace societies and promote the concept of peaceful settlement of international disputes», the Bureau was, in its early years, virtually synonymous with the popular peace movement of that time—that is to say, with all the peace organizations affiliated with it and with their then homogeneous ideology and program. Figuring prominently in this program were such matters as arbitration procedures, bilateral peace treaties, the creation of a permanent court of international justice and of some kind of intergovernmental or even supranational body or bodies for cooperation and negotiation between nations. To disseminate and promote these ideas, the Bureau arranged the annual peace congresses, formulated their agenda, and implemented their decisions. It also provided a means of communication between the various individuals and organizations working for peace, and collected and issued information, often through its fortnightly publication *Correspondance bimensuelle* and its yearbook *Annuaire du mouvement pacifiste*. Until the Bureau received the Nobel Peace Prize in 1910, its funds for these activities were limited, varying each year «from 8,000 to 9,000 francs»[2].

Along with the Interparliamentary Union, with which it had a close relationship, the International Peace Bureau was influential in bringing the concern for peace to the attention of both public opinion and politicians,

* This history is based on the IPB's pamphlet *The International Peace Bureau: History, Aims, Activity*, written by Dr.Ulrich Herz, secretary-general of the IPB (Geneva, 1969) and on the IPB's six-page mimeographed document entitled «General Background» and dated Summer, 1970. The editor gratefully acknowledges the IPB's kind permission to use this material freely, both substantively and verbally.
1. Fredrik Bajer (1837–1922), co-recipient of the Nobel Peace Prize for 1908.
2. Élie Ducommun, «The Permanent International Bureau of Peace», p.661.

being very successful in promoting what eventually took form as the League of Nations.

World War I not only hindered the work of the Bureau but brought the International Union of Peace Societies to an end. Consequently, after the war was over, «the IPB was not able to keep the same predominant position amongst international organizations and institutions. Since an intergovernmental body existed – tentative and defective though it was – and since the ideas of arbitration, mediation, etc., were accepted by many governments, it was no longer necessary for a nongovernmental organization to focus its own activities on these matters. The international peace movement, furthermore, developed into a more complex and diversified pattern of ideologies, interests, and projects, and it was no longer either possible or even desirable to have only one coordinating body. The IPB, therefore, had to try to find its own image. It concentrated its efforts mainly on attempting to communicate certain ideas and proposals of the peace movement which represented the broad outlines of opinion within nongovernmental organizations concerned with questions of peace and humanitarian welfare, to those circles responsible for decisions on the governmental and intergovernmental level»[1].

In order to facilitate this reconstruction of activity and to work in closer contact with the new League of Nations, the Bureau moved in 1924 to Geneva, which is still the site of its headquarters. It continued to organize annual conferences, build up the library, and publish a periodical.

During World War II, for technical and ideological reasons, the work of the International Peace Bureau came to a halt, and its assets were temporarily placed under the supervision of the Swiss authorities. In 1946 some of its former member organizations met to reestablish the Bureau and its work. The result was a new international organization called International Liaison Committee of Organizations for Peace (ILCOP) which, after several years of negotiations, was recognized on January 20, 1961, by the Swiss Federal Council as the legal successor to the old International Union of Peace Societies; the assets of the Bureau were given to the ILCOP and its library deposited with the UN in Geneva. Shortly afterwards, ILCOP readopted the name International Peace Bureau which now stands for the international organization as such and for its secretariat in Geneva; administration of its funds was transferred to the newly established Foundation

1. IPB, «General Background», p. 2.

ILCOP which has the character and function of a legal body under Swiss law.

Today membership is open to:

(a)   international organizations working primarily for peace and international cooperation;

(b)   national peace councils or other federations coordinating the peace movement of their respective countries;

(c)   international organizations having the promotion of peace and international cooperation as one of their aims;

(d)   national and local organizations working directly for peace and international cooperation, or having the work for peace as one of their aims.

Associate membership without voting right is open to organizations and individuals who support the aim of the International Peace Bureau[1].

The present aim of the International Peace Bureau is «to serve the cause of peace by the promotion of international cooperation and nonviolent solution of international conflicts». This is much the same as its original objective, but must now in most cases be interpreted and implemented differently to meet the current international situation. The Bureau still works to facilitate communication between different national and international peace organizations, and between these organizations and governmental and intergovernmental bodies, doing so in accordance with its established principle of non-alignment with such bodies. It still acts as a clearing house for ideas, and it still coordinates the activities of different peace organizations, but only insofar as member groups desire it–it no longer acts as a permanent agent, decision-maker, or spokesman for the peace movement as a whole. It still makes the organization of international conferences the core of its activity, but such conferences are now more «working parties or seminars» than congresses, and they concentrate on the different aspects of one specific subject or project rather than trying to give a general survey of all problems, as former conferences normally did.

In recent years the Bureau has adopted four procedural steps in handling these projects: preparation of available documentation in a «Working Paper»; the conference itself (often preceded by a smaller preparatory seminar), whose participants are recruited to secure attendance from three categories: «(1) representatives of governments and governmental bodies, (2) peace research workers and other experts in the specific field, (3) representatives

1. Taken from Ulrich Herz, *The International Peace Bureau*, p. 10.

of peace organizations and other national and international organizations concerned with the specific subject of the conference»[1]; the editing, publishing, and distributing of the Conference Report, completed with any further documentation collected; and the final follow-up on the Conference findings and decisions, which in many cases involves transmitting proposals to certain governments or certain intergovernmental bodies.

Such projects require an average of two to four years for completion, with the Bureau being able to handle a maximum of two at one time. Recent projects have included that on UN peace-keeping operations, initiated by the Bureau, and the NGO [Non-Governmental Organizations] Information Seminar on Disarmament, which it co-sponsored; the Seminar's other sponsors have continued action in this field, and since February, 1970, IPB has been the secretariat for the Special NGO Committee on Disarmament. In process are projects entitled «The Right to Refuse Military Service and Orders» (begun in 1968 as IPB's contribution to the «International Year for Human Rights» when the UN so designated that year) and «Alternatives to Military Defense».

Selected Bibliography

Ducommun, Élie, «The Permanent International Bureau of Peace» in *The Independent*, 55 (March 19, 1903) 660–661.

Gobat, Albert, *Développement du Bureau international permanent de la paix*. Bern, 1910.

Herz, Ulrich, *The International Peace Bureau: History, Aims, Activities*. Geneva, 1969.

International Peace Bureau, «General Background (Summer, 1970)» [mimeographed document].

La Fontaine, Henri, *Bibliographie de la paix et de l'arbitrage international*. Tome 1, *Mouvement pacifique*, pp. 150–152. Monaco, Institut International de la Paix, 1904.

1. IPB, *op.cit.*, p. 4.

Peace 1911

TOBIAS MICHAEL CAREL ASSER

ALFRED HERMANN FRIED

Presentation

by Jørgen Gunnarsson Løvland*, Chairman of the Nobel Committee

Tobias Michael Carel Asser was born in 1838 in Amsterdam where he became professor of commercial law and later of international law from 1862 to 1893 when he was named a member of the Council of State. He soon became legal counselor to the Dutch Foreign Office and in 1904 minister of state. He holds honorary doctorates from the Universities of Cambridge, Edinburgh, and Bologna. He was a Dutch delegate at the two Peace Conferences at The Hague[1] and, among other things, arbitrator in the dispute between Russia and the U.S.A. on the Bering Straits, which he heard in 1902[2], and in the dispute between the U.S.A. and Mexico on the Pious Fund of the Californias, which was brought to the Arbitration Court at The Hague (1902)[3].

* Mr. Løvland welcomed the audience to the award ceremony held on December 10, 1911, in the auditorium of the Nobel Institute and then called upon Prof. Fredrik Stang (later a member of the Committee himself), who addressed the assembly on «Nordic Cooperation in Unifying Civil Law». This address was followed by Mr. Løvland's announcement that the Nobel Peace Prize for 1911 was to be shared by Mr. Asser and Mr. Fried, neither of whom was able to be present at the ceremony and neither of whom delivered a Nobel lecture. Mr. Løvland then gave a biographical account of each laureate and, since 1911 was the tenth anniversary of the first prize presentation, concluded with some brief comments on the basis used for awarding the prizes. His account of Mr. Asser is given here as the presentation speech. The translation is based on the Norwegian text of it (insofar as the reporter was able to reproduce it) in the Oslo *Aftenposten* of December 11, 1911.

1. Held in 1899 and 1907.
2. Mr. Asser decided in favor of the U.S. which had contended that damages for Russian seizure of 5 sealing vessels should be assessed on the basis of the average annual catch; although not taken to the Hague Tribunal, the case was settled according to the code of that court.
3. The so-called Pious Fund, which was set up in the 18th century to aid Catholicism in the Californias and which, after 1842, was controlled by Mexico, became the cause of a dispute when Mexico, having ceded Upper California to the U.S. in 1848, thereafter refused to pay the bishops of Upper California their share of the Fund's interest. The laureate was one of the 4 arbitrators in the case, the first ever submitted to the Hague Tribunal; the award was to the U.S. and the bishops.

He was one of the founders of the Institut de droit international (1873)[1] and has been one of its most active and influential members.

Asser has above all been a practical legal statesman. He holds a position in the sphere of international private law similar to that enjoyed by the famous French jurist Louis Renault[2] in international public law. Indeed, his public activity has overshadowed his scholarly writing, which is of great importance in its own right. As a pioneer in the field of international legal relations, he has earned a reputation as one of the leaders in modern jurisprudence. It is therefore only natural that his countrymen should see him as a successor to or reviver of The Netherlands' pioneer work in international law in the seventeenth century[3].

It was at his instigation that the Dutch government summoned the four conferences at The Hague in 1893, 1894, 1900, and 1904 on international private law; all presided over by Asser, they prepared the ground for conventions which would establish uniformity in international private law and thus lead to greater public security and justice in international relations. The responsibility then passed to individual countries to bring their national legislation into line. Asser has also proposed that other nations follow The Netherlands' example by appointing permanent commissions to prepare the work of the Conferences. «By doing this», he said in 1900, «the foundations will be laid for an international organization which, without interfering with the complete autonomy of the nations in the domain of legislation, would contribute greatly to the codification of international civil law within the not too distant future.» As a result of these conferences, seven Conventions have been concluded on different aspects of civil procedure (legal aid) and of family law; five of these have been subscribed to by Norway.

1. Recipient of the Nobel Peace Prize for 1904.
2. Louis Renault (1843–1918), co-recipient of the Nobel Peace Prize for 1907.
3. The first definitive text on international law, *De jure belli ac pacis* (1625), was written by a Dutchman, Hugo Grotius (1583–1645).

Biography

Tobias Michael Carel Asser (April 28, 1838–July 29, 1913) was born in Amsterdam into a family with a tradition in the field of law, both his father and his grandfather having been well-established lawyers and his uncle having served as the Dutch minister of justice. A brilliant student, young Asser won a competition in 1857 with his thesis *On the Economic Conception of Value*. Although this achievement may have confirmed an early decision to take up a career in the business world, he changed his mind and went on to study law at the Athenaeum in Amsterdam, taking a doctor's degree in 1860 at the age of twenty-two. In that same year, the Dutch government appointed him a member of an international commission which was to negotiate the abolition of tolls on the Rhine River.

Asser practiced law for a brief period but devoted his life mainly to teaching, scholarship, and politics. In 1862 he accepted a teaching position at the Athenaeum as professor of private law; in 1876, when the institution became the University of Amsterdam, he continued as a professor of international and commercial law while continuing a reduced legal practice.

Early in his scholarly career, Asser turned to the problems of international law, dedicating himself particularly to the area of international private law in which he soon acquired a position of leadership. Believing that legal conflicts between nations could best be solved by international conferences which would agree on common solutions to be implemented by each participating nation, he persuaded the Dutch government to call several conferences of European powers to work out a codification of international private law. Attended by representatives of most of the countries of Europe, the first two of these conferences, held at The Hague in 1893 and 1894 and over which Asser presided, drew up a treaty, made effective in May, 1899, establishing a uniform international procedure for conducting civil trials. Asser also presided over the conferences of 1900 and 1904, which resulted in several important treaties governing international family law, including matters relating to marriage, divorce, legal separation, and guardianship of minors.

Asser's interest in international law led him, along with the Belgian Gustave Rolin-Jaequemyns and the Englishman John Westlake, to found a journal of international law, *Revue de droit international et de législation comparée* in 1869. Four years later he was one of those invited by Rolin-Jaequemyns to take part in the small international conference at Ghent which founded the Institute of International Law, an organization which Asser later headed. Active in efforts to establish an academy of international law, Asser died before such an academy became a reality at The Hague in 1923.

Asser's contributions to the literature of law were a vital part of his efforts. Among his more important works are *Schets van het internationaal Privaatrecht* (1877) and *Schets van het Nederlandsche Handelsrecht* (1904).

Asser also participated in the practical politics of international affairs. He accepted a position as legal adviser to the Netherlands Ministry of Foreign Affairs in 1875; became a member of the Council of State, the highest administrative body in the government, in 1893; served as president of the State Commission for International Law beginning in 1898; acted as his country's delegate to the Hague Peace Conferences of 1899 and 1907, there urging that the principle of compulsory arbitration be introduced in the economic area; held a post as minister without portfolio from 1904 until his death.

Noted as a negotiator, Asser was involved during this period from 1875 to 1913 in virtually every treaty concluded by the Dutch government. One of his triumphs was the securing of a seat for Spain and for The Netherlands beside France, England, Germany, Austria, Italy, Russia, and Turkey on the Suez Canal Commission, the body that drew up the Suez Canal Convention of 1888 guaranteeing the canal's neutrality. Noted also as an arbiter of international disputes, he sat as a member of the Permanent Court of Arbitration that heard the first case to come before that court–the Pious Fund dispute between the United States and Mexico (1902).

Asser was an accomplished linguist, handling effectively the German, French, and English languages, as well as his native Dutch. For his scholarship and its application to the affairs of government he was awarded honorary degrees by the Universities of Edinburgh, Cambridge, Bologna, and Berlin. Housed in the Peace Palace at The Hague, a library of international law which he gathered with the help of contributions from twenty countries has been named «The Asser Collection».

Selected Bibliography

Asser, Tobias M. C., *La Convention de La Haye du 14 novembre 1896 relative à la procédure civile*. Haarlem, Bohn, 1901.

Asser, Tobias M. C., *Schets van het Internationaal Privaatrecht*. Haarlem, Bohn, 1877.

Asser, Tobias M. C., *Schets van het Nederlandsche Handelsrecht*. Haarlem, Bohn, 1904.

Asser, Tobias M. C., *Studiën op het Gebied van Recht en Staat (1858–1888)*. Haarlem, Bohn, 1889.

Encyclopaedia Judaica.

«Der Nobelpreis 1911», in *Die Friedens-Warte*, 13 (December, 1911) 373–374.

«T. M. C. Asser», in *American Journal of International Law*, 8 (1914) 343–344.

Presentation

by Jørgen Gunnarsson Løvland*, Chairman of the Nobel Committee

Alfred Hermann Fried was born in Vienna in 1864, but most of his activities have been carried on in Germany. Since 1891 he has devoted his whole life to work for peace, one of the few men to do so. Fried, who was first a bookseller and then a journalist, is a self-educated man who, with true German persistence and application, worked his way up until he had mastered scholarly writing. He has probably been the most industrious literary pacifist in the past twenty years. In 1892 he founded the Deutsche Friedensgesellschaft [German Peace Society] and for a time edited its journals. Since 1899 he has been publishing his own monthly periodical *Die Friedenswarte*[1], which he has gradually turned into the best journal in the peace movement, with excellent leading articles and news of topical international problems. Fried has considered it his task to win over the German university faculties of international law and history to the cause of peace and to persuade them to contribute to his periodical, and he may now be said to have succeeded. Among the many who have lent their support to Fried's candidacy for the Nobel Peace Prize are Professors L. von Bar, Lamprecht, Niemeyer, Schucking, Rehm, and Lentner[2]. Fried's name was also proposed by the Swedish Parliamentary Peace Group through Baron Bonde and by the Swedish Peace and Arbitration Association through another member of Parliament.

According to Fried, the foundation of the peace movement should be

* Mr. Løvland gave biographical data on both prizewinners for 1911 in his presentation speech at the award ceremony in the Norwegian Nobel Institute on December 10, 1911. The second part of the speech, that concerning Mr. Fried, is given here. The translation is based on the Norwegian text of it (insofar as the reporter was able to reproduce it) in the Oslo *Aftenposten* of December 11, 1911. (For a note on other details of the occasion, see p. 233.) Mr. Fried was not present and never delivered a Nobel lecture.

1. This replaced *Die Waffen Nieder*, published by Fried and edited by Bertha von Suttner.
2. All of these were scholars and experts in law (particularly international law) or in history and political science.

the legal and political *organization* of international life. He finds the beginnings of an efficient organization in the existing international bureaus and wants new ones to be created for all fields of international relations. The existing international anarchy (armed peace) will gradually disappear with increased organization and be succeeded by an ordered state of peace. Because of this viewpoint Fried places less emphasis on combating war; the method generally employed by friends of peace, that of arousing disgust at the idea of war, is not in his opinion sufficient. Instead of fighting the symptoms of war, he wants first and foremost to fight its cause, namely, the anarchy in international relations. Fried has argued his theory in a work entitled *The Basis of Pacifism*[1] (Freiburg, 1908).

In addition to innumerable contributions to the Austro-German press, Fried has published a large number of individual monographs and books on pacifism. Among these are: *Das Abrüstungs-Problem* (Berlin, 1904); *Der kranke Krieg* (Leipzig, 1909), a collection of his best leading articles in *Die Friedenswarte*; and *Pan-Amerika* (Berlin, 1910), a meritorious scholarly account of the efforts organized by the Pan-American Bureau[2] in Washington. His best known work is his *Handbuch der Friedensbewegung* (1905) of which Part I came out this year in a new and expanded edition. It is an account of the fundamental problems of the peace movement, giving reports on peace conferences and the position of arbitration, and containing an interesting historical review of the peace movement, with biographies of outstanding friends of peace and a list of societies and other organizations belonging to the movement.

Fried's agitation played a part in bringing about the Morocco Pact[3].

---

1. The original German title was *Die Grundlagen des revolutionären Pacifismus* (Tübingen: Mohr, 1908). Later editions were entitled *Die Grundlagen des ursächlichen Pazifismus*.
2. The International Bureau of American Republics became the Pan American Union in 1910; today it serves as the secretariat of the Organization of American States (OAS) formed in 1948.
3. The latest of several Moroccan crises–brought on by European rivalry, especially between Germany and France, for territorial power in Morocco–had just been settled by the Convention of November 4, 1911, which provided that Germany would allow France a free hand in Morocco in exchange for part of the French Congo.

Biography

Alfred Hermann Fried (November 11, 1864–May 5, 1921) was born in Vienna, but pursued most of his active journalistic career in Germany. Leaving school at the age of fifteen, he worked in his native city as a bookseller, then a few years later went to Berlin where he opened his own press in 1887.

Influenced by Bertha von Suttner, Fried became interested in the peace movement, founded the Deutsche Friedensgesellschaft [German Peace Society], and edited its major publication, *Monatliche Friedenskorrespondenz* [Monthly Peace Correspondence], from 1894 to 1899. Having persuaded Baroness von Suttner to serve as editor, he started a peace journal, naming it *Die Waffen Nieder!* [Lay Down Your Arms], the title of the Baroness' famous antiwar novel[1]. In 1899 this was replaced by *Die Friedenswarte* [The Peace Watch], which he edited and which Norman Angell called «the most efficient periodical of the Pacifist movement in the world»[2]. This publication, which was addressed to an audience of intellectuals, has had a continuous history to the present time; edited by Fried until his death in 1921, then by Hans Wehberg, it was moved to Zürich in 1933. In 1905 Fried founded another journal, *Annuaire de la vie internationale*, which reflected his growing interest in international cooperation, particularly as exemplified by the Pan-American movement and the work of the Hague Conferences.

The peace literature which flowed from his pen–reports, editorials, essays, pamphlets, books–was extensive, but he also contributed to the cause his capacity as an organizer. He was a member of the Bern Peace Bureau, secretary of the International Conciliation for Central Europe, and secretary-general of the Union internationale de la presse pour la paix.

The Hague Peace Conference of 1899 was a turning point in the devel-

1. *Die Waffen nieder!* (Leipzig: Pierson, 1889) was translated into every major language and published in hundreds of editions; Bertha von Suttner was the recipient of the Nobel Peace Prize for 1905.
2. In the Preface to Fried's *The German Emperor and the Peace of the World*, p. x; Norman Angell was the recipient of the Nobel Peace Prize for 1933.

opment of Fried's philosophy of pacifism. Thereafter, in his appeals to the German intellectual community he placed more reliance on economic co-operation and political organization among nations as bases for peace, and less upon limitation of armaments and schemes for international justice[1]. «War is not in itself a condition so much as the symptom of a condition, that of international anarchy», he said. «If we wish to substitute for war the settlement of disputes by justice, we must first substitute for the condition of international anarchy a condition of international order.»[2]

Fried's efforts were partly responsible for the founding of the Verband für internationale Verständigung [Society for International Understanding] in 1911. His theory of internationalism did not preclude nationalism. In the Pan-American movement he perceived a model for the preservation of national identity within international organization[3]. In keeping with this position, Fried defended Germany before World War I by chronicling Wilhelm II's positive attitude toward world peace and during the war by refuting what he considered to be unreasonable criticism of Germany in the French, British, and American press.

Fried was in Vienna when war broke out in 1914. Since pacifist activities there were curtailed by government censorship and intolerant public opinion, Fried shifted his organizational and journalistic work to Switzerland. He was active in efforts to ameliorate the conditions of prisoners of war and continued to publish *Die Friedenswarte* as a rallying point for international peace efforts. Accused of treason by the Austrian government, he was unable to return to Vienna until the war's end.

The war over, Fried published *Mein Kriegstagebuch* [My War Journal], a «diary» which he kept during the war years to record his sentiments and his activities, along with those of his colleagues in the peace movement; he expressed dissatisfaction with the peace settlement and organized a journalistic campaign against the Versailles Treaty; he tirelessly pressed the point in his propaganda for peace that the war was proof of the validity of the pacifistic analysis of world politics.

Fried lost what wealth he possessed in the collapse of Austria-Hungary and died in poverty of a lung infection in Vienna at the age of fifty-seven.

---

1. See Alfred Fried, *Die Grundlagen der modernen Wirtschaft und der Krieg* (Berlin, 1908).
2. Alfred Fried, *International Cooperation*, p.3.
3. See Alfred Fried, *Pan-Amerika*.

Selected Bibliography

Fried's library was purchased by Stanford University (Palo Alto, Calif., U.S.A.); a collection of his manuscripts is housed in the Peace Archives of the United Nations Library in Geneva.

Encyclopaedia Judaica.

Fried, Alfred Hermann, *Das Abrüstungs-Problem: Eine Untersuchung.* Berlin, Gutman, 1904.

Fried, Alfred Hermann, *The German Emperor and the Peace of the World,* with a Preface by Norman Angell. London, Hodder & Stoughton, 1912.

Fried, Alfred Hermann, *Die Grundlagen des revolutionären Pacifismus.* Tübingen, Mohr, 1908. Translated into French by Jean Lagorgette as *Les Bases du pacifisme: Le Pacifisme réformiste et le pacifisme «révolutionnaire».* Paris, Pedone, 1909.

Fried, Alfred Hermann, *Handbuch der Friedensbewegung.* Wien, Oesterreichischen Friedensgesellschaft, 1905. 2nd ed., Leipzig, Verlag der «Friedens-Warte», 1911.

Fried, Alfred Hermann, «Intellectual Starvation in Germany and Austria», in *Nation,* 110 (March 20, 1920) 367–368.

Fried, Alfred Hermann, *International Cooperation.* Newcastle-on-Tyne, Richardson [1918].

Fried, Alfred Hermann, *Das internationale Leben der Gegenwart.* Leipzig, Teubner, 1908.

Fried, Alfred Hermann, «The League of Nations: An Ethical Institution», in *Living Age,* 306 (August 21, 1920) 440–443.

Fried, Alfred Hermann, *Mein Kriegstagebuch.* 4Bde. Zürich, Rascher, 1918–1920.

Fried, Alfred Hermann, *Pan-Amerika.* Zürich, Orell-Füssli, 1910.

Fried, Alfred Hermann, *The Restoration of Europe,* transl. by Lewis Stiles Gannett. New York, Macmillan, 1916.

Fried, Alfred Hermann, ed., *Der Weltprotest gegen den versailler Frieden.* Leipzig, Verlag der Neue Geist, 1920.

Fried, Alfred Hermann, *Die zweite Haager Konferenz: Ihre Arbeiten, ihre Ergebnisse, und ihre Bedeutung.* Leipzig, Nachfolger [1908].

Goldscheid, Rudolf, *Alfred Hermann Fried: Eine Sammlung von Gedenkblättern.* Leipzig, 1922.

Schou, August, *Histoire de l'internationalisme III: Du Congrès de Vienne jusqu'à la première guerre mondiale (1914),* pp. 365–368. Publications de l'Institut Nobel Norvégien, Tome VIII. Oslo, Aschehoug, 1963.

Verzeichnis von 1000 Zeitungsartikeln A.H.Frieds zur Friedensbewegung. Berlin, 1908.

Wehberg, Hans, «Alfred Hermann Fried», in *Deutsches Biographisches Jahrbuch.* Band III, 1921.

Wehberg, Hans, «Alfred H.Fried», in *Die Führer der deutschen Friedensbewegung,* pp. 19–23. Leipzig, Oldenburg, 1923.

Wehberg, Hans, «Alfred H.Fried und seine Bedeutung für die pacifistische Wissenschaft», in *Erste Ethische Rundschau* (1914) 10.

Peace 1912

(Prize awarded in 1913)

ELIHU ROOT

Presentation

by Ragnvald Moe*, Secretary to the Nobel Committee

Elihu Root was born on February 15, 1845, in the State of New York and took his degree in law at New York University in 1867. At a later date he studied international law and took his doctorate[1] in 1894. For some years he practiced as an attorney in New York, becoming one of the best in the profession. In August, 1899, he was appointed secretary of war by President McKinley[2] and held that office until 1904. In the following year Roosevelt[3] persuaded him to take over the State Department where he remained until his election to the Senate in 1909.

Root is a man of engaging personality who has tried, with determination and independence, to put his ideals into practice.

In the ten years during which he held office [as secretary of war and secretary of state], he had to settle a number of particularly difficult problems, some of an international character. It was he who was chiefly responsible for organizing affairs in Cuba and in the Philippines after the Spanish-American War[4]. Even more important was his work in bringing about better understanding between the countries of North and South America. When he visited South America in the summer of 1906, he did a great deal to strengthen the Pan-American movement, and in 1908 he founded the

---

* Mr. Moe delivered this speech on the laureate's political career on December 10, 1913, in the Norwegian Nobel Institute after Mr. Løvland, chairman of the Committee, had announced that the Nobel Peace Prize for 1912, reserved in that year, was being awarded to Mr. Root and the prize for 1913 to Henri La Fontaine. Neither laureate was present. The translation is based on the Norwegian reporting of the speech appearing in the Oslo *Morgenposten* of December 11, 1913.

1. It seems likely that this refers, not to a degree resulting from formal study, but to the honorary degree of LL.D. conferred upon the laureate in 1894 by Hamilton College.

2. William McKinley (1843–1901), president of the U.S. (1897–1901).

3. Theodore Roosevelt (1858–1919), president of the U.S. (1901–1909); recipient of the Nobel Peace Prize for 1906.

4. 1898.

Pan-American Bureau in New York[1]. His strenuous efforts to improve relations between the small Central American countries have borne splendid
fruit. The most difficult problem with which Root had to deal while secretary of state, however, was the dispute with Japan over the status of Japanese
immigrants. Although a final solution of this dispute eluded him, his work[2]
on it was nevertheless of great value.

After he had left the government, Root gave himself heart and soul to
the cause of peace, and he is now president of the great Carnegie Peace
Foundation[3]. [As a senator] Root was one of the most energetic champions
of Taft's[4] proposal for an unconditional arbitration treaty between the
U.S.A. and Great Britain; and in the dispute concerning tolls for the Panama Canal, he supported the English interpretation of the Hay-Pauncefote
Treaty, opposing special privileges for American shipping[5]. When he spoke
on this in the Senate last spring, he gained the admiration of all friends of
peace.

1. Washington, D.C., rather than New York, would be correct here if, as seems probable, the reference is to the laureate's part in the 1908 cornerstone ceremonies for the
Pan-American building which thereafter housed the Bureau; Root had proposed the
building and had solicited the money for it from Andrew Carnegie.
2. The so-called Gentlemen's Agreement, negotiated by Root in 1908, was superseded
by the Immigration Bill of 1924.
3. Founded by Andrew Carnegie (1835–1919), American industrialist, in 1910 with
a gift of $10,000,000.
4. William Howard Taft (1857–1930), president of the U.S. (1909–1913).
5. The Hay-Pauncefote Treaty (1901) between the U.S. and Great Britain provided
that the Panama Canal be open to all nations on equal terms; the U.S. Panama Canal
Act (passed in 1912 and repealed in 1914) exempted U.S. ships from tolls.

ELIHU ROOT

Towards Making Peace Permanent

*Nobel Lecture**

The humanitarian purpose of Alfred Nobel in establishing the peace prize which bears his name was doubtless not merely to reward those who should promote peace among nations, but to stimulate thought upon the means and methods best adapted, under the changing conditions of future years, to approach and ultimately attain the end he so much desired.

The apparent simplicity of the subject is misleading. Recognition of the horrors of war and the blessings of peace, acceptance of the dogma «War is wrong and to keep the peace a duty», are so universal that upon the surface it seems only necessary to state a few incontrovertible truths and to press them upon the attention of mankind, in order to have war end and peace reign perpetually.

Yet the continual recurrence of war and the universally increasing preparations for war based upon expectation of it among nations all of whom declare themselves in favor of peace, indicate that intellectual acceptance of peace doctrine is not sufficient to control conduct, and that a general feeling in favor of peace, however sincere, does not furnish a strong enough motive to withstand the passions which lead to war when a cause of quarrel has arisen. The methods of peace propaganda which aim at establishing peace doctrine by argument and by creating a feeling favorable to peace in general seem to fall short of reaching the springs of human action and of dealing with the causes of the conduct which they seek to modify. It is much like

* In 1913, Mr. Root was awarded the Nobel Peace Prize for the year 1912, the prize having been reserved in that year. Mr. Root agreed to speak in Oslo on September 8, 1914, but was prevented from doing so by the outbreak of World War I. This text is taken from Elihu Root's *Addresses on International Subjects*, edited by Robert Bacon and James B. Scott (Cambridge: Harvard University Press, 1916), pp. 153–174. Of this speech, the editors say: «The address prepared by Mr. Root for that occasion [acknowledging the prize in Oslo on September 8] is here printed exactly as it was prepared for delivery before the outbreak of the war, without the change of a word or syllable» (p. 154). The speech was not given a title; the title used here is a thematic phrase taken from the eighth paragraph.

treating the symptoms of disease instead of ascertaining and dealing with the cause of the symptoms. The mere assemblage of peace loving people to interchange convincing reasons for their common faith, mere exhortation and argument to the public in favor of peace in general fall short of the mark.

They are useful, they serve to strenghten the faith of the participants, they tend very gradually to create a new standard of conduct, just as exhortations to be good and demonstrations that honesty is the best policy have a certain utility by way of suggestion. But they do not, as a rule, reach or extirpate or modify the causes of war.

Occasionally some man with exceptional power of statement or of feeling and possessed by the true missionary spirit, will deliver a message to the world, putting old truths in such a way as to bite into the consciousness of civilized peoples and move mankind forward a little, with a gain never to be altogether lost. But the mere repetition of the obvious by good people of average intelligence, while not without utility and not by any means to be despised as an agency for peace, nevertheless is subject to the drawback that the unregenerate world grows weary of iteration and reacts in the wrong direction. The limitation upon this mode of promoting peace lies in the fact that it consists in an appeal to the civilized side of man, while war is the product of forces proceeding from man's original savage nature. To deal with the true causes of war one must begin by recognizing as of prime relevancy to the solution of the problem the familiar fact that civilization is a partial, incomplete, and, to a great extent, superficial modification of barbarism. The point of departure of the process to which we wish to contribute is the fact that war is the natural reaction of human nature in the savage state, while peace is the result of acquired characteristics. War was forced upon mankind in his original civil and social condition. The law of the survival of the fittest led inevitably to the survival and predominance of the men who were effective in war and who loved it because they were effective. War was the avenue to all that mankind desired. Food, wives, a place in the sun, freedom from restraint and oppression, wealth of comfort, wealth of luxury, respect, honor, power, control over others, were sought and attained by fighting. Nobody knows through how many thousands of years fighting men have made a place for themselves while the weak and peaceable have gone to the wall. Love of fighting was bred in the blood of the race because those who did not love fighting were not suited to their environment and perished. Grotius himself sets war first in the title of his great work,

De jure belli ac pacis [1], as if, in his mind, war was the general and usual condition with which he was to deal, and peace the occasional and incidental field of international relations. And indeed the work itself deals chiefly with war and only incidentally with peaceful relations.

In attempting to bring mankind to a condition of permanent peace in which war will be regarded as criminal conduct, just as civilized communities have been brought to a condition of permanent order, broken only by criminals who war against society, we have to deal with innate ideas, impulses, and habits, which became a part of the caveman's nature by necessity from the conditions under which he lived; and these ideas and impulses still survive more or less dormant under the veneer of civilization, ready to be excited to action by events often of the most trifling character. As Lord Bacon says, «Nature is often hidden, sometimes overcome, seldom extinguished.»[2] To eradicate or modify or curb the tendencies which thus survive among civilized men is not a matter of intellectual conviction or training. It is a matter primarily of development of character and the shifting of standards of conduct – a long, slow process in which advance is to be measured, not by days and years, but by generations and centuries in the life of nations.

The attractive idea that we can now have a parliament of man with authority to control the conduct of nations by legislation or an international police force with power to enforce national conformity to rules of right conduct is a counsel of perfection. The world is not ready for any such thing, and it cannot be made ready except by the practical surrender of the independence of nations, which lies at the basis of the present social organization of the civilized world. Such a system would mean that each nation was liable to be lawfully controlled and coerced by a majority of alien powers. That majority alone could determine when and for what causes and to what ends the control and coercion should be exercised. Human nature must have come much nearer perfection than it is now, or will be in many generations, to exclude from such a control prejudice, selfishness, ambition, and injustice. An attempt to prevent war in this way would breed war, for it would destroy local self-government and drive nations to war for liberty. There is no nation in the world which would seriously consider a proposal so shocking to the national pride and patriotism of its people.

1. Hugo Grotius (1583–1645), Dutch jurist; published *De jure belli ac pacis* (1625), the first definitive text on international law.
2. From «Of Nature in Men», *Essays* (1597) by Francis Bacon.

To help in the most practical and efficient way towards making peace permanent, it is needful to inquire with some analysis what are the specific motives and impulses, the proximate causes which, under the present conditions of the civilized world, urge nations to the point where the war passion seizes upon them. And then we should inquire what are the influences which naturally tend or may be made to tend towards checking the impulse, destroying the motive, preventing the proximate cause, before passion has become supreme and it is too late.

It is to be observed that every case of war averted is a gain in general, for it helps to form a habit of peace, and community habits long continued become standards of conduct. The life of the community conforms to an expectation of their continuance, and there comes to be an instinctive opposition to any departure from them.

The first and most obvious cause for international controversy which suggests itself is in the field of international rights and obligations. Claims of right and insistence upon obligations may depend upon treaty stipulations, or upon the rules of international law, or upon the sense of natural justice applied to the circumstances of a particular case, or upon disputed facts. Upon all these there are continually arising controversies as to what are the true facts; what is the rule of international law applicable to the case; what is the true interpretation of the treaty; what is just and fair under the circumstances. This category does not by any means cover the entire field out of which causes of war arise, but no one should underestimate its importance. Small differences often grow into great quarrels, and honest differences of opinion frequently produce controversies in which national *amour propre* is involved and national honor, dignity, and prestige are supposed to be at stake. Rival claimants to an almost worthless strip of land along a disputed boundary, a few poor fishermen contesting each others' rights to set nets in disputed waters, may break into violence which will set whole nations aflame with partisanship upon either side. Reparation demanded for injury to a citizen or an insult to a flag in foreign territory may symbolize in the feeling of a great people their national right to independence, to respect, and to an equal place in the community of nations. The people of a country, wholly mistaken as to their national rights, honestly ignorant of their international obligations, may become possessed of a real sense of injustice, of deep resentment, and of a sincere belief that the supreme sacrifice of war is demanded by love of country, its liberty and independence, when in fact their belief has no just foundation whatever.

In this field the greatest advance is being made towards reducing and preventing in a practical and effective way the causes of war, and this advance is proceeding along several different lines. First, by providing for the peaceable settlement of such controversies by submission to an impartial tribunal. Up to this time that provision has taken the form of arbitration, with which we are all familiar. There have been occasional international arbitrations from very early times, but arbitration as a system, a recognized and customary method of diplomatic procedure rather than an exceptional expedient, had its origin in the Hague Conference of 1899. It is interesting to recall the rather contemptuous reception accorded to the Convention for the Pacific Settlement of International Disputes concluded at that conference, and to the Permanent Court at The Hague which it created[1]. The convention was not obligatory. No power was bound to comply with it. The cynicism with which the practical diplomatist naturally regards the idealist pronounced it a dead letter. But the convention expressed, and, by expressing, established a new standard of international conduct which practical idealism had long been gradually approaching, for which thoughtful men and women in all civilized lands had been vaguely groping, which the more advanced nations welcomed and the more backward nations were ashamed to reject. Let me quote the recitals with which the delegates prefaced their work:

«Animated by a strong desire to concert for the maintenance of the general peace;

Resolved to second by their best efforts the friendly settlement of international disputes;

Recognizing the solidarity which unites the members of the society of civilized nations;

Desirous of extending the empire of law, and of strengthening the appreciation of international justice;

Convinced that the permanent institution of a Court of Arbitration, accessible to all, in the midst of the independent Powers, will contribute effectively to this result;

Having regard to the advantages attending the general and regular organization of arbitral procedure;

Sharing the opinion of the august initiator of the International Peace

1. See Gobat's Nobel lecture and Renault's Nobel lecture, pp. 31–35; 155–158.

Conference that it is expedient to record in an international agreement the principles of equity and right, on which are based the security of states and the welfare of peoples...»[1].

These declarations, although enforced by no binding stipulation, nevertheless have become principles of action in international affairs because, through the progress of civilization and the influence of many generations of devoted spirits in the cause of humanity, the world had become ready for the setting up of the standard. The convention would have been a dead letter if the world had not been made ready for it, and, because the world was ready, conformity to the standard year by year has become more universal and complete. Since this convention, which was binding upon no state, 113 obligatory general treaties of arbitration have been made between powers who have taken part in the Hague Conferences, and sixteen international controversies have been heard and decided, or are pending before that tribunal according to the last report of the Administrative Council of the Court.

Quite apart from the statistics of cases actually heard or pending, it is impossible to estimate the effect produced by the existence of this court, for the fact that there is a court to which appeal may be made always leads to the settlement of far more controversies than are brought to judgment. Nor can we estimate the value of having this system a part of the common stock of knowledge of civilized men, so that, when an international controversy arises, the first reaction is not to consider war but to consider peaceful litigation.

Plainly, the next advance to be urged along this line is to pass on from an arbitral tribunal, the members of which are specifically selected from the general list of the court for each case, and whose service is but an incident in the career of a diplomatist or a publicist, to a permanent court composed of judges who devote their entire time to the performance of judicial duties and proceed in accordance with a sense of judicial obligation, not to adjust or compromise differences, but to decide upon rights in accordance with the facts and the law.

Long steps in this direction were made in the Second Hague Conference by the convention for the establishment of a permanent international prize court and by the formulation and adoption of a draft convention relative to

1. These «recitals» constitute the preamble to the Convention for the Pacific Settlement of International Disputes.

the creation of a general judicial arbitration court. This draft convention lacked nothing of completion except an agreement upon the method by which the judges were to be selected. Towards the creation of such a court the best efforts of those who wish to promote peace should be directed.

The second line of advance in this same field of international controversy is in pressing forward the development of international law and the agreement of nations upon its rules. Lord Mansfield[1] described the law of nations as «founded upon justice, equity, convenience, the reason of the thing, and confirmed by long usage». There are multitudes of events liable to occur frequently in the intercourse of nations, regarding which there has never been any agreement as to what is just, equitable, or convenient, and, as to many of the classes of controversy, different views are held by different nations, so that in a large part of the field with which an arbitral tribunal or international court should deal there is really no law to be applied. Where there is no law, a submission to arbitration or to judicial decision is an appeal, not to the rule of law, but to the unknown opinions or predilections of the men who happen to be selected to decide. The development of the peaceable settlement of international disputes by the decision of impartial tribunals waits therefore upon the further development of international law by a more complete establishment of known and accepted rules for the government of international conduct.

In this direction also great progress has been made within recent years. The ordinary process of reaching rules of international law through the universal assent of nations, expressed as particular cases arise from time to time in the ordinary course of international affairs, is so slow that, instead of making progress towards a comprehensive law of nations by such a method, the progress of the law has been outstripped by the changes of condition in international affairs, so that the law has been growing less and less adequate to settle the questions continually arising. The Declaration of Paris, in 1856, by a few simple rules[2], dealing not with particular cases but looking to the future through an agreement of the powers signing the convention, was a new departure in the method of forming international law. That method

1. William Murray, first Earl of Mansfield (1705–1793), British jurist and member of Parliament.
2. The «rules» were: (1) privateering is abolished; (2) the neutral flag covers enemy goods, except for contraband; (3) neutral goods, except for contraband, are not liable to seizure when under an enemy flag; (4) a blockade to be binding must be effective in fact.

has developed into the action of the two Hague Conferences of 1899 and 1907, which were really lawmaking bodies, establishing, by the unanimous vote of the powers, rules of conduct[1] for the future, covering extensive portions of the field of international conduct. The action of the Hague Conferences would have been impossible if it had not been for the long continued and devoted labors of the Institut de droit international[2], which, in its annual meetings for forty years, has brought together the leaders of thought in the science of the law of nations in all the countries of the civilized world to discuss unofficially, with a free and full expression of personal opinion, the unsettled problems as to what the law is and ought to be. The conclusions of that body furnished to the successive Hague Conferences the matured results of years of well-directed labor and bore the same relation to the deliberations of the conferences as the report of a committee of a legislative body in furnishing the basis for deliberation and action. Their work should be encouraged and their example should be followed.

Further Hague Conferences should be insisted upon. They should be made to recur at regular periods without requiring the special initiative of any country. The process of formulating and securing agreement upon rules of international law should be pressed forward in every direction.

There is a third line of progress, little, if any, less important than the two already mentioned, and that is the instruction of students and of the great bodies of the people of civilized countries in the knowledge of international law. Under the modern development of constitutional governments, with varying degrees of extension of suffrage, more and more the people who cast the ballots determine the issues of peace and war. No government now embarks in war without the assurance of popular support. It is not uncommon in modern times to see governments straining every nerve to keep the peace, and the people whom they represent, with patriotic enthusiasm and resentment over real or fancied wrongs, urging them forward to war. Nothing is more important in the preservation of peace than to secure among the great mass of the people living under constitutional government a just conception of the rights which their nation has against others and of the duties their nation owes to others. The popular tendency is to listen approvingly to the most extreme statements and claims of politicians and orators who seek popularity by declaring their own country right in every-

1. For a discussion of many of these rules of conduct, see the Nobel lectures given by Gobat and Renault, pp. 30–38; 143–166.
2. Founded in 1873, the Institute received the Nobel Peace Prize for 1904.

thing and other countries wrong in everything. Honest people, mistakenly believing in the justice of their cause, are led to support injustice. To meet this tendency there should be not merely definite standards of law to be applied to international relations, but there should be general public understanding of what those standards are. Of course it is not possible that all the people of any country can become familiar with international law, but there may be such knowledge and leadership of opinion in every country on the part of the most intelligent and best educated men that in every community mistaken conceptions can be corrected and a true view of rights and obligations inculcated. To attain this end much has been done and much is in contemplation. Societies of international law have been formed in many countries for the discussion of international questions and the publication and distribution of the results. Many journals of international law have been established and are rapidly increasing their circulation and influence. More and more colleges and universities are establishing chairs and giving instruction in international law to their students. A further step is about to be taken at The Hague by the establishment there of an international school of international law[1] to which scholars from all over the civilized world will come and in which the great masters of the science have undertaken to give instruction. There can be no better augury for the success of the new institution than the fact that it found its origin in the general enthusiasm of Ludwig von Bar of Göttingen, of Otfried Nippold of Frankfort, of Demetrius Sturdza of Roumania, and of T.M.C. Asser of Holland; and that it has for its president Louis Renault of France[2]. The distinctive feature of this new departure is that it will bring together teachers and students from many countries so that their intercourse and instruction will tend towards the unification of rules and the establishment of a general standard of law, instead of perpetuating the differing and often antagonistic conceptions which obtain within the limits of different nations.

Along all these lines of practical effort for peace in the development of

---

1. The Academy of International Law was established at The Hague in 1923, with an administrative council made up of members of different nations.
2. Karl Ludwig von Bar (1836–1913), German jurist and scholar of international law; Otfried Nippold (1864–1936), German jurist, pacifist, and internationalist; Demetrius Sturdza (1833–1914), premier of Roumania (1895–1896; 1897–1899; 1901–1906; 1907–1909) and writer on international issues; Tobias M.C. Asser (1838–1913), co-recipient of the Nobel Peace Prize for 1911; Louis Renault (1843–1918), co-recipient of the Nobel Peace Prize for 1907.

arbitration and judicial decision in the development of a definite system of law, determining the rights and obligations of nations, and in the enlightenment of the civilized nations as to what their rights and obligations are, the present generation has rendered a service in the cause of peace surpassing that of many centuries gone before, and in further development along these same lines the present generation has before it a golden opportunity for further service.

There is, however, another class of substantive causes of war which the agencies I have described do not reach directly. This comprises acts done or demanded in pursuance of national policy, and ordinarily either for the enlargement or protection of territory or for trade or industrial advantage. The conduct of a nation under such a policy is often regarded by other nations as unwarranted aggression or as threatening their safety or their rights. Illustrations of this kind of question are to be found in the protean forms of the Eastern question and of the balance of power in Europe, in the assertion of the Monroe Doctrine by the United States; in the position of Germany regarding the settlement of Morocco before the Conference of Algeciras; in the attitude of Great Britain regarding Agadir after that conference. It is plain that, under the present organization of civilization in independent nationalities, questions of public policy supposed to be vital cannot be submitted to arbitration because that would be an abdication of independence and the placing of government *pro tanto* in the hands of others. The independence of a state involves that state's right to determine its own domestic policy and to decide what is essential to its own safety.

It does not follow, however, that we are without opportunity to promote and strengthen specific influences tending to diminish or prevent causes of war of this description. In the first place, when there is a policy of intentional aggression, inspired by a desire to get possession of the territory or the trade of another country, right or wrong, a pretext is always sought. No nation now sets forth to despoil another upon the avowed ground that it desires the spoils. Some ground of justification is always alleged. The wolf always charges the lamb with muddying the stream. The frank and simple days of the Roman proconsul and of the robber baron have passed, and three things have happened: first, there has come to be a public opinion of the world; second, that opinion has set up a new standard of national conduct which condemns unjustified aggression; and third, the public opinion of the world punishes the violation of its standard. It has not been very long since the people of each country were concerned almost exclusively with their own affairs, and, with but few individual exceptions, neither knew nor cared what was going on outside their own boundaries. All that has changed. The spread of popular education; the enormous increase in the production and circulation of newspapers and periodicals and cheap books; the competition of the press, which ranges the world for news; the telegraph, which carries instantly knowledge of all important events everywhere to all parts of the world; the new mobility of mankind, which, availing itself of the new means of travel by steamship and railroad, with its new freedom under the recently recognized right of expatriation and the recently established right of free travel, moves to and fro by the million across the boundaries of the nations; the vast extension of international commerce; the recognition of interdependence of the peoples of different nations engendered by this commerce and this intercourse; their dependence upon each other for the supply of their needs and for the profitable disposal of their products, for the preservation of health, for the promotion of morals and for the increase of knowledge and the advance of thought–all these are creating an international community of knowledge and interest, of thought and feeling. In the hundreds of international associations reported by Senator La Fontaine's L'Office central at Brussels[1], men of all nations are learning to think internationally about science and morals and hygiene and religion and society and business. Gradually, everything that happens in the world is coming to be of interest everywhere in the world, and, gradually, thoughtful men and women everywhere are sitting in judgment upon the conduct of all nations. Some very crass and indefensible things have been done by nations within the past few years, but no one can read the discussions about those national acts without seeing that the general judgment of mankind has sunk deep into the hearts of the people of the countries responsible; that a great new force is at work in international affairs; that the desire for approval and the fear of condemnation by the contemporary opinion of the civilized world is becoming a powerful influence to control national conduct. True, we are but at the beginning, but it is the beginning of a great new era in which the public opinion of mankind renders judgment, not upon peace and war, for a vast majority of mankind is in favor of war when that is necessary for the preservation of liberty and justice, but upon the just and unjust conduct of nations, as the public opinion of each community passes upon the just and unjust conduct of its individual members. The chief force which

1. Henri La Fontaine (1854–1943), recipient of the Nobel Peace Prize for 1913.

makes for peace and order in the community of individuals is not the police officer, with his club, but it is the praise and blame, the honor and shame, which follow observance or violation of the community's standards of right conduct. In the new era that is dawning of the world's public opinion we need not wait for the international policeman, with his artillery, for, when any people feels that its government has done a shameful thing and has brought them into disgrace in the opinion of the world, theirs will be the vengeance and they will inflict the punishment.

Two conclusions from all these considerations are quite obvious. First, that the development and understanding of international law and the habit of submitting international controversies to judicial decision will continually tend to hinder wanton aggression because it will tend to make it more difficult to find pretexts, excuses, or justification. Second, that quite apart from argument and exhortation concerning war and peace, there is a specific line of effort along which those who seek to promote peace may most usefully proceed: by insisting upon a willingness to do justice among nations, and this, not justice according to the possibly excited and warped opinion of the particular nation, but according to the general public judgment of the civilized world; by condemning injustice on the part of nations as we condemn injustice on the part of individuals; by pressing upon the peoples of the earth a consciousness that if they are arrogant and grasping and overbearing and use their power to oppress and despoil the weak, they will be disgraced in the estimation of mankind. Such an effort is not a denial of the innate impulses of the race but is an appeal to them. It accords with the line of historic development. The taboo of savage tribes is nothing else. The social penalties of civilized communities are the same thing. The theoretical postulate of all diplomatic discussion between nations is the assumed willingness of every nation to do justice. The line of least resistance in the progress of civilization is to make that theoretical postulate real by the continually increasing force of the world's public opinion.

Yet there are other influences tending in the same direction which may be usefully promoted. The self-interest which so often prompts nations to unjust aggression can no longer safely assume that its apparent profit is real; for a nation which has been built up by the industry and enterprise of its people, which depends upon its products and the marketing of them, upon its commerce and the peaceful intercourse of commerce for its prosperity, the prize of aggression must be rich indeed to counterbalance the injury sustained by the interference of war with both production and commerce.

At the same time, freedom of trade regardless of political control is diminishing the comparative value of extension of territory. The old system of exploitation of colonies and the monopolization of their trade for the benefit of the mother country has practically disappeared. The best informed men are coming to understand that, under modern conditions, the prosperity of each nation is enhanced by the prosperity of all other nations; and that the government which acquires political control over new territory may gratify pride and minister to ambition but can have only a slight effect to advance the welfare of its people.

The support of these statements rests upon the facts of economic science. If they are true, as I am sure we all believe them to be, they should be forced upon the attention of the peoples, not by mere assertion, which avails but little, but by proof drawn from the rich stores of evidence to be found in the history of mankind. For the accomplishment of this purpose a meeting of eminent economists and publicists was held three years ago at Bern. They came from Denmark, Holland, Belgium, Great Britain, France, Germany, Switzerland, Italy, Austria-Hungary, the United States, and Japan. For some weeks they devoted themselves to the preparation of a program for systematic, scientific investigation into the historical and economic causes and effects of war. For the three years which have ensued they have been engaged, with ample and competent assistance, in pursuing their investigations. The first installments of their work are ready for publication, and they reconvened last month to review what has been done and to lay down the lines of further work. The results of their labors, when made available, should be eagerly sought by every lover of peace who is competent by tongue or pen to be a teacher of his fellowmen, for we may be confident they will show that while the sacrifice of war may be demanded for justice, for liberty, for national life, yet war is always a sacrifice, and never is a rational mode of promoting material prosperity.

There yet remain certain disposing causes, which, quite apart from real substantive questions in controversy, operate upon national feeling and give injurious effect to trifling or fancied occasions for offense. There is no international controversy so serious that it cannot be settled if both parties really wish to settle it. There are few controversies so trifling that they cannot be made the occasion for war if the parties really wish to fight. Among these disposing causes which create an atmosphere of belligerency are:
(a) Race and local prejudice, breeding dislike and hatred between the peoples of different countries.

(b) Exaggerated national *amour propre*, which causes excessive sensitiveness and excessive resentment of foreign criticism or opposition.

(c) With these go the popular assumption, often arrogant, often ignorant, that the extreme claims of one's country are always right and are to be rigidly insisted upon as a point of national honor. With them go intolerance of temperate discussion, of kindly consideration, and of reasonable concession.

Under these feelings, insulting words and conduct towards foreign governments and people become popular, and braggart defiance is deemed patriotic. Under them the ambitious aspirants of domestic politics seek preferment through avenues of military success.

And under them deep and real suspicions of the sinister purpose of other nations readily take possession of a people, who become ready to believe that an attack by their own country is the only recourse to guard effectually against an attack upon their country by others, and that patriotism requires them to outstrip other countries in armament and preparation for war.

Prejudice and passion and suspicion are more dangerous than the incitement of self-interest or the most stubborn adherence to real differences of opinion regarding rights. In private life more quarrels arise, more implacable resentment is caused, more lives are sacrificed, because of insult than because of substantial injury. And it is so with nations.

The remedy is the same. When friends quarrel we try to dissipate their misunderstandings, to soften their mutual feelings, and to bring them together in such a way that their friendship may be renewed. Misunderstanding and prejudice and dislike are, as a rule, the fruits of isolation. There is so much of good in human nature that men grow to like each other upon better acquaintance, and this points to another way in which we may strive to promote the peace of the world. That is by international conciliation through intercourse, not the formal intercourse of the traveler or the merchant, but the intercourse of real acquaintance, of personal knowledge, of little courtesies and kindly consideration; by the exchange of professors between universities, by the exchange of students between countries; by the visits to other countries on the part of leaders of opinion, to be received in private hospitality and in public conference; by the spreading of correct information through the press; by circulating and attracting attention to expressions of praise and honor rather than the reverse; by giving public credit where credit is due and taking pains to expose and publish our good opinions of other peoples; by cooperation in the multitude of causes which are worldwide in their interest; by urging upon our countrymen the duty of international civility and kindly consideration; and by constant pressure in the right direction in a multitude of ways–a slow process, but one which counts little by little if persisted in.

Each separate act will seem of no effect, but all together they will establish and maintain a tendency towards the goal of international knowledge and broad human sympathy. There is a homely English saying, «Leg over leg the dog went to Dover.» That states the method of our true progress. We cannot arrive at our goal *per saltum*[1]. Not by invoking an immediate millennium, but by the accumulated effects of a multitude of efforts, each insignificant in itself but steadily and persistently continued, we must win our way along the road to better knowledge and kindliness among the peoples of the earth which the will of Alfred Nobel describes as «the fraternity of nations».

There are many reasons to believe that progress toward the permanent prevalence of peace may be more rapid in the future than in the past.

Standards of conduct are changing in many ways unfavorable to war.

Civilized man is becoming less cruel. Cruelty to men and to the lower animals as well, which would have passed unnoticed a century ago, now shocks the sensibilities and is regarded as wicked and degrading. The severity of punishments for minor offenses which formerly prevailed now seems to us revolting. The torture of witnesses or of criminals has become unthinkable. Human life is held in much higher esteem, and the taking of it, whether in private quarrel or by judicial procedure, is looked upon much more seriously than it was formerly. The social reaction from the theories of the individualistic economists of the last century has brought with it a very widespread sense that men have some sort of responsibility to cause affairs to be so ordered in civilized communities that their fellowmen have a chance to live. The Hague Conventions to regulate the conduct of war and the Geneva Conventions[2] to ameliorate its horrors have a significance which goes beyond their professions. They mark the changing attitude of the world towards the subject to which they relate; and they introduce into the business of warfare obligatory considerations of humanity and respect for human rights which tend to destroy the spirit upon which alone the business itself can continue. No one can read those conventions closely without being

1. «by leaps».
2. The Hague Conventions of 1899 and 1907. The Geneva Conventions of 1864 and 1906.

struck by the similarity of the process of regulation and limitation which they exhibit with the historic process by which private war was ultimately regulated out of existence in the greater part of the civilized world. The growth of modern constitutional government compels for its successful practice the exercise of reason and considerate judgment by the individual citizens who constitute the electorate. The qualities thus evoked in the training schools of domestic affairs are the qualities which make for national self-restraint and peace in international affairs. History is being rewritten, and the progress of popular education is making men familiar with it; and as the world, which worships strength and has most applauded military glory, grows in knowledge, the great commanding figures rising far above the common mass of mere fighters, the men who win the most imperishable fame have come to be the strong, patient, greathearted ones like Washington, and Lincoln, and William the Silent, and Cavour[1], whose genius, inspired by love of country and their kind, urges them to build up and not to destroy. The sweetest incense offered to the memory of the soldier is not to the brutal qualities of war but to the serene courage ennobled by sympathy and courtesy of a Bayard or a Sidney[2]. The hero-worshipper is gradually changing from the savage to the civilized conception of his divinities. Taken all in all, the clear and persistent tendencies of a slowly developing civilization justify cheerful hope.

We may well turn from Tripoli and Mexico and the Balkans with the apocryphal exclamation of Galilei, «And still the world moves.»

1. George Washington (1732–1799), first president of the U.S.(1789–1797); Abraham Lincoln (1809–1865), president of the U.S.(1861–1865); William I (1533–1584), Prince of Orange, called the Silent, leader of the Dutch struggle for independence from Spanish rule; Count Camillo Cavour (1810–1861), premier of Sardinia (1852–1859; 1860–1861), leader of movement for Italian unification.
2. Possibly Pierre Terrail de Bayard (c. 1473–1524), French hero known as «Chevalier sans peur et sans reproche», killed in battle at Sesia River in Italy. Possibly Sir Philip Sidney (1554–1586), brilliant English soldier, statesman, and poet; wrote *Apologie for Poetrie*; died from effect of a wound received at the battle of Zutphen.

Biography

Elihu Root (February 15, 1845–February 7, 1937), who became one of the most brilliant administrators in American history, was born in Clinton, New York, son of a professor of mathematics at Hamilton College. Perhaps it was inevitable that the father and Elihu's elder brother, who was also a mathematician, should be nicknamed «Cube» and «Square». At Hamilton College, Elihu was graduated first in his class in 1864 at the age of nineteen. He taught school for one year, was graduated from the Law School of New York University in 1867, founded a law firm after one year of practice, and by the age of thirty had established himself as a prominent lawyer specializing in corporate affairs. He became a wealthy man in the thirty or so years which he devoted to legal practice, acting as counsel to banks, railroads, and some of the great financiers of the day. His comprehensive grasp of legal principles, his formidable power of analysis, his creative genius in discovering solutions to problems, his disciplined attention to detail, and his skill in expression, whether written or oral, earned him recognition from his colleagues as the leader of the American bar.

Although he had participated in local Republican politics in New York, he was little known as a political figure when, in 1899, President McKinley invited him to become his secretary of war. Since the nation was just emerging from the Spanish-American War, it seemed an unlikely appointment. But President McKinley, with remarkable insight, said that he needed a lawyer in the post, not a military man, and Root accepted the call of what he called «the greatest of all our clients, the government of our country»[1].

As secretary of war from 1899 to 1904, Root performed the services that moved Henry L. Stimson, himself a later secretary of war, to say that «no such intelligent, constructive, and vital force» had occupied that post in American history[2]. He reorganized the administrative system of the War Department, established new procedures for promotion, founded the War College, enlarged West Point, opened schools for special branches of the

1. Quoted by Henry L. Stimson in *Addresses Made in Honor of Elihu Root*, p. 25.
2. *Ibid.*, p. 29.

service, created a general staff, strengthened control over the National Guard, restored discipline within the department. He was most concerned, however, about the three dependencies acquired as a result of the war. He devised a plan for returning Cuba to the Cubans; wrote a democratic charter for the governance of the Philippines, designing it to insure free government, to protect local customs, and to bring eventual self-determination; and eliminated tariffs on Puerto Rican goods imported into the United States.

He returned to his private legal practice in 1904, but in 1905 at President Theodore Roosevelt's invitation, accepted the post of secretary of state. His record is impressive. He brought the consular service under Civil Service, thus removing it from the «spoils system»; maintained the «open door» policy in the Far East, a policy he had helped to formulate as secretary of war; negotiated the so-called «Gentlemen's Agreement» with Japan which dealt with emigration of Japanese to America; strengthened amicable relations with South America in 1906 during an unprecedented diplomatic tour; sponsored the Central American Peace Conference held in Washington in 1907 which resulted in the creation of the Central American Court of Justice, an international tribunal for the judicial settlement of disputes; negotiated some forty reciprocal arbitration treaties; along with Lord Bryce, resolved current American-Canadian problems and instituted the Permanent American-Canadian Joint High Commission for the settlement of future problems.

A United States senator from 1909 to 1915, Elihu Root took an active role in settling the North Atlantic fisheries dispute, in opposing a bill which would have exempted U.S. shipping from paying tolls to use the Panama Canal while levying charges against other nations' shipping, and in pressing for international arbitration.

In 1915 he declined candidacy for reelection to the Senate and even declined, at least publicly, nomination by the Republican Party for the presidency of the United States. Although seventy years of age, he continued to be active as an elder statesman. He opposed Woodrow Wilson's neutrality policy but supported him during the war; he accepted Wilson's appointment as ambassador extraordinary to head a special diplomatic mission to Russia in 1917; on the 1919 Treaty of Versailles and the League of Nations he took a middle stance between Wilson on the one hand and the «irreconcilables» on the other; as a delegate to the Washington Naval Conference of 1921–1922, he took a leading role in drafting the Five-Power Treaty limiting naval armament.

Root dedicated a large portion of his life to the cause of international arbitration. He, more than any other, formulated the plan to create the Central American Court of Justice. In 1907 he instructed the American delegates to the Hague Conference to support the founding of a World Court; in 1920, at the request of the Council of the League of Nations, he served on a committee to devise plans for the Permanent Court of International Justice which was set up in 1921; in 1929 after intermittent discussion between the League and the United States concerning certain reservations the Senate had insisted upon in its 1926 ratification of the Protocol for U.S. participation in the court, Root, on his eighty-fourth birthday, left for Geneva where he convinced the delegates from fifty-five nations to accept a revised Protocol; he later appeared before the Senate Foreign Relations Committee to urge ratification, but the Senate failed to act at that time and eventually declined to ratify at all.

Root was the first president of the Carnegie Endowment for International Peace and helped to found its European counterpart. He believed that international law, along with its accompanying machinery, represented mankind's best chance to achieve world peace, but like the hardheaded realist he was, he also believed that it would take much time, wisdom, patience, and toil to implement it effectively.

Selected Bibliography

Addresses Made in Honor of Elihu Root. New York, The Century Association, 1937. The introductory address by Royal Cortissoz deals mainly with Root's relations to the arts; that by Henry L. Stimson with an assessment of Root's career as secretary of war and secretary of state; that by Nicholas Murray Butler with the story of the 1916 Republican convention in Chicago.

Jessup, Philip C., *Elihu Root.* Vol. I, *1845–1909*; Vol. II, *1905–1937*. New York, Dodd, Mead, 1938.

Leopold, Richard W., *Elihu Root and the Conservative Tradition.* Boston, Little, Brown, 1954.

Root, Elihu. The papers of Elihu Root are held by the Library of Congress, Washington, D.C.

Root, Elihu. The eight volumes of Root's addresses and writings collected and edited by Robert Bacon and James B. Scott and published by the Harvard University Press between 1916 and 1925 are titled as follows:

Addresses on American Government and Citizenship (1916)

Addresses on International Subjects (1916)

The Military and Colonial Policy of the United States: Addresses and Reports (1916)
Latin America and the United States (1917)
Miscellaneous Addresses (1917)
North Atlantic Coast Fisheries Arbitration at The Hague (1917)
The United States and the War, the Mission to Russia, Political Addresses (1918)
Men and Policies (1925)

Scott, James B., «Elihu Root», in *American Secretaries of State and Their Diplomacy*, ed. by S.F.Bemis. Vol.IX, pp.193–282. New York, Knopf, 1929.

Peace 1913

HENRI MARIE LA FONTAINE

Presentation

by Ragnvald Moe*, Secretary to the Nobel Committee

Henri La Fontaine is the true leader of the popular peace movement in Europe. Since 1907 he has been president of the International Peace Bureau in Bern[1]. He is also a prominent member of the Interparliamentary Union[2]. La Fontaine was born on April 22, 1854, in Brussels, where he is counsel at the Court of Appeal and a professor of international law. He entered the Senate in 1895 and has been working for the cause of peace since 1889. La Fontaine is also a member of the Brussels City Council, a member sponsored by the Socialist Party. He is one of the best informed men working for peace, and his initiative and energy have done much to promote the international peace movement, particularly in the interparliamentary and peace conferences of recent years, where he has contributed to the practical organization of the movement and to the framing of international law. In 1899, for example, his activities included participation in a Peace Congress in Oslo. In 1895 he founded the International Institute of Bibliography and [later] the Central Office of International Associations[3]. La Fontaine has also been very active in the literary field, an example being his great documentary

* At the award ceremony in the Norwegian Nobel Institute on December 10, 1913, Mr. Løvland, chairman of the Nobel Committee and at this time president of the Norwegian Parliament, welcomed the audience and announced the Nobel prizewinner for 1912 (Elihu Root) and for 1913 (Henri La Fontaine). Neither laureate was present. Mr. Moe then spoke on both laureates and their contributions to peace. The second part of his speech, that on Mr. La Fontaine, is given here. The translation is based on the Norwegian reporting of it in the Oslo *Morgenposten* of December 11, 1913.
1. Recipient of the Nobel Peace Prize for 1910.
2. In effect founded in 1888 but formally constituted in 1889, the Union is composed of parliamentarians from the various nations who discuss problems of international relations and law, and of peace, promoting their solution through governmental channels; at this time it was primarily interested in encouraging arbitration of international disputes.
3. The creation of both the Institute in 1895 and the Central Office twelve years later must be credited to the initiative of two Belgian internationalists: La Fontaine and his friend Paul Otlet.

work on arbitration cases from 1794 to 1900[1]. There is no one who has contributed more to the organization of peaceful internationalism, and his outstanding talent for administration has been invaluable to the peace movement. La Fontaine belongs to the moderate wing of the Socialist Party; he is the first Social Democrat to receive the Nobel Peace Prize.

The laureate did not deliver a Nobel lecture.

1. *Pasicrisie internationale: Histoire documentaire des arbitrages internationaux, 1794–1900* (1902).

Biography*

Henri Marie La Fontaine (April 22, 1854–May 14, 1943) was born in Brussels. A professor of international law, a senator in the Belgian legislature for thirty-six years, a renowned bibliographer, a man of wide-ranging cultural achievements, he was noted, most of all, for his fervent and total internationalism.

In 1877 at the age of twenty-three, La Fontaine registered as counsel with the Brussels Court of Appeal after reading law at the Free University of Brussels, from which he later received a doctorate in law. For the next sixteen years, he practiced law, becoming one of Belgium's leading jurists; wrote a technical work on the rights and duties of contractors of public works (1885) and collaborated on another concerning counterfeiting (1888); began his long work in the cause of peace; and participated in liberal reform causes.

His interest in reform eventually led him into politics. A socialist, La Fontaine wrote for the movement, spoke at meetings, joined in founding *La Justice*, a socialist paper. Elected to the Belgian Senate as a Socialist, he represented Hainaut from 1895 to 1898, Liège from 1900 to 1932, and Brabant from 1935 to 1936. He was secretary of the Senate for thirteen years (1907–1919) and a vice-president for fourteen years: third vice-president (1919–1921), second vice-president (1921–1922), and first vice-president (1923–1932).

Throughout his career in the Senate he showed an abiding interest in education, labor, and foreign affairs. As a freshman senator, he introduced a bill to reform primary education and in his last year in the Senate spoke on the budget for public instruction. In labor legislation, he submitted a bill on mine inspection in 1897 and in 1926 supported the adoption of the eight-hour day and forty-hour week. In foreign affairs, he spoke almost every year on the foreign affairs budget, asked the Belgian government to demand

* The editor wishes to acknowledge his debt to Professor J. Vanderlinden, Faculté de Droit, Université Libre de Bruxelles, for his kindness in collecting research information on which much of this biographical notice is based.

arbitration between the combatants of the Boer War (1901), introduced a bill approving the treaty of obligatory arbitration with Italy (1911), and gave his legislative support to the League of Nations, the establishment of an economic union with Luxembourg, the Locarno Pacts, the Kellogg-Briand Pact, disarmament, and the legal means of settling international disputes.

La Fontaine was a member of the Belgian delegation to the Paris Peace Conference in 1919 and a delegate to the First Assembly of the League of Nations in 1920–1921. To those deliberations he brought his uncompromising internationalism. For example, during a plenary meeting that was considering Article 16 of the Covenant – the article which provided that members of the League must unite in diplomatic pressure, sanctions, or, if necessary, armed force to prevent a resort to aggressive war in breach of the Covenant – he spoke against an amendment releasing from commitment those countries which deemed themselves endangered should they take part in sanctions, saying: «Belgium thinks that however great the peril which a country might have to undergo under the system which we seek to establish here, that country ought to do its duty. It was thus that Belgium understood her obligations in 1914... We fully admit that, in circumstances of this nature, powerful countries may take certain measures, but in our opinion it would be impossible, on the pretext that they would suffer more than others, for some countries to hold aloof from the sacred task of defending justice, even at the peril of their own existence. ‹Fais ce que dois, advienne que pourra.›»[1]

Ideas for some of the auxiliary bodies of the League of Nations and of such affiliated bodies as the Institute of Intellectual Cooperation may have been influenced by La Fontaine's plan for an international intellectual union, along with which he proposed the creation of international agencies that logically follow from the acceptance of the international idea – among them, a university, a library, a language, a parliament, a court, a bank, and clearing houses for labor, trade, immigration, and statistical information[2].

La Fontaine entered the organized peace movement when Hodgson Pratt, the British pacifist, came to Belgium in the early 1880's to establish a branch

1. Quoted by William E. Rappard, *The Quest for Peace since the World War* (Cambridge, Mass.: Harvard University Press, 1940), pp. 227–228, from *Records of the First Assembly*, Plenary Meetings, p. 409.
2. Noted by Mortimer Lipsky, *The Quest for Peace: The Story of the Nobel Award* (New York: A. S. Barnes, 1966), pp. 57–58.

of his International Arbitration and Peace Association. Becoming the secretary-general of the Société belge de l'arbitrage et de la paix in 1889, La Fontaine thereafter participated actively in virtually all of the peace congresses held in the next twenty-five years. In 1907, he succeeded Fredrik Bajer (one of the two Nobel Peace laureates for 1908) as president of the International Peace Bureau (winner of the 1910 Peace Prize), an organization he helped to found and whose titular head he remained until his death.

La Fontaine became a member of the Interparliamentary Union as soon as he attained eligibility by virtue of being elected to a national legislature. To La Fontaine the Union was an embryo world parliament, the precursor of a world government. An enthusiastic member, he was chairman of its Juridical Committee prior to World War I and a member of two of its important commissions – that on preparation of a model world parliament and that on drafting a model treaty of arbitration.

In the two decades between 1894 and 1915, La Fontaine's literary efforts were prodigious, with much of his more important work associated with internationalism. The *Manuel des lois de la paix: Code de l'arbitrage* (1894) was approved by the International Peace Congress held at Antwerp. Published in 1902, the immense volume, *Pasicrisie internationale: Histoire documentaire des arbitrages internationaux, 1794–1900*, is a source book of 368 documents on arbitration, including agreements, rules of procedure, and case decisions, printed in whole or in part in their original languages. A complementary work, *Histoire sommaire et chronologique des arbitrages internationaux, 1794–1900*, provides commentary on *Pasicrisie*. His exhaustive and carefully edited *Bibliographie de la paix et de l'arbitrage international*, containing 2,222 entries, appeared in 1904. *The Great Solution: Magnissima Charta* (1916) offers a set of principles for organized international relations, not for a «World State» which he considered many years away, and sketches a «constitution» embodying the necessary institutions that would fit the times while preventing future wars. In «International Judicature» (1915) he outlines the essentials for a supreme court of the world. Not that he was very optimistic at this time. From Washington, D.C., where he lived following his flight to England and then to the United States after the German invasion of Belgium in 1914, he wrote in a private letter: «The peoples are not awake...[There are dangers] which will render a world organization impossible. I foresee the renewal of...the secret bargaining behind closed doors. Peoples will be as before, the sheep sent to the slaughterhouses or to the meadows as it pleases the shepherds. International institutions ought to be, as the national ones in democratic countries, established by the peoples and for the peoples.»[1]

In the period before World War I, La Fontaine inaugurated an ambitious bibliographical scheme. In 1895, in collaboration with Paul Otlet, he established the Institut international de bibliographie. This «House of Documentation», as it came to be called, was a vast informational retrieval scheme, in which he proposed to file, index, and provide information for retrieval on anything of note published anywhere in the world. With the help of a subsidy from the Belgian government, he went some distance in bringing his plan into reality, for the House developed a methodology of universal classification and produced some reference works, particularly bibliographies of social sciences and peace.

From the work of the Institute came the idea for the Union of International Associations, which he founded with Paul Otlet in 1907, and, as secretary-general, directed thereafter. Still located in Brussels, the Union was granted consultative status with the Economic and Social Council of the United Nations in 1951 and with UNESCO in 1952. As the «only centre in the world devoted to documentation, research and promotion of international organizations, particularly the voluntary (nongovernmental) variety»[2] and as the publisher of *The Yearbook of International Organizations*, the first of which appeared in 1909, and of a host of reference works of proceedings, documents, bibliographies, directories, and calendars of meetings of international organizations, it carries on in a sophisticated manner the embryonic conceptions of its founder.

Throughout his life La Fontaine was concerned with education. He occupied the chair of international law from 1893 to 1940, first at the Université Nouvelle, a branch of the Free University of Brussels, and then at the Institut des Hautes Études after the branch merged with the University following World War I. He taught courses on the elements of international law and on the evolution of the judicial structures of the world, and, as occasion required, offered courses of lectures on various subjects–among them, disarmament, the League of Nations, international misunderstandings, world federation, the law in relation to political and moral crises in the world.

1. Letter to David Starr Jordan, president of Stanford University, dated December 29, 1916. Archives of the Hoover Institution of War, Revolution, and Peace, Stanford University.
2. *Yearbook of International Organizations*, 1968–1969 edition, p. 1023.

A zealous reformer, La Fontaine was a leading spokesman for women's rights. He was appointed secretary of a technical school for young women in 1878; he wrote *La Femme et le barreau* in 1901, taking an advanced position on the place of women in the legal profession; and for some time he was president of the Association for the Professional Education of Women.

La Fontaine's talents and energy led him to explore many interests. A mountaineer, he wrote about climbing, compiled an international bibliography of «Alpinism», and served as president of the Club alpin belge. He translated portions of Wagner's operas, published essays on American libraries and the status of American women, founded the review *La Vie internationale*, lectured to adult education classes on modern movements in the arts, served on the Brussels City Council from 1904 to 1908, and even, in his young manhood, produced a volume of poetry.

Henri La Fontaine lived to see his native Belgium invaded once again but not to see it liberated, for he died in 1943.

Selected Bibliography

«Activité parlementaire de M. Henri La Fontaine, Sénateur de 1895 à 1898, de 1900 à 1932 et de 1935 à 1936.» A sixteen-page reference list in typescript of bills introduced, bills discussed, and special speeches delivered by La Fontaine, prepared by the Services d'étude et de documentation du sénat de Belgique.

«The Award of the Nobel Peace Prize to Senator Henri La Fontaine», in *American Journal of International Law*, 8 (January, 1914) 137–138.

Davis, Hayne, «Henri La Fontaine», in *Among the World's Peace-Makers: An Epitome of the Interparliamentary Union with Sketches of Eminent Members of This International House of Representatives*, pp. 118–126. New York, Progressive Publishing Co., [1906?]

«Enseignement de Monsieur Henri La Fontaine.» A two-page list in typescript of courses taught and lectures delivered as professor of international law from 1898 to 1940. Prepared by J. Vanderlinden, Faculté de Droit, Université Libre de Bruxelles.

«Essai de bibliographie de M. Henri La Fontaine, ancien vice-président du sénat de Belgique.» A nine-page list in typescript, prepared by the Services d'étude et de documentation du sénat de Belgique.

La Fontaine, Henri, *Bibliographie de la paix et de l'arbitrage international*. Tome premier: *Mouvement pacifique*. Bruxelles, Institut international de bibliographie, 1904.

La Fontaine, Henri, *Des droits et obligations des entrepreneurs de travaux publics nationaux, provinciaux, et communaux*. Bruxelles, Ferdinand Larcier, 1885.

La Fontaine, Henri, *La Femme et le barreau*. Rapport à la Fédération des avocats belges; assemblée générale ordinaire du samedi 27 avril 1901, à Charleroi. Bruxelles, Ferdinand Larcier, 1901

La Fontaine, Henri, *The Great Solution: Magnissima Charta*. Boston, World Peace Foundation, 1916.

La Fontaine, Henri, *Histoire sommaire et chronologique des arbitrages internationaux (1794–1900)*. Bruxelles, Bureau de la Revue de droit international et de législation comparée, 1902.

La Fontaine, Henri, «International Judicature», *Judicial Settlement of International Disputes*, No.22. Baltimore, American Society for Judicial Settlement of International Disputes, 1915.

La Fontaine, Henri, *Manuel des lois de la paix: Code de l'arbitrage*. Congrès international de la paix, 1894, Anvers. Bruxelles, Lombaerts, 1894.

La Fontaine, Henri, *Pasicrisie internationale: Histoire documentaire des arbitrages internationaux, 1794–1900*. Bern, Stämpfli, 1902.

La Fontaine, Henri, et Paul Otlet, *L'État actuel des questions bibliographiques et l'organisation internationale de la documentation*. Bruxelles, 1908.

Moi (pseudonyme de Henri La Fontaine), *Premières rimes*. Bruxelles, Ferdinand Larcier, 1886.

Olin, X., et Henri La Fontaine, *Traité de contrefaçons*. Bruxelles, Ferdinand Larcier, 1888.

Peace 1914–1916

Prizes not awarded

Peace 1917

THE INTERNATIONAL COMMITTEE
OF THE RED CROSS

The International Committee of the Red Cross–1917

The only Nobel Peace Prize awarded during the years of World War I was that for 1917 given to the International Committee of the Red Cross. The award ceremony took place on December 10, 1917, at the Nobel Institute in Oslo, with Mr. Jørgen Gunnarsson Løvland, chairman of the Nobel Committee, presiding. After the award announcement, Mr. Ragnvald Moe, secretary to the Nobel Committee, delivered the only speech of the occasion, an account of the origins and development of the International Committee of the Red Cross and of the Prisoners of War Agency it had established in 1914.

The speech is briefly reported in the Oslo newspapers, but there is no text of the speech available. However, an account of the Committee and its work, covering what is apparently much the same subject matter, appears in *Les Prix Nobel en 1914–1918*. Since the usual Nobel lecture given by the prize-winner was not delivered in this case, the *Les Prix Nobel* account, translated from its French text, is given here in order to provide more specific information about the International Committee and its work (from 1863 through this period of WWI) than is given in the brief «history» of the Red Cross on p.284.

The International Committee of the Red Cross was founded in Geneva in 1863 to work for the realization of the magnanimous sentiments expressed the year before in the famous book *Un Souvenir de Solférino* [*A Memory of Solferino*] by a young idealist from Geneva, Henri Dunant[1]. The Committee's objectives were: the creation, in all countries, of societies devoted to aiding the sick and wounded in time of war; the establishment of an international convention for the reciprocal protection of soldiers wounded on the battlefield; and the proclamation of the neutrality and inviolability of ambulances and hospitals. The first president was General Dufour who was, upon his

1. Jean Henri Dunant (1828–1910), co-recipient of the Nobel Peace Prize for 1901. See biography, p.5.

death in 1875, succeeded by Gustave Moynier, who held this post until 1910[1].

The result of the efforts of Henri Dunant and of the Geneva Committee was the *Geneva Convention*[2] concluded in 1864 by an international conference of sovereign governments.

In the years that followed until the 1914 War, the Geneva Committee faithfully pursued the implementation of its program by encouraging the organization of Red Cross Societies, which were successively established in nearly all the civilized countries. Since 1869, by publishing an *International Bulletin*, it has tried to serve as a link between the various national societies and has furthermore periodically organized international conferences of Red Cross Societies. As the provisions of the Geneva Convention appeared, from the first, to be incomplete, the Committee has made continuous efforts to improve them and to extend their principles to naval warfare. The desired revision was made at Geneva in 1906 when an international conference adopted the text of a new Convention[3].

During the World War from 1914 to 1919, the International Committee took up the role of moral guardian of the Geneva Convention. It tactfully but firmly reminded the governments of the belligerent nations of the principles of the Convention and sent protests in cases of clear violation of these principles. It collected the funds necessary for the development of Red Cross organizations in the belligerent countries. It sent delegations to the various war fronts to investigate and to improve the situation of the wounded. The Committee took the initiative in the exchange of seriously wounded prisoners sent back through Switzerland to their own countries; it also took the initiative in arranging for the internment in Switzerland of wounded officers of the belligerent parties. The president of the Committee from 1910 until 1917 was Gustave Ador, who was then succeeded by Édouard Naville[4].

1. Guillaume Henri Dufour (1787–1875) was active president 1863–1864 and honorary president from 1864 until his death. Gustave Moynier (1826–1910) was active president 1864–1910. See history, p.284.
2. See history, p.285.
3. Acting after the 1899 Hague Peace Conference adopted a convention for the adaptation to maritime warfare of the principles of the Geneva Convention of 1864, the Geneva Congress of 1906, with representatives from over thirty nations present, expanded the original 10 articles of the 1864 Convention to 33.
4. Gustave Ador (1845–1928), Swiss statesman, resumed the Committee presidency for the period 1920–1928. Vice-President Édouard Naville (1844–1926), Swiss Egyptologist, was acting president in the three-year interval, 1917–1920, while Mr. Ador was a federal councillor and in 1919 president of the Swiss Confederation.

The most important new measure taken by the Committee during the war, however, was the establishment in Geneva in August, 1914, of an Agence internationale de secours et de renseignements en faveur des prisonniers de guerre [Central Prisoners of War Agency]. One of the principal objects of this agency was to supply information to families concerning the whereabouts and welfare of the prisoners. Its importance has been universally recognized from the outset. The detaining powers regularly sent official lists of prisoners to the Agency and authorized it to apply for information to the commandants of prison camps and to the directors of hospitals. The Agency had to limit its operations to the western front; but the Committee also organized similar institutions for the eastern front.

History of the Red Cross

Since the Red Cross has figured four times in the award of the Nobel Peace Prize (1917, 1944, and 1963), as well as in the award to Henri Dunant (1901), and has therefore been made the subject of various presentation speeches and Nobel lectures which give details of its inception, history, and activities, the following brief summary of its origins and present organization is intended as a frame of reference for all four of these awards rather than as the typical history ordinarily included for each award to an organization.

Origins

In February of 1863 in Geneva, Switzerland, the Société genevoise d'utilité publique [Geneva Public Welfare Society] set up a committee of five Swiss citizens to look into the ideas offered by Henri Dunant in his book *Un Souvenir de Solférino*[1]–ideas dealing with protection of the sick and wounded during combat. The committee had as its members: Guillaume Henri Dufour (1787–1875), a general of the Swiss army and a writer of military tracts who became the committee's president for its first year and its honorary president thereafter; Gustave Moynier (1826–1910), a young lawyer and president of the sponsoring Public Welfare Society, who from this time on devoted his life to Red Cross work; Louis Appia (1818–1898) and Théodore Maunoir (1806–1869), both medical doctors; and Henri Dunant himself.

Guided by Moynier's talent for organization, the committee called an international conference for October of 1863 which, with sixteen nations represented, adopted various pertinent resolutions and principles, along with an international emblem, and appealed to all nations to form voluntary units to help wartime sick and wounded. These units eventually became the National Red Cross Societies, and the Committee of Five itself eventually became the International Committee of the Red Cross, with Gustave Moynier as its president (1864–1910) both before and after it took this name.

1. See Dunant's biography, p. 6.

As a result of the 1863 Conference, which hoped to see its Red Cross principles become a part of international law, an international diplomatic meeting was held at Geneva the following year at the invitation of the Swiss government. The assembly formulated the Geneva Convention of 1864. This international «Convention for the Amelioration of the Condition of the Wounded and Sick in Armed Forces in the Field» included provisions guaranteeing neutrality for medical personnel and equipment and officially adopting the red cross on a field of white as the identifying emblem. It was signed on August 22, 1864, by twelve states and was later accepted by virtually all.

The work of the Red Cross had been inaugurated.

Three other conventions were later added to the first, extending protection to victims of naval warfare, to prisoners of war, and to civilians. Revisions of these conventions have been made from time to time, the most extensive being that of 1949.

Although the Red Cross has always given major service and often accomplished herculean tasks during time of war, it has achieved even greater service in its gradual development and operation of humanitarian programs that serve continuously in both peace and war.

Organization

The Red Cross, a strictly neutral and impartial worldwide organization dedicated to humanitarian interests in general and to alleviating human suffering in particular, is composed of three basic elements.

1. The self-governing National Red Cross Societies, including the Red Crescent (in Muslim countries) and the Red Lion and Sun (in Iran), operate on the national level through their volunteer members, although they also participate in international work. Each must be recognized by the International Committee. Today numbering 114, these societies all have Junior Red Cross Societies as well. Virtually all have disaster relief programs, and many carry on welfare programs, with community health and safety instruction, and so on. Since World War II, many of the European and Asian societies have also established refugee services.

2. The League of Red Cross Societies, a coordinating world federation of these societies, was established in 1919 as the result of proposals made by Henry P. Davison (1867–1922) of the American Red Cross. The League maintains contacts between the societies; acts as a clearinghouse for informa-

tion; assists the societies in setting up new programs and in improving or expanding old ones; coordinates international disaster operations. It functions under an executive committee and a board of governors on which every national society has representation.

3. The International Committee of the Red Cross [ICRC], a private, independent group of Swiss citizens chosen by co-optation (limited to twenty-five in number), acts during war or conflict whenever intervention by a neutral body is necessary, such action constituting its special field of activity. As guardian of the Geneva Conventions and of Red Cross principles, it promotes their acceptance by governments, suggests their revision, works for further development of international humanitarian law, and recognizes new Red Cross Societies; it sends its Swiss delegates into prisoner-of-war camps, supervises repatriation, operates the Central Tracing Agency, supplies material relief, and the like.

The International Red Cross Conference, which met for the first time in 1867, is the highest legislative body. It is composed of representatives of the National Societies, the League, the International Committee, and the governments that have signed the Geneva Conventions. Meeting every four to six years, it reviews Red Cross activities and the operation of the Conventions in practice, taking under consideration, whenever necessary, any suggested revision of the Conventions or the adoption of new ones. (Actual revision and adoption are matters for a diplomatic conference convened by the Swiss government in its role as the custodian of the Conventions; texts submitted to such a diplomatic conference would be prepared by the ICRC with expert assistance and previously approved by an International Conference of the Red Cross.) Between Conferences, coordination of the work of the League with that of the Committee is ensured by the Standing Commission of the International Red Cross.

Selected Bibliography

This bibliography, like the preceding «history», is intended for reference in connection with all awards to the Red Cross: to the International Committee of the Red Cross (1917, 1944, and 1963) and to the League of Red Cross Societies (1963).

Boissier, Pierre, *Histoire du Comité international de la Croix-Rouge de Solférino à Tsoushima*. Paris, Plon, 1963.

Buckingham, Clyde E., *For Humanity's Sake: The Story of the Early Development of the League of Red Cross Societies.* Washington, D.C., Public Affairs Press, 1964.

Cousier, Henri, *The International Red Cross*, transl. by M.C.S.Phipps. Geneva, ICRC [International Committee of the Red Cross], 1961.

Draper, G.I.A.D., *The Red Cross Conventions.* New York, Praeger, 1958.

Dunant, Jean Henry, *A Memory of Solferino*, English translation of *Un Souvenir de Solférino.* Washington, D.C., American National Red Cross, 1939.

Huber, Max, *Principles and Foundations of the Work of the International Committee of the Red Cross, 1939–1946.* Geneva, ICRC, 1947.

International Review of the Red Cross. English edition (since 1961) of the *Revue internationale de la Croix-Rouge*, monthly publication of the ICRC, Geneva (since 1919).

Joyce, James Avery, *Red Cross International and the Strategy of Peace.* London, Hodder & Stoughton, 1959. New York, Oceana Publications, 1959.

Junod, Marcel, *Warrior without Weapons*, with a Preface by Max Huber. Transl. by Edward Fitzgerald of *Le Troisième Combattant.* New York, Macmillan, 1951.

Liste des publications du Comité international de la Croix-Rouge de 1863 à 1944, compiled by Élie Moray, G.Vuagnat, and Daniel Clouzot. Genève, 1945.

Manuel de la Croix-Rouge internationale. Genève, Comité international de la Croix-Rouge et Ligue des sociétés de la Croix-Rouge, 1951.

Patrnogic, Jovica, «The Red Cross as a Factor of Peace», in *International Review of the Red Cross*, 87 (June, 1968) 283–294.

Pictet, Jean S., ed., *Commentary: The Geneva Conventions of 12 August 1949.* 4 vols. Geneva, ICRC, 1952, 1958, 1960.

Pictet, Jean S., *Red Cross Principles.* Geneva, ICRC, 1956.

Red Cross World. Publication of the League of Red Cross Societies, Geneva (since 1919). [Title varies prior to 1952.]

Report of the International Committee of the Red Cross on Its Activities during the Second World War, Sept.1, 1939–June 30, 1947. Geneva, ICRC, 1948.

Siordet, Frédéric, «A Hundred Years in the Service of Humanity», in *International Review of the Red Cross*, 29 (August, 1963) 393–428.

Peace 1918

Prize not awarded

Peace 1919

(Prize awarded in 1920)

THOMAS WOODROW WILSON

Remarks at the Award Ceremony

by Anders Johnsen Buen*, President of the Norwegian Parliament

The letter from the Nobel Committee of the Norwegian Parliament reads as follows: «The Nobel Committee of the Norwegian Parliament has the honor of announcing herewith its decision to award the Nobel Peace Prize for 1919 to the President of the United States of America Mr. Woodrow Wilson and that for 1920 to Mr. Léon Bourgeois, president of the French Senate and president of the Council of the League of Nations.»

Today, Gentlemen, as the Norwegian Parliament meets to present the Nobel Peace Prize for the first time since the World War[1], it is with the conviction that the great ideal of peace, so deeply rooted in the hopes for survival of the nations, will gain fresh ground in the minds of men as a result of the recent tragic events.

As the name of President Wilson comes to the fore on this occasion as the recipient of the Peace Prize, I know that the award is accompanied by the thanks of the people of Norway, because in his celebrated Fourteen Points[2] the President of the United States has succeeded in bringing a design for a fundamental law of humanity into present-day international politics. The basic concept of justice on which it is founded will never die, but will steadily grow in strength, keeping the name of President Wilson fresh in the minds of future generations.

[In a final brief paragraph, President Buen refers to Léon Bourgeois, the laureate for 1920.]

---

* Mr. Buen addressed these remarks to the Parliament at an official session on December 10, 1920, doing so after the Nobel Committee had announced its decision and after the diplomatic representatives of the two absent laureates had been officially admitted to the meeting. He then gave the Nobel diplomas and medals to the two ministers. No presentation speech, in the usual sense of the term, was made. The translation is based on the Norwegian text in *Forhandlinger i Stortinget* (nr. 502) for December 10, 1920 [Proceedings of the Norwegian Parliament].

1. World War I (1914–1918).

2. Wilson's framework for peace discussions–eight points involve more or less specific territorial and political problems, and six deal with general principles of international relations: «open covenants», «freedom of navigation», removal of economic barriers, reduction of armaments, adjustment of colonial claims, and–most famous–«a general association of nations».

Acceptance

by Albert G. Schmedeman, American Minister

The Peace Prize for 1919, reserved in that year, was awarded in 1920 to Woodrow Wilson in recognition of his Fourteen Points peace program and his work in achieving inclusion of the Covenant of the League of Nations in the 1919 Treaty of Versailles. Since President Wilson was not present at the award ceremony on December 10, 1920, Albert G. Schmedeman, United States minister in Oslo, accepted the prize in his behalf. Mr. Schmedeman's speech[1], which included the reading of a message from President Wilson, follows:

Mr. President, I have the honor to inform you that I am the bearer of a telegram from Woodrow Wilson, President of the United States, in which he requests me to express his thanks and appreciation for the honor which has been conferred upon him by the Nobel Peace Committee of the Storting in awarding him the prize for the year 1919. Therefore, I have the honor, Mr. President, to request that permission will be granted me to read the message and make a few remarks to the honorable body.

I have been instructed by President Wilson to convey the following message[2] of appreciation to President [Chairman] Løvland and the members of the Nobel Peace Committee of the Storting:

«In accepting the honor of your award I am moved not only by a profound gratitude for the recognition of my [sincere and] earnest efforts in the cause of peace, but also by a very poignant humility before the vastness of the work still called for by this cause.

May I not take this occasion to express my respect for the far-sighted wisdom of the founder in arranging for a continuing system of awards? If

1. Taken from the text in *Les Prix Nobel en 1919–1920*, with two minor emendations based on the text in *Forhandlinger i Stortinget* (nr. 502) for December 10, 1920 [Proceedings of the Norwegian Parliament].
2. The text and punctuation of the telegram are taken from *Les Prix Nobel en 1919–1920* and verified in *Forhandlinger i Stortinget* (nr. 502); the words in brackets are from the *New York Times* (December 11, 1920) version of the text.

there were but one such prize, or if this were to be the last, I could not of course accept it. For mankind has not yet been rid of the unspeakable horror of war. I am convinced that our generation has, despite its wounds, made notable progress. But it is the better part of wisdom to consider our work as one[1] begun. It will be a continuing labor. In the indefinite course of [the] years before us there will be abundant opportunity for others to distinguish themselves in the crusade against hate and fear and war.

There is indeed a peculiar fitness in the grouping of these Nobel rewards. The cause of peace and the cause of truth are of one family. Even as those who love science and devote their lives to physics or chemistry, even as those who would create new and higher ideals for mankind in literature, even so with those who love peace, there is no limit set. Whatever has been accomplished in the past is petty compared to the glory and promise of the future.

Woodrow Wilson»

I regret that I am unable to address this honorable body in the Norwegian language; even if I were, there are no words which can fully express my appreciation for the high honor conferred upon my country by the award of the Nobel Peace Prize for the year 1919 by the Nobel Committee of the Storting to one of America's greatest statesmen, Woodrow Wilson, President of the United States of America. This honor which has been bestowed on President Wilson is one of significance and of utmost satisfaction to me – an occasion which will always remain in my memory. To have the privilege of accepting, on behalf of the President of the United States, this evidence of appreciation of his efforts to replace discord with harmony by appealing to the highest moral forces of each nation, is an event to be cherished.

It is unnecessary for me to dwell upon any of those achievements of President Wilson which justify the bestowal of this honor upon him; his comprehensive understanding of international affairs and his discerning and convincing methods of procedure in matters affecting the welfare and success of entire peoples, which, due to his earnest and forceful endeavors, resulted in the formation of the League of Nations, are well known to us all. He, perhaps as much as any public man, is conscious of the fact that the time is

---

1. *Les Prix Nobel* and *Forhandlinger i Stortinget* read «one»; *N. Y. Times* reads «only»; the context suggests «only» as the proper reading.

past when each nation can live only unto itself, and his labors have been inspired with the idea and hope of making peace universal a living reality. It is impossible to make a proper estimate of Woodrow Wilson and his great work for international peace until time has revealed much that must, for the present, be a sealed book.

Let me assure you, members of the Norwegian Storting, that words fail to convey the deep emotion which stirs within me at this time, when it falls within my province to receive this testimonial on behalf of the President of the United States of America. No more fitting word of appreciation could be voiced than that contained in the President's message, in which he acknowledges the great honor that has been conferred upon him by the Nobel Peace Committee of the Storting.

President Wilson, who notified the Nobel Committee that ill health prevented his visiting Oslo, did not deliver a Nobel lecture.

Biography

Thomas Woodrow Wilson (December 28, 1856–February 3, 1924) was born in Staunton, Virginia, to parents of a predominantly Scottish heritage. Since his father was a Presbyterian minister and his mother the daughter of a Presbyterian minister, Woodrow was raised in a pious and academic household. He spent a year at Davidson College in North Carolina and three at Princeton University where he received a baccalaureate degree in 1879.

After graduating from the Law School of the University of Virginia, he practiced law for a year in Atlanta, Georgia, but it was a feeble practice. He entered graduate studies at Johns Hopkins University in 1883 and three years later received the doctorate. In 1885 he published *Congressional Government*, a splendid piece of scholarship which analyzes the difficulties arising from the separation of the legislative and executive powers in the American Constitution.

Before joining the faculty of Princeton University as a professor of jurisprudence and political economy, Wilson taught for three years at Bryn Mawr College and for two years at Wesleyan College. He was enormously successful as a lecturer and productive as a scholar.

As president of Princeton University from 1902 to 1910, Wilson became widely known for his ideas on reforming education. In pursuit of his idealized intellectual life for democratically chosen students, he wanted to change the admission system, the pedagogical system, the social system, even the architectural layout of the campus. But Wilson was a thinker who needed to act. So he entered politics and as governor of the State of New Jersey from 1911 to 1913 distinguished himself once again as a reformer.

Wilson won the presidential election of 1912 when William Howard Taft and Theodore Roosevelt split the Republican vote. Upon taking office he set about instituting the reforms he had outlined in his book *The New Freedom*, including the changing of the tariff, the revising of the banking system, the checking of monopolies and fraudulent advertising, the prohibiting of unfair business practices, and the like.

But the attention of this man of peace was forced to turn to war. In the early days of World War I, Wilson was determined to maintain neutrality. He protested British as well as German acts; he offered mediation to both sides but was rebuffed. The American electorate in 1916, reacting to the slogan «He kept us out of war», reelected Wilson to the presidency. However, in 1917 the issue of freedom of the seas compelled a decisive change. On January 31 Germany announced that «unrestricted submarine warfare» was already started; on March 27, after four American ships had been sunk, Wilson decided to ask for a declaration of war; on April 2 he made the formal request to Congress; and on April 6 the Congress granted it.

Wilson never doubted the outcome. He mobilized a nation – its man-power, its industry, its commerce, its agriculture. He was himself the chief mover in the propaganda war. His speech to Congress on January 8, 1918, on the «Fourteen Points» was a decisive stroke in winning that war, for people everywhere saw in his peace aims the vision of a world in which freedom, justice, and peace could flourish.

Although at the apogee of his fame when the 1919 Peace Conference assembled in Versailles, Wilson failed to carry his total conception of an ideal peace, but he did secure the adoption of the Covenant of the League of Nations. His major failure, however, was suffered at home when the Senate declined to approve American acceptance of the League of Nations. This stunning defeat resulted from his losing control of Congress after he had made the congressional election of 1918 virtually a vote of confidence, from his failure to appoint to the American peace delegation those who could speak for the Republican Party or for the Senate, from his unwillingness to compromise when some minor compromises might well have carried the day, from his physical incapacity in the days just prior to the vote.

The cause of this physical incapacity was the strain of the massive effort he made to obtain the support of the American people for the ratification of the Covenant of the League. After a speech in Pueblo, Colorado, on September 25, 1919, he collapsed and a week later suffered a cerebral hem-orrhage from the effects of which he never fully recovered. An invalid, he completed the remaining seventeen months of his term of office and lived in retirement for the last three years of his life.

Selected Bibliography

Axson, Stockton, « Woodrow Wilson as Man of Letters », in *The Rice Institute Pamphlet*, 22 (October, 1935) 195–270. Three lectures on Wilson: « Heredity and Environment », « The Political Philosopher », and « The Literary Historian ».

Bailey, Thomas A., *Woodrow Wilson and the Peacemakers*. New York, Macmillan, 1947. This book combines two books previously published separately: *Woodrow Wilson and the Lost Peace* (1944) and *Woodrow Wilson and the Great Betrayal* (1945).

Baker, Ray Stannard, *Woodrow Wilson: Life and Letters*. 8 vols. New York, Doubleday, 1927–1939.

Daniels, Josephus, *The Wilson Era*. 2 vols. Chapel Hill, N.C., University of North Carolina Press, 1946.

Link, Arthur S., *Wilson*. Princeton, Princeton University Press, 1947—. The five volumes published to date are: *The Road to the White House* (1947); *The New Freedom* (1956); *The Struggle for Neutrality: 1914–1915* (1960); *Confusions and Crises: 1915–1916* (1964); *Campaigns for Progressivism and Peace: 1916–1917* (1965).

Phifer, Gregg, « Woodrow Wilson's Swing around the Circle in Defense of His League », in *Florida State University Studies*, No. 23, pp. 65–102. Tallahassee, Fla., Florida State University, 1956.

Seymour, Charles, *The Intimate Papers of Colonel House*. 4 vols. New York, Houghton Mifflin, 1926.

Wilson, Woodrow, *Congressional Government*. New York, Houghton Mifflin, 1885. A modern edition of this book, Wilson's first and best, may be found in Vol. 4 of *The Papers of Woodrow Wilson*, ed. by A. S. Link, pp. 6–179.

Wilson, Woodrow, *A History of the American People*. 5 vols. New York, Harper, 1902.

Wilson, Woodrow, *The New Freedom: A Call for the Emancipation of the Generous Energies of a People*. New York, Doubleday, 1913.

Wilson, Woodrow, *The Papers of Woodrow Wilson*, ed. by Arthur S. Link. Princeton, Princeton University Press, 1966– . Eight volumes of this definitive work, covering the years 1856 to 1894, have been published to date.

Wilson, Woodrow, *The Public Papers of Woodrow Wilson*, ed. by Ray Stannard Baker and William E. Dodd. 6 vols. New York, Harper, 1925–1926.

Peace 1920

LÉON VICTOR AUGUSTE BOURGEOIS

Remarks at the Award Ceremony

by Anders Johnsen Buen*, President of the Norwegian Parliament

The letter from the Nobel Committee of the Norwegian Parliament reads as follows: «The Nobel Committee of the Norwegian Parliament has the honor of announcing herewith its decision to award the Nobel Peace Prize for 1919 to the President of the United States of America Mr. Woodrow Wilson and that for 1920 to Mr. Léon Bourgeois, president of the French Senate and president of the Council of the League of Nations.»

Today, Gentlemen, as the Norwegian Parliament meets to present the Nobel Peace Prize for the first time since the World War[1], it is with the conviction that the great ideal of peace, so deeply rooted in the hopes for survival of the nations, will gain fresh ground in the minds of men as a result of the recent tragic events.

[President Buen then speaks of Woodrow Wilson–included in the section on Wilson.]

And the other Peace Prize, awarded to Léon Bourgeois, is accompanied by a salute from Norway to the will for peace of the French people, whom he has represented with great distinction for many years through good days and bad.

---

* Mr. Buen addressed these remarks to the Parliament at an official session on December 10, 1920, doing so after the Nobel Committee had announced its decision and after the diplomatic representatives of the two absent laureates had been officially admitted to the meeting. He then gave the Nobel diplomas and medals to the two ministers. Mr. Pralon, the French minister, accepted on behalf of Mr. Bourgeois, expressing the laureate's regret at not being there to speak for himself and his gratitude, along with that of France, for the recognition given. The translation of Mr. Buen's comments is based on the Norwegian text in *Forhandlinger i Stortinget* (nr. 502) for December 10, 1920 [Proceedings of the Norwegian Parliament].

1. World War I (1914–1918).

LÉON BOURGEOIS

The Reasons for the League of Nations

Communication to the Nobel Committee, December, 1922*

Some weeks ago, Mr. Branting[1] went to Oslo to fulfill the obligation incumbent upon every Nobel Peace Prize laureate. I wish to offer my apologies
for not having been able to do the same this last year. The state of my
health has not permitted me to make the journey to Norway, and this has
caused me the most profound regret.

Your Chairman informed me that you would permit me to address you
in writing. I now send you my sincere gratitude and an account of certain
ideas of mine, which I would much prefer to have offered you in person.
Gentlemen, please accept my heartfelt thanks.

I

I am in full agreement with the views Mr. Branting expressed to you last
June. With great perspicacity, he analyzed and placed in proper perspective
«the great disillusionment» which the Great War of 1914–1918 had engendered in the minds of men. Certainly, this sudden unleashing of a cataclysm unequalled in the past, appeared to be the direct negation of the
hopes which Nobel had nurtured when he founded the Peace Prize. But
in place of the discouragement which had taken hold of the public, Mr.
Branting offered reasons for believing that we could still derive confidence
from the catastrophe. He showed that, under the ruins left behind by the
bitter times we have just experienced, there were to be found far too many

* Mr. Bourgeois, awarded the prize for 1920, was unable to attend the ceremony on
December 10 of that year. He later told the Nobel Committee that he would deliver
his Nobel lecture sometime between May and September of 1922. Because of illness,
he cancelled this intended appearance but in December of 1922 sent to the Committee
a manuscript that is called a «communication». The text of this communication in
French which appears in the «Nobel Conférences» [Lectures] section of *Les Prix Nobel
en 1921–1922* is used for this translation.
1. Hjalmar Branting (1860–1925), co-recipient of the Nobel Peace Prize for 1921,
gave his Nobel lecture on June 19, 1922.

signs of rejuvenation to allow us to discount the present years as a period of regression.

The victory had been, above all, a victory for law and order, and for civilization itself. The collapse of three great monarchies based largely upon military power had given birth to a number of young nations, each representing the right of peoples to govern themselves, as well as to enjoy the benefits of democratic institutions which, by making peace dependent on the will of the citizens themselves, infinitely reduced the risk of conflict in the future.

The same movement had brought not only the resurrection of oppressed nations, but also the reintegration in political unity of races hitherto torn apart by violence.

Finally, one singularly important fact had succeeded in giving true significance to the victory of free nations. Out of the horror of four years of war had emerged, like a supreme protest, a new idea which was implanting itself in the minds of all people: that of the necessity for civilized nations to join together for the defense of law and order and the maintenance of peace. The League of Nations, heralded in 1899 and 1907 by the Hague Peace Conferences, became, through the Covenant[1] of June 28, 1919, a living reality.

But, can it furnish us at last with a stable instrument of peace? Or shall we again encounter, at the very moment when we think we are reaching our goal, the same obstacles which for centuries have blocked the way of those pilgrims of every race, creed, and civilization who have struggled in vain toward the ideal of peace?

II

To answer this question, which touches upon all the anguish of the human race, and to understand the causes of the upheavals which have beset mankind, we must delve not only into the history of peoples but into that of man himself, into the history of the individual, whose passions are no different from those of his community and in whom we are certain to find all propensities, good or bad, enlarged as in a mirror.

Human passions, like the forces of nature, are eternal; it is not a matter

---

1. A provision of the Treaty of Versailles, 1919.

of denying their existence, but of assessing them and understanding them. Like the forces of nature, they can be subjected to man's deliberate act of will and be made to work in harmony with reason. We see them at work in the strife between nations just as we see them in struggles between individuals, and we realize at last that only by using the means for controlling the latter can we control the former.

To assert that it is possible to establish peace between men of different nations is simply to assert that man, whatever his ethnical background, his race, religious beliefs, or philosophy, is capable of reason. Two forces within the individual contribute to the development of his conscience and of his morality: reason and sensitivity.

His sensitivity is twofold. At first, it is merely an expression of the instinct of self-preservation, springing from the need of all beings to develop at the expense of their surroundings, to the detriment of other beings whose death seems essential to their very existence. But there is also another manifestation of the instinct, which makes him sensitive to the suffering of others: it is this which creates a moral bond between mother and child, then between father and son, and later still between men of the same tribe, the same clan. It is this instinct of sympathy which enables man to fight against and to control his brutish and selfish instincts.

A great French philosopher, criticizing the doctrine according to which «one could wish no more for a race than that it should attain the fullest development of its strength and of its capacity for power», has pointed out that this is only an incomplete concept of what man is. «This is to place man in isolation and to see in him a noble animal, mighty and formidable. But to be seen as a complete whole, man must be viewed in the society which developed him: The superior race is the one best adapted to society and to communal progress.»

In this respect, goodness, the need for sociability, and, to a higher degree, a sense of honor, are spontaneous attributes, valuable beyond all other instincts but just as natural. Now these feelings are present in a national community just as they are in the individuals who compose it. To place them above the gratification of individual egotism is the task of civilization. Never should the power of an individual be allowed to impede the progress of the rest of the nation; never should the power of a nation be allowed to impede the progress of mankind.

Man has a sensitivity which can be either selfish or altruistic; but it is *reason* which is his essence. It is not his violent and contradictory impulses, but rather his reason which, at first hesitant and fragile in childhood, then growing in strength, finally brings man to reconcile the two sides of his sensitivity in conscious and lasting harmony. It is reason which, from the beginning of history, has led mankind little by little in the course of successive civilizations to realize that there is a state preferable to that of the brutal struggle for life, not only a less dangerous state, but the only one capable of conforming to the dictates of conscience; and that is, in its ever increasing complexity and solidity, the truly social state.

The rise of man from the animal to the human level was prolonged by the necessity of rising from a state of barbarism and violence to one of order and peace. In this process too, it was *reason* that finally persuaded man to define, under the name of law, some limits within which each individual must confine himself if he wishes to be worthy of remaining in the social state.

At first, laws evolved out of religious doctrines. It followed that they were recognized only when advantageous to those who practiced the same religion and who appeared equals under the protection of the same gods. For the members of all other cults, there was neither law nor mercy. This was the age of implacable deities, of Baal and of Moloch; it was also the age of Jehovah, preaching to his people the extermination of the conquered.

The torch of *reason* was first held up to the world by Greek philosophy, which led to the stoicism according to which all men are equal and «are the members of a single body», and in which the human will, regulated by law, is regarded as the guiding mechanism of man's activity.

This doctrine of the human will was expressed in Roman law of the Imperial Age by that admirable theory of obligations which, in private law, makes the validity of contracts dependent upon the free consent of the contractors.

What a gulf there still exists between these affirmations of private law and the recognition of the same law as the guiding force for the policies of nations!

Then came Christianity which gave to man's natural capacity for sympathy a form and a forcefulness hitherto unknown. The doctrine of Christ enjoins men, all brothers in His eyes, to love one another. It condemns violence, saying: «He who lives by the sword shall die by the sword.»[1]

1. See Matthew 26:52.

It preaches a Christian communion superseding all nationalities and offering to the Gentiles – in other words, to all nations of the earth – the hope of a better life in which justice will finally rule.

The Middle Ages, on the whole, embodied the history of the development of this doctrine, and for several centuries the efforts of the Papacy reflected a persistent desire to bring to the world, if not justice itself, which seemed still to be beyond the human grasp and which was generally left «in the hands of God», at least a temporary, relative state of peace, «the Truce of God»[1], which gave unhappy humanity a respite from its suffering, a brief moment of security.

But a new period of conflict arrived in its turn to upset Europe with religious wars[2]. These were perhaps the more cruel because they obliged the conscience itself to repudiate compassion and seemed to incite conflict between the two forces which had hitherto shared the world between them: *sensitivity* and *reason*. Not until the eighteenth century were they finally reconciled.

The Declaration of the Rights of Man[3] at last set down for all of mankind the principles of justice without which it would never be possible to lay any foundations for true and lasting peace.

But how much suffering, how much blood had to be squandered for more than a century before we could finally hope to see the application of the truly humanitarian, moral principles proclaimed by the French Revolution! It has been necessary, as Taine[4] says, «to multiply ideas, to establish earlier thinking in the conscious mind, to marshal thoughts around accepted precepts: in a word, to reshape, on the basis of experience, the interior of the human head».

Was not the greatest revolution in history that which allowed *reason* to regard the whole of humanity as being subject to law and to acknowledge the status of «man» in every human being?

All men equal in rights and duties, all men equally responsible for the destiny of mankind – what a dream!

---

1. An effort by the church to limit fighting to certain days and seasons of the year.
2. Especially the struggles between Huguenots and Catholics in France (1562–1598) and the Thirty Years War (1618–1648).
3. Drawn up by the French revolutionists in 1789 and made the preamble of the French constitution of 1791, the Declaration proclaimed the equality of men, the sovereignty of the people, and the individual's right to «liberty, property, security».
4. Hippolyte Adolphe Taine (1829–1893), French critic and historian.

Will the concept of law as mistress of the world finally make reason reasonable?

III

Have we arrived at a stage in the development of universal morality and of civilization that will allow us to regard a League of Nations as viable? If its existence is feasible, what characteristics and what limitations should it have in order to adapt itself to the actual state of affairs in the world?

Certainly, immense progress has already been made in the political, social, and moral organization of most nations.

The spreading of public education to nearly every corner of the globe is producing a powerful effect on many minds.

The prevalence of democratic institutions is evident in every civilized nation.

We are witnessing a weakening of the class prejudice so obstructive to social progress and we see, even in Russia, a rejection of Communist systems that seek to stifle personal liberty and initiative.

Finally, there is an increasing number of social institutions offering assistance, insurance, and fellowship, whose object is the protection of the rights of the individual and, in a broader sense, the propagation of the concept of an increasingly humanitarian justice under which the individual's responsibility for his conduct will no longer be dissociated from that of society itself.

In every nation, all these factors are preparing the way for the intellectual revolution of which we speak, a revolution that will lead people to appreciate and to understand the superiority, indeed the absolute necessity, of having international organizations which will recognize and apply the same principles.

It is true, of course, that there still remain outside the movement to bring civilization to this superior state of conscience, vast territories whose populations, held for centuries in slavery or servitude, have not yet felt the stir of this awakening influence and for whom a period, and undoubtedly a long one at that, of moral and intellectual growth is imperative.

Nevertheless, it is a new and significant fact that the civilized nations, alert to «the sacred trust of civilization», have, within the terms of Article 22 of the Covenant of the League of Nations, undertaken the task of educating the backward peoples so that they may become «able to stand by themselves under the strenuous conditions of the modern world».

Progress has been made not only in terms of institutions, organizations, and customs, but also in a purely political way from the standpoint of the map of Europe and of the world itself.

When the Hague Peace Conference of 1899, meeting at the instigation of the Czar, set before the civilized world the problem of disarmament and of peace, and for the first time mentioned the name «League of Nations», it was *a priori* certain that the problem could not be solved at that time. The political geography of Europe was far too firmly founded on violations of the rights of peoples. How could anyone use it as a basis for organizing peace in the face of this fact?

Today, war has served to eliminate most of the injustices of that time. In Europe, Alsace-Lorraine has been returned to France; Poland has been restored as an independent entity; and the Czechoslovaks, Danes, Belgians, Slavs, and Latins have regained their respective rights of self-government or have been returned to their homelands.

Even in Asia a great effort is being made right now to find, in legality and in peace, a durable balance between the historic rights of the various races.

Does this mean, then, that in Europe or, for that matter, in other parts of the world all sources of trouble have disappeared? We are far from being blindly confident of the future; indeed, we have before our very eyes signs of trouble too obvious and too certain for us even to dream of denying them.

In the first place, certain powers that were defeated in the Great War have not been wholehearted in their acceptance of the moral disarmament which is the primary condition for any peace. Some turbulent minorities of uncertain character, too weak to form a state of their own but resistant to the majority in the societies of which they are a part, are seeking support outside the natural frontiers within which communal life thrives, thus threatening to create areas of friction and violence where there should be mutual tolerance and trust.

In the second place, artificial movements are springing up which seek to cross national boundaries, and to bring together in inorganic bodies the most varied of peoples. Movements such as the Pan-Germanic, Pan-Islamic, or Pan-Negro justify themselves on the basis of their common language, or their common religion, or their color. But since the undefined masses involved in these movements lack the essential and real unity of background or community of purpose, they become a grave danger to general peace.

Yet all this may be of transient significance, for it seems to be mainly part of the last tremors of the cataclysm that has shaken the world.

But there is something more profound that must be taken into account about any international organization. Mr. Branting, in his speech to you a few months ago, showed that there was a world of difference between the International of the classes as envisaged by certain Socialist congresses and the true International of nations, and that only through the latter could peace be truly established among men, instead of being merely longed for against all reasonable hope.

The concept of patriotism is not incompatible with that of humanity; on the contrary, let me state emphatically that he who best serves pacifism, serves patriotism best. The nation is and can be no more than the vital basic unit of any international league. Just as the formation of the family is basic to the formation of the state, so the states themselves are the only units that can form the basic constitution of a viable international organization.

The 1914–1918 War, being a war of liberation of nationalities, could not help overstimulating nationalistic sentiment. It gave greater impetus to the moral and intellectual tendencies conducive to patriotism; it made this feeling, as well-founded as any other, more zealous. As a result, the proposed international organization must, in the final analysis, be based not only on the intangible sovereignty of each nation, but also on the equality of rights of them all, regardless of their strength, weakness, or relative size. It is only among properly constituted states that the reign of law and order can be established.

For these same reasons, it was impossible even to dream of any organization being forced on the nations from without. The idea of a «superstate» whose will could be imposed on the governing bodies of each nation might have brought about a revolt of patriotism. What was and is necessary and at the same time sufficient, is that each nation understand that mutual consent to certain principles of law and to certain agreements, acknowledged to be equally profitable to the contracting parties, no more implies a surrender of sovereignty than a contract in private business implies a renunciation of personal liberty. It is, rather, the deliberate use of this very liberty itself and an acknowledged advantage for both parties.

But what, then, is the fundamental condition necessary for such an agreement, what is the indispensable condition that insures consent without reservation, that gives confidence to all sides that nothing essential, no vital interest, will be sacrificed by any of the contracting parties?

There must be a paramount rule, a sovereign standard, by which each settlement may be measured and checked, just as in the scientific world, man, distrusting his own fallible senses, refers for comparison and evaluation of phenomena to the evidence of standardized instruments free of personal error.

On a moral plane it is law, devoid of individual or national bias and immune to the fluctuations of opinion which will be the instrument, the unprejudiced registrar of claims and counterclaims. By its absolute impartiality and its authoritative evidence, the law will appease passions, disarm ill will, discourage illusory ambitions, and create that climate of confidence and calm in which the delicate flower of peace can live and grow.

Does such a sovereign and unassailable law in fact exist? The history of the past centuries suggests an affirmative answer.

Now and henceforth there exists an international law whose doctrine is firm and whose jurisprudence is not contested by a single civilized nation. The nineteenth century, which introduced the Hague Peace Conferences and generated numerous international conferences on a variety of subjects, also brought an increasing number of applications of international law. If this law was all too obviously violated in 1914 and during the war years, the victory has righted the wrong done. Should such violations ever happen again, then indeed we must despair of the future of mankind.

Of a purely theoretical and doctrinal nature at first, international law is gradually being enriched by numerous conventions containing essential obligations of a judicial order, which can be precisely defined and codified and made legally binding and subject to sanctions. The scope of these conventions grows continuously, gradually embracing moral concepts which constitute what I have called in a recent study, international ethics; it concerns everything that touches on the life, the health, and the well-being, material and spiritual, of all human beings.

International law does in fact exist.

But, can we hope that a juridical body vested with such sovereignty will ever constitute a faithful interpreter of the law as unbiased and dispassionate as the law itself?

The recent course of the deliberations in the League of Nations and the creation of the Court of International Justice[1] enable us to say yes once again!

IV

Let us summarize the three conditions necessarily basic to any international organization which would be in step with contemporary civilization.

In the first place, there must exist among the associated states a community of thought and feeling and a development of ideas which, if not actually identical, should at least be sufficiently analogous to allow a common understanding of the principles of international order and to produce general agreement on the laws which give them effectiveness.

Second, each one of these laws must have received the free and unqualified consent of each state; and if sanctions have been proclaimed in the event of the violation of such a law, these sanctions should have been agreed upon by all in the same way that the laws themselves were, so that no nation can claim to have been forced into participating in a collective action to which it would not have given its consent at the outset.

Finally, there should be a centrally located tribunal to define for each individual case the findings of international law and to rule on their application. Such a tribunal must be one of unquestionable impartiality which compels recognition of its moral authority by virtue of the expert ability and moral caliber of the judges who occupy its benches.

If these three conditions are met—and it will be immediately apparent that all three are in effect contained in one primary condition: the freely given consent of each of the participants—if these conditions are met, then the League of Nations will be able to function, on the one hand with a flexibility which will allow its members to feel secure and at ease within its authority and, on the other hand with the kind of moral force that will preclude the members from even thinking of evading its decisions.

We talk of moral force. But this does not mean that we exclude the use of material force when necessary in extreme cases against nations found guilty of violating the Covenant. We regard it, however, as a last resort

1. The Permanent Court of International Justice, popularly known as the World Court, was set up by the League of Nations in 1921; it was superseded after 1945 by the International Court of Justice, the principal judicial organ of the United Nations.

and if these cases do arise, we are convinced that such force must not be employed until it can be established beyond doubt that an act of violence or aggression has been committed, and then only when the guilt of the alleged aggressor is universally acknowledged.

Moreover, the meaning of Article 10 and of Articles 12, 13, 15, and 16 of the Covenant of the League of Nations in no way contradicts the interpretation we have placed upon them. Our American friends have voiced the fear that Article 10 could involve their country in military operations to which it would not have given its consent. To be sure, Article 10 provides a general guarantee preserving the integrity of the territories of each nation [1]. But none of the articles that follow permits us to conclude that any nation could find itself suddenly involved against its will in a military operation without the explicit consent of the agencies which embody its national sovereignty.

In connection with the difficult problem of limitation of armaments neither the Council nor the Assembly has ever believed it possible to enact relevant statutes without the express support of every nation. Each nation remains free to define and determine the conditions necessary to its internal or external security. In the same way, each nation remains free to give or to withhold its consent to any concerted military action. In the final analysis, the one penalty which can result from the provisions of the Covenant is the loss of the benefits of membership in the League of Nations.

We may be sure that nations will not become attuned in one day to the basic truths which we have tried to define. This will take time and unceasing propaganda, as well as clear evidence of the advantages of association.

We are concerned here with the only kind of propaganda which is truly successful, which–to borrow an expression which has often been used in an execrable sense, and which we would now like to restore to its better and more edifying connotation–might be called: the propaganda of fact. The fact which we have to impress upon everyone's mind, a fact powerful enough to triumph over prejudice, to overcome all resistance and disarm any ill will, is the actual fact of international life itself.

1. Article 10 of the League of Nations Covenant reads as follows: «The Members of the League undertake to respect and preserve as against external aggression the territorial integrity and existing political independence of all Members of the League. In case of any such aggression or in case of any threat or danger of such aggression the Council shall advise upon the means by which this obligation shall be fulfilled.»

Even now there exists in the world an international way of life so power-ful and so complex that nobody can avoid its effects. The protection of public health, the provision of transport facilities, the lowering of customs barriers, the creation of an international credit organization—all these are aspects of internationalism from which no nation, however powerful, can claim to be dissociated. In spite of her size, her extensive industrial and commercial influence, America has suffered no less from unemployment than have the nations of Europe. We have only to recall the terrible effects of speculation on the currency exchange to see how impossible it now is to set up anywhere in the world a watertight bulkhead against the flow of international movements.

Exemplifying the necessity of the international way of life by devising instruments for such a life, learning to live together with men of different nations and different races, and highlighting the universal phenomenon of the solidarity of nations and of men—these will constitute the best, the most effective, and the most persuasive lesson it is possible to imagine.

A lesson concerned with such facts would be invaluable. It is not, how-ever, irrelevant to add another. Propaganda must be organized in all civilized countries to impress upon public opinion the true purpose of the League of Nations, the limitations of its power, the true respect which it holds for the laws and the sovereignty of states, that is to say, for the nations themselves, and at the same time the great moral power it wields in the world through the certitude of its principles.

Fortunately, there are already in nearly all nations large associations which disseminate these teachings far and wide, cutting through political bias to the very heart of popular sentiment.

One of the latest creations of the League of Nations bears this significant title: intellectual cooperation [1]. A committee composed of the most eminent scholars, men of vast learning and brilliant intellect, was set up at one of our recent sessions. Its name is full of promise.

What is intellectual cooperation if not the pooling of all intellectual re-sources for mutual and equitable exchange, just as material and political interests are pooled? All living organisms must have a driving force, a moving spirit. From all these diverse forces arising from nations and races, is it not possible to give birth to a communal soul, to a common science

1. The Assembly of the League adopted a resolution presented by Bourgeois con-cerning the establishment of the Commission on Mutual [Intellectual] Cooperation in September of 1921.

for a communal life, associating but not absorbing the traditions and hopes of every country in a concerted thrust for justice?

To climb by all roads originating from all points of the world to the pinnacle where the law of man itself holds sway in sovereign rhythm – is this not the ultimate end of mankind's painful and centuries-long ascent of calvary?

To be sure, many years of trial must yet elapse, and many retrogressions yet occur before the rumble of human passions common to all men yields to silence; but if the road toward the final goal is clearly marked, if an organization like the League of Nations realizes its potential and achieves its purpose, the potent benefits of peace and of human solidarity will triumph over evil. This at least we may dare to hope for; and, if we will consider how far we have come since the dawn of history, then our hope will gather strength enough to become a true and unshakable faith.

Biography

Léon Victor Auguste Bourgeois (May 21, 1851–September 29, 1925), the «spiritual father» of the League of Nations, was a man of prodigious capabilities and diversified interests. A statesman, jurist, artist, and scholar, Léon Bourgeois, in the course of a long career, held almost every major office available in the French government of the Third Republic.

The son of a clock-maker of Jurassian and Burgundian descent, Bourgeois lived most of his life in Paris in an eighteenth-century townhouse on the rue Palatine. He was an insatiable student, reflective, diligent, enthusiastic, and possessed of a happy propensity for becoming involved in whatever he did. Concerned throughout his life with the improvement of man's condition through education, justice under the law, medical care, and the abolition of war, he was that political anomaly, a politician without personal ambition, who twice refused to run for the presidency of the Republic despite assurances that he could easily capture it.

As a schoolboy at the Massin Institution in Paris, Bourgeois displayed his intelligence, leadership, and oratorical flair early. He continued his education at the Lycée Charlemagne, and, after fighting in an artillery regiment during the Franco-Prussian War, enrolled in the Law School of the University of Paris. His education was remarkably broad. He studied Hinduism and Sanskrit, worked in the fine arts, becoming knowledgeable in music and adept in sculpture–indeed, at the height of his political career he exercised his talent as a draftsman, so it is reported, by drawing caricatures of his colleagues in cabinet meetings.

In 1876, after having practiced law for several years, he assumed his first public office as deputy head of the Claims Department in the Ministry of Public Works. In rapid succession he became secretary-general of the Prefecture of the Marne (1877), under-prefect of Reims (1880), prefect of the Tarn (1882), secretary-general of the Seine (1883), prefect of the Haute-Garonne (1885), director of personnel in the Ministry of the Interior (1886), director of departmental and communal affairs (1887). In November of 1887, at the age of thirty-six, he was appointed chief commissioner of the Paris police.

When in February, 1888, Bourgeois defeated the formidable General Boulanger to become deputy from the Marne, his political future was assured. He joined the Left in the Chamber, attending the congresses of the Radical-Socialist Party and rapidly becoming their most renowned orator. He was named undersecretary of state in Floquet's cabinet (1888), elected deputy from Reims (1889), chosen minister of the Interior in the Tirard cabinet (1890).

As minister of public instruction in Freycinet's cabinet from 1890 to 1892 and again in 1898 under Brisson, Bourgeois instituted major reforms in the educational structure, reconstituting the universities by regrouping the faculties, reforming both the secondary and primary systems, and extending the availability of postgraduate instruction. When he gave up the education portfolio in 1892, he accepted that of the Ministry of Justice for two years.

On November 1, 1895, Bourgeois formed his own government. His political program included the enactment of a general income tax, the establishment of a retirement plan for workers, and implementation of plans for the separation of church and state, but his government succumbed, not quite six months old, to a constitutional fight over finances.

Chairman of the French delegation to the first Hague Peace Conference in 1899, Bourgeois presided over the Third Commission, which dealt with international arbitration, and, together with the chairmen of the British and American delegations, was responsible for the success of the proposal adopted by the Conference to establish a Permanent Court of Arbitration. In early 1903, after the Court had become a reality, he was designated a member.

Bourgeois became president of the Chamber of Deputies in 1902; briefly withdrew from public life in 1904 because of poor health; traveled for a time in Spain, Italy, and the Near East; resisted the urging of his friends to run for the presidency; sought and won election as senator from the Marne in 1905, an office to which he was continuously elected until his death; became minister of foreign affairs under Sarrien in 1906.

In 1907, Bourgeois represented his country at the second Hague Peace Conference where he served as chairman of the First Commission on questions relating to arbitration, boards of inquiry, and pacific settlement of disputes. His speeches at The Hague and at other peace conferences were published in 1910 under the title *Pour la Société des Nations*.

Soon after the turn of the century, Bourgeois twice declined the invitation of the president of the Republic to form governments, but he continued his services to the nation in other posts. He was minister of public works under Poincaré (1912), minister of foreign affairs under Ribot (1914), minister of state during the war, minister of public works (1917).

In January of 1918, heading an official commission of inquiry on the question of a League of Nations, he presented a draft for such an organization. President of a newly formed French Association for the League of Nations, he attended the 1919 international congress, convened in Paris, of various organizations interested in establishing a League, and in the same year served as the French representative on the League of Nations Commission chaired by Woodrow Wilson. He brought out another collection of his speeches at this time, *Le Pacte de 1919 et la Société des Nations*.

The culmination of Bourgeois' career came in 1920 when he assumed the presidency of the French Senate, was unanimously elected the first president of the Council of the League of Nations, and was awarded the Nobel Peace Prize.

Because of deteriorating health and approaching blindness, he was unable to travel to Oslo to accept the prize in person, and in 1923 he retired from the Senate. He died at Château d'Oger, near Epérnay, of uremic poisoning at the age of seventy-four. The French people honored him with a public funeral.

Selected Bibliography

Boulen, Alfred-Georges, «Exposé de la doctrine de M. Bourgeois: La Pente socialiste», in *Les Idées solidaristes de Proudhon*, pp. 23–74. Paris, Marchal & Godde, 1912.

Bourgeois, Léon, *L'Oeuvre de la Société des Nations, 1920–1923*. Paris, Payot, 1923.

Bourgeois, Léon, *Le Pacte de 1919 et la Société des Nations*. Paris, Charpentier, 1919.

Bourgeois, Léon, *Pour la Société des Nations*. Paris, Charpentier, 1910.

Bourgeois, Léon, *Solidarité*. Paris, Colin, 1896.

Brisson, Adolphe, «M. Léon Bourgeois», in *Les Prophètes*, pp. 268–286. Paris, Tallandier & Flammarion, [1903].

Buisson, Ferdinand, *La Politique radicale: Étude sur les doctrines du parti radical et radical-socialiste*. Paris, Giard & Brière, 1908.

Dictionnaire de biographie française.

Hamburger, Maurice, *Léon Bourgeois, 1851–1925*. Paris, Librairie des sciences politiques et sociales, 1932.

Obituaries: *Journal des Économistes*, 82 (octobre, 1925) 247–249; (London) *Times* (September 30, 1925); *New York Times* (September 30, 1925).

Schou, August, *Histoire de l'internationalisme III: Du Congrès de Vienne jusqu'à la pre-*

mière guerre mondiale (1914), pp. 449–451. Publications de l'Institut Nobel Norvégien, Tome VIII. Oslo, Aschehoug, 1963.

Scott, James Brown, «Léon Bourgeois, 1851–1925», in *American Journal of International Law*, 19 (October, 1925) 774–776.

Peace 1921

KARL HJALMAR BRANTING

CHRISTIAN LOUS LANGE

Report of the Speech by Halvdan Koht*

Professor Koht made a long speech today on the occasion of the award of the Nobel Prize to Branting and Lange. He outlined their activities in the cause of peace, stressing Branting's political work, starting with the Socialism which had made him a practical statesman and an international pioneer for peace. He had demonstrated this in practice by his efforts for a peaceful settlement in the matter of the union between Sweden and Norway.

The speaker drew a fascinating picture of Lange's contribution to the work for peace, a contribution which followed completely different lines from that of Branting. He described him as the great organizer with a practical grasp of things, an unswerving idealism, a wealth of knowledge, and a determination to do his duty in good times and bad. He had given evidence of the last during the war[1] – as no other man had.

Branting and Lange were both worthy recipients of the Peace Prize, and it was an honor and a pleasure for us that they should be representatives of two kindred neighboring nations determined to live at peace with each other.

---

* The award ceremony held in the auditorium of the Norwegian Nobel Institute on December 10, 1921, the twenty-fifth anniversary of Alfred Nobel's death, was opened by Mr. Jørgen Gunnarsson Løvland, the chairman of the Nobel Committee, who announced the joint prizewinners for 1921, Mr. Branting and Mr. Lange, and then reviewed Nobel's life and the aims and organization of the Nobel Foundation. His presentation of the diplomas and medals followed. Since Mr. Branting was unable to be present because of official duties, Baron Ramel, the Swedish minister, accepted in his behalf, reading a telegram of thanks from Mr. Branting. After Mr. Lange's acceptance, Professor Halvdan Koht, a member of the Committee, spoke on the life and work of each laureate. There is no text of his speech available. The report given here is a brief summary of it carried (in Norwegian) by the Oslo *Aftenposten* of December 10, 1921.
1. World War I (1914-1918).

Fraternity among Nations

Nobel Lecture*, June 19, 1922

In the fundamental clauses of the Nobel testament concerning the Peace Prize, it is stated that it should be awarded to the men or women who have sought to work for «fraternity among nations, for the abolition or reduction of standing armies and for the holding and promotion of peace congresses».

«Fraternity among nations» is placed first. It sets forth the great goal itself. The other points cover some of the prerequisites and methods of attaining this end, expressed in the light of the striving and longing which prevailed at the time the testament was drawn up. The formulation itself mirrors a particular epoch in history. Fraternity among nations, however, touches the deepest desire of human nature. It has stood as an ideal for some of the most highly developed minds for a millennium; yet in spite of all the progress of civilization, nobody can step forward today and claim with any certainty that this goal will be reached in the near future. However unnoticed before, the clefts and gulfs lying between nations were fully exposed and deepened even further by the World War[1]. And the courageous work of bridging these gaps across the broken world has scarcely been begun.

No matter how far off this high goal may appear to be, no matter how violently shattered may be the illusion entertained at times by many of us that any future war between highly civilized nations is as inconceivable as one between the Scandinavian brothers, we may be certain of one thing: that for those who cherish humanity, even after its relapse into barbarism these past years, the only road to follow is that of the imperishable ideal of the fraternity of nations.

I am sure that I do not, in this connection, have to deal in any detail

---

* This lecture was delivered in the Auditorium of the University of Oslo. The translation is based on the Swedish text published in *Les Prix Nobel en 1921–1922*. The lecture is not given a title in *Les Prix Nobel*; the one provided here embodies in a phrase its central theme.

1. World War I (1914–1918).

with the subject of nationalism and internationalism. The sort of internationalism which rejects the sovereignty of a nation within its own borders and which aims ultimately at its complete obliteration in favor of a cosmopolitan unity, has never been other than a caricature of the true international spirit. Even when supported by quotations out of context—for example, by the well-known words of the *Communist Manifesto*[1], «The worker has no fatherland», or by those of Gustave Hervé who, before becoming violently nationalistic during the war, exhorted French workers to plant the French flag on a dunghill[2]—even then, such ideas have found no real roots in the spirit of people anywhere.

The kind of support encouraged by such modes of expression has always arisen basically from confusing the fatherland itself with the social conditions which happened to prevail in it. How often, recalls Jaurès[3] in his book *The New Host* [*L'Armée nouvelle*], have the socially and politically privileged believed or pretended to believe that their own interests coincided with those of the fatherland: «The customs, traditions, and the primitive instinct of solidarity which contribute to the formation of the concept of patriotism, and perhaps constitute its physiological basis, often appear as *reactionary* forces. The revolutionaries, the innovators, the men who represent a higher law have to liberate a new and superior nation from the grip of the old... When the workers curse their native country, they are, in reality, cursing the social maladjustments which plague it, and this apparent condemnation is only an expression of the yearning for the new nation.»

Who can now deny, after the experiences of the World War, that this view was correct! The contradiction between nationalism and internationalism, which appears so stark when seen in the light of a warped and one-sided exposition of the duties and significance of each, is in reality non-existent. «The same workers,» wrote this great man, «who now misuse paradoxical phrases and hurl their hatred against the very concept of a fatherland, will rise up to a man the day their national independence is in danger.» Prophetic words, confirmed on both sides of the battlefront; yet,

1. The basic formulation of Marxist communism written by Karl Marx and Friedrich Engels (1848).
2. Gustave Hervé (1871–1944), French journalist and founder of the socialist journal *La Guerre Sociale* (1908), left the Socialist Party after the outbreak of W W I, changed his journal's name to *La Victoire*, supported Clemenceau's policies.
3. Jean Léon Jaurès (1859–1914), French Socialist leader; editor of *L'Humanité* (1904–1914).

it had actually been supposed, before any issue was at stake, that the countries on both sides could be invaded with impunity.

It is precisely this deeply rooted feeling for the importance of the nation that later becomes the basis and starting point for true internationalism, for a humanity built not of stateless atoms but of sovereign nations in a free union.

As a result of the World War and of a peace whose imperfections and risks are no longer denied by anyone, are we not even further away from the great aspirations and hopes for peace and fraternity than we were one or two decades ago?

I have already mentioned that recent years have brought with them much disillusionment concerning what has so far been achieved by humanity. But it is possible that, in the days ahead, these years we have lived through may eventually be thought of simply as a period of disturbance and regression.

The signs of renewal are far too numerous and promising to allow of despair. Never since the dawn of history, with its perpetual wars between wild tribes, never up to the present day throughout the unfolding of the ages, during which wars and devastation have occurred with such frequency and with interruptions for only such short periods of peace and recovery, never has our race experienced such a concentrated period of disturbance or such devastation of a large part of the world as that which began in 1914.

Yet in spite of the unique extent of the devastation, we should not forget that this hard labor constituted the birthpangs of a *new Europe*. Three great military monarchies based essentially on a feudal order have collapsed[1] and been replaced by states whose constitutions assert more strongly than ever before the principles of nationality and of a people's right to self-determination. We must remember that the people for whom this change represents a first taste of freedom and a new and brighter future did not allow their resolution to falter, no matter how great the suffering by which they bought this independence. On our own eastern frontiers where we have witnessed with joy the birth of a free Finland[2]; down along the Baltic coast with its three new Baltic states[3]; throughout the newly risen Poland, land of martyrs of freedom[4]; in Czechoslovakia, the fatherland of John Huss and

1. The laureate probably refers to Austria-Hungary, Germany, and Russia.
2. Russia recognized Finland's independence early in 1918.
3. Lithuania, Latvia, and Estonia.
4. A Polish republic was proclaimed in 1918.

Comenius[1]; and in all of southeast Europe's more or less reconstituted states – in all of these, we have rich additions, for each of them will now enjoy a great opportunity to develop nationally, to the ultimate benefit of all that part of the world which we can call our own!

I do not overlook the fact that the appearance of these new, free nations in the European political community not only celebrates the return of the prodigal son but also creates new sources of friction here and there. There is all the more reason, therefore, to concentrate on the other great benefit which has resulted from the past years of darkness: the beginning development of a *League of Nations* in which disputes between members are to be solved by legal methods and not by the military superiority of the stronger.

It is a commonplace that the League of Nations is not yet what its most enthusiastic protagonists intended it to be. The absence of President Wilson's own country[2] and of the great, though vanquished, nations, Germany and Russia[3], so obviously circumscribes its ability to fulfill its task that when its critics speak of the League as a League of the Victorious Powers, they do so with some justification. Even with its faults, which can and must be remedied if our civilization is to survive, the League of Nations is succeeding – for the first time after a huge military catastrophe – in opening perspectives of a durable peace and of justice between the free and independent nations of the world, both large and small.

It is remarkable to see how Alfred Nobel's fundamental ideas reappear in the Covenant of the League of Nations. I have already quoted from his testament, with reference to the road leading toward fraternity among nations; namely, reduction in armaments and promotion of peace congresses. The reduction of armaments is positively enjoined throughout Article 8, although in cautious terms. And the annual meetings of the League's Assembly are in effect official peace congresses binding on the participating states to an extent that most statesmen a quarter of a century ago would have regarded as utopian. But the similarities in their respective lines of thought go even further. In her lecture here in Oslo in 1906, Bertha von

1. Czechoslovakia became an independent republic in 1918. John Huss [Jan Hus] (1369?–1415), religious reformer. John Amos Comenius [Jan Amos Komenský] (1592–1670), theologian and educational innovator.
2. Thomas Woodrow Wilson (1856–1924), recipient of the Nobel Peace Prize for 1919. The U.S. Senate, objecting to certain articles in the League Covenant, voted against ratification, and the U.S. never joined the League.
3. Germany eventually gained admission in 1926; Russia joined in 1934.

Suttner quoted[1] from a private communication addressed to her by Alfred Nobel: «It could and should soon come to pass that all states pledge themselves collectively to attack an aggressor. That would make war impossible and would force even the most brutal and unreasonable Power to appeal to a court of arbitration, or else keep quiet. If the Triple Alliance included every state instead of only three, then peace would be assured for centuries.»

Here we encounter the idea of *sanctions* in an acutely sharp form. Article 16 of the Covenant fortunately contains a considerably toned down version of it. Last year, the Assembly of the League, as a result of the initiative taken by the Scandinavian nations, further limited and clarified all the provisions of the clause prescribing the duty of states to participate in sanctions. But Nobel's basic idea has been realized. The whole collective force of the League is to be turned against the aggressor, with more or less pressure according to the need. Without envisaging any supranational organization, for which the time is not yet ripe, the present approach is as analogous as circumstances permit to that of an earlier age when the state first exercised authority over individual leaders unaccustomed to recognizing any curbs on their own wills.

These last observations about a League comprising all states instead of only a few, should encourage us even today to remain firm in the demand which we small, so-called neutral countries should make at Geneva and everywhere: the demand that the League of Nations become *universal* in order truly to fulfill its task.

No nation is so great as to be able to afford, in the long run, to remain outside an increasingly universal League of Nations. However, in the nature of things, the *smaller* states have a special reason for doing all they can to promote its existence and development.

The equality among all members of the League, which is provided in the statutes giving each state only one vote, cannot of course abolish the actual material inequality of the powers concerned. The great powers which, from various motives, direct the development of the world toward good or evil, either forging the links of a higher concept of humanity or pandering to the greed of the few, will always exert an influence far greater than their individual votes, regardless of any permanent support they may or may not receive from the votes of dependent states. A formally recognized equali-

1. Bertha von Suttner (1843–1914), recipient of the Nobel Peace Prize for 1905. See pp. 85–86 of this volume for the quotation.

ty does, however, accord the smaller nations a position which they should be able to use increasingly in the interest of humanity as a whole and in the service of the ideal. The prerequisite is merely that they try as far as possible to act *in unison*.

We here in the North have for many years had a natural tendency to feel that when our representatives come together at an international meeting, we embark on the quest of mutual understanding and support. In this quest, there has truly been no desire on the part of any one of us to encroach upon the freedom of the others to use their own ways of thinking in arriving at the opinions they wish to hold. No one who has shared this experience, however, has failed to sense that considerable strength arose out of our coalition. It has, moreover, fortunately been the rule, at any rate recently, that the views of the spokesmen for our three peoples have essentially coincided.

Furthermore, the nature of European problems has not infrequently extended our agreement beyond the confines of the North. Other nations, not involved in the World War, have held very similar views on the measures to be taken to ensure better times. This identity of views has of itself led to the creation of a considerable coalition of powers who were neutral during the war. At Geneva, the neutral states were often in agreement concerning the preliminaries for Genoa, and Genoa itself was marked by a quite natural mutual exchange of ideas[1]. This unity of approach to the problem confronting us had become so much a matter of course in other conferences of powers, that the «neutrals», as we were still called, were specially represented in the most important subcommittee.

As long as the problem of world reconstruction remains the center of interest for all nations, blocs having similar attitudes will form and operate even within the League itself. There is no reason why agreement on particular points should not be both possible and advantageous to the so-called neutrals and to one or more of the blocs, either existing or in the process of formation, within the League of Nations. With Finland and with the Baltic states we in the North have strong cultural affinities; the states of the Little Entente[2] often advance views that differ from the unilateral ones of the great powers; and the representatives of the South American nations are likewise evincing a strong tendency to act together. All in all, the League of Nations is not inevitably bound, as some maintain from time to time, to

1. The international Genoa Conference, to which the laureate was a Swedish delegate. was held in the spring of 1922 to consider the economic reconstruction of Europe,
2. An alliance formed after WWI by Czechoslovakia, Yugoslavia, and Rumania.

degenerate into an impotent appendage of first one, then another of the competing great powers. If we all do our best to work for that real peace and reconciliation between peoples which it is our first duty to promote within the League of Nations, then the power to command attention will be available to us, even though, as small nations, we are so isolated and powerless that individually we can exert little influence on the great powers in world politics.

Allow me one other observation. The League of Nations is not the only organization, albeit the most official, which has inscribed the maintenance of peace through law on its banner. Before the war there were many who were more or less ignorant of the international labor movement but who nevertheless turned to it for salvation when the threat of war arose. They hoped that the workers would never permit a war.

We now know that this hope was futile. The World War broke out with such elemental violence, and with such resort to all means for leading or misleading public opinion, that no time was available for reflection and consideration. But after all those horrors, does it follow that the present sentiment of the workers against war, now more widely held, will exhibit the same impotence in every new situation? To be sure, the political International is at present weakened by the split which Bolshevism has caused in the ranks of labor everywhere[1], but the trade-union International at Amsterdam[2] is stronger than ever before. Its twenty million workers are a force to be reckoned with, and their propaganda against war and the danger of war continues ceaselessly among the masses. Some years hence it may well turn out that when the question is asked, Who has in the recent past done most for the cause of peace in the spirit of Alfred Nobel? the answer may be: The Amsterdam International.

Let us return, however, to the League of Nations. To create an organization which is in a position to protect peace in this world of conflicting interests and egotistic wills is a frighteningly difficult task. But the difficulties must not hold us back. I conclude with a few lines from James Bryce[3],

1. In 1921 the international labor movement had been split politically into three Internationals: the Second International, revived in 1919 after WWI; the Third International (Communist), formed in 1919 in Moscow; and the so-called Vienna International, newly created in 1921 by parties which had left the Second International but were not prepared to join the Third International.
2. The International Federation of Trade Unions, founded in 1919 with headquarters at Amsterdam, replaced the old organization of the same name which had disintegrated during WWI.
3. James Bryce (1838–1922), English historian, statesman, and jurist.

which could be said to epitomize the testament of this venerable champion of peace and humanity:

«The obstacles are not insuperable. But whatever they may be, we must tackle them head on, for they are much less than the dangers which will continue to menace civilization if present conditions continue any longer. The world cannot be left where it is at present. If the nations do not try to annihilate war, then war will annihilate them. Some kind of common action by all states who set a value on peace is a compelling necessity, and instead of shrinking from the difficulties, we must recognize this necessity and then go forward.»

Biography

The «father» of socialism in Sweden, Karl Hjalmar Branting (November 23, 1860–February 24, 1925) was born in Stockholm, the only child of Professor Lars Branting, one of the principal developers of the Swedish school of gymnastics. He was educated at the exclusive Beskow School in Stockholm, passing his matriculation examination at the age of seventeen, with a distinguished record in mathematics and Latin. After studying at the University of Uppsala for the next five years, concentrating on mathematics and astronomy, he accepted a position in 1882 as an assistant to the director of the Stockholm Observatory.

But Branting was a social scientist as well as a natural scientist. By 1880 he had adopted liberal views, which had their origin in his studies and observations on social and cultural questions. In 1881 when he learned that the Stockholm Workers Institute, which provided lectures and courses of study for workingmen, had been denied financial support by the city, he contributed from his personal funds the amount necessary to keep the Institute open. For Branting the year of 1883 proved decisive. In Paris he heard the lectures of the French Socialist, Paul Lafargue; in Zurich he learned about German socialist doctrine from Eduard Bernstein, who was publishing *Der Sozial-Demokrat* while in self-imposed exile; wherever he went–including Russia–he tested his thinking in discussion with workingmen and social philosophers.

Giving up his scientific career in 1884, Branting joined the staff of the radical Stockholm paper *Tiden* [The Times] as foreign editor. He became editor-in-chief the next year but, like his predecessor in that office[1], was unable to solve the financial crises which periodically afflicted the paper. Upon its demise in 1886, Branting became chief editor of another socialist newspaper, *Socialdemokraten*, making this journal, in the course of his thirty-one years' association with it, a textbook for the education of the workers and a potent force in Swedish politics. Radical though Branting was, he

---

1. K.P.Arnoldson, co-recipient of the Nobel Peace Prize for 1908.

taught evolution rather than revolution, believing that true democracy could not exist without the active involvement of the workingmen and that any socialist philosophy not based on the democratic concept was a mockery. Branting was not a utopian doctrinaire then or afterwards. Thirty years later, in 1918 for instance, he contended that socialism was an applied theory of democratic development and that communism, on the contrary, was an oligarchy, an enemy of democracy and an enticement to economic disaster in its demand for destruction of proprietary rights.

Branting was not only the schoolmaster of the movement, he was also its recruiter and field marshal. He formed workingmen's clubs, helped to organize unions, supported strikes, directed strategy. In demand as a speaker at innumerable meetings, he became one of the most skillful speakers in the land, noted for his logical argument, precision of style, blunt honesty, warmth of personality.

He was the directing genius behind the formation of the Social Democratic Labor Party in 1889, serving as its president from 1907 until his death. To advance the aspirations of the workingman, political action should, he believed, be enmeshed with industrial action, not superimposed upon it.

Elected to the Lower Chamber of the Parliament in 1896 from a workingmen's constituency in Stockholm, Branting was the sole Social Democrat to hold a seat until 1902. In Parliament he gave visibility to the rights of workers, decried legislation against unions, pled for universal suffrage, supported national defense, and advocated peaceful solution of the crisis between Sweden and Norway over the dissolution of the union in 1905. Meanwhile, the power of his party grew: in 1902 there were four Social Democrats out of a total membership of 230 in the Lower Chamber of the Parliament; in 1903, thirteen; in 1908, thirty-four; in 1911, sixty-four; in 1914, seventy-two; in 1921, a hundred and ten.

By 1917, the Social Democrats were a strong third party in what had traditionally been a two-party system. In that year the Social Democrats joined the Liberals in a coalition government, with Branting as minister of finance. The coalition sponsored the constitutional reform of 1919, extending the franchise to all males (women receiving the vote in 1921 under Branting's government), but it was dissolved when the Liberals refused to support the Social Democrats' demands for tax reform, unemployment insurance, and nationalization.

Branting then formed his first government, depending upon Liberal support since he did not command a majority in Parliament. When the power of the Liberal Party appeared to be diminishing, he dissolved the Parliament in October of 1920, but the ensuing elections went against him. He returned to the prime ministry in October, 1921, retaining the foreign affairs portfolio and departed in April, 1923, when faced by a combination of the Liberals and Conservatives. When the elections of 1924 gave the Social Democrats a majority over each of the other two parties, Branting, for the third time, became prime minister, resigning in January, 1925, when his health failed.

Branting's lifelong interest in international affairs was intensified during and after World War I. He supported the Allied position but insisted upon Swedish neutrality, tried to preserve the international solidarity of the labor-union movement, served as Sweden's representative to the Paris Peace Conference in 1919, advocated adoption of the Covenant of the League of Nations. He led the successful movement to bring Sweden into the League, served as the Swedish delegate to the League, and was named to the Council of the League in 1923. Branting was chairman of the Assembly's Committee on Disarmament in 1920–1921 and a member of the Council's Committee on Disarmament in 1924; he participated in the settlement of the Greek-Italian conflict of 1923 and served as «rapporteur» in the Mosul dispute between Britain and Turkey in 1924; he was involved in the drafting of the Geneva Protocol, a proposed international security system requiring arbitration between hostile nations.

Branting was a «constitutional pacifist». He believed that security should be based on functional principles of justice, that truth in dispute could best be found through arbitrament by a judicial body, not through survival in trial by combat.

By the age of sixty-five, through his continuous and exacting labors, he had worn out a powerful physique bequeathed to him by heredity and strengthened by the discipline of gymnastics. He died in February, 1925, and was buried in Stockholm.

Selected Bibliography

Alsterdal, Alvar, och Ove Sandell, red., *Hjalmar Branting: Socialism och demokrati.* Stockholm, Prisma, 1970.

Branting, Anna (Jäderin), *Min långa resa: Boken om Hjalmar och mig.* Stockholm, Medén, 1945.

Branting, Hjalmar, *Demokratins genombrott.* Stockholm, Tidens Förlag, 1919.

Branting, Hjalmar, *Den politiska krisen: Dess innebörd, uppkomst och första förlopp.* Stockholm, Tidens Förlag, 1914.

Branting, Hjalmar, *Socialdemokratiens århundrade.* Första bandet: *Frankrike, England.* Andra bandet: *Tyskland, Sverige, Danmark, Norge.* Stockholm, Aktiebolaget Ljus, 1904, 1906.

Branting, Hjalmar, *Tal och skrifter i urval,* utgåvos i 11 delar. Z. Höglund [o. fl.], red. Stockholm, Tidens Förlag, 1927–1930.

Branting, Hjalmar, *Varför det var rätt att antaga pensionförsäkringslagen.* Stockholm, Tidens Förlag, 1913.

Branting, Hjalmar, och Per A. Hansson, *Demokratisk linje: Tal och artiklar.* Stockholm, Tidens Förlag, 1948.

Hjalmar Branting: Statsmannen och människan. Stockholm, Morgon-Tidningen, 1950.

Höglund, Zeth, *Hjalmar Branting.* Stockholm, Folket i bilds Förlag, 1949. A condensation of the two-volume biography by the same author.

Höglund, Zeth, *Hjalmar Branting och hans livsgärning.* 2 band. Stockholm, Tidens Förlag, 1928–1929.

Lindgren, John, *Från Per Götrek till Per Albin: Några drag ur den svenska socialdemokratiens historia.* Stockholm, Bonniers, 1946.

MacDonald, Ramsay, «Ebert and Branting: Helmsmen in Europe's Storm and Stress Period», in *Living Age,* 325 (June 6, 1925) 487–495. Reprinted from *Nineteenth Century and After,* 97 (April, 1925) 465–475.

Magnusson, Gerhard, *Socialdemokratien i Sverige.* Första bandet: I brytningstider. Andra bandet: I kamptider. Tredje bandet: I ansvarstider. Stockholm, Norstedt, 1920–1924.

Nerman, Ture, *Hjalmar Branting: Fritänkaren.* Stockholm, Tidens Förlag, 1960.

Nerman, Ture, *Hjalmar Branting: Kulturpublicisten.* Stockholm, Tidens Förlag, 1958.

Vallentin, Hugo, «Hjalmar Branting: A Character Sketch of the Swedish Socialist Leader», in *Fortnightly Review,* 108 (July, 1917) 62–68.

CHRISTIAN L. LANGE

Internationalism

Nobel Lecture*, December 13, 1921

I

In accordance with the Statutes of the Nobel Foundation, every prizewinner is supposed to deliver a public lecture on the work which earned him the prize. It has seemed natural for me, when fulfilling this obligation today, to try to give an account of the theoretical basis of the work which is being done for international peace and law, work of which my efforts form a part. It is probably superfluous to mention that this account is not original in any of its details; it must take its material from many fields in which I am only a layman. At best it can claim to be original only in the manner in which the material is assembled and in the spirit in which it is given.

I shall discuss *Internationalism*, and not «Pacifism». The latter word has never appealed to me – it is a linguistic hybrid, directing one-sided attention to the negative aspect of the peace movement, the struggle against war; «antimilitarism» is a better word for this aspect of our efforts. Not that I stand aside from pacifism or antimilitarism; they constitute a necessary part of our work. But I endow these words with the special connotation (not universally accepted) of a *moral* theory; by pacifism I understand a moral protest against the use of violence and war in international relations. A pacifist will often – at least nowadays – be an internationalist and vice versa. But history shows us that a pacifist need not think internationally. Jesus of Nazareth was a pacifist; but all his utterances, insofar as they have survived, show that internationalism was quite foreign to him, for the very reason that he did not think politically at all; he was apolitical. If we were to place him in one of our present-day categories, we should have to call him an antimilitarist and an individualistic anarchist.

Internationalism is a *social* and *political* theory, a certain concept of how human society ought to be organized, and in particular a concept of how the nations ought to organize their mutual relations.

* Dr. Lange delivered this lecture at the Norwegian Nobel Institute in Oslo. This translation is based on the Norwegian text in *Les Prix Nobel en 1921–1922*.

The two theories, *nationalism* and *internationalism*, stand in opposition to each other because they emphasize different aspects of this question. Thus, they often oppose each other on the use of principles in everyday politics, which for the most part involve decisions on individual cases. But there is nothing to hinder their final synthesis in a higher union–one might say in accordance with Hegel's dialectic[1]. On the contrary. Internationalism also recognizes, by its very name, that nations do exist. It simply limits their scope more than one-sided nationalism does.

On the other hand, there is an absolute conflict between nationalism and *cosmopolitanism*. The latter looks away from and wants to remove national conflicts and differences, even in those fields where internationalism accepts, and even supports, the fact that nations should develop their own ways of life.

II

Like all social theories, internationalism must seek its basis in the economic and technical fields; here are to be found the most profound and the most decisive factors in the development of society. Other factors can play a role –for example, religious beliefs, which have often influenced the shaping of societies, or intellectual movements–but they are all of subsidiary importance, and sometimes of a derivative, secondary nature. The most important factors in the development of society are, economically, the possibility of a division of labor, and technically, the means of exchanging goods and ideas within the distribution system–in other words the degree of development reached by transport and communications at any particular time.

From ethnography and history we can discern three stages in the development of social groups, limited by the possibilities provided through economic and technical development: the nomadic horde whose members live from hand to mouth; the rural community (county) or city-state where the scope of the division of labor is restricted; the territorial state and the more or less extensive kingdom in which the division of labor and the exchange of goods reach larger proportions. Every time economic and technical development takes a step forward, forces emerge which attempt to

1. Georg Wilhelm Friedrich Hegel (1770–1831), German philosopher in whose view a concept (thesis) interacts with another concept (antithesis) to form a new concept (synthesis) which in turn becomes a new thesis.

create political forms for what, on the economic-technical plane, has already more or less become reality. This never comes about without a struggle. The past dies hard because the contemporary political organizations or holders of power seldom bend themselves willingly to the needs of the new age, and because past glories and traditions generally become transformed into poetic or religious symbols, emotional images, which must be repudiated by the practical and prosaic demands of the new age. Within each such social group, a feeling of solidarity prevails, a compelling need to work together and a joy in doing so that represent a high moral value. This feeling is often strengthened by the ruling religion, which is generally a mythical and mystical expression of the group feeling. War within the group is a crime, war against other groups a holy duty.

Today we stand on a bridge leading from the territorial state to the world community. Politically, we are still governed by the concept of the territorial state; economically and technically, we live under the auspices of worldwide communications and worldwide markets.

The territorial state is such an ancient form of society—here in Europe it dates back thousands of years—that it is now protected by the sanctity of age and the glory of tradition. A strong religious feeling mingles with the respect and the devotion to the fatherland. The territorial state today is always ready to don its «national» costume: it sees in national feeling its ideal foundation. Historically, at least in the case of the older states, nationalism, the fatherland feeling, is a product of state feeling. Only recently, during the nineteenth century, and then only in Europe, do we meet forms of the state which have been created by a deliberate national feeling. In particular, the efforts to reestablish peace after the World War have been directed toward the formation of states and the regulation of their frontiers according to a consciously national program.

It is characteristic that this should take place just when it is becoming more and more clear to all who think about the matter, that technically and economically we have left the territorial state behind us. Modern techniques have torn down state frontiers, both economical and intellectual. The growth of means of transport has created a world market and an opportunity for division of labor embracing all the developed and most of the undeveloped states. Thus there has arisen a «mutual dependence» between the world's different peoples, which is the most striking feature of present-day economic life. Just as characteristic, perhaps, is the intellectual interdependence created through the development of the modern media of communication: post, telegraph, telephone, and popular press. The simultaneous reactions elicited all over the world by the reading of newspaper dispatches about the same events create, as it were, a common mental pulse beat for the whole of civilized mankind. From San Francisco to Yokohama, from Hammerfest to Melbourne, people read at the same time about the famine in Russia, about the conference in Washington, about Roald Amundsen's trip to the North Pole[1]. They may react differently, but they still react simultaneously.

The free trade movement in the middle of the last century represents the first conscious recognition of these new circumstances and of the necessity to adapt to them. Some years before the war, Norman Angell coined the word «interdependence»[2] to denote the situation that stamps the economic and spiritual culture of our time, and laid down a program for internationalism on the political level.

Inherent in the very idea of politics is the notion that it must always «come after». Its task is to find external organizational forms for what has already been developed as a living reality in the economic, technical, and intellectual fields. In his telegram to the Nobel Committee recently, Hjalmar Branting[3] formulated the task of internationalism in exactly the right words when he described it as «working toward a higher form of development for world civilization».

The World War showed how very necessary it is that this work be brought to a victorious conclusion. It is a matter of nothing less than our civilization's «to be or not to be». Europe cannot survive another world war.

Moreover, if the territorial state is to continue as the last word in the development of society, then war is inevitable. For the state by its nature claims *sovereignty*, the right to an unlimited development of power, determined only by self-interest. It is by nature anarchistic. The theoretically unrestricted right to develop power, to wage war against other states, is

---

1. The Russian famine of 1921–1922, the Washington Conference on naval armaments and Far-Eastern questions (November 12, 1921–February 6, 1922), and the Arctic expedition of the Norwegian explorer, Roald Amundsen (1872–1928), were all in the news at the time of the laureate's lecture.

2. Norman Angell (1872–1967), recipient of the Nobel Peace Prize for 1933, in *The Great Illusion* (1910).

3. Hjalmar Branting (1860–1925), co-recipient, with Lange, of the Peace Prize for 1921.

antisocial and is doubly dangerous, because the state as a mass entity represents a low moral and intellectual level. It is an accepted commonplace in psychology that the spiritual level of people acting as a crowd is far lower than the mean of each individual's intelligence or morality.

Therefore, all hope of a better future for mankind rests on the promotion of «a higher form of development for world civilization», an all-embracing human community. Are we right in adopting a teleological viewpoint, a belief that a radiant and beneficent purpose guides the fate of men and of nations and will lead us forward to that higher stage of social development? In propaganda work we must necessarily build upon such an optimistic assumption. Propaganda must appeal to mankind's better judgment and to the necessary belief in a better future. For this belief, the valley of the shadow of death is but a war station on the road to the blessed summit.

But teleological considerations can lead no further than to a belief and a hope. They do not give certainty. History shows us that other highly developed forms of civilization have collapsed. Who knows whether the same fate does not await our own?

III

Is there any real scientific basis for the concept of internationalism apart from the strictly sociological approach?

For thousands of years, prophets and thinkers have pointed to the *unity of mankind* as constituting such a basis. The idea was developed in theory by the Greek philosophers, especially by the Stoics, and from them early Christianity took it up as a moral-religious principle, preaching the doctrine of God as the universal father, and that of the brotherhood of man. The idea was revived as a confirmed maxim at the beginning of more recent times by a number of writers–among them, the heretical Sebastian Franck[1], the Jesuit Suárez, one of the founders of modern international law[2], and Amos Comenius, the last bishop of the Moravian Brethren and the father of modern teaching. With Comenius, the concept actually acquires a physio-

1. Sebastian Franck [Franck von Wörd] (1499?–1543), German free thinker and religious writer who left Catholic priesthood to join the Lutheran Church but later separated from it.
2. Francisco Suárez (1548–1617), Spanish theologian and scholastic philosopher who refuted the patriarchal theory of government.

logical tinge when he writes: «Thus we human beings are like a body which retains its individuality throughout all its limbs.»[1] Thereafter, the idea was kept alive in Western cultures. It dominated the leading minds during the seventeenth, eighteenth, and nineteenth centuries, from William Penn and Leibnitz to Wergeland and Emerson[2].

In recent times, biology has found a totally rational and genuinely scientific basis for the concept. The unity of mankind is a physiological fact. It was the German Weismann's[3] study of jellyfish (1883) that opened the approach to such an understanding. Other scholars went on to prove that the law which Weismann had applied to jellyfish applied equally to all species of animals, including man. It is called the law of «continuity of the germ plasm».

Upon the union of the male germ cell with the female egg cell, a new cell is created which almost immediately splits into two parts. One of these grows rapidly, creating the human body of the individual with all its organs, and dies only with the individual. The other part remains as living germ plasm in the male body and as ova in the female. In this way there live in each one of us actual, tangible, traceable cells which come from our parents and from their parents and ancestors before them, and which–through conception–can in turn become our children and our children's children. Each of us is, literally and physiologically, a link in the big chain that makes up mankind.

All analogies break down at some point. And yet it seems to me appropriate to look upon mankind as a mighty tree, with branches and twigs to which individuals are attached as leaves, flowers, and fruit. They live their individual, semi-independent lives; they

> *Wake, grow and live,*
> *Change, age and die.*[4]

The tree, however, remains and continues, with its branches and twigs and

1. John Amos Comenius (1592–1670), Czech theologian and educational innovator; the quotation is from his *Panegersia* (1645).
2. William Penn (1644–1718), English Quaker and founder of Pennsylvania in North America. Baron Gottfried Wilhelm von Leibnitz (1646–1716), German philosopher and mathematician. Henrik Arnold Wergeland (1808–1845), Norwegian poet, playwright, and patriot. Ralph Waldo Emerson (1803–1882), American essayist, poet, and philosopher.
3. August Weismann (1834–1914), German biologist.
4. «vekkes, spirer og födes,/skifter, eldes og dödes.»

shoots, and with constantly renewed leaves, flowers, and fruit. The latter have their small, short, personal lives. There are leaves that wither and fall unnoticed to the ground; there are flowers which gladden with their scent and color; there are fruits which can give nourishment and growth. Leaves, flowers, and fruit come and go in countless numbers; they establish connections with each other so that a net, with innumerable intersections, embraces the whole tree. It is at this point that our analogy breaks down – but the tree is one, and mankind is one single organism.

During the World War, two natural scientists, independently but with the same purpose in mind, developed and clarified the significance for internationalism of this biological conception[1]. Their work, especially the second author's application of the theory, with which many natural scientists disagree, need not concern us here. Of sole use to us is the fact on which it is based. I wish only to draw a single conclusion: if mankind is a physiological entity, then war – international war no less than civil war – is suicide, a degradation of mankind. Hence, internationalism acquires an even stronger support and a firmer foundation to build on than that which purely social considerations can give.

IV

The consequences and applications of the theory of internationalism, as it is here defined and supported, are not difficult to establish. They appear in the economic and political fields. But their fundamental importance in the purely spiritual fields is limited.

Economically, the consequences of internationalism are obvious and have already been hinted at. The main concept is that of an international solidarity expressed in practice through worldwide division of labor: free trade is the principal point in the program of internationalism. This also agrees with the latest ideas and theories in the field of natural science. Concord, solidarity, and mutual help are the most important means of enabling animal species to survive. All species capable of grasping this fact manage better in the struggle for existence than those which rely upon their own strength alone: the wolf, which hunts in a pack, has a greater chance of survival than the

1. Chalmers Mitchell, *Evolution and the War* (London, 1915). G.F.Nicolai, *Die Biologie des Krieges* (2nd ed., Zurich, 1919; the second edition, but not the first, was supervised by the author himself).

lion, which hunts alone. Kropotkin[1] has fully illustrated this idea with examples from animal life and has also applied it to the social field in his book *Mutual Aid* (1902).

It is necessary to linger in a little more detail over the *political* consequences of internationalism. Here the task is to devise patterns of organization for the concept of world unity and cooperation between the nations. That, in a word, is the great and dominating political task of our time.

Earlier ages fortified themselves behind the sovereign state, behind protectionism and militarism. They were subject to what Norman Angell called the «optical illusion» that a human being increased his stature by an inch if the state of which he was a citizen annexed a few more square miles to rule over, and that it was beneficial for a state to be economically self-supporting, in the sense that it required as few goods as possible from abroad. This national protectionism was originally formulated by the American Alexander Hamilton[2], one of the fathers of the United States Constitution; it was then transplanted by the German Friedrich List[3] from American to European soil where it was converted to use in the protectionist agitation in all the European countries.

Hand in hand with nationalist economic isolationism, militarism struggles to maintain the sovereign state against the forward march of internationalism. No state is free from militarism, which is inherent in the very concept of the sovereign state. There are merely differences of degree in the militarism of states. A state is more militaristic the more it allows itself to be guided by considerations of military strategy in its external and internal policies. The classic example here is the Prussian-German kaiser-state before, and especially during, the World War. Militarism is basically a way of thinking, a certain interpretation of the function of the state; this manner of thinking is, moreover, revealed by its outer forms: by armaments and state organization.

It is against this concept of the sovereign state, a state isolated by protectionism and militarism, that internationalism must now engage in decisive battle. The sovereign state has in our times become a lethal danger to human civilization because technical developments enable it to employ an infinite

---

1. Prince Peter Alexeivich Kropotkin (1842–1921), Russian geographer, social philosopher, and revolutionary.
2. Alexander Hamilton (1757?–1804), first U.S. secretary of the treasury (1789–1795).
3. Georg Friedrich List (1789–1846), German-born economist, naturalized American citizen who returned to Germany as U.S. consul.

number and variety of means of destruction. Technology is a useful servant but a dangerous master. The independent state's armaments, built up in a militaristic spirit, with unlimited access to modern methods of destruction, are a danger to the state and to others. From this point of view we can see how important work for disarmament is; it is not only a task of economic importance, which will save unproductive expenditure, but also a link in the efforts to demilitarize – or we might say, to civilize – the states, to remove from them the temptation to adopt an arbitrary anarchical policy, to which their armaments subject them.

If the sovereign state were supported only by the narrow, self-serving ideas embodied in economic isolationism and militarism, it would not be able to count on a secure existence, for internationalism could wage a fairly effective fight against it. But the sovereign state is also sustained by a spiritual principle: it claims to be «national», to represent the people's individuality as a distinct section of mankind.

It has already been said that in most states the «nation» is a product of the state, not the basis for the creation of the state. And when it is asserted that these «nations» have anthropological character of their own, a «racial» character, the answer must be that the state which is inhabited by an anthropologically pure race is yet to be found. Scientific investigations prove that there is in all countries an endless crossbreeding between the various constituents of the population. A «pure race» does not exist at all. Furthermore, although various external anthropological distinctions – the shape of the head, the hair, the color of skin – are exact enough in themselves, we cannot prove that any intellectual or spiritual traits are associated with them.

And «nationality» is nothing if not a spiritual phenomenon. Renan has given the valid definition: «A nation is a part of mankind which expresses the will to be a nation; a nation's existence is a continuous, daily plebiscite – un plébiscite de tous les jours.»[1] The first clause is a circular definition. It is both sharply delimited and totally exhaustive because it puts the emphasis on the *will* to be a nation. The concept of nationality thus moves into the realm of the spiritual. There it belongs, and there it should stay.

Internationalism will not eradicate these spiritual distinctions. On the contrary, it will develop national characteristics, protect their existence, and free their development. Internationalism differs in this from cosmopolitan-

1. Ernest Renan (1823–1892), French philologist, historian, and philosopher; the quotation is from «Qu'est-ce que c'est qu'une nation?» (1882), a lecture delivered at the Sorbonne.

ism. The latter wants to wipe out or at least to minimize all national characteristics, even in the spiritual field. Internationalism on the other hand
admits that spiritual achievements have their roots deep in national life;
from this national consciousness art and literature derive their character and
strength and on it even many of the humanistic sciences are firmly based.

Diversity in national intellectual development, distinctive character in
local self-government – both of these are wholly compatible with internationalism, which indeed is really a prerequisite for a rich and varied development.

It is the political authority over *common interests* that internationalism
wants to transfer to a common management. Thus, a world federation, in
which individual nations linked in groups can participate as members, is
the political ideal of internationalism. Before the war, a first groping step
was taken in this direction with the work at The Hague[1]. *The League of
Nations* marks the first serious and conscious attempt to approach that goal.

V

A definition of internationalism along the lines which have here been discussed could take the following form:

Internationalism is a community theory of society which is founded on
economic, spiritual, and biological facts. It maintains that respect for a
healthy development of human society and of world civilization requires
that mankind be organized internationally. Nationalities should form the
constitutive links in a great world alliance, and must be guaranteed an independent life in the realm of the spiritual and for locally delimited tasks,
while economic and political objectives must be guided internationally in
a spirit of peaceful cooperation for the promotion of mankind's common
interests.

VI

One last word.

Has this theory of internationalism any relevance to our religious needs,

1. The Hague Peace Conferences of 1899 and 1907.

to the claim to eternity that irresistibly arises in the soul of every thinking and feeling person?

There are surely many of us who can only regard the belief in personal immortality as a claim which must remain unproved—a projection of the eternity concept onto the personal level.

Should we then be compelled to believe that the theory of materialism expressed in the old Arab parable of the bush whose leaves fall withered to the ground and die without leaving a trace behind, truly applies to the family of man?

It seems to me that the theory of mankind's organic unity and eternal continuity raises the materialistic view to a higher level.

The idea of eternity lives in all of us. We thirst to live in a belief which raises our small personality to a higher coherence—a coherence which is human and yet superhuman, absolute and yet steadily growing and developing, ideal and yet real.

Can this desire ever be fulfilled? It seems to be a contradiction in terms.

And yet there is a belief which satisfies this desire and resolves the contradiction.

It is the belief in the unity of mankind.

Biography

In the first third of the twentieth century, Christian Lous Lange (September 17, 1869–December 11, 1938) became one of the world's foremost exponents of the theory and practice of internationalism. His career from his school days to his death was closely focused on international affairs.

Lange was born in Stavanger, an old city on Norway's southwestern coast. His paternal grandfather had been an editor and historian; his father was an engineer in the armed services. After graduating from the local schools in 1887, Lange studied history, French, and English at the University of Oslo, traveled and studied in France and England, and received the Master of Arts degree from the University of Oslo in 1893. For some years thereafter he taught in the secondary schools of Oslo. In 1919 he was granted the Ph.D. degree by the University of Oslo.

Lange's first official connection with internationalism came in 1899 when he was appointed secretary of the committee on arrangements for the Conference of the Interparliamentary Union to be held that year in Oslo. His capacity for organization having been noted, Lange was the next year appointed secretary to the Norwegian Parliament's Nobel Committee and to the nascent Norwegian Nobel Institute. He resigned from this position in 1909 but served as an adviser to the Institute from then until 1933, and from 1934 until his death as a member of the Committee itself. Lange was involved in the planning of the Institute's building, which was opened in 1905, as well as in the founding of its library the year before. He looked upon the Institute as a «scientific» institution, a «peace laboratory, a breeding place of ideas and plans for the improvement and development of international relations»[1].

Lange's association with the Interparliamentary Union, auspiciously begun in 1899, was continued in 1909 when he was appointed its secretary-general, holding this office until 1933 when he declined reappointment. The organization which he was called to administer, still flourishing today, was ini-

1. Christian L. Lange, «The Future of the Norwegian Nobel Institute», p. 1063.

tiated in 1888 by William Randal Cremer and Frédéric Passy, both destined
to become Nobel Peace Prize laureates[1]. Its members are active parliamentarians who form groups within the structure of national legislative bodies—
there are sixty-eight such groups at present. Broadly stated, its objectives,
then and now, are to promote personal relations among the world's legis-
lators and to strengthen democratic institutions throughout the world; its
more specific objective is that of encouraging efforts on behalf of peace
and international intercourse, especially by substituting processes of adju-
dication for force in the resolution of international conflicts.

As the first paid, nonparliamentary secretary-general, Lange administered
the affairs of the Interparliamentary Bureau, met with parliamentary groups
in various countries, helped to formulate the agenda for the annual meetings,
edited the official publications of the Union, raised money (Norway was
the first country to provide an annual subvention to the Union), and kept
the Union in the public eye by lecturing and publishing on his own account.
To this job in which personal diplomacy was a necessity, Lange brought
tact, personal magnetism, and a character that elicited trust.

Lange supervised the reorganization of the Bureau after it was moved
from Bern to Brussels in 1909, and in 1914, when Germany overran Belgium, installed the office in his own home in Oslo. That the Union continued
to exist during and after the war when so many international organizations
became casualties is a tribute to Lange's persistence. Since the Union's funds
in Brussels had been impounded by the Germans and most of the parliamentary groups were no longer providing contributions, Lange made ends
meet by obtaining loans from the Carnegie Endowment for International
Peace and by cutting expenses, even carrying on correspondence in his own
hand. The war over, he convened the Council of the Union in Geneva
in 1919, and the Council, in turn, convened the first postwar conference
of the Union in Geneva in 1921. To be close to the League of Nations and
its vast array of international activities, Lange moved the administrative and
editorial headquarters of the Union to Geneva.

Either as private citizen or as governmental representative, Lange participated in numerous other international activities. In 1907 he was a technical delegate of the Norwegian government to the second Hague Peace
Conference; in 1915 and later he was active in the work of the Central
Organization for a Lasting Peace, an organization founded by the Dutch;

1. Cremer in 1903 and Passy in 1901.

in 1917, at the invitation of the Carnegie Endowment for International Peace, he prepared a report, later published both separately and in the *New York Times*, on conditions in the warring countries, especially in Russia; from 1916 to 1929 he was a «special correspondent» for the Carnegie Endowment.

From the opening of the League of Nations until his death, Lange was a delegate or an alternate delegate from Norway, always «a sort of standing adviser». The author of those words, Oscar J. Falnes, lists some of Lange's official League duties: in 1920 Lange provided a general orientation for the Assembly's Committee VI (Disarmament); in 1932 he headed the Assembly's Committee VI (Political Questions); in 1933 headed the Advisory Committee which kept the Assembly informed on the Sino-Japanese situation; in 1936 chaired the Assembly's Committee III (Arms Reduction); in 1938 served on the Assembly's committee on armament problems[1].

Lange was a liberal in social philosophy, buttressing his progressive beliefs with sound historical knowledge and wide acquaintance with contemporary culture. He believed in free speech, free trade, universal suffrage, the mobility of labor and the workers' right to organize. An international defender of democratic doctrine, he pinpointed its special characteristic as «the subordination of the executive to the legislature»[2]. He was an expert on the complicated subjects of arbitration and control of armament. He treated the subjects of internationalism and pacifism theoretically, but, perhaps more habitually, historically. His book-length history of pacifist doctrine surveys the subject from antiquity to the period immediately after World War I. The first volume of his *Histoire de l'internationalisme*, published in 1919, initiated a projected survey from classical times to his own day. Volume II, for which he had written the early chapters before his death, was completed and published in 1954 by August Schou, the present director of the Norwegian Nobel Institute, who himself did the research and the writing of Volume III, published in 1963. Of Lange's theory of internationalism defined in the *Histoire*, as well as in many of his other publications and speeches, including his Nobel lecture, Schou has remarked that it «agrees with the principle that had become the basis of the League of Nations» and that Lange «made an important contribution by participating in the work of ideological preparation for the League»[3].

1. Falnes, «Christian L. Lange and His Work for Peace», p. 272.
2. Lange, «Parliamentary Government and the Interparliamentary Union», p. 3.
3. August Schou, «The Peace Prize», in *Nobel: The Man and His Prizes* (Amsterdam: Elsevier, 1962), p. 565.

Lange died at the age of sixty-nine on December 11, 1938, one day after the seventeenth anniversary of his being awarded the Nobel Peace Prize.

Selected Bibliography

Falnes, Oscar J., «Christian L. Lange and His Work for Peace», *American-Scandinavian Review*, 57 (1969) 266–274.

Fett, Harry, «Christian Lange», in *Godviljens menn*, pp. 124–152. Oslo, 1948.

Lange, Christian L., *The Conditions of a Lasting Peace: A Statement of the Work of the Union*. Oslo, Interparliamentary Union, 1917. This work has appeared in French, German, and Scandinavian editions.

Lange, Christian L., *Den europaeiske borgerkrig*. Oslo, Aschehoug, 1915.

Lange, Christian L., «The Future of the Norwegian Nobel Institute», *The Independent*, 62 (May 9, 1907) 1060–1064.

Lange, Christian L., «Histoire de la doctrine pacifique et de son influence sur le développement du droit international», dans *Recueil des cours* (Académie de droit international), 1926, III, Tome 13 de la Collection, pp. 171–426. Paris, Hachette, 1927. Contains a bibliography of Lange's principal publications up to 1926.

Lange, Christian L., *Histoire de l'internationalisme I: Jusqu'à la Paix de Westphalie (1648)*. Christian L. Lange et August Schou, *Histoire de l'internationalisme II: De la Paix de Westphalie jusqu'au Congrès de Vienne (1815)*. August Schou, *Histoire de l'internationalisme III: Du Congrès de Vienne jusqu'à la première guerre mondiale (1914)*. Publications de l'Institut Nobel Norvégien, Tomes IV, VII, VIII. Oslo, Aschehoug, 1919, 1954, 1963.

Lange, Christian L., *Organisation centrale pour une paix durable: Exposé des travaux de l'organisation*. La Haye, Organisation centrale pour une paix durable, 1917.

Lange, Christian L., «Parliamentary Government and the Interparliamentary Union», in World Peace Foundation Pamphlet Series, Vol. 1, No. 3, Part III. Boston, World Peace Foundation, 1911. Originally a paper read at the First Universal Races Congress, London, July 26–29, 1911, entitled «Tendencies towards Parliamentary Rules».

Lange, Christian L., *Russia, the Revolution and the War: An Account of a Visit to Petrograd and Helsingfors in March, 1917*. Washington, D.C., Carnegie Endowment for International Peace (Division of Intercourse and Education, No. 12), 1917.

Lange, Christian L., *Union interparlementaire: Résolutions des conférences et décisions principales du conseil*, 2e éd. Bruxelles, Misch & Thron, 1911.

Norsk biografisk leksikon.

Obituary, *New York Times* (December 12, 1938).

Peace 1922

FRIDTJOF NANSEN

Presentation

by Fredrik Stang*, Chairman of the Nobel Committee

I take pleasure in announcing that this year's Peace Prize has been awarded to Professor Fridtjof Nansen.

Work of an international character carried out by Mr. Nansen during these past years has brought him the Peace Prize. I might especially mention his work in the repatriation of prisoners of war, his work for the Russian refugees, his work in aiding the millions in Russia struggling against famine, and now his work for the refugees in Asia Minor and Thrace. Although this activity has been in progress for only a few years, its extent and significance are such that the Nobel Committee has felt it worthy of the great distinction of the Nobel Peace Prize.

Those of us who have remained at home, following events only through the newspapers, have had but isolated glimpses of all this. We have seen how great international tasks have again and again been entrusted to Nansen. We have seen him appear as the High Commissioner of the League of Nations[1], its representative and plenipotentiary. We have seen him negotiating with representatives of nearly every country in Europe or with agencies created under his administration. We see him incessantly on the move: one day we read in a cable that he is having talks with Lloyd George[2] in London;

* Mr. Stang, newly elected chairman of the Nobel Committee and at this time rector of the University of Oslo and professor of jurisprudence, delivered this speech in the auditorium of the Nobel Institute in the afternoon of December 10, 1922. Mr. Halvdan Koht, a member of the Committee, preceded Mr. Stang, giving a brief eulogy on Jørgen Gunnarsson Løvland, recently deceased, who had been a member of the Committee since its beginning and its chairman since 1901. At the conclusion of his own address, Mr. Stang presented the Nobel medal and diploma to the laureate who responded with a short speech of acceptance. This translation of Mr. Stang's speech is based on the Norwegian text published in the Oslo *Morgenbladet* of December 11, 1922, collated with the French text carried by *Les Prix Nobel en 1921–1922*.

1. The League of Nations created the office of High Commissioner for Refugees on June 27, 1921; Nansen held the position from August 20, 1921, until his death in May, 1930.
2. David Lloyd George (1863–1945), prime minister of Great Britain (1916–1922).

then we suddenly learn that he has gone to Rome for a conference with the Pope. Next he is in Russia to study the famine at first hand and to negotiate with the Soviet government; typhus claims some of his closest collaborators, but he himself, as so often before, emerges safe and sound from the danger. Another day he is to be found in the League of Nations Assembly in Geneva, pleading the cause of humanity in the face of all political prejudices. Then he is off once more on his travels, most recently to Constantinople and Greece, until he now stands for a moment among us, in his homeland, to receive the Peace Prize awarded to him without his even having been aware of his candidacy.

Nansen's reports to the League of Nations and the records of its debates provide an authentic and comprehensive account of his activities during these years[1]. I shall try, with the aid of this material, to give an outline of the principal facts.

In April, 1920, the League of Nations charged Professor Nansen with the direction of the repatriation of the prisoners of war who had not yet been exchanged. He was authorized to negotiate with the various governments and to cooperate with the organizations which had already begun this work.

There were then about half a million people languishing in Europe and Asia, still waiting to return to their homes. The greater part of them had been made prisoners during the gigantic struggle between Russia and Germany in the early years of the war. So they had been waiting for four, five, and even six years. Most of them had suffered exceedingly, both physically and mentally. Homeless, starved, tortured, unwanted where they were, they longed to return to the homes from which they had been torn and where they were now anxiously awaited.

As representative of the League of Nations, Nansen immediately approached the Soviet and German governments, as well as those of a number of other states, and concluded agreements for the delivery of the prisoners and for their board and transport. Relying particularly on using the Baltic route, he succeeded, after considerable difficulty, in chartering some of the ships which Germany was to deliver to England under the terms of the peace treaty[2]. These were used for the repatriation of the prisoners which now

1. For a listing of the major Nansen reports to the League of Nations and the sources of their texts, see Hans Aufricht, *Guide to League of Nations Publications* (New York: Columbia University Press, 1951), pp. 192–194.
2. The Treaty of Versailles (1919).

proceeded quickly and at unexpectedly low cost. Some of the prisoners, those from Eastern Siberia, had to be sent home via Vladivostok, others through the Black Sea, thus creating more serious problems as well as entailing more time.

The greatest difficulty, however, was in raising the required funds, for it was necessary to arrange governmental loans to a number of the Central European states whose prisoners were to be returned. This took some time but was successfully accomplished in the end.

In September, 1921, Nansen was able to report to the League of Nations that it had been possible to repatriate 350,000 prisoners via the Baltic, 12,000 via Vladivostok, and 5,000 via the Black Sea. His task was practically finished.

But even before it could be concluded, Nansen was given another and still more difficult one.

Russian refugees had settled all over Europe, their number being estimated at one and a half million. Some of them had managed to obtain work and put down roots where they were. But many were without work or resources and consequently were a burden to the countries in which they lived.

In June, 1921, the Council of the League of Nations decided to appoint a High Commissioner whose assignment would be to promote mutual cooperation between nations, with a view to transferring unemployed and needy prisoners to countries where work was available. In August, 1921, Nansen took over this post of High Commissioner.

His first job was to obtain a clear picture of this multitude of scattered and homeless human beings and to consider what future possibilities could be opened up for them. Having done this, he had to negotiate with countries which might be willing to accept Russian refugees and provide them with work and opportunity. Obviously, it was here that the greatest difficulties would be encountered.

Nansen started negotiations with a number of governments, and also appointed representatives who could negotiate on his behalf. As had to be expected, a number of states refused to accept any refugees. But many others responded favorably. Moreover, a large number of refugees originally from countries which were separated from Russia after the war – for example, many Estonians – were taken back home.

This work has already achieved a large measure of success. It has been hampered and delayed, however, by the inadequacy of the funds available.

In one of his reports to the Council of the League of Nations, Nansen says that the whole problem could have been solved much more quickly if he had had at his disposal only a fraction of the huge sums which the governments paid out during a single year to support the Russian refugees.

With this work still in progress, Nansen received his third and most formidable mission.

The famine in Russia had assumed enormous proportions and threatened to ravage vast areas. The lives of twenty to thirty million people were at stake.

In August, 1921, Nansen was asked to direct the famine relief work. This time the request came not from the League of Nations but from a conference of governments and private organizations held in Geneva[1].

From one point of view, Nansen's task was not so difficult; for although millions in Russia were starving and approaching certain ruin unless they were given aid, there were huge quantities of grain in other countries. In the United States, for example, the wheat lay rotting for lack of buyers, and in Argentina there was such an abundance of maize that it was used as fuel for railway engines. Nor did the shipment of the grain to Russia present a great problem, since whole fleets of ships were lying idle. Moreover, the transport network inside Russia itself was adequate for the distribution of the grain, especially if it arrived before winter closed rivers and lakes.

There was, however, another and greater difficulty to be faced. In a world where nations, social classes, and individuals fought each other to further their own ideas and ambitions, there had to be created a feeling of solidarity strong enough to transcend national frontiers and political differences.

Nansen immediately approached the Soviet government and concluded an agreement on two points: first, that the grain sent would reach those for whom it was intended and, second, that Nansen would be empowered on behalf of the Soviet government to ask the European governments for a credit of ten million pounds.

The work of obtaining the grain supplies started without delay. Considerable sums of money were raised through private and semiofficial organizations and from private donations; and large shipments were made.

To solve the problem completely, it was essential to arrange a loan to Russia since it was decided that the scheme could not and should not be

1. Held on August 15, 1921; see Nansen's lecture, p.371.

based on charity alone. This matter of a loan met with a serious obstacle, for the Soviet government was not recognized, nor the political system which it represented approved, by the other governments[1]. Consequently, in spite of the agreements concluded by Nansen, there were many who remained unconvinced that the aid given would really benefit those for whom it was intended.

Nansen's hardest task was to break down this opposition. Time and again he turned to the League of Nations for moral support in his demand that credit be granted to the Russian state. In a powerful speech, the words of which still ring in our ears, he argued before the League of Nations that the rescue of millions from death by starvation should not be impeded by political considerations. Even if political considerations are taken into account, he says, they too indicate that aid must be given. For it is the very areas in Europe that have hitherto yielded the largest exports of grain which are now being devastated. Can Europe do without the Volga districts? Can it do without Russia? Some argue that to send grain to Russia is to aid the Soviet government. Nansen answers: I do not believe that we are supporting the Soviet simply because we are showing the Russian people that there is compassion in Europe. But suppose that such aid would support the Soviet—is there any man who dares come forward and say: It is better to allow twenty million people to die of starvation than to support the Soviet government?

It has not been possible to obtain the credit for Russia. States have contributed, Norway among others; private and semiofficial organizations have raised large sums of money; but the help which could have halted the disaster in the beginning has been withheld.

The consequence is that the work has not yielded the results which could have been achieved. Millions, it is true, have been helped, and in the end nearly ten million were being kept alive. But many have succumbed – between two and four million of them. And since the harvest this year was poor because the spring sowing was done by people who were starving and short of both seed corn and working beasts, we can predict that the distress will again be appalling when spring approaches.

Nansen has now been entrusted with a fourth mission of an international character. As the High Commissioner of the League of Nations, he is going

1. Great Britain recognized the Soviet government on February 1, 1924, being followed shortly thereafter by most of the other European powers; by Japan in January, 1925; by the United States in November, 1933.

to direct the work of aiding the unfortunate people of all races and religions who have become victims of *the Greco-Turkish War*. It is necessary above all to help the refugees who are now streaming in from Eastern Thrace and Asia Minor to the Balkan countries and Greece[1]. This work is now in progress, and the newspapers carry reports of it every day.

These are the missions with which Nansen has been charged and the work that he has accomplished, an account of which we wished to give here. He has found at his side, however, not only a great number of individuals, but also a series of organizations with which he has worked and which deserve a large share of the credit for the results obtained[2].

The human mind cannot visualize this enormous activity any more than it can grasp astronomical figures. One starving person, one human being lying like forgotten wreckage on a street corner, wasting away bit by bit–this we understand; here our feeling is so strong it becomes compassion. One refugee, even a crowd of refugees, if you like, pushing their children and their possessions in wheelbarrows in front of them–this we understand. But millions of these, hunted like game from country to country, behind them the fires of their burning homes, before them the emptiness of a future over which they have no control–here our minds stop dead; instead of producing images, they merely play back the statistics presented to them. Charity on an intimate scale, even charity on a larger scale, for our countrymen or for our provinces–this is within our reach; this we understand. But a program whose aim is to rescue a continent's millions from misery and death–this presents proportions so immense and involves such a myriad of jumbled details that we give up and allow our minds to rest.

It will be the task of future generations to give this work its proper place in world history. We who have lived through it can merely make a few observations upon it.

And that is what I wish to do now.

What is it that has sustained the work? Is it the functioning of the ordinary machinery of nations? Is it the stirring of the consciences of politicians and statesmen which has found such magnificent expression? Oh, no! The source lies deeper. It lies in the fact that it was to the people themselves, to their deepest and broadest stratum, that the appeal was addressed and from them a world opinion crystallized. Indeed, war had to be declared

1. See biography.
2. This paragraph appears in the French text of the speech in *Les Prix Nobel en 1921– 1922*, p. 116, but not in the Norwegian text in the *Morgenbladet*.

against all political considerations to enable the idea and the feeling to break through the barriers erected by nations, classes, and individuals. The appeal had to reach those innermost depths in man which no statecraft can enter.

Men's deepest feelings are often invoked, and often by politics. But the feelings politics stirs up are most frequently those which divide: national self-interest, class consciousness, suspicion, lust for power. There are times, it is true, when politics appeals to that which unites, not only to what unites nations and social classes, but also to what binds mankind together most closely. But this does not happen often. For me one of the most important aspects of the work before us is that it has penetrated the very depths of the human feeling which lies buried within all of us, the feeling that the family of man is *one*, whatever its national or social divisions. As Nansen says in one of his speeches, it is love for one's neighbor that he has wished to enroll in the service of his work. And he has succeeded. Progress has not been rapid, and the goal is still far away. This wave of warmth rising from so deep within has struck ice and cold. Nevertheless, it has advanced far enough that the work it has supported has become an event in the history of mankind.

In the forefront of it all we see a number of combatants, each stationed at his post: organizations and individuals engaged year after year in the struggle to clear a path through all the barriers which stand between the victims of misfortune and their rescuers. At their head we see first and foremost one single man. What burdens he has borne upon his shoulders! What organizing ability his work has demanded, what energy and initiative, what self-sacrificing patience, what talent for coming straight to the heart of any problem! What he has lived through, this man who has seen Europe's misery at first hand and who has felt a sense of responsibility for it!

Seeing him in our midst today awakens many memories. Behind him is a life which we have all, in our thoughts, lived with him.

Perhaps what has most impressed all of us is his ability to stake his life time and time again on a single idea, on one thought, and to inspire others to follow him.

We remember a young boy, for he was but little more than that, crossing Greenland on skis. He thought that up there in the North where the costly expeditions from great nations always suffered shipwreck, Norwegian sports equipment and Norwegian familiarity with ice and snow would be able to succeed. He did succeed, and his trip became a landmark in the history of Arctic exploration.

We recall too a mature man who, on the basis of his scientific knowledge, developed the theory that a current flows from east to west across the Polar Sea. Nearly all the scientists believed that he was wrong. But he staked his life on the theory; he allowed himself to be frozen into the eastern ice to be carried over the Pole. The current was there and carried him forward to his goal[1].

And is it not much the same thing that we have now witnessed? An undercurrent in which few have believed has again carried Nansen forward: the deep current of human feeling which lies beneath the layer of ice in which nations and individuals encase themselves during the daily struggles and the trials of life. He believed in this current and because he did, his work has triumphed. May this current also carry much for the future!

1. See biography.

FRIDTJOF NANSEN

The Suffering People of Europe

Nobel Lecture*, December 19, 1922

In the Capitoline Museum in Rome is a sculpture in marble which, in its simple pathos, seems to me to be a most beautiful creation. It is the statue of the «Dying Gaul». He is lying on the battlefield, mortally wounded. The vigorous body, hardened by work and combat, is sinking into death. The head, with its coarse hair, is bowed, the strong neck bends, the rough powerful workman's hand, till recently wielding the sword, now presses against the ground in a last effort to hold up the drooping body.

He was driven to fight for foreign gods whom he did not know, far from his own country. And thus he met his fate. Now he lies there, dying in silence. The noise of the fray no longer reaches his ear. His dimmed eyes are turned inward, perhaps on a final vision of his childhood home where life was simple and happy, of his birthplace deep in the forests of Gaul.

That is how I see mankind in its suffering; that is how I see the suffering people of Europe, bleeding to death on deserted battlefields after conflicts which to a great extent were not their own.

This is the outcome of the lust for power, the imperialism, the militarism, that have run amok across the earth. The golden produce of the earth has been trampled under iron feet, the land lies in ruins everywhere, and the foundations of its communities are crumbling. People bow their heads in silent despair. The shrill battle cries still clamor around them, but they hardly hear them anymore. Cast out of the lost Eden, they look back upon the simple basic values of life. The soul of the world is mortally sick, its courage broken, its ideals tarnished, and the will to live gone; the horizon is hazy, hidden behind burning clouds of destruction, and faith in the dawn of mankind is no more.

Where is the remedy to be sought? At the hands of politicians? They

* The laureate delivered this Nobel lecture in the Auditorium of the University of Oslo. For this translation the text used is that published in Norwegian in *Les Prix Nobel en 1921–1922*. The lecture was not given a title; the one used here is taken from the third paragraph of the speech.

may mean well enough, many of them at any rate, but politics and new political programs are no longer of service to the world–the world has had only too many of them. In the final analysis, the struggle of the politician amounts to little more than a struggle for power.

The diplomats perhaps? Their intentions may also be good enough, but they are once and for all a sterile race which has brought mankind more harm than good over the years. Call to mind the settlements arranged after the great wars – the Treaty of Westphalia[1], the Congress in Vienna with the Holy Alliance[2], and others. Has a single one of these diplomatic congresses contributed to any great extent to the progress of the world? One is here reminded of the famous words of Oxenstjerna[3] to his son when he complained about the negotiations in Westphalia: «If you only knew, my son, with how little wisdom the world is ruled.»

We can no longer look to traditional leadership for any hope of salvation. We have of late experienced one diplomatic and political congress after another; has any one of these brought the solution any nearer? There is at present one in progress in Lausanne[4]. Let us hope that it will bring us the longed-for peace in the East so that at least one delicate question may be resolved.

But what of the main evil itself, the heart of the disease? It is whispered that France does not want to reach a final settlement with Germany, does not want Germany to finish paying her indemnities. For in that case, the pretext for occupying the western side of the Rhine would be removed, and she could no longer unsettle German industry with threats against the Ruhr district. This is naturally only malicious slander, but how common are such rumors!

It is also whispered that neither do the industrial leaders of Germany desire a final agreement with France. They would prefer the uncertainty to continue so that the value of the mark will fall steadily, enabling German industry to survive longer. For, if a settlement were to come, then the mark

1. The Treaty of Westphalia (1648) ended the Thirty Years War (1618–1648).
2. The Congress of Vienna attempted (1814–1815) to settle the political affairs of Europe after the first abdication of Napoleon I; the Holy Alliance, formed in 1815 primarily to maintain the status quo in Europe, lasted until 1848.
3. Count Axel Gustavsson Oxenstjerna (1583–1654), chancellor of Sweden (1612–1654), prominent figure in Thirty Years War.
4. The Lausanne Conference (1922–1923) resulted in a new treaty of peace between the Allies and Turkey.

would be stabilized or even rise in value, and German industry would be ruined since it would no longer be competitive.

Whether these things are true or not, the mere fact that they are uttered at all reflects the manner in which the whole European community and its way of life have been and still are toys in the hands of reckless political and financial speculators – perhaps largely bunglers, inferior men who do not realize the outcome of their actions, but who still speculate and gamble with the most valuable interests of European civilization.

And for what? Only for power. This unfortunate struggle, this appalling trampling of everything and everyone, this destructive conflict between the social classes and even between peoples exists for power alone!

When one has stood face to face with famine, with death by starvation itself, then surely one should have had one's eyes opened to the full extent of this misfortune. When one has beheld the great beseeching eyes in the starved faces of children staring hopelessly into the fading daylight, the eyes of agonized mothers while they press their dying children to their empty breasts in silent despair, and the ghostlike men lying exhausted on mats on cabin floors, with only the merciful release of death to wait for, then surely one must understand where all this is leading, understand a little of the true nature of the question. This is not the struggle for power, but a single and terrible accusation against those who still do not want to see, a single great prayer for a drop of mercy to give men a chance to live.

Surely those who have seen at first hand the destitution pervading our misgoverned Europe and actually experienced some of the endless suffering must realize that the world can no longer rely on panaceas, paper, and words. These must be replaced by action, by persevering and laborious effort, which must begin at the bottom in order to build up the world again.

The history of mankind rises and falls like the waves. We have fallen into wave-troughs before in Europe. A similar trough occurred a hundred years ago after the Napoleonic Wars. Everyone who has read the excellent work of Worm-Müller[1] describing the conditions here in Norway during that time must have noticed the many remarkable similarities between the situation then and now. It may be a consolation to know that the abyss of those times disappeared and that Norway struggled upward again; but it took a depressingly long time, thirty to forty years.

This time, as far as I can see, the trough is even deeper and more exten-

1. Jacob S. Worm-Müller (Norwegian historian and politician, 1884–1963), *Christiania og krisen efter Napoleonskrigene* (Oslo: Grøndahl and Sons, 1922).

sive, embracing the major part of Europe, and, in addition, exists under conditions that now are more complex. It is true that industry did exist at that time, but people lived off the land to a far greater extent. Now industry has come into its own, and it is more difficult to bring recovery to industry after a depression than to agriculture. A few good years will put farming back on its feet, but many years are required to develop new markets for industry. All the same, we may reasonably hope that the process of revival will be more rapid this time, for everything happens more quickly in our day because of our systems of communication and the vast apparatus of economic facilities that we now possess. But there are as yet few signs of progress. We have still not reached the bottom of the wave-trough.

What is the basic feeling of people all over Europe? There is no doubt that for a great many it is one of despair or distrust of everything and everyone, supported by hate and envy. This hatred is each day disseminated among nations and classes.

No future, however, can be built on despair, distrust, hatred, and envy.

The first prerequisite, surely, is understanding–first of all, an understanding of the cause and the nature of the disease itself, an understanding of the trends that mark our times and of what is happening among the mass of the population. In short, an understanding of the psychology of every characteristic of our apparently confused and confounded European society.

Such an understanding is certainly not attainable in a day. But the first condition for its final establishment is the sincere will to understand; this is a great step in the right direction. The continuous mutual abuse of groups holding differing views, which we witness in the newspapers, will certainly never lead to progress. Abuse convinces no one; it only degrades and brutalizes the abuser. Lies and unjust accusations achieve still less; they often finally boomerang on those who originate them.

It must also always be remembered that there is hardly a trend or movement in the community which does not in some degree possess a reason and right of its own, be it socialism or capitalism, be it fascism or even the hated bolshevism. But it is because of blind fanaticism for and against– especially against–that conflicts come to a head and lead to heartrending struggles and destruction; whereas discussion, understanding, and tolerance might have turned this energy into valuable progress.

An expansion of this subject is not possible here; suffice it to say that the parable about seeing the mote in your neighbor's eye while not aware of the beam in your own[1] is valid for all times, and not least for the age in which we live.

But when understanding is absent and especially when the will to understand is lacking, then that fermenting uncertainty, which threatens us with total destruction, arises. No one knows what tomorrow will bring. Many people live as though each day were the last, thus sliding into a state of general decadence. From this point the decline is steady and inexorable.

Moreover, the worst that this insecurity, this speculation in uncertainty, creates, is the fear of work; it was bred during the war, and it has grown steadily since. It was bred by the stock-jobbing and the speculation familiar to us all, whereby people could make fortunes in a short time, thinking they could live on them for the rest of their lives without having to work and toil. This created an aversion to work which has lasted to this very day. There are still some who will honestly and wholeheartedly settle down to hard toil, but the only places where I have met this sincere will to work are those where the angel of death by starvation is reaping his terrible harvest.

I shall always remember a day in a village east of the Volga to which only one-third of its inhabitants had returned; of the remaining two-thirds, some had fled and the rest had died of starvation. Most of the animals had been slaughtered; but courage had still not been completely extinguished, and although their prospects were bleak, the people still had faith in the future. «Give us seed», they said, «and we will sow it in the soil.» «Yes», we replied, «but what will you do without animals to pull the plough?» «That does not matter», they said; «if there are no animals, we will put ourselves and our women and children to the plough.» It was not selfindulgence that was speaking here, not extravagance, not mere showmanship – it was the very will to stay alive, which had not given in.

Must we all live through the bitter pangs of hunger before we learn the real value of work?

I might also mention conditions in Germany. I have been told that because of short working hours and restricted output, Germany does not produce the coal needed for her own requirements and must therefore buy coal from England – I believe a figure of one million tons a month was mentioned – and pay for it with foreign currency. But if the working hours were increased to ten hours a day, Germany could herself produce an adequate supply of coal. That is but one example.

1. Matthew 7:3 – 5.

In Switzerland where everything is grinding to a halt, where industry is ruined because it can no longer produce at prices attractive to world markets, I was told that if the daily working hours were to be increased to ten, with reasonable pay, the workers would find employment for the whole week instead of for the three days during which the factories are now running at a loss merely to stay in existence. Moreover, the workmen themselves would gladly work longer if they dared, but they cannot do so lest they contravene their union's program. Such is the situation.

This sad state of affairs can, it is true, be blamed partly on the unpredictable fluctuations in the value of money. These are characteristic problems which, it appears to me, not even the experts can satisfactorily explain.

But below the surface of these obvious factors there are, quite plainly, greater internal ones. It is an undeniable fact that people cannot live without working, and there has been too little work for too long. It will be asked: «What is the purpose of work if there is no market for the products?» And markets are indeed not there. But neither can markets be created without work. If no work is done, if markets are not created where they should exist, then no purchasing power will be developed, and everyone must suffer in consequence. The universal disease is, in fact, lack of work. Even honest work cannot thrive, however, except where there are peace and confidence: confidence in one's self, confidence in others, and confidence in the future.

Here we strike at the heart of the matter. How then can this confidence in peace be inspired? Can it proceed from politicians and diplomats? I have already expressed my opinion of them. They can, perhaps, do something, but I am not particularly convinced of that, nor of the ability of politicians of the individual countries to achieve anything in this situation. In my opinion, the only avenue to salvation lies in cooperation between all nations on a basis of honest endeavor.

I believe that the only road to this goal lies through the League of Nations. If this fails to introduce a new era, then I see no salvation, at any rate at present. But are we right in placing so much faith in the League of Nations? What has it done so far to promote peace and confidence? In asking this question we must remember that the League is still a young plant that can easily be damaged and prevented from growing by the frost of doubt. We should bear in mind that the League can attain full powers only when it embraces all nations, including the big ones still outside[1]. But

1. At the time of this lecture: Germany and Russia, which joined later, and the United States, which never joined.

even in its short lifetime, it can claim credit for actions which point to a brighter future. It has already in its short active life settled many controversial questions which would otherwise have led, if not to war, at least to serious disturbances.

One example was the Åland controversy between Sweden and Finland. Though there were some who were dissatisfied with the solution[1], they nevertheless accepted it, thus preventing further trouble.

A serious frontier dispute arose between Yugoslavia and Albania. Serbian troops had already crossed the border. The League of Nations intervened, settled the question, and both parties accepted the solution[2] without further bloodshed.

Mention can also be made of the Silesian question which threatened serious trouble between Germany and Poland. This too has been settled– very badly according to some, while others maintain that any other solution would have been impossible in view of previous agreements reached in the Treaty of Versailles[3]. But the fact is that the settlement has been sanctioned by both parties and that it has not led to any further trouble.

Another example is that of Poland and Lithuania. It is true that the League of Nations did not in this case reach any settlement, the problem having proved too difficult because of various reasons which I am not going to delve into here. The fact is, however, that the act of investigation by the League of Nations in itself prevented the two parties from taking up arms[4].

It may be claimed that these were controversies between small nations, but what if real issues arose between greater powers–would they yield to the arbitration of the League of Nations? Well, I point to the Silesian question again. Germany is no small nation, and it is moreover a fact that

1. In 1921 the League settled the dispute over the Åland Islands by awarding them to Finland, with autonomous status and an agreement against militarization.
2. Under pressure by the League, the Conference of Ambassadors on November 9, 1921, confirmed the frontiers of 1913 for Albania, also making some concessions to Yugoslavia.
3. By the terms of the Versailles Treaty, a plebescite to determine the frontier in Upper Silesia was held on March 20, 1921; disputes followed, and after study by a committee, the Council of the League made recommendations on October 12, 1921, and named a negotiator; a convention of settlement was signed at Geneva on May 15, 1922.
4. The city of Vilna was assigned to Lithuania by the Paris Peace Conference in 1919, but in the following year was occupied by Poland and annexed in 1922. Bad relations continued from this time, when the laureate was speaking, until 1927–1931 when, over a period of four years, agreements were reached on several issues.

the victorious great powers which set out to settle the question were unable to reach agreement; so the matter was referred to the League of Nations. Recently, however, we have had an even better example of great powers submitting to the judgment of the League of Nations in an issue between Great Britain and France.

In 1921 the French government issued a decree declaring that everyone living in Tunisia and Morocco was compelled to do national service. Thus British subjects living in the French protectorates were liable to conscription in the French army. The British government objected strongly, while the French maintained that this was an internal problem. Neither would give in and the controversy became serious. Nine years ago such a question could only have ended in a war or at best in an expensive diplomatic conference. At that time there was no world organization which could have dealt with such a question. Now, however, it was referred to the League of Nations, and the tension was immediately released[1].

The mere fact that the League of Nations has set up the Permanent Court of International Justice[2] constitutes a great and important step toward the more peaceful ordering of the world, a step in the direction of creating confidence among nations.

If any doubt still exists about the position now occupied by the League of Nations in the minds of people, reference can be made to the last election in Great Britain. Of the 1,386 candidates standing, only three dared to face their electors with a declaration that they were opponents of the League of Nations. Two or three more made no mention of the subject, but all the rest expressed their faith in the League.

In my opinion, however, the greatest and most important achievement of the League so far, and one which presages a really new and better future for Europe, is the measure initiated at the last Assembly in Geneva, that of arranging an international loan to Austria[3] to give her a chance of surviving the threat of economic ruin. This action raises hope for yet more;

1. The League submitted the dispute to the Permanent Court of International Justice which, in February, 1923 (two months after the laureate's lecture), found that this question was not a purely internal affair, whereupon the two governments made an amicable agreement.
2. The Permanent Court of International Justice (1921–1945), provided judgments on international disputes voluntarily submitted to it; popularly called the World Court, it was supplanted by the International Court of Justice.
3. On October 4, 1922.

it is the prelude to a new and promising trend in the economic politics of Europe.

It is my conviction that the German problem, the intricate differences between Germany and her opponents, cannot and will not be solved until it too has been laid before the League of Nations[1].

In addition, the difficult question of total or partial disarmament was first broached at the last meeting in Geneva. Here, as well as in most other fields of the League's activity, there is one name which stands out, namely that of Lord Robert Cecil[2]. Again we must keep in mind, particularly in the matter of partial disarmament, the serious difficulties arising from the fact that there are important military powers which are not yet members of the League.

But more important by far than any partial disarmament of armies and fleets, is the «disarmament» of the people from within, the generation, in fact, of sympathy in the souls of men. Here too, in the great and important work that has been carried on, the League of Nations has taken an active part.

I must, however, first mention the gigantic task performed by the Americans under the remarkable leadership of Hoover[3]. It was begun during the war with the Belgian Relief, when many thousands of Belgians, children and adults, were supported. After the war, it was extended to Central Europe, where hundreds of thousands of children were given new hope by the invaluable aid from the Americans, and finally, but not least, to Russia. When the whole story of this work is written, it will take pride of place as a glorious page in the annals of mankind, and its charity will shine like a brilliant star in a long and dark night. At the same time, the Americans have, through other organizations such as the American Red Cross and the Near East Relief, achieved the unbelievable in the Balkans, in Asia Minor, and now, finally, in Greece. Many European organizations must also not be forgotten. In particular, divisions of the Red Cross in different countries, among them our own, have contributed much during and after the war.

1. Germany, not a member of the League at this time, was admitted in September, 1926.
2. Edgar Algernon Robert Cecil (1864–1958), recipient of the Nobel Peace Prize for 1937.
3. Herbert Clark Hoover (1874–1964), president of the United States (1929–1933); director of food administration and war relief bureaus during and after World War I.

The League of Nations sponsored activities of this nature soon after its formation. Its first task was the repatriation of the many thousands of prisoners of war still scattered round the world two years after the war, mostly in Siberia and Eastern and Central Europe. I do not intend to dwell on this theme since it has already been mentioned at the meeting in the Nobel Institute. I shall say only that, as a result of this effort, nearly 450,000 prisoners were sent back to their homes and, in many instances, to productive work.

Immediately after this, the League took up the fight against epidemics which were then threatening to spread from the East, and worked to control disease in Poland, along the Russian border, and in Russia itself. The League has, through its excellent Commission on Epidemics[1], worked effectively to prevent the spread of epidemics and has saved thousands from destitution and annihilation.

Efforts are now being made, through a special organization sponsored by the League of Nations[2], to provide subsistence aid for destitute Russian refugees, more than a million of whom are scattered all over Europe.

Mention must also be made of the work now in progress in support of famine-stricken refugees in Asia Minor and Greece[3]. It is true that it has still barely begun, but this work too can be of the greatest importance. Under the present conditions in these areas, there is a threat of disorganization and despair worse than anywhere else in Europe. If this danger can be averted or at least reduced, if this malignant growth can to some extent be eradicated, then there will be one such cancer the less in the European community, one risk the less of unrest, of disturbance, of dissolution of states in the future.

Having already emphasized the significance of this type of work, I must do so once more. The relief in thousands of homes in seeing the return of their menfolk, the help received by them in their distress; the gratitude this inspires, the confidence in people and in the future, the prospect of sounder working conditions–all this is, I believe, of greater importance for the cause of peace than many ambitious political moves that now seldom reach far beyond a limited circle of politicians and diplomats.

1. Established May 19, 1920.
2. The High Commission for Refugees was established by the League on June 27, 1921, with the laureate appointed as High Commissioner.
3. See biography.

Finally, a few words about the assistance to Russia[1]. In this the League of Nations did not participate, a fact which I deeply regret because I cannot but believe that had the League, with its great authority, lent its support while there was still time, the situation in Russia would have been saved, and conditions in both Russia and Europe would now be totally different and much better.

I shall not go into greater detail on the work that has been done. I wish only to emphasize that the difficulty certainly did not lie in finding the food or transporting it to those who were starving. No, there was more than enough grain in the world at that time, and adequate distribution facilities were available. The problem lay in obtaining funds, an obstacle which has always bedeviled such attempts to supply aid—not least so at this moment.

European governments were unwilling to sanction the loan of ten million pounds sterling which appeared indispensable if the starving millions of Russia were to be saved and the famine prevented from turning into a tragedy, not only for Russia, but for all Europe. The only alternative, therefore, was to rely on private contributions and to institute an appeal for charity to individuals all over the world.

The result exceeded every expectation. Donations poured in from all countries, and not least from our own. In spite of the existence of people here at home who thought it right to oppose the collection, the contribution of our little country was still so great, thanks to the Norwegian Parliament, the Norwegian government, and the excellent work of the Famine Committee, that had the big countries contributed in proportion, the famine in Russia would now be a thing of the past.

One notable exception outside Europe must be mentioned. Once again, the American people contributed more than any other, first through the Hoover organization and then through the government itself, which donated twenty million dollars to the fight against famine on the condition that the Russian government would provide ten million for the purchase of seed. Altogether, America has certainly contributed fifty to sixty million dollars to the struggle against the Russian famine, and has thus saved the lives of countless millions.

But why were there some who did not want to help? Ask them! In all probability their motives were political. They epitomize sterile self-im-

1. On August 15, 1921, an international conference of representatives of certain governments and of delegates from forty-eight Red Cross and charitable organizations had appointed Nansen to direct the relief effort in famine-stricken Russia.

portance and the lack of will to understand people who think differently, characteristics which now constitute the greatest danger in Europe. They call us romantics, weak, stupid, sentimental idealists, perhaps because we have some faith in the good which exists even in our opponents and because we believe that kindness achieves more than cruelty. It may be that we are simpleminded, but I do not think that we are dangerous. Those, however, who stagnate behind their political programs, offering nothing else to suffering mankind, to starving, dying millions–they are the scourge of Europe.

Russia is not alone in being threatened by a new and terrible famine. The situation in Europe also looks black enough. No one knows yet where it will end. The destitution is so great, so nearly insurmountable, the conditions so desperate, even in the rich fertile area of Russia, not to mention other countries, that in spite of widespread private generosity, what can be provided constitutes only a drop in the ocean.

Everyone must join in this work. We must take up the fiery cross and light the beacons so that they shine from every mountain. We must raise our banner in every country and forge the links of brotherhood around the world. The governments too must stand shoulder to shoulder, not in a battle line, but in a sincere effort to achieve the new era.

The festival of Christmas is approaching when the message to mankind is: Peace on earth.

Never has suffering and bewildered mankind awaited the Prince of Peace with greater longing, the Prince of Charity who holds aloft a white banner bearing the one word inscribed in golden letters: «Work».

All of us can become workers in his army on its triumphant march across the earth to raise a new spirit in a new generation–to bring men love of their fellowmen and an honest desire for peace–to bring back the will to work and the joy of work–to bring faith in the dawn of a new day.

Biography

Fridtjof Nansen (October 10, 1861–May 13, 1930) was born at Store Frøen, near Oslo. His father, a prosperous lawyer, was a religious man with a clear conception of personal duty and moral principle; his mother was a strong-minded, athletic woman who introduced her children to outdoor life and encouraged them to develop physical skills. And Nansen's athletic prowess was to prove of the utmost importance to his career. He became expert in skating, tumbling, and swimming, but it was his expertise in skiing that was to play such a large role in his life. Not massively built, Nansen was tall, supple, strong, hard. He possessed the physical endurance to ski fifty miles in a day and the psychological self-reliance to embark on long trips, with a minimum of gear and only his dog for company.

In school Nansen excelled in the sciences and in drawing and, upon entering the University of Oslo in 1881, decided to major in zoology. In the next fifteen years he united his athletic ability, his scientific interests, his yearning for adventure, and even his talent for drawing in a series of brilliant achievements that brought him international fame.

In 1882 he shipped on the sealer *Viking* to the east coast of Greenland. On this trip of four and a half months, the scientist in him made observations on seals and bears which, years later, he updated and turned into a book; but at the same time the adventurer became entranced by this world of sea and ice.

Obtaining the post of zoological curator at the Bergen Museum later that year, Nansen spent the next six years in intensive scientific study, punctuating his work with visits to some of the great laboratories on the Continent and once by an extraordinary trek across Norway from Bergen Oslo and back on skis. In 1888 he successfully defended his dissertation on the central nervous system of certain lower vertebrates for the doctorate at the University of Oslo.

For a long time Nansen had been evolving a plan to cross Greenland, whose interior had never been explored. He decided to cross from the uninhabited east to the inhabited west; in other words, once his party was put ashore, there could be no retreat. In 1926, explaining his philosophy to the students at St. Andrews in his rectorial address, Nansen said that a line of retreat from a proposed action was a snare, that one should burn his boats behind him so that there is no choice but to go forward. The party of six survived temperatures of −45° C, climbed to 9,000 feet above sea level, mastered dangerous ice, exhaustion, and privation to emerge on the west coast early in October of 1888 after a trip of about two months, bringing with them important information about the interior.

In the next four years, Nansen served as curator of the Zootomical Institute at the University of Oslo, published several articles, two books, *The First Crossing of Greenland* (1890) and *Eskimo Life* (1891), and planned a scientific and exploratory foray into the Arctic. Basing his plan on the revolutionary theory that a current carried the polar ice from east to west, Nansen put his ship, the *Fram* [Forward], an immensely strong and cunningly designed ship, into the ice pack off Siberia on September 22, 1893, from which it emerged thirty-five months later on August 13, 1896, into open water near Spitzbergen. Nansen was not aboard.

Realizing that the ship would not pass over the North Pole, Nansen and one companion, with thirty days' rations for twenty-eight dogs, three sledges, two kayaks, and a hundred days' rations for themselves, had set out in March of 1895 on a 400-mile dash to the Pole. In twenty-three days they traveled 140 miles over oceans of tumbled ice, getting closer to the Pole than anyone had previously been. Turning back, they made their way southwest to Franz Josef Land, wintered there in 1895–1896, started south again in May, reached Vardo, Norway, the same day the *Fram* reached open water and were reunited with the crew on August 21 at Tromsø.

The voyage was a high adventure but it was also a scientific expedition, the *Fram* serving as an oceanographic-meteorological-biological laboratory. Holding a research professorship at the University of Oslo after 1897, Nansen published six volumes of scientific observations made between 1893 and 1896. Continuing thereafter to break new ground in oceanic research, he was appointed professor of oceanography in 1908.

Nansen interrupted his research in 1905 to urge the independence of Norway from Sweden and, after the dissolution of the Union, served as his country's minister to Great Britain until May of 1908. In the next few years he led several oceanographic expeditions into polar regions, but once the world was plunged into war in 1914 and exploration was halted, he became increasingly interested in international political affairs.

For almost a year in 1917–1918, as the head of a Norwegian delegation in Washington, D.C., Nansen negotiated an agreement for a relaxation of the Allied blockade to permit shipments of essential food. In 1919, he became president of the Norwegian Union for the League of Nations and at the Peace Conference in Paris was an influential lobbyist for the adoption of the League Covenant and for recognition of the rights of small nations. From 1920 until his death he was a delegate to the League from Norway.

In the spring of 1920, the League of Nations asked Nansen to undertake the task of repatriating the prisoners of war, many of them held in Russia. Moving with his customary boldness and ingenuity, and despite restricted funds, Nansen repatriated 450,000 prisoners in the next year and a half.

In June, 1921, the Council of the League, spurred by the International Red Cross and other organizations, instituted its High Commission for Refugees and asked Nansen to administer it. For the stateless refugees under his care Nansen invented the «Nansen Passport», a document of identification which was eventually recognized by fifty-two governments. In the nine-year life of this Office, Nansen ministered to hundreds of thousands of refugees–Russian, Turkish, Armenian, Assyrian, Assyro-Chaldean–utilizing the methods that were to become classic: custodial care, repatriation, rehabilitation, resettlement, emigration, integration.

The Red Cross in 1921 asked Nansen to take on yet a third humanitarian task, that of directing relief for millions of Russians dying in the famine of 1921–1922. Help for Russia, then suspect in the eyes of most of the Western nations, was hard to muster, but Nansen pursued his task with awesome energy. In the end he gathered and distributed enough supplies to save a staggering number of people, the figures quoted ranging from 7,000,000 to 22,000,000.

In 1922 at the request of the Greek government and with the approval of the League of Nations, Nansen tried to solve the problem of the Greek refugees who poured into their native land from their homes in Asia Minor after the Greek army had been defeated by the Turks. Nansen arranged an exchange of about 1,250,000 Greeks living on Turkish soil for about 500,000 Turks living in Greece, with appropriate indemnification and provisions for giving them the opportunity for a new start in life.

Nansen's fifth great humanitarian effort, at the invitation of the League in 1925, was to save the remnants of the Armenian people from extinction. He drew up a political, industrial, and financial plan for creating a national home for the Armenians in Erivan that foreshadowed what the United Nations Technical Assistance Board and the International Bank of Development and Reconstruction have done in the post-World War II period. The League failed to implement the plan, but the Nansen International Office for Refugees later settled some 10,000 in Erivan and 40,000 in Syria and Lebanon.

Nansen died on May 13, 1930, and was buried on May 17, Norway's Independence Day.

Selected Bibliography

Christensen, Christian A.R., *Fridtjof Nansen: A Life in the Service of Science and Humanity*. Geneva, UN High Commissioner for Refugees, 1961.

Høyer, Liv Nansen, *Nansen: A Family Portrait*, translated from the Norwegian by Maurice Michael. New York, Longmans, Green, 1957.

Innes, Kathleen E., *The Story of Nansen and the League of Nations*. London, Friends Peace Committee, 1931.

Lange, Halvard, «Nestekjaerlighet er realpolitikk: Fridtjof Nansen og internasjonal solidaritet i handling», with an English summary. Nansen Memorial Lecture. Oslo, Universitetsforlaget, 1967.

Nansen, Fridtjof, *Adventure and Other Papers*. London, L. & V. Woolf, 1927.

Nansen, Fridtjof, *Armenia and the Near East*. London, Allen & Unwin, 1928. (*Gjennem Armenia*. Oslo, Dybwad, 1927.)

Nansen, Fridtjof, *Brev*. Utgitt av Steinar Kjaerheim. 5 vols.: 1882–1895; 1896–1905; 1906–1918; 1919–1925; 1926–1930. Oslo, Universitetsforlaget, 1961–1971.

Nansen, Fridtjof, *Eskimo Life*, translated by William Archer. London, Longmans, Green, 1893. (*Eskimoliv*. Oslo, Aschehoug, 1891.)

Nansen, Fridtjof, *Farthest North: Being the Record of a Voyage of Exploration of the Ship «Fram», 1893–1896, and of a Fifteen Months' Sleigh Journey by Dr. Nansen and Lt. Johansen*. 2 vols. New York, Harper, 1897. (*Fram over Polhavet: Den norske polarfaerd, 1893–1896*. 2 vols. Oslo, Aschehoug, 1897.)

Nansen, Fridtjof, *The First Crossing of Greenland*, translated by Hubert M. Gepp. London, Longmans, Green, 1890. (*På ski over Grønland*. Oslo, Aschehoug, 1890.)

Nansen, Fridtjof, *Nansens røst: Artikler og taler*. 3 vols. Oslo, Dybwad, 1944.

Nansen, Fridtjof, ed., *The Norwegian North Polar Expedition, 1893–1896: Scientific Results*. 6 vols. London, Longmans, Green, 1900–1906.

Nansen, Fridtjof, *Russia and Peace*. London, Allen & Unwin, 1923. («Russland og freden.» 12 artikler i *Tidens Tegn*, 1923.)

Nansen, Fridtjof, *Verker*. Revidert utgave ved Marit Greve og Odd Nansen. Oslo, Aschehoug, 1961.

Noel-Baker, Philip, «Nansen's Place in History.» Nansen Memorial Lecture. Oslo, Universitetsforlaget, 1962.

Ristelhueber, René, *La Double Aventure de Fridtjof Nansen: Explorateur et philanthrope.* Montreal, Éd. Variétés, 1945.

Schou, August, «Fra Wergeland til Nansen: Internasjonalismens idé i Norge», with an English summary. Nansen Memorial Lecture. Oslo, Universitetsforlaget, 1964.

Shackleton, Edward, *Nansen: The Explorer.* London, Witherby, 1959.

Sørensen, Jon, *The Saga of Fridtjof Nansen*, translated from the Norwegian by J.B.C. Watkins. New York, Norton, 1932. Contains a bibliography.

Vogt, Per, *Fridtjof Nansen: Explorer, Scientist, Humanitarian.* Oslo, Dreyers Forlag, 1961.

Peace 1923 - 1924

Prizes not awarded

Peace 1925

(Prize awarded in 1926)

JOSEPH AUSTEN CHAMBERLAIN

CHARLES GATES DAWES

No More War

Speech at Award Ceremony by Fridtjof Nansen*, Peace Laureate for 1922

We still remember it vividly, that event of over eight years ago. For four long years the world had resounded with the fearful din of the battlefields, the piercing cries of the dying, the forlorn laments of parents and widows over the bloody corpses of their sons and husbands.

Then suddenly the terrible nightmare faded, the roar of the cannons was stilled; the unbelievable had really happened—*the world war had ended!*

Europe breathed again, raised its head, gazed out over the disconsolate fields of battle, over the endless mounds of smoldering ruins, toward the horizon and the breaking day. But the day would not be hurried. Dark clouds gathered from all sides and spread from country to country; stormy skies cast their menacing shadows first in one place, then in another. It was as if everyone was waiting for a dawn which would not come. Now insidious doubt seeps into men's minds, breeding a melancholy uneasiness. Fear takes hold, and the powers of darkness gain sway. Suspicion and distrust

---

* Mr. Nansen delivered this speech on December 10, 1926, in the auditorium of the Nobel Institute in Oslo to a distinguished audience convened to witness the presentation of the Peace Prizes for 1925 and 1926. After an orchestral overture, Mr. Fredrik Stang, chairman of the Nobel Committee, announced that the prize for 1925, having been reserved in that year, was awarded equally to Sir Austen Chamberlain and to Charles G. Dawes and that the prize for 1926 was awarded equally to Aristide Briand and to Gustav Stresemann. Mr. Ragnvald Moe, secretary to the Committee, spoke briefly on Dr. Nobel, this day being the thirtieth anniversary of his death. Mr. Nansen then delivered the speech printed here. It is not the typical «presentation speech». But it serves the purpose of such a speech since it deals with the 1924 plan of reparations prepared by the so-called Dawes Committee and with the Locarno Pact in which the other three laureates played leading roles. In a sense, therefore, it is a presentation speech for four laureates, but it departs from the usual form of such a speech by developing a theme derived from the speaker's own thinking. Since none of the laureates was present on this occasion, the diplomatic representatives of the four nations concerned accepted the prizes on their behalf. The text of Mr. Nansen's speech does not appear in *Les Prix Nobel*; the text published in Norwegian in *Eventyr-lyst—Ingen krig mere: To taler av Fridtjof Nansen* (Oslo: Jacob Dybwad, 1927), pp. 71–100, has been used for this translation.

grow between nations, between classes, and only thistles prosper in such soil. Hatred grows; increasing insecurity and fear paralyze all initiative, opening the way to every kind of blunder. There is talk of another war. It is as if the world, which had once before hovered on the brink and peered down into the abyss but which had at the eleventh hour dragged itself onto safer ground, is once again in perilous darkness being drawn back into the depths.

What is wrong? What is missing? It is the good human qualities that can grow only in the light of day: forbearance, confidence, compassion, the sincere desire for full cooperation in rebuilding the world.

A peace settlement following a ruinous war can easily degenerate into the imposition by the victors of more or less humiliating conditions upon the vanquished. Such terms, in their turn, can easily bear fruit which will in time ripen into a fresh war. The Peace of Versailles can certainly not be said to constitute an exception to this rule. The more protracted the withering trial of war, the harsher the conditions imposed; so when victory is finally won, the demands are difficult, or even impossible, to fulfill. The coercion used to compel the vanquished to give beyond their capabilities only breeds greater hatred and the thirst for revenge. Failure to receive what the victors consider their just compensation for the wounds suffered in war begets disappointment and frustration. To these is added the insecurity and fear of possible consequences when forcible and oppressive means must be used to recover claims. The difficulties mount steadily; nations move further and further apart; insecurity, fear, anxiety foster rearmament.

Such is the picture that Europe presented in 1923, more than four years after the ending of the war. When Germany found herself unable to pay the reparations to which the French felt entitled, French troops marched into and occupied the Ruhr. The result was the disruption of the entire production of Europe. Hatred of France flared up in Germany more violently than ever. Paralyzing despondency spread among people of all European nations, and talk of the next war became more and more common.

Then, when the darkness was deepest, America extended a helping hand. The United States had hitherto kept out of the situation and was thus able to observe the unhappy events in Europe calmly and in perspective. The Americans now felt obliged to try to help Europe back onto her feet. An idea which had already been voiced by U.S. Secretary of State Hughes[1] in December, 1922, now gained increasing support. This was that Germany's

---

1. Charles Evans Hughes (1862–1948), U.S. secretary of state (1921–1925).

capacity to pay reparations should be investigated by a competent committee in order to obtain an expert scientific basis for future deliberations.

The idea eventually found favor with Poincaré and the French, and it was then agreed to appoint a committee of experts; the American government sent Owen D. Young and Charles G. Dawes, the latter becoming chairman of the committee[1].

The first meeting took place in Paris on January 14, 1924. By April 9 of the same year the committee had drafted a plan, later known as the Dawes Plan. The committee proposed that the reparations should be paid by an altogether different system and that a moratorium should first be applied. It further proposed, among other measures, the complete reorganization of Germany's finances and the granting of a foreign loan. The plan also regarded as an economic necessity the return of the Ruhr to Germany.

The importance of this plan was already evident from the fact that when it became apparent at the end of July, 1924, that it would be accepted by the Allied governments, confidence in the European economy immediately began to revive, and there was a consequent and marked improvement in the strength of European currency.

It is true that the plan envisaged a substantial reduction in the war reparations which Germany was to pay, but it did at least seek to ensure a considerable payment each year. Its adoption contributed to the decision to evacuate the Ruhr. It also brought a temporary halt to the endless conflicts about Germany's reparations, which had been largely responsible for the pessimistic outlook in Europe and for the anxiety and insecurity which had characterized the first five years of peace.

The plan was important not only for Germany, France, and the Allies, but, both economically and politically, for the whole of Europe and consequently for America as well. It restored confidence in the economy and future of Europe. It brought her safely through an acute crisis which could have resulted in the most serious danger to peace. But its greatest significance lies in the fact that it was a symptom of a psychological change in European mentality and at the same time a powerful impetus for continued change. It marked the beginning of the policy of reconciliation and peace which led

1. Raymond Poincaré (1860–1934), president of France (1913–1920); premier (1912; 1922–1924; 1926–1929). Owen D. Young (1874–1962), American lawyer and corporation executive, chairman of the Reparations Conference of 1929; the Young Plan of reparation payments which replaced the Dawes Plan took its name from him.

to the Locarno agreements. This was the first dawning of the day after the long darkness.

Another memorable step along the path of peace was the Geneva Protocol adopted by the League of Nations Assembly in the autumn of 1924[1]. For the first time the delegates of nations from all parts of the world declared aggressive war to be a crime. They also adopted the principle that all international controversies without exception must be settled by peaceful means, either by arbitration or before a court of law.

It is true that the Protocol was not ratified by the governments; nevertheless it is an important milestone in history, and its spirit should not be ignored by the statesmen of the future. For it was this spirit which prepared the way for what was to be accomplished later.

The next great milestone bears the name of Locarno. The initiative on this occasion came from Germany, from Chancellor Luther and Foreign Minister Stresemann[2].

During the negotiations which preceded the Geneva Protocol the French, and especially Briand, its warm advocate, strongly urged the necessity of guarantees to provide security against aggression and war. In a note dated February 9, 1925, Germany outlined the security guarantees which she believed were required and suggested a possible form for a security treaty which could «prepare the ground for a world convention of all states similar to that arranged for the Geneva Protocol by the League of Nations for the peaceful settlement of international disagreements».

Following extensive negotiations, a meeting took place in Locarno from October 5 to October 16 of 1925. France was represented by Briand, Germany by Luther and Stresemann, Great Britain by Chamberlain, Italy by Mussolini, Belgium by Vandervelde, Poland by Skrzyński, and Czechoslovakia by Beneš[3]. A treaty clarifying the question of the Rhineland was concluded between Germany, Belgium, France, Great Britain, and Italy, and four arbitration agreements were made between Germany on the

1. See Henderson's lecture, Vol.2, p.194, fn.1.
2. Hans Luther (1879–1962), chancellor of Germany (1925–1926); and see Stresemann's lecture, Vol.2, p.13, fn.3.
3. Benito Mussolini (1883–1945), Italian premier and dictator (1922–1943). Émile Vandervelde (1866–1938), Belgian minister of foreign affairs (1925). Count Aleksander Skrzyński (1882–1931), Polish prime minister (1925–1926). Eduard Beneš (1884–1948), foreign minister of Czechoslovakia (1918–1935); president (1935–1938; in exile 1939–1945; 1946–1948).

one side and Belgium, France, Poland, and Czechoslovakia on the other.

I shall not go into greater detail on the provisions of these treaties, for they are well known. Of the Rhineland treaty it has been said that for the first time since Louis XIV[1], the Rhine has ceased to be a cause of dissension in European politics. So closes a chapter in history. Under the four arbitration agreements the nations undertake to submit to peaceful settlement through impartial mediation or arbitration all disputes except those «arising out of past events which took place prior to the present agreement».

The Locarno agreements mark a radical and complete change in European politics, transforming the relations between the former antagonists in the war and infusing them with an entirely new spirit. This spirit derives from the almost unprecedented attempt to base politics on the principle of mutual friendship and trust.

What inspires one's confidence is that it was neither idealism nor altruism, but a sense of necessity which prompted those concerned to make the attempt. The men who met at Locarno are no idealistic pacifists; they are realistic politicians and responsible statesmen who, having originally pursued directly conflicting policies, have come to the realization that the only chance of creating a real future for mankind is to stand united in a sincere desire to work together.

In a speech he made after the signing of the agreements, Briand aptly remarked: «The war has taught us one thing, namely, that a common fate binds us together. If we go under, we go under together. If we wish to recover, we cannot do so in conflict with each other, but only by working together.»[2]

Both Briand and Stresemann have rightly emphasized that every individual must first be a good citizen of his own country–a good Frenchman, a good German, a good Briton–but still a good European bound to other Europeans by the great ideals of the European civilization so gravely menaced by the events of the last war.

If we are to appreciate fully what these statesmen accomplished at Locarno for the peace of Europe, then we must not overlook the violent nationalistic opposition in their own countries which several of them had to overcome

1. Louis XIV (1638–1715), king of France (1643–1715).
2. According to Vallentin-Luchaire in *Stresemann* (New York: Smith, 1931), p.211, and according to the (London) *Times* of December 2, 1925, p.16, these words are from the speech made by Gustav Stresemann after the official signing of the Locarno Pacts in London on December 1, 1925.

in order to push through the peace program. They strode ahead fearlessly in the conviction that they had now found the right road.

With Locarno an accomplished fact, it seemed as though a new day would be breaking and renewed courage and confidence would be returning to Europe with ever increasing tempo. But the agreements were not yet activated. One of their provisions was that Germany should enter the League of Nations. This step, however, was to encounter more serious difficulties than had been anticipated. Still fresh in our memory is that distressing special session of the Assembly at Geneva last March when the delegates met for the sole purpose of admitting Germany into the League, only to depart without having been able to do it.

But these events were followed by the Assembly meeting at Geneva last September when Germany's delegates, with Stresemann at their head, were able to enter honorably and take their places among the members of the League. No one who was present will forget that moment.

Germany's admission was welcomed in a remarkable speech by Briand. Among other things, he said: «No more war!... From now on it will be for the judge to decide what is right. Just as individual citizens settle their disagreements before a judge, so shall we also resolve ours by peaceful means. Away with rifles, machine guns, cannons. Make way for conciliation, arbitration, peace!»[1]

On this point we can now see daylight again. Is it not almost as if we are seeing the new earth turn green again after Armageddon[2]?

The Locarno Pacts, together with Germany's entry into the League of Nations and the speeches which followed it, hold much promise for the future—they all tend to build up confidence and to strengthen the will to carry on the good work. But all this must not blind us to the fact that there is still a long way to go before the goal is reached and lasting peace really secured. Noble words and noble intent on the part of leaders are a great encouragement, but they are not enough. Words must be translated into action, intent into earnest toil, for shining promises have often come to nothing in the past and the blue skies of hope have again been filled by storm clouds.

1. From Briand's speech to the Seventh Plenary Meeting of the Assembly, September 10, 1926 (League of Nations, *Official Journal*, Special Supplement 44, p. 53); for text in French see Achille Elisha, *Aristide Briand: Discours et écrits de politique étrangère* (Paris: Plon, 1965), pp. 176–184.
2. The Norwegian word here translated as *Armageddon* is *Ragnarokk* which in Norse mythology refers to the end of the world.

Our watchword must be: «No more war!» And what does this mean? It does not mean «no more world war», with everyone, and especially the principal powers, free to indulge in small private wars whenever they are so disposed. It does not mean «no more war» except when a power is able, without any great effort on its part, to crush a weak neighbor that falls easy prey to superior force. It does not mean «no more war» except when what we used to call national honor is at stake.

It means none of these. What it does mean is no more war of any kind whatsoever, no more aggression, no more of the bloody and futile clashes which have tarnished the history of mankind for so long. It means working to eradicate the use of force from national policies; to stamp out suppression of others in whatever form it appears; to liberate ourselves now and for all time–as we in this generation can do if we so resolve–from the hideous corruption of warfare between different groups of the human race, be it between nations or within nations.

I say without hesitation that this is the greatest of all the causes which now command our attention. The question of how we can put an end to all war is the vital problem of our time, not only for international politics, but for national politics as well.

This may strike many people as an exaggeration, even as a misuse of language. To them such problems as those of miners' strikes, social reform, customs barriers, prohibition, or whatever, seem far more important. I say with utter conviction that those who think so are wrong.

War, preparation for war, the burden of armament, particularly in the case of the larger countries–these are the first and vital problems. If we can erect barriers against war, if we can abolish the armament burdens which Europe suffers today, if we can destroy the evil specter of militarism which still haunts the world and so vouchsafe complete security for all time, then we shall obtain, and swiftly at that, the social reforms we desire, the development of our resouces, the many forms of progress we hope for; we shall move forward toward a new and better life.

But if we do not get rid of war, if we do not put a complete end to it, if Europe does not reduce and limit its armaments, then we shall have no reforms and no progress of any significance.

We can be certain that in the future, just as in the past, armament will call forth counterarmament, alliances and counteralliances; it will engender suspicion and distrust, bringing fear to men's hearts; it will lead to international crises; it will lead to war, perhaps to small local wars at first, but, finally and inescapably, it will bring down upon us a great world war no less frightful than the last.

If the work for disarmament which the League of Nations has now begun does not produce results, if the level of armaments is maintained, then war will result. It seems to me that all our past experience shows this to be incontrovertible. But do not take my word for it. Listen to what more qualified authorities have to say.

Lord Grey, foreign minister of Great Britain at the outbreak of the war[1], has said, and he has said it time and time again, that it was Europe's steadily increasing armaments which led to the war in 1914. He has warned us that if armaments in Europe are maintained, if the nations of the world embark on a new contest in military preparedness, we will bring upon ourselves a new war as inevitably as we did the last one. And he has told us that a new war will mean the end of our civilization as we know it today.

Who will question Lord Grey's authority to speak on this subject? Many other leading statesmen have uttered the same sentiments on several occasions. Let me mention just one. As recently as January of this year, Mr. Baldwin, the present prime minister of Great Britain[2], said: «A new war in the West and the civilization of our era will collapse in a fall as great as that of Rome.»

These men I have mentioned are not fanatics, indeed not even pacifists; they are responsible statesmen who have exercised or who will in the future exercise great power in the leadership of the world. If they mean their statements seriously, then it seems to me to follow that there is scarcely any other political problem worth discussing until the problem of the next war is resolved.

Let us pause for a moment to consider what they have said. It may seem fantastic to state that our civilization can be obliterated.

We have a sense of vitality and strength, a feeling that a great future lies ahead of us. But let us not forget that civilizations have been wiped out before. Powerful nations, which seemed as strong then as the most powerful states of our time seem to us now, have vanished. The Roman Empire, which ruled Europe for a period hundreds of years longer than the lifetime of our modern Western civilization, was swept away by the invasion of barbaric hordes.

1. Sir Edward Grey (1862–1933), secretary of state for foreign affairs (1905–1916).
2. Stanley Baldwin (1867–1947), British prime minister (1923–1924; 1924–1929; 1935–1937).

You have no sense of any impending disaster, you are too conscious of the forces of life around you. I feel the same. I too feel these forces. But I also sense that the last war inflicted upon our civilization a terrible wound, a painful wound that is still far from healed. It was as if the very foundations shook under Europe. And, worst of all, most Europeans still do not understand the true nature and significance of the last war. They are already about to forget it before they have learned the lesson it should teach them. They are forgetting their dead.

Of course, there are still millions of people in practically every country of Europe who cannot forget the horrors of the war. The carnage of the battlefields, once seen, is not easily forgotten. These people can tell of the merciless slaughter on the lovely countryside of France; of the agony of mind, the terror inspired by the big bombardments and the ceaseless rattle of gunfire in a modern offensive; of the inconceivable suffering of wounded and broken men hanging perhaps for days on barbed wire, crying out for the death which they themselves had not the strength to inflict. Of such horrors and worse can these people tell, and if Europe would only heed them, if all its people would only remember the war's bestiality, its barbaric cruelty, they would see to it that war would never occur again.

But there are other aspects of war which I, perhaps more than most people, have had the opportunity to observe. For more than six years now, it has been my task, on behalf of the League of Nations[1], to investigate and as far as possible to alleviate the terrible aftereffects of war. During all these years I have had to deal with hundreds of thousands of prisoners of war, with famine, with refugees – frightened refugees, each with his own story of endless heartrending tragedy, the old, the women, the little helpless children left alone because of the vicissitudes of war, and all of them lost, plundered, bereft of everything of value in this world.

I wish I could give you a picture of what I have seen and experienced. I wish I could just for one moment make you feel what it is to see a whole nation fleeing in wild terror along the country roads; or to travel among a people struck down by famine; to enter huts where men, women, and children lie still, no longer complaining, waiting only for death in countries where corpses are dug up out of their graves and eaten, where maddened mothers slay their own children for food. But no, I cannot attempt it now.

All this endless misfortune, all this misery and incredible suffering, these

1. As the League's High Commissioner for Refugees.

hundreds of thousands of forsaken prisoners of war, these famines, these millions of helpless refugees – they are all, directly or indirectly, the results of the war. But, believe me, all these calamities cannot occur without undermining our entire social system; they sap the vitality of nations and they inflict wounds so deep that they will take a long time to heal, if they ever do.

And still, even still, people talk about the probability of another war.

Do we not stop to think what this would mean? Even if the next war is no worse than the last, I believe it will destroy our European civilization. But of course the next war will not be like the last. It will be incomparably worse.

I shall not weary you by going further into that. It is enough to say that in the event of a new war we face the threatening fact that our civilization can be annihilated, just as other civilizations have been annihilated in the past.

But we also have the means to avert this threat. War does not come unless we wish it upon ourselves. War is not the result of some uncontrollable catastrophe of nature; it is the result of man's will. It is his own shame. And truly, with reasonable policies, it would be comparatively easy to put an end to war.

Let me suggest the course which I believe can lead us forward. The governments of Europe must unite around and stake their all on what I shall, for the sake of brevity, call the League of Nations policy.

Do not misunderstand me here. The League of Nations is no longer a remote or abstract idea. It is a living organism. Its institutions are now an essential part of the machinery of world control. If we can put the full force of the combined power of individual governments behind these institutions, behind the policy of disarmament, behind all the policies pursued by the League, then we shall put an end to war.

But the governments, whether of large countries or of small, must stake everything on this policy without reservations. There must be no clinging to ancient rights to wage private wars. There must be no secret hopes that, if the League is weak in certain areas, it can be made to serve private interests.

We must follow the new road in international politics mapped out at Locarno, and we must burn behind us the bridges that lead back to the old policies and the old systems which have failed us so tragically. It has always been my conviction that, in the great things of life, it is of decisive importance to have no line of retreat – a principle which certainly holds good here.

By the very nature of things, progress will depend essentially on the actions of the great powers. But small nations like our own can also do much. For the large states must take into account such a variety of factors, such a multitude of conflicting interests, that their leaders may often find it difficult to follow their own convictions, assessing all the time, as they must, the political currents among their electorates, the national self-interests of their countries, not to mention the complex intrigues which frequently surround them. All these circumstances can often restrict their freedom to act.

Small nations and their leaders enjoy greater latitude in this respect; they have fewer conflicting interests, and for them a policy of peace without restrictions or reservations is a natural one. If all the small nations will work together resolutely and systematically in the League of Nations to lay the ghost of war, they can achieve much, greatly strengthening the League in the process.

Certainly, it cannot be denied that the great powers can give and on occasion have given the impression of acting somewhat arbitrarily and without proper consideration for the views of the other members of the League. But the small nations have ample opportunity to state their case if they will just confidently take it. And when they fail to do so, the blame falls chiefly on themselves. As Briand said in his splendid speech to the last Assembly, there must in future be no more resorting to «methods of negotiation which are inconsistent with the true spirit of the League of Nations», and «the League's work shall in future take place in the full light of day and with the collaboration of all its members.»[1]

It is, then, the duty of all members, and not least of the small nations, to unite in the task of abolishing war, to participate positively in this work, not to wait passively but to act.

If we really want to put an end to war, if we want to be rid of heavy armaments, the governments must, as I have said, stake everything upon the policy of the League of Nations without thinking about any lines of retreat. They must work in every way and at every opportunity to build up the power and strength of the League. If they do so and if their peoples support them in the same spirit, then shall the evil monster of war be felled and our future secured for the work of peace, that of building, not tearing down.

1. See p.388, fn.1.

Acceptance

by Joseph Austen Chamberlain

The Peace Prize for 1925, reserved in that year, was awarded on December 10, 1926, half of it to Sir Austen Chamberlain, the British foreign minister, and half to Charles Gates Dawes. In Sir Austen's case, the prize recognized his work on the Locarno Pacts of 1925. Since he was not present at the award ceremony in the Norwegian Nobel Institute at Oslo, Sir Francis O. Lindley, Great Britain's minister in Oslo, accepted the prize for him. Sir Francis read the following telegram from Sir Austen:

«I should like you to express to the Chairman of the Nobel Committee my deep appreciation of the honor just done me by this award.

I had the good fortune to have, in my work, the collaboration of two statesmen both remarkable for the magnanimity of their spirit, for the independence of their judgment, and for their love of peace. Without their help I would have been able to do nothing. My feeling of gratitude for the award acknowledging my part in the common effort is heightened by the fact that the Committee has recognized in the same manner the important roles played by Mr. Briand and Mr. Stresemann. The outstanding work of the Dawes Committee, which preceded us, greatly facilitated our task, and I am proud to be associated with the distinguished American statesman whose name will always be remembered in connection with the great work of European reconstruction.»[1]

Sir Austen did not deliver a Nobel lecture.

1. Translated from the French text in *Les Prix Nobel en 1926*.

Biography

Sir Joseph Austen Chamberlain (October 16, 1863–March 17, 1937) was the eldest son of Joseph Chamberlain, the great British statesman known as the «Empire-builder»; he was a half-brother of Neville Chamberlain, prime minister from 1937 to 1940. Like William Pitt the Younger, son of a famous father a hundred years earlier, he was trained for statesmanship. It was said of Austen that he did not choose a career, he accepted one. Having completed his boyhood schooling at Rugby and his university studies at Cambridge, he spent nine months at the École des Sciences Politiques in Paris and twelve months in Berlin. When he returned to Birmingham in 1887, he became, in effect, his father's private secretary. Consequently, in 1892, when Austen Chamberlain was twenty-nine years old, he was well equipped to take a seat in the House of Commons, representing East Worcestershire, a constituency near the family home in Birmingham. Upon his father's death in 1914, Austen became the member for West Birmingham, holding this seat until his own death in 1937.

Austen Chamberlain's forty-five year career in the House of Commons may be divided into two periods: the first from his entry into the House in 1892 to 1922 when Lloyd George resigned as prime minister; and the second from 1922 to his death in 1937. In the first period he was concerned primarily with domestic questions; in the second, with international questions.

Chamberlain made his mark quickly. His maiden speech in 1893 was praised by William Gladstone; from 1895 to 1900 he was civil lord of the Admiralty; from 1900 to 1902, financial secretary to the Treasury; for one year, 1902–1903, the postmaster general; from 1903 to 1906, he was chancellor of the Exchequer.

In the wartime coalition government formed by Herbert Asquith in 1915, Chamberlain accepted the position of secretary of state for India, resigning in 1917. When David Lloyd George formed a coalition government after the election of 1918, he made Chamberlain his chancellor of the Exchequer. Chamberlain filled this post from 1919 to 1921 with distinction, paying the enormous debts accumulated during the war, maintaining a stable currency, and strengthening the national credit.

Upon Bonar Law's retirement from the leadership of the Conservative Party in 1921, Chamberlain succeeded him for eighteen months. By this time Lloyd George's coalition was tottering and the rank and file of the Conservative Party wanted to break away from it. When Chamberlain stood by the prime minister, the party, withdrawing from the coalition, first placed Bonar Law in the prime ministry and then Stanley Baldwin.

In the Baldwin government of 1924 to 1929, Chamberlain was secretary of state for foreign affairs. His brilliant tenure in office reflected the brilliant qualities he brought to it. In establishing policy, he was philosophically realistic and morally fearless; in pursuing a course of action he was patient, determined, resourceful; in personal negotiation he was linguistically fluent, faultlessly polite, charming in manner and elegant in appearance.

His first important act as foreign secretary shocked some diplomatic circles. In 1925 on behalf of his government he rejected the proposed Geneva Protocol in a speech to the Council of the League of Nations, not so much because it required compulsory arbitration of international disputes as because it was the Council which was to decide what action member states should take to enforce the authority of the League in time of crisis. He tempered the effect of this rejection by suggesting that the best way in theory to deal with situations as they arose was to «supplement the Covenant by making special arrangements in order to meet special needs».

The road to Locarno now lay open. Gustav Stresemann, the German foreign minister, and Aristide Briand, the French foreign minister, were willing to travel the road with him. After meticulous preparation during the summer of 1925, representatives of seven powers–Great Britain, Germany, France, Belgium, Italy, Poland, and Czechoslovakia–met at Locarno in southern Switzerland on October 5, 1925. On Chamberlain's birthday, October 16, the foreign ministers initialed the documents known as the Locarno Agreements. Eight treaties or agreements in all, they included the Rhine Guarantee Pact (or «Locarno Pact») with Germany, Belgium, France, Great Britain, and Italy as signatories; individual treaties of arbitration between Germany and former enemy nations; guarantee treaties involving France, Poland, and Czechoslovakia; and a collective note on the entry of Germany into the League of Nations.

Upon his return to London after the triumph at Locarno, Chamberlain was given an immense ovation, was made Knight of the Garter, and a year later, along with Stresemann and Briand, his two companions in diplomacy, was awarded the Nobel Peace Prize.

In his later years in the foreign office Chamberlain dealt with vexing questions in China and Egypt. He displayed what firmness he could in defending British interests against encroachments of the Chinese Nationalists, but, lacking full cooperation from the United States and Japan, could forge no long-range solutions. To provide some permanent pattern for Anglo-Egyptian relations, Chamberlain drew up a draft of a treaty in 1927 which anticipated the treaty signed in the mid-thirties.

Out of office in his last years, partly because he chose to provide opportunity for the young men in Parliament, Chamberlain still spoke with a commanding voice in the Commons. He was among the first to see potential danger in Hitler; he favored both the imposition of sanctions against Italy during the Abyssinian crisis and their removal when they failed to prevent an Italian victory.

During these years he was also writing with a graceful pen. His *Down the Years* is part reminiscence, part character studies of great men he had known, part familiar essays. His *Politics from Inside* consists chiefly of letters he wrote to his stepmother from 1906 to 1914 to keep his ailing father informed of governmental and diplomatic events.

On March 17, 1937, Austen Chamberlain died of apoplexy, the same affliction that had killed his father a month before World War I began.

Selected Bibliography

Chamberlain, Sir Austen, *Down the Years*. London, Cassell, 1935. Reminiscences, character sketches (including one of Briand and one of Stresemann).

Chamberlain, Sir Austen, *The League of Nations*. Glasgow, Jackson, Wiley, 1926.

Chamberlain, Sir Austen, *Peace in Our Time: Addresses on Europe and the Empire*. London, Allen, 1928.

Chamberlain, Sir Austen, *Politics from Inside: An Epistolary Chronicle, 1906–1914*. London, Cassell, 1936. A full account of political events written for his father after his illness in 1906. This book and *Down the Years* were translated and published in one volume: *Englische Politik: Erinnerungen aus fünfzig Jahren*. Übers. von Fritz Pick. Essen, Essener Verlagsanstalt, 1938.

Chamberlain, Sir Austen, *Speeches on Germany*. London, Friends of Europe Publications, 1933.

Coudurier de Chassaigne, Joseph Louis, *Les Trois Chamberlain: Une Famille de grands parlementaires anglais*. Paris, 1939.

Dictionary of National Biography.

Pensa, Henri, *De Locarno au Pacte Kellogg: La Politique européenne sous le triumvirat Chamberlain-Briand-Stresemann, 1925–1929.* Paris, 1930.

Petrie, Sir Charles A., *The Chamberlain Tradition.* New York, Stokes, 1938.

Petrie, Sir Charles A., *The Life and Letters of the Right Hon. Sir Austen Chamberlain.* 2 vols. London, Cassell, 1939.

Stern-Rubarth, Edgar, *Three Men Tried: Austen Chamberlain, Stresemann, Briand and Their Fight for a New Europe.* London, Duckworth, 1939.

Acceptance

by Charles Gates Dawes

Charles Dawes, vice-president of the United States, was not present to receive the Peace Prize for 1925, which he shared with Sir Austen Chamberlain. Given in recognition of his work as chairman of the Dawes Committee handling the problem of German reparations, the award (reserved in 1925) was made on December 10, 1926, at the Nobel Institute in Oslo. The prize was accepted on his behalf by Laurits Selmer Swenson, the United States minister in Oslo, who read the following telegram[1] from Mr. Dawes:

«This award, which is in recognition of the work of the First Committee of Experts, Reparation Commission, of which I was chairman, is gratefully acknowledged. The committee was composed of Owen D. Young, Sir Josiah C. Stamp, Sir Robert M. Kindersley, Jean Parmentier, Edgard Allix, Alberto Pirelli, Frederico Flora, Emile Francqui, Baron Maurice Houtart, and myself. It was the endeavor of the experts to found their plan upon the principles of justice, fairness, and mutual interest, relying for its acceptance thus prepared upon that common good faith which is the enduring hope for the universal safeguarding of peace. That the results achieved under it have merited in your judgment this high recognition is a tribute to the united efforts of the committee.»

Mr. Dawes did not deliver a Nobel lecture.

1. This telegram to the American Legation in Oslo, dated December 8, 1926, and sent in English, is the original text in the files of the Nobel Institute. It appears in French translation in *Les Prix Nobel en 1926*.

Biography

Charles Gates Dawes (August 27, 1865 – April 23, 1951) pursued two careers during his lifetime, one in business and finance, the other in public service. He was at the height of his fame in both in 1926 when he was awarded the Nobel Peace Prize for 1925. He was the vice-president of the United States; he had achieved worldwide recognition for his report on German reparations in 1924; he had a secure reputation as a financier.

By ancestry he was destined for a life of such duality. His father had distinguished himself in the Civil War, achieving the rank of brevet brigadier general; an uncle had given his life. Four generations earlier, William Dawes had ridden with Paul Revere on April 18, 1775, to warn the Massachusetts colonists of the British advance which signalized the opening of the American Revolution; and seven generations earlier in 1628 the first William Dawes had been among the Puritans who came to America. Financial acumen was just as natural a heritage as active patriotism. Dawes's father owned and managed a lumber company in Marietta, Ohio; an uncle was a prosperous banker.

Since Charles Dawes's mother had graduated from Marietta College and his father was on its Board of Trustees, it was almost inevitable that he would enroll there. He received his bachelor's degree in 1884 at the age of nineteen, studied for two years in the Law School of the University of Cincinnati, and returned to Marietta to earn a master's degree.

In 1887 he moved to Lincoln, Nebraska, more to participate in the advantages of a fast-growing economy than to engage in the practice of law. In the seven years he lived there he earned a reputation as an intelligent, ingenious, persuasive, alert businessman. He controlled a city block of business offices, controlled a meat packing company, acted as director of a bank, and was an investor in land and in bank stocks. He laid the foundation for his large personal fortune in 1894, however, when he purchased control of a plant manufacturing artificial gas in LaCrosse, Wisconsin, and of another plant immediately to the north of Chicago. Eventually, he and his brothers controlled twenty-eight gas and electric plants in ten states. To be near his main business office, he made his home in Evanston, a suburb to the north of Chicago, residing there until his death.

In 1902, turning over to his brothers the management of the utilities, he entered the third phase of his business career, that of banking. He founded and became president of the Central Trust Company of Illinois, often referred to as the «Dawes Bank», and spent virtually full time in its management until he enlisted in the army in 1917.

The comptrollership of the currency was Dawes's first official governmental position. President William McKinley, for whom he had acted as a fund raiser in the 1896 campaign, had appointed him in 1898, and in 1901 promised to support him as a candidate for the Senate from Illinois. When McKinley was assassinated, Dawes, shorn of presidential support, withdrew his candidacy.

In 1917 Dawes enlisted as a major in the army and twenty-six months later was discharged as a brigadier general. While on General Pershing's staff he integrated the system of supply procurement and distribution for the entire American Expeditionary Force and later performed an analogous service for the Allies by devising an inter-Allied purchasing board, as well as a unified distribution authority. In 1919, despite the opposition raised by his own Republican Party, he strongly urged the Congress to accept the Treaty of Versailles and the League of Nations.

In 1920, appointed to the newly inaugurated position of Director of the Budget, Dawes applied his conceptions of efficiency and unity to the reform of budgetary procedures in the United States government. His most important reform resulted from his insistence that each department of the government prepare a true budget projecting future expenditures and stay within it. It is estimated that this reform and others, notably the unification of purchasing, saved the government about two billion dollars in the first year.

The League of Nations late in 1923 invited Dawes to chair a committee to deal with the question of German reparations. The «Dawes Report», submitted in April, 1924, provided facts on Germany's budget and resources, outlined measures needed to stabilize the currency, and suggested a schedule of payments on a sliding scale. For his masterly handling of this crucial international problem, he was awarded the Nobel Peace Prize; he donated the money to the endowment of the newly established Walter Hines Page [1] School of International Relations at Johns Hopkins University.

1. W. H. Page (1855–1918), American writer, editor, and diplomat; cofounder of Doubleday, Page & Co., a publishing firm; ambassador to Great Britain (1913–1918).

From 1924 to 1932, Dawes devoted his entire attention to public service. He was elected to the vice-presidency of the United States in 1924, serving in office from 1925 to 1929. In 1929, when the Dominican Republic request-ed advice on improving the financial operation of its government, Dawes headed a commission whose extensive recommendations for reform were later adopted. From June of 1929 to January of 1932, Dawes was the U.S. ambassador to Great Britain. In 1930 he was a delegate to the London Naval Conference; in 1932 he accepted the chairmanship of the American delega-tion to the Disarmament Conference in Geneva but resigned to accept the chairmanship of the Reconstruction Finance Corporation, a governmental agency empowered to lend money to banks, railroads, and other businesses in an effort to prevent total economic collapse during the depression.

Dawes was a disciplined and productive man. He led a full life in the commercial and political world until the age of sixty-seven; he wrote nine books; he discharged countless civic duties. Even in music he excelled. He performed on the flute and piano; composed a melody that Fritz Kreisler, the noted violinist, often played as an encore; combined his interest in music and his acumen in business to establish grand opera in Chicago. Withal he found time for family life. He admired his father and uncle; he brought his brothers into his business enterprises; and he was devoted to his wife and to his son and daughter, suffering intensely when his son was rowned in Lake Geneva, Wisconsin, while on summer vacation from Princeton University.

Dawes was a forthright man given to forthright talk. His nickname, «Hel and Maria» Dawes, came from some words uttered before a congressional committee investigating charges of waste and extravagance in the conduct of World War I. When a member of the committee asked Dawes if it was true that excessive prices were paid for mules in France, he shouted «Helen Maria, I'd have paid horse prices for sheep if the sheep could have pulled artillery to the front!»[1]

He died of a coronary thrombosis at his Evanston home on April 23, 1951.

1. Apparently «Helen Maria» was an expletive in common usage in Nebraska. The newspapers printed it as «Hell and Maria», and that form stuck. Timmons tells the story in detail in *Portrait of an American*, pp.193–198; Dawes also tells the story but leaves out the crucial phrase in *Notes as Vice President*, pp.9–13.

Selected Bibliography

Bliven, Bruce, «Dawes: Supersalesman», in *The New Republic*, 53 (1928) 263–267. A brief but excellent contemporaneous account of Dawes's career.

Dawes, Charles Gates. The Dawes papers are deposited in the Library of Northwestern University, Evanston, Ill. His books are listed here chronologically by date of publication.

Dawes, Charles Gates, *The Banking System of the United States and Its Relation to the Money and Business of the Country*. Chicago, Rand McNally, 1894.

Dawes, Charles Gates, *Essays and Speeches*. New York, Houghton, 1915.

Dawes, Charles Gates, *Journal of the Great War*, 2 vols. New York, Houghton, 1921.

Dawes, Charles Gates, *The First Year of the Budget of the United States*. New York, Harper, 1923.

Dawes, Charles Gates, *Notes as Vice President, 1928–1929*. Boston, Little, Brown, 1935.

Dawes, Charles Gates, *How Long Prosperity?* New York, Marquis, 1937.

Dawes, Charles Gates, *Journal as Ambassador to Great Britain*. New York, Macmillan, 1939.

Dawes, Charles Gates, *A Journal of Reparations*. New York, Macmillan, 1939.

Dawes, Charles Gates, *A Journal of the McKinley Years*, ed. by Bascom N. Timmons. La Grange, Ill., Tower, 1950.

Leach, Paul Roscoe, *That Man Dawes*. Chicago, Reilly and Lee, 1930.

National Cyclopedia of American Biography.

Obituary, the *New York Times* (April 24, 1951).

Sherman, Richard Garrett, *Charles G. Dawes: An Entrepreneurial Biography, 1865–1951*. Unpublished Ph.D. dissertation. Iowa City, Iowa, University of Iowa, 1960.

Timmons, Bascom Nolly, *Portrait of an American: Charles G. Dawes*. New York, Holt, 1953.

Name Index

Index of Biographies

Appendix A

Awards and other annual actions by the
Norwegian Nobel Committee (1901–1970)

1901   Jean Henri Dunant (1828–1910), *Switzerland*; and Frédéric Passy
(1822–1912), *France*

1902   Élie Ducommun (1833–1906), *Switzerland*; and Charles Albert
Gobat (1843–1914), *Switzerland*

1903   William Randal Cremer (1828–1908), *Great Britain*

1904   The Institute of International Law (1873–   )

1905   Bertha von Suttner (1843–1914), *Austria*

1906   Theodore Roosevelt (1858–1919), *United States*

1907   Ernesto Teodoro Moneta (1833–1918), *Italy*; and Louis Renault
(1843–1918), *France*

1908   Klas Pontus Arnoldson (1844–1916), *Sweden*; and Fredrik Bajer
(1837–1922), *Denmark*

1909   Auguste Marie François Beernaert (1829–1912), *Belgium*; and Paul
Henri Benjamin Balluet, Baron d'Estournelles de Constant de
Rebecque (1852–1924), *France*

1910   The Permanent International Peace Bureau (1891–   )

1911   Tobias Michael Carel Asser (1838–1913), *The Netherlands*; and Alfred
Hermann Fried (1864–1921), *Austria*

1912   The Prize was reserved in that year and in 1913 was awarded to: Elihu
Root (1845–1937), *United States*

1913   Henri Marie La Fontaine (1854–1943), *Belgium*

1914   The Prize was reserved in that year and in 1915 the prize money was
allocated to the Special Funds of the Committee.

1915   The Prize was reserved in that year and in 1916 the prize money was
allocated to the Special Funds of the Committee.

1916   The Prize was reserved in that year and in 1917 the prize money was
allocated to the Special Funds of the Committee.

1917   The International Committee of the Red Cross (1863–   )

1918   The Prize was reserved in that year and in 1919 the prize money was
allocated to the Special Funds of the Committee.

1919   The Prize was reserved in that year and in 1920 was awarded to:
       Thomas Woodrow Wilson (1856–1924), *United States*

1920   Léon Victor Auguste Bourgeois (1851–1925), *France*

1921   Karl Hjalmar Branting (1860–1925), *Sweden*; and Christian Lous
       Lange (1869–1938), *Norway*

1922   Fridtjof Nansen (1861–1930), *Norway*

1923   The Prize was reserved in that year and in 1924 the prize money was
       allocated to the Special Funds of the Committee.

1924   The Prize was reserved in that year and in 1925 the prize money was
       allocated to the Special Funds of the Committee.

1925   The Prize was reserved in that year and in 1926 was awarded to:
       Austen Joseph Chamberlain (1863–1937), *Great Britain*; and Charles
       Gates Dawes (1865–1951), *United States*

1926   Aristide Briand (1862–1932), *France;* and Gustav Stresemann
       (1878–1929), *Germany*

1927   Ferdinand Edouard Buisson (1841–1932), *France*; and Ludwig Quidde
       (1858–1941), *Germany*

1928   The Prize was reserved in that year and in 1929 the prize money was
       allocated to the Special Funds of the Committee.

1929   The prize was reserved in that year and in 1930 was awarded to: Frank
       Billings Kellogg (1856–1937), *United States*

1930   Lars Olof Jonathan [Nathan] Söderblom (1866–1931), *Sweden*

1931   Jane Addams (1860–1935), *United States*, and Nicholas Murray Butler
       (1862–1947), *United States*

1932   The Prize was reserved in that year and in 1933 the prize money was
       allocated to the Special Funds of the Committee.

1933   The Prize was reserved in that year and in 1934 was awarded to:
       Norman Angell (1872–1967), *Great Britain*

1934   Arthur Henderson (1863–1935), *Great Britain*

1935   The Prize was reserved in that year and in 1936 was awarded to:
       Carl von Ossietzky (1889–1938), *Germany*

1936   Carlos Saavedra Lamas (1878–1959), *Argentina*

1937   Edgar Algernon Robert Cecil, Viscount Cecil of Chelwood (1864–
       1958), *Great Britain*

1938   The Nansen International Office for Refugees (1930–1938)

1939   The Prize was reserved in that year and again in 1940; in 1941 it was
       suspended and the prize money allocated to the Main Fund of the
       Nobel Foundation.

1940   The Prize was reserved in that year; in 1941 it was suspended and the prize money allocated to the Main Fund of the Nobel Foundation.

1941   The Prize was suspended in that year and the prize money allocated to the Main Fund of the Nobel Foundation.

1942   The Prize was suspended in that year and the prize money allocated to the Main Fund of the Nobel Foundation.

1943   The Prize was suspended in that year and two-thirds of the prize money allocated to the Special Funds of the Committee and one-third to the Main Fund of the Nobel Foundation.

1944   After the Norwegian Nobel Committee ceased to function in 1944, the Board of Directors of the Nobel Foundation reserved the prize for that year; in 1945 the reconstituted Committee awarded it to: The International Committee of the Red Cross (1863–   )

1945   Cordell Hull (1871–1955), *United States*

1946   Emily Greene Balch (1867–1961), *United States*; and John Raleigh Mott (1865–1955), *United States*

1947   The Friends Service Council (1927–   ), *Great Britain* and *Ireland*; and The American Friends Service Committee (1917–   ), *United States*

1948   The Prize was not awarded in that year; two-thirds of the prize money was allocated to the Special Funds of the Committee and one-third to the Main Fund of the Nobel Foundation.

1949   Lord John Boyd Orr of Brechin (1880–1971), *Great Britain*

1950   Ralph Johnson Bunche (1904–1971), *United States*

1951   Léon Jouhaux (1879–1954), *France*

1952   The Prize was reserved in that year and in 1953 was awarded to: Albert Schweitzer (1875–1965), *France*

1953   George Catlett Marshall (1880–1959), *United States*

1954   The Prize was reserved in that year and in 1955 was awarded to: The Office of the United Nations High Commissioner for Refugees (1951–   )

1955   The Prize was reserved in that year and in 1956 two-thirds of the prize money was allocated to the Special Funds of the Committee and one-third to the Main Fund of the Nobel Foundation.

1956   The Prize was reserved in that year and in 1957 two-thirds of the prize money was allocated to the Special Funds of the Committee and one-third to the Main Fund of the Nobel Foundation.

1957   Lester Bowles Pearson (1897–   ), *Canada*

1958   Georges Pire (1910–1969), *Belgium*

1959   Philip John Noel-Baker (1889–   ), *Great Britain*

1960   The Prize was reserved in that year and in 1961 was awarded to:
Albert John Lutuli (1898?–1967), *Union of South Africa*

1961   Dag Hjalmar Agne Carl Hammarskjöld (1905–1961), *Sweden*

1962   The Prize was reserved in that year and in 1963 was awarded to:
Linus Carl Pauling (1901–   ), *United States*

1963   The International Committee of the Red Cross (1863–   ); and
The League of Red Cross Societies (1919–   )

1964   Martin Luther King, Jr. (1929–1968), *United States*

1965   The United Nations Children's Fund (1946–   )

1966   The Prize was reserved in that year and in 1967 two-thirds of the
prize money was allocated to the Special Funds of the Committee
and one-third to the Main Fund of the Nobel Foundation.

1967   The Prize was reserved in that year and in 1968 two-thirds of the
prize money was allocated to the Special Funds of the Committee
and one-third to the Main Fund of the Nobel Foundation.

1968   René-Samuel Cassin (1887–   ), *France*

1969   The International Labor Organization (1919–   )

1970   Norman Ernest Borlaug (1914–   ), *United States*

Appendix B

Summary of Awards (1901–1970)
Laureates by Nationality; Organizations Honored

Country	Name and Year	Number
Argentina	Saavedra Lamas (1936)	1
Austria	Suttner (1905), Fried (1911)	2
Belgium	Beernaert (1909), La Fontaine (1913), Pire (1958)	3
Canada	Pearson (1957)	1
Denmark	Bajer (1908)	1
France	Passy (1901), Renault (1907), d'Estournelles de Constant (1909), Bourgeois (1920), Briand (1926), Buisson (1927), Jouhaux (1951), Schweitzer (1952), Cassin (1968)	9
Germany	Stresemann (1926), Quidde (1927), Ossietzky (1935)	3
Great Britain	Cremer (1903), Chamberlain (1925), Angell (1933), Henderson (1934), Cecil (1937), Boyd Orr (1949), Noel-Baker (1959)	7
Italy	Moneta (1907)	1
The Netherlands	Asser (1911)	1
Norway	Lange (1921), Nansen (1922)	2
Sweden	Arnoldson (1908), Branting (1921), Söderblom (1930), Hammarskjöld (1961)	4
Switzerland	Dunant (1901), Ducommun (1902), Gobat (1902)	3
Union of South Africa	Lutuli (1960)	1
United States	Roosevelt (1906), Root (1912), Wilson (1919), Dawes (1925), Kellogg (1929), Addams (1931), Butler (1931), Hull (1945), Balch (1946), Mott (1946), Bunche (1950), Marshall (1953), Pauling (1962), King (1964), Borlaug (1970)	15

Total number of individual awards   54

Organizations   Institute of International Law (1904), Interna-
                   tional Peace Bureau (1910), International Com-
                   mittee of the Red Cross (1917), Nansen Inter-
                   national Office for Refugees (1938), Inter-
                   national Committee of the Red Cross (1944),
                   American Friends Service Committee (1947),
                   Friends Service Council (1947), Office of the
                   UN High Commissioner for Refugees (1954),
                   International Committee of the Red Cross
                   (1963), League of Red Cross Societies (1963),
                   United Nations Children's Fund (1965), Inter-
                   national Labor Organization (1969)

                   Total number of organizational awards   12
                   (Ten different organizations)

Grand total of awards (1901–1970)   66

Awards not made 1914, 1915, 1916, 1918, 1923, 1924, 1928, 1932,
                1939, 1940, 1941, 1942, 1943, 1948, 1955, 1956,
                1966, 1967   18